ALIBIS OF EMPIRE

ALIBIS OF EMPIRE

HENRY MAINE AND THE
ENDS OF LIBERAL IMPERIALISM

Karuna Mantena

PRINCETON UNIVERSITY PRESS   PRINCETON AND OXFORD

Copyright © 2010 by Princeton University Press
Published by Princeton University Press, 41 William Street,
Princeton, New Jersey 08540
In the United Kingdom: Princeton University Press, 6 Oxford Street,
Woodstock, Oxfordshire OX20 1TW

Library of Congress Cataloging-in-Publication Data
Mantena, Karuna, 1974–
Alibis of empire : Henry Maine and the ends of liberal imperilism / Karuna Mantena.
        p.   cm.
Includes bibliographical references and index.
ISBN 978-0-691-12816-0 (hardcover : alk. paper)
1. Imperialism. 2. Great Britain—Colonies. 3. Maine, Henry Sumner, Sir,
1822-1888—Political and social views. I. Title.
JC359.M277 2009
325′.22—dc22   2009019884

British Library Cataloging-in-Publication Data is available

This book has been composed in Sabon with Gill Sans.

Printed on acid-free paper. ∞

press.princeton.edu

Printed in the United States of America

1   3   5   7   9   10   8   6   4   2

For my parents

SURYANARAYANA RAJU AND ANASUYA MANTENA

Contents

Acknowledgments   ix

INTRODUCTION
The Ideological Origins of Indirect Rule   1

CHAPTER ONE
The Crisis of Liberal Imperialism   21

CHAPTER TWO
**Inventing Traditional Society: Empire and the Origins
of Social Theory**   56

CHAPTER THREE
Codification in the East and West   89

CHAPTER FOUR
The Nineteenth-Century Debate on Property   119

CHAPTER FIVE
**Native Society in Crisis: Conceptual Foundations
of Indirect Rule**   148

CODA
Liberalism and Empire Reconsidered   179

Notes   189

Bibliography   227

Index   255

Acknowledgments

RESEARCH FOR THIS BOOK was made possible by grants from the Social Science Research Council, the Minda de Gunzburg Center for European Studies, the Department of Government, and the Graduate School of Arts and Sciences at Harvard University. This book grew out of a dissertation project that was encouraged and shepherded from its earliest stages by Richard Tuck and Pratap Bhanu Mehta. Their unrestrained erudition and originality of insight inspired and shaped this enterprise more deeply, and in many more ways, than they know. I am grateful also to Seyla Benhabib and Glyn Morgan for their formative criticism, counsel, and unfailing support. Sudipta Kaviraj and Istvan Hont, in addition to being to exemplary scholars and teachers, have been exceptionally generous with their time and wisdom. All have taught me about the challenge and value of working creatively and seriously at the intersection of politics, political theory, and the history of political thought, for which I thank them with gratitude and admiration.

The thinking, research, and writing of this book have been with me for over a decade, during which time I have benefited enormously from the generosity and guidance of friends, mentors, and colleagues. I have incurred special debts to Danielle Allen, David Apter, Katy Arnold, Asli Bali, Barney Bate, Duncan Bell, Clarisse Berthezène, Richard Bourke, David Bromwich, Susan Buck-Morss, Chris Chekuri, Noah Dauber, Nick Dirks, Munis Faruqui, Jason Frank, Bryan Garsten, Michael Gasper, Will Glover, Manu Goswami, Duncan Kelly, Arang Kesharvarzian, Sanjay Krishnan, David Lieberman, Michael Lobban, Jonathan Magidoff, Mahmood Mamdani, Tomaz Mastnak, Tom McCarthy, Uday Mehta, Farina Mir, Molly Moloney, Jeanne Morefield, Sam Moyn, Darra Mulderry, Sankar Muthu, Ranjit Nahal, Isaac Nakhimovsky, Nauman Naqvi, Paulina Ochoa, Steve Pincus, Jennifer Pitts, Teena Purohit, Aziz Rana, Anupama Rao, Nadia Rasheed, Sanjay Reddy, Mel Richter, Emma Rothschild, Greta Scharnweber, Jean-Frédéric Schaub, Melissa Schwartzberg, David Scott, Nermeen Shaikh, Ian Shapiro, Kristin Smith, Steven Smith, Travis Smith, Verity Smith, Annie Stilz, Prakash Upadhyay, Nadia Urbinati, Frédéric Vandenberghe, Milind Wakankar, and Cheryl Welch. The faculty, staff, and students at the Government Department and Committee on Social Studies at Harvard University; the Department of Government at Cornell University; and the Department of Political Science, Program in Ethics, Politics, and Economics, and Directed Studies at Yale University provided wonderfully stimulating and convivial intellectual environments for the completion of this project. David Armitage and Barbara Arneil graciously read the manuscript for the press; their incisive and thorough reviews were invaluable. Ian Malcolm has been an ideal editor; his acumen and enthusiasm sustained me throughout the publication process.

The ideas and arguments of this book have greatly benefited from comments and criticisms offered when presented at the Political Theory Colloquium at Harvard University; the "South Asia: Histories of the Present" conference at the University of Michigan; the Law and History Colloquium at University College London; the "Victorian Visions of Global Order" workshop at Cambridge University; the "Empire and Modern Political Thought" workshop at the Bellagio Study and Conference Center; the British Historical Studies Colloquium and Political Theory Workshop at Yale University; the History of Political Ideas seminar at the Institute for Historical Research, University of London; "The Idea of the Political in India" workshop at Columbia University/Barnard College; the "Lineages of Empire" conference at the British Academy; the "Revolution, Empire, Race: Experiences of British Modernity" seminar at the École des Hautes Études de Sciences Sociales; the Political Theory Colloquium at Concordia University; the "Imperial Models in the Early-Modern World: From Early-Modern to Modern Empire and from Empire to Nation-State" conference at UCLA's Clark Memorial Library; the Faculty Seminar on Social and Political Thought at Columbia University; the Critical Perspectives on South Asia Seminar at New York University; and the History and Economics Seminar at Harvard University.

Rama Mantena, Sunil Agnani, and Kavita Datla, beyond well-worn and ineffable filial ties, have been my most cherished intellectual companions. I am grateful to Narender, Purnima, Aman, and Dhanush Mantena for indulging me whenever I needed respite from work. The depth of my obligations to my parents, Suryanarayana Raju and Anasuya Mantena, is immeasurable. I thank them for their patience, support, and care—but most of all, for their trust in me to make my way in the world.

A condensed and earlier version of chapter one has been published as "The Crisis of Liberal Imperialism," in *Victorian Visions of Global Order: Empire and International Relations in Nineteenth-Century Political Thought*, ed. Duncan Bell (Cambridge, 2007). Sections of chapter one have appeared in "Mill and the Imperial Predicament," in *J. S. Mill's Political Thought: A Bicentennial Reassessment*, ed. Nadia Urbinati and Alex Zakaras (Cambridge, 2007).

INTRODUCTION

THE IDEOLOGICAL ORIGINS

OF INDIRECT RULE

ON MAY 10, 1857, native troops of the Bengal army mutinied against their British commanders, instigating the largest indigenous rebellion against European empire in the nineteenth century. In addition to the revolt of over 130,000 Indian soldiers, the "Sepoy Mutiny" brought together a wide array of disaffected groups into popular insurrection against British rule, temporarily shattering the imperial edifice across northern India and provoking a brutal response by the British. In strictly military terms, the war and the final suppression of the insurgency were both short-lived and less catastrophic relative to other major armed conflicts of the era. Yet, in Henry Sumner Maine's view, it would prove to be "the greatest fact in all Anglo-Indian history."[1] For Britain, the rebellion was a rude awakening and a deeply disillusioning affair, shaking the growing self-confidence in its imperial mission that had attended the steady expansion and consolidation of the British Empire in India over the prior hundred years. Moreover, the Indian Mutiny signaled the beginning of a particularly turbulent and violent decade in imperial politics during which a number of key uprisings broke out across the empire, most momentously among the oldest and most important of Britain's colonies and dependencies—Ireland, Jamaica, and India. Coming in quick succession, the Mutiny, the Maori Wars, the Morant Bay Rebellion in Jamaica, and the Fenian Rising in Ireland (and corollary bombings in England), together produced a threatening portrait of native disaffection and imperial instability that dramatically reshaped metropolitan attitudes toward subject peoples and gave rise to an anxiety about the meaning, character and future trajectory of the British Empire. In this manner, the 1857 Rebellion would come to mark a definitive turning point in the transformation of British imperial ideology.[2] More precisely, it would mark the decisive *turning away* from an earlier liberal, reformist ethos that had furnished nineteenth-century empire its most salient moral justification.

The liberal model of empire, in which imperial domination was argued to be an effective and legitimate tool of moral and material progress, has been the subject of sustained scholarly interest, and, most recently, a key focus of philosophical and theoretical discussions of empire.[3] Yet, while the nineteenth century was certainly the critical period in which *liberal imperialism* came to be most clearly articulated and assuredly defended, the marked tendency to treat the liberal model of progressive empire as definitive of British imperial ideology obscures the fact that imperial justifications and governing strategies underwent fundamental revision in the course of the century. In many ways, the remarkable feature of nineteenth-century empire was how the era of its greatest geographic expansion in Asia and Africa—the period between 1857 and 1914—directly coincided with a phase of liberal retrenchment and the repudiation of central assumptions and imperatives underlying the "civilizing mission." Whereas earlier, reform-oriented, imperial ideologies conceived of native societies as in need of radical reconstruction along Western lines, late imperial thinking questioned both the practicality and the theoretical underpinnings of such an interventionist agenda. In place of the universalist project of civilization, a new emphasis on deep-seated "cultural" differences between peoples came to the fore. Rather than eradicated or aggressively modernized, native social and political forms would now be patronized as they became inserted into the institutional dynamics of imperial power, most notably in the theory and practice of *indirect rule* in colonial Africa.

This book studies the conceptual developments that enabled this broad transition from a *universalist* to a *culturalist* stance in nineteenth-century imperial ideology. As dramatic forms of rebellion, resistance, and instability in the colonies—such as the 1857 Rebellion—occasioned important reassessments of past imperial policy, this, in turn, led to a fundamental rethinking of the nature and purpose of imperial rule. Significantly, these reassessments were premised upon and generated new theories of native society as a way to account for the fact of native disaffection as well as to explain the failure of past imperial policy to modernize subject peoples. On the one hand, postemancipation political crises in the British Caribbean provoked new forms of racialization and racial categorization; the failures of "the Great Experiment" in abolition, for example, were understood as stemming from deficiencies inherent in ex-slave populations, as an innate inability to reform themselves in line with liberal political and economic models.[4] On the other hand, in India (and later in Southeast Asia and Africa), that is, in areas where imperial rule was not coincident with the prior eradication of indigenous societies, the new racial categorization of extant native societies in the wake of 1857 took the form of a distinct theory of *traditional society*, as a cohesive, cultural whole that likewise was seen to resist the logic of modern society. Intellectually, this reorientation was closely linked to the development of modern social theory, namely its stark historical contrast between traditional and modern societies, and the holistic models of *culture* and *society* that sustained this dichotomy. Late imperial ideology[5] relied upon the social-theoretic account of traditional society both as the displaced site of imperial legitimation and the rubric through which to formulate distinct strategies of ruling. The most influential articulation of this model of traditional society in its practical connection to late imperial ideology appears in the social and political theory of Henry Maine and, thus, his work figures centrally in this study.

Maine is perhaps best remembered as a theorist of legal modernity, for the famous contention advanced in *Ancient Law* that legal evolution could be conceptualized in terms of a movement "from Status to Contract."[6] This formulation, which is premised upon a distinct account of relationship between kinship and law in primitive societies, continues to mark Maine as a founding figure of modern anthropology and sociology. However, for political theory, Maine's historical and anthropological work has always been more or less ignored in favor of his late writings on popular government; thus defining Maine as primarily, a conservative critic of democracy. In his own time, Maine was a leading jurist and legal historian of Victorian Britain who served as Law Member in the Viceroy's Council in India during the crucial period of post-Mutiny consolidation. As a highly visible member of imperial administration and a preeminent scholar of Indian law and society, Maine's ideas would fundamentally shape the trajectory of late imperial ideology. As a critical conduit between emerging social theory and the imperatives of imperial governance, no intellectual was more influential in shaping the practical work of nineteenth-century British empire (with the possible exception of James Mill).[7] Maine's seminal contribution to imperial policy debates stemmed from his evocative account of the unique dynamics of primitive, ancient societies, of which India was a prime example. Maine's account of status and contract not only emphasized the radical and systemic difference between ancient and modern society but also drew attention to the customary basis of ancient society. In doing so, Maine constructed a generic model of native society, newly defined as *traditional society* in opposition to modern society, that stressed the primacy of the "social" in understanding and explaining the nature of native society. In contrast to earlier conceptions of non-Western societies as politically dysfunctional (embodied in various theories of Oriental despotism), Maine's social-theoretical model conceptualized native society as an apolitical, functional whole, held together by stable bonds of custom and structures of kinship.

Historically, this model of traditional society came to prominence in the aftermath of the 1857 Rebellion, in the context of a fundamental rethinking of the future character of British rule in India. While the conflict ended with the final abolition of the East India Company and the official transfer of the Government of India to the Crown, this institutional change was arguably less momentous than the deeper shift brought about in political, cultural, and moral attitudes toward empire and its subjects. Among imperial administrators and metropolitan observers alike, it would both generate a crisis of imperial legitimacy and occasion reassessments of past imperial governance, especially those policies that were seen to have precipitated revolt. In seeking to make sense of native disaffection and resistance, these critical reassessments drew upon and elicited new ethnographic and sociological accounts of the nature of native society.

The most prominent imperial perceptions of the rebellious native were framed by notions of ingratitude and inscrutability. The fact of resistance was itself taken as evidence of a derisive and perverse rejection by Indians of the civilizational benefits proffered by imperial rule. Because the progressive and moral character of the British Empire in India was taken as given, its rejection could only appear as irrational, for which a specific kind of accounting was required. In the case of 1857, the trope of inscrutability was often linked to a reading of the revolt as "an outburst of terrified fanaticism."[8] Maine had no doubt "that it was a genuine fanatical rising"[9] rooted in deep religious and caste fears of pollution. This account would give great causal weight to, firstly, the specific grievance that provoked the outbreak of the Mutiny, namely the refusal of native troops to use newly issued rifle cartridges greased with beef and pork fat and, secondly, the more pervasive fear of conversion generated by the increase in missionary activity. Moreover, the religious interpretation of the revolt was given substantive confirmation in the Queen's Proclamation of 1858, which made the principle of noninterference into native religious beliefs and customs the cornerstone of post-Mutiny imperial policy. In a very obvious sense, the more jingoistic portrayals of the conflict as fueled by obscurantist, religious sentiments clearly functioned to justify a "war of retribution" and elide recognition of the political character of the rebellion.[10] Yet, even among more critical observers who argued that the trajectory of past imperial policy had significantly contributed to the upheavals, the notion of native inscrutability played a central role.

At one level, specific policies connected to the pre-Mutiny administration of Lord Dalhousie—such as "the doctrine of lapse" (which enabled the aggressive annexation of princely states) and the expansion of officially sanctioned missionization—were seen in hindsight to have been premised on mistaken judgments about the content, character, and strength of native customs and beliefs.[11] This was supplemented with a more general skepticism about previous trajectories of imperial policy, especially its more progressive currents that had attempted to place the modernization of Indian society as the pivot of Britain's imperial project. The Mutiny was seen as a sign of the failure of liberal, utilitarian, and evangelical reforms to either transform, civilize, and emancipate the native or lend security to the imperial order. The altering of native habits

and beliefs as well as the reshaping of native economic and social structures were now viewed as more difficult and more protracted than advocates had previously assumed, and as themselves potentially fomenting
instability. In this vein, Maine argued that

> it is a question of the gravest practical importance for the rulers of India how
> far the condition of religious and social sentiment revealed by the Mutiny
> survives in any strength. . . . It is manifest that, if the belief in caste continues
> unimpaired or but slightly decayed, some paths of legislation and of executive
> action are seriously unsafe: it is possible to follow them, but it is imperative
> to walk wearily.[12]

The status of native belief had "a direct bearing on the structure of government which it may be possible to give to the Indian possessions of this
country."[13] The emerging post-Mutiny consensus sought to curtail the
transformative ambition implied in the civilizing mission and reconstitute the imperial order on a more conservative basis, in line with the
"traditional" imperatives of native society. If the native of reform was
figured as a child amenable to education, conversion, and assimilation,
by contrast, the native of late empire was construed as tenaciously bound
to custom, whose acquiescence to British rule would depend on protecting the traditional basis of native society. The inscrutability of the
native in revolt would be overcome by attentiveness to and deep knowledge of the unique (cultural) logic of native society, a logic that purport-
edly made imposed radical change impossible and/or undesirable.
Maine's work was crucial here, both in terms of providing a methodological foundation for supposedly better ethnographic knowledge of traditional India and in formulating a distinct, substantive account of the customary basis of native society (through his influential conceptualization
of the Indian village-community).

In metropolitan debates, the seeming ingratitude of the native in revolt
provoked a deep sense of disappointment and hostility, a hostility that
worked to harden racial attitudes toward non-European peoples. The
growing sense that subject peoples might be "irredeemably savage" displaced earlier attempts—especially prominent in abolitionist, missionary,
and liberal discourses—to construe native peoples as intrinsically amenable to reform and civilization.[14] In this sense, coupled with the Morant
Bay Rebellion of 1865, the Mutiny was a crucial episode in the making
of Victorian racism.[15] Politically, the disillusionment with the agenda of
reform and the concomitant racialization of subject peoples, led, in the
case of Jamaica, to the dramatic turning away from the principle of representative government with the voluntary dissolution of the Assembly in
the aftermath of the 1865 Rebellion. The transformation of Jamaica from
a self-governing to Crown colony signaled not only the turn to more stra-

tegically defined and overtly authoritarian rule in the West Indies, but also cemented a racialization of the constitutional trajectories of the Empire as a whole. Race now defined an increasingly precise institutional division between white settler colonies oriented toward greater degrees of self-government and colonies/dependencies of predominately nonwhite populations in which representative government was aggressively disavowed. In India, the political analogue of racialization was a heightened sense of a fundamental difference between English and Indian institutions such that the attempt to rejuvenate Indian society on Western models was considered to be both futile and disruptive. The strategic abandonment of the liberal agenda in this case implied the turn to a very different philosophy of imperial governance, one in which the native was thought to be best ruled through his/her own institutions and structures of authority. Ruling was thought to require a more precise knowledge of the dynamics of native society, and an adjustment to the supposedly natural and traditional foundations of native society. As an ostensibly less intrusive and less disruptive mode of power, *indirect rule*, the rule through native institutions, was often championed as both more efficient and more fruitful for stabilizing the imperial order. It would be normatively defended as a deference to native agency, and, in more enlightened self-descriptions, as a form of cosmopolitan pluralism, one that recognized and respected the cultural specificity of native society.[16]

One of the most important conceptual innovations Maine provided to the theory of indirect rule was his provocative account of the ways in which native societies were increasingly threatened under the rubric of modern imperial rule. While Maine detailed the internal coherence of native institutions, he also argued that this structural integrity was rendered increasingly fragile with greater contact with modern institutions. And, in practical terms, the rapidity of the process of disintegration, for Maine, engendered the gravest consequences for the stability of imperial rule. This warning about the potential "dissolution of society" under the imperative of modern empire proved to be the ideological linchpin of the theory and practice of indirect rule. For advocates of native institutions, Maine's cogent account of the disruptive, structural impact of colonial/modern institutions upon native society vividly demonstrated the urgent need for protection. The call for the protection or rehabilitation of native society was committed not only to the idea that native society contained within itself the resources for its maintenance and reproduction, but also that this unity was threatened by and yet in need of imperial rule. For it was the portrayal of native society as simultaneously *intact* and *vulnerable* that underpinned the paternalistic impulse of late imperial rule.

What began in India as a principle of noninterference into native religious practices in the wake of 1857 had, by the turn of the century, meta-morphosed into an array of arguments for the protection and rehabilitation of native institutions. *Indirect rule* became the foundational principle of late imperial administration and philosophy in Asia and Africa, articulated in different forms, for example, in Swettenham's vision for Malaya, Cromer's policy in Egypt, and, most famously, Lugard's account of the dual mandate for tropical Africa. In all these various manifestations, Maine's account of a traditional society in crisis supplied a rationale and an impetus for indirect imperial rule, a rule to protect native society from the traumatic impact of modernity. Maine thus stands as the progenitor of a distinct and powerful line of imperial thinking, and emerges as a pivotal figure in the intellectual history of empire.[17]

Maine's work provided the intellectual grounds for the consolidation of a distinctive pattern of rule, one whose influence and importance, moreover, would only increase with the dramatic expansion of European empires throughout the nineteenth century. As the percentage of the world controlled by European imperial powers increased from 35 percent to 84 percent,[18] with the most significant increase coming with partition of Africa at the turn of the century, the models for ruling alien subjects forged during Britain's Indian experience, in the period of high empire, would become transportable in key respects. Indirect rule was not only the dominant model of British imperialism in Africa and Southeast Asia, it would also come to be emulated in French, Portuguese, and German colonial practice.[19] In this manner, indirect rule had a profound impact on the reshaping of indigenous societies, one whose institutional legacy continues to be felt in many contentious arenas of postcolonial politics across Asia and Africa.

FROM UNIVERSALIST JUSTIFICATIONS TO CULTURALIST ALIBIS

Recent scholarly work in the intellectual history of empire and the history of political thought has drawn attention to the intimate and indeed constitutive relationship between the development of modern political theory and the history of European expansion. A growing body of literature has begun to reckon with the ways in which modern political thought has been shaped by, on the one hand, political arguments about the legitimacy of conquest and colonization, and, on the other, attempts to comprehend the global diversity of life practices, knowledge of which increased with five centuries of European expansion. Studies of the conquest and settlement of the Americas, for example, have examined how many prominent early-modern thinkers were drawn into a host of debates about the nature and legitimate grounds of sovereignty (*imperium* in the classic sense) and property (*dominium*). Debates around such pivotal, practical questions about the right to expropriate land and assert authority over native peoples generated conceptual innovations central to the development of modern theories of sovereignty and property, especially in the emergence of early-modern natural rights theories. The problem of empire and foundations of liberalism appear in a profound sense to be coeval.[20]

Studies of empire in nineteenth-century political thought have also focused on the particularly salient and paradoxical relationship between liberalism and empire. Scholars have sought to understand how a liberalism ostensibly grounded in universal and democratic principles generated, at the same time, justifications of imperial rule. In analyzing the ways in which J. S. Mill denied the applicability of representative government to India, or how Alexis de Tocqueville lent support to the conquest of Algeria, these studies have investigated theoretical tensions in liberalism that could justify a variety of forms of political exclusion. In doing so, they have undermined everyday assumptions about the relationship of empire to political thought which either presume that questions about empire, expansion, and colonization were merely incidental to the development of liberal thought or that any contradictions were contingent accommodations to contemporary opinions and prejudices. In demonstrating that the potential for exclusionary practices was compatible with the theoretical core of liberalism, these studies raise fundamental philosophical and political questions about the limits of liberal political theory.[21]

At the same time, studies of liberalism and empire have only unevenly addressed the question of how justifications of empire historically evolved in relation to the practices and politics of imperial rule on the ground. On the one hand, this has led to a privileging of the progressive civilizing mission as the paradigmatic ideological form of nineteenth-century empire, thus eclipsing other salient features of imperial thought and practice. In particular, a singular focus on liberal justifications of empire elides the manner in which, at the height of imperial power, moral and political justifications of imperial rule gave way to the ascendancy of elaborate social, cultural, and racial explanations and alibis of European imperial domination. On the other hand, liberalism and liberal imperialism are often analyzed as static theoretical constructs, in which core ideas about human nature and human diversity are seen to propel the variation in stances—critical, justificatory, or otherwise—taken by thinkers vis-à-vis empire and imperial projects. Rather, I want to suggest, liberal imperialism is better understood as a historical constellation such that conceptualizations of moral universalism and cultural diversity ought to be seen as evolving in response to a changing set of imperial dilemmas. This recognition compels us to consider how philosophical claims about human unity and diversity were negotiated, contested, and reconstituted on the practical terrain of imperial politics.[22]

Moreover, attending more closely to the fate of liberal imperial thought—to the ways that liberal justifications of empire and liberal ideologies of rule came to be increasingly questioned and criticized—reveals a more general dynamic underlying modern imperial ideology, especially universalistic defenses of empire. At the peak of imperial confidence in nineteenth-century Britain, when the project of liberal reform (and its program of remaking the world in its own image) encountered resistance, its universalism easily gave way to harsh attitudes about the intractable differences among people, the inscrutability of other ways of life, and the ever-present potential for racial and cultural conflict. That is, when empire faced opposition or produced consequences that did not fit neatly into its vision of progress, the error was understood to lie less with the structure of imperial power (and the contradictions that ensue from its attempt to elicit social transformation through force) than in the nature of colonized societies. Resistance, especially political resistance, when refracted through the imperial lens, was redescribed as a deep-seated cultural intransigence to universal norms of civilization. The ways in which liberal confidence and capaciousness could slide into moral disavowal, disillusionment, and an unforgiving stance toward others, I would argue, reveals a theoretically significant instability *internal* to the structure of imperial ideology.

The oscillation between universalist justifications and culturalist alibis, between viewing colonized societies as either amenable or resistant to transformation, may prove to be a necessary and general feature of the political dynamic of modern empire. The turn from liberal justifications to culturalist alibis in nineteenth-century discourses of imperial legitimation was not in any strict sense necessitated by the internal logic of liberalism, but rather emerges as a political reaction and reconfiguration. It intimates a temporal logic and entailment between universalism and culturalism, a systematic connection that should not be dismissed as a mere historical contingency. Understanding the transformation of nineteenth-century ideology, moreover, signals a cautious lesson for the contemporary revival of theories of benevolent empire and trusteeship today, for it draws attention to the ways in which revitalized imperial politics seemingly go hand in hand with heightened forms of cultural conflict.

Late imperial ideology, and especially indirect rule, has always been difficult to conceptualize straightforwardly as *ideology*, since it was more often defended in practical and strategic terms as founded less upon ideas than expediency. The mainstream of British imperial historiography has tended to contest the notion that the British Empire had any sort of ideological unity, even going so far as to question whether *the* Empire as such

ever existed as a coherent unit.[23] Imperial historians have especially under-
played (even dismissed) the role of ideas and ideology in shaping the structure and pattern of the British Empire.[24] Since Gallagher and Robinson's
influential critique of Eurocentric theories of imperialism, imperial historiography has shown a marked tendency to emphasize local developments
and local (imperial and native) actors as the primary agents that both
propel imperial expansion and shape governance patterns (the latter predominately understood as regimes of collaboration and accommodation
with powerful native agents).[25] In this perspective, the emergence of indirect rule in Africa is understood to result from the constraints and limitations imposed on imperial administration by rapid territorial expansion
and limited manpower. Indirect rule is thus rendered a rarefied name for
a political necessity, a practical institutional solution that accommodated
itself with "facts on the ground," that is, with local conditions and structures of power. In the self-understanding of imperial administrators, indirect rule was likewise conceived of as emblematic of the practical, anti-
ideological orientation of British imperial policy, routinely contrasted to
the militancy of the French *mission civilisatrice*.

In contrast to the orientation of imperial historiography, one of the
central aims of this book is to explore indirect rule as a distinctive ideological formation, whose conceptual roots are linked to the rejection of earlier liberal models of empire and to developments in modern social theory.
The emergence of indirect rule as the dominant form of British imperial
practice was a historical formation, forged through the long experience
of empire and rebellion in British India, and specifically devised as a critique of earlier assimiliationist strands of imperial policy. It was premised
on an ideological shift, one that interpreted what was *practically* necessary in strikingly new ways. What was deemed expedient depended on a
distinct account of the nature of imperial order and what would be construed as threats to that order. Whereas for liberal reformers the corruption and degeneration that imperial rule was meant to overcome was associated with "premodern" or "traditional" forms of hierarchy, patronage,
and domination (i.e., institutions of slavery, feudalism, and caste), for
advocates of indirect rule, threats to the imperial order were broadly
linked to the problem of modernization, which was seen as socially disruptive and thus politically unwieldy. Yet, in claiming to accommodate
imperial rule to the facts on the ground, ideological work was also required in inventing a particular view of native society, and the designation
of particular sets of actors and institutions deemed to be "natural" and
essential to the stability of the imperial order.

Indirect rule also came to function as ideology in a more classic sense,
as a way to conceal and justify the consolidation of imperial power. But
as a form of justification, it was of a peculiar kind, and one that differed

markedly in its ethical/moral character from earlier and more well known liberal justifications of empire. With the turn away from reform-oriented imperial policy in the aftermath of 1857, late empire became severed from any clear ethical justification, in effect generating a crisis of imperial legitimation. British imperial ideology in India as it came to be constituted in the early nineteenth century had been closely tied to the ideals of *trusteeship* and *improvement*, which taken together conferred a moral imperative to the imperial mission. It was an ethical horizon that was defined by a sense of needing to atone for the injustice/violence of conquest through the active rejuvenation of Indian society. This ethical horizon, which in its most progressive formulations would be linked to the goal of eventual self-government by Indians, was broadly shared by political thinkers from Edmund Burke to John Stuart Mill, and policymakers from Charles Grant to T. B. Macaulay. While liberal justifications of empire always had their detractors, after 1857 both their prominence and efficacy were dramatically eclipsed. And with their decline, a more general waning of ethical arguments and moral justifications of empire ensued. Imperial policy debates would be overwhelmingly framed by questions of stability and order, remaining remote from, even dismissive of, concerns about the moral purpose and legitimacy of imperial rule. The idea of educating India for eventual self-government as the telos of empire was almost entirely eclipsed, and only reemerged in the twentieth century in response to the demands of Indian nationalism.

In the late nineteenth century, in the absence of overt and ambitious justifications of imperial rule, the burden of legitimation was increasingly shifted onto native societies. Imperial rule was often construed as a necessity for curtailing the tendency of native societies toward dissolution, born of endemic internecine conflict, or (more subtly) from contact with modern civilization. Moreover, the remedy to these crises would be sought through the protection and reinvigoration of native society. Native society here functioned both as pretext and solution, as an *alibi* for the fait accompli of empire. To contrast late imperial alibis to earlier justifications is not to imply that these prior forms were *less* ideological, more authentic, purer, or necessarily more attractive models of imperial rule. Liberal imperialism, and the universalism that underpinned its agenda of reform, harbored its own contradictions, exclusions, and deferrals, often premised upon profoundly distorted visions of indigenous societies. But the distinction relies less on whether one ideological formation was either more descriptively accurate or normatively superior, than on what each postulated the purpose of empire to be, and thus the conceptual terrain upon which imperial legitimacy would be constituted and contested. For liberal reformers modern empire had to be decisively severed from older, extractive and oppressive forms of conquest, and rendered just by becoming an agent of civilizing progress. Legitimacy would be defined by the ethical character of the imperial regime, given by its motivating logic and elevated ideals. With the collapse of the liberal model and its moral vision, however, the legitimacy of empire became disassociated from avowed metropolitan imperatives and, instead, enframed and mediated by the immanent properties of subject societies. In the process, native society was given an altered and heightened ideological function, not strictly as a pathology to be overcome but as a structure to be accommodated and contained.

The term *alibi* is meant to mark the ways in which late imperial ideology worked through this definitive form of displacement, in which the sources of imperial legitimacy, power, and authority are refracted *elsewhere*—in this case from metropole to colony. Rather than as a self-consciously willed project, empire would be reactively and retrospectively defended; the continuity of imperial domination would be construed as the lesser evil to leaving native societies to collapse on their own. Moreover, as a form of rule, empire was depicted as merely an epiphenomenal construct *indirectly* ruling through preexisting native institutions and structures of authority. Native society as alibi, thus, was "an *alleged* elsewhere,' "[26] an ideological construct that made possible the deferral and disavowal of moral and political responsibility for imperial domination.

SOCIAL THEORY, TRADITIONAL SOCIETY, AND THE "CULTURAL" LIMITS OF POLITICS

While indirect rule emerged from a set of imperial debates about how to rule native societies, these debates were also shaped by intellectual developments in the ways in which non-European societies were conceptualized, linked especially to the rise of modern social theory. Therefore, another preoccupation of the book is the analysis of the reciprocal impact of social theory, and the expanding scope of colonial knowledge, on imperial thought and practice. As was noted above, recent studies of empire in political theory have not only been interested in how major political thinkers developed arguments about the legitimacy of imperial expansion, but have also explored the ways in which modern political thought has been shaped by the attempt to comprehend the global diversity of life practices, knowledge of which increased in tandem with the growth of European empires. From the "discovery" of the New World, the encounter with Oriental languages and civilizations, to the "scramble for Africa," imperial encounters have engendered theoretical reflection on the nature of human diversity. These encounters generated new modes of comparison—new frameworks by which Europe would be related to other social and political formations, and unfamiliar cultures and practices would be made scientifically (and morally) comprehensible. As Richard Tuck has argued,

> the extraordinary burst of moral and political theorizing in terms of natural rights which marks the seventeenth century, and which is associated particularly with the names of Grotius, Hobbes, Pufendorf, and Locke, was primarily an attempt by European theorists to deal with the problem of deep cultural differences, both within their own community (following the wars of religion) and between Europe and the rest of the world (particularly the world of the various pre-agricultural peoples encountered around the globe).[27]

In the eighteenth century, the encounters with, and growing knowledge of, different societies in the East and West challenged major Enlightenment thinkers to reconceptualize the nature of human diversity in a globalizing world. Thinkers such as Montesquieu, Diderot, Kant, Herder, and the Scottish philosophical historians, all took up this challenge directly, developing philosophical and historical methods to rethink and account for the diversity of ways of living and the historical development of societies. Enlightenment thinkers understood that the new age demanded new philosophic anthropologies and histories (from ancient times to modern commercial society), but ones that were truly global in nature.[28]

With the institutionalization of the modern social sciences and the concurrent expansion and intensification of modern technologies of imperial governance, the nineteenth century witnessed a veritable explosion of historical and anthropological research on the non-European world. In this period, the records and reports of expanding colonial bureaucracies ascended to the rank of evidentiary knowledge for the anthropologist and sociologist. This expansion of colonial knowledge was to have profound consequences for the development of modern social science, indeed laying the groundwork of modern disciplines of anthropology and sociology. It brought forth a variety of new facts to be confronted and comprehended, and generated methodological innovations in the ways societies would be conceptualized, classified, and compared. Ideas about comparison and "the comparative method" were given a heightened investment in the nineteenth century, as a subject for philosophical elucidation as well as a privileged model for attaining scientific certainty with a universal scope.[29] Two of the most ambitious theoretical endeavors to emerge in response to the challenge of universal comparison were nineteenth-century social theory (or classical sociology) and evolutionary anthropology. While classical social theory focused more squarely on analyzing the unprecedented nature and dynamics of industrializing societies, the attempt to chart the unique trajectory of Western modernity necessarily involved making

large-scale and conceptually bold comparisons with other social formations, past and present. The disciplinary birth of anthropology can be
readily seen as intimately linked to the rapidly expanding scope of historical and ethnographical researches, and its striking feature was the prominence of grand schemes of social evolution that attempted to enfold and
categorize the radical diversity of social practices across time and space.[30]
Moreover, nineteenth-century responses to the problem of incommensurability—such as sociological narratives of transition, evolutionary and
comparative methodologies, and hierarchical scales of civilization—were
closely tied to the development of holistic conceptions of kinship, culture,
and society.

   Maine's work contributed to the development of both theoretical traditions, and he is often acknowledged as a founder figure of both sociology
and anthropology. Maine's distinction between societies based upon status and contract was representative of the dualistic construction of traditional and modern societies typical of nineteenth-century social theory.
Maine's contrast between the corporate nature of ancient/primitive society and the individualist basis of modern society not only directly shaped
Ferdinand Tönnies's evocative rendering of this binary in *Gemeinschaft
und Gesellschaft*,[31] but also closely resonated with many of Durkheim's
early formulations about the differences between mechanical and organic
solidarity in simple and complex societies, respectively.[32] For anthropology, Maine was one of the earliest to theorize kinship as the structuring
principle of social interaction, as a cornerstone of a holistic model of society. And even as anthropology came to reject speculative, evolutionary
theories about the earliest forms of society, Maine's "jural" model of kinship, kinship as enacting a set of reciprocal rights and duties, was substantively revived in twentieth-century anthropology, especially in British
social-functionalism.

   In the context of late nineteenth-century empire, sociological and anthropological theories made available a generic model of native society,
newly defined as *traditional society* in opposition to modern society.
Maine outlined many of the central features of this model—kinship as a
central structuring principle of society, the intermingling of law and religion in early jurisprudence, the predominance of rigid, ritual codes of
conduct circumscribing individual action, the hold of custom on both
modes of action and conceptual imagination, and finally the moral and
functional priority of community or the social whole—that would become commonplace assumptions about traditional society carried forward into twentieth-century anthropology and sociology, especially in
theories of sociocultural modernization. Most importantly, nineteenth-
century theorists such as Maine produced a distinctively *apolitical* model
of traditional society, one that embodied a substantive and methodologi-

cal investment in viewing societies as functional, cultural wholes. It was a view that stressed the internal cohesiveness and the communal/corporate orientation of native society, prioritizing the cultural determination of individual action and thought, and thus, de-emphasizing political conflict, change, and agency. This model of native society as an integral whole, held together by reciprocal bonds of custom and structures of kinship, would provide the theoretical foundation, and even a normative justification, for late imperial ideologies of protection, preservation, and collaboration.

In contrast to the dynamism of modern society, traditional society in social theory was often construed as fundamentally static, dominated by nonrational forms of politics and economics, themselves pervaded by religious, kin-based, customary ties. And while it was in this model of traditional society that modern social theory elaborated its most deterministic model of social behavior, social theory initiated a more general shift toward a view of society that emphasized the nonrational bases of sociability, that is, in terms of either the external force of social and economic structures or pervasive cultural attachments and historical habits. In important ways, then, social theory sought to project a model of the social as the privileged arena for understanding the nature and dynamics of society. The concept of *society* is for sociology what the concept of *culture* is for anthropology, namely a relatively autonomous entity that affects, limits, and even determines the character of social, political, and economic institutions. With the rise of social theory, the question of politics was thus reframed in a context that increasingly emphasized the limits of political action in relation to social, cultural, and historical imperatives. This shift toward a view of human behavior as a product of collective learning, social conditioning, and historically informed custom would have important legacies for twentieth-century social science. Not only is the modern anthropological concept of culture[33] indebted to this model of society, but also the sociological tradition notably retained many of these elements in its general account of social integration.[34]

In exploring how social theory shaped the intellectual foundations of late imperial ideology, this study draws attention to the imperial context of the origins of social theory, both in terms of how social theory influenced the theory and practice of nineteenth-century empire and how empire, in turn, shaped the central concepts of modern social theory. Finally, as the concept of culture has become a central category in contemporary politics, political science, and political theory, interrogating a key moment in its political and theoretical emergence has become evermore vital. Contemporary debates in political theory around the question of culture often conceptualize culture as the definitive site of difference, rooted in alternative forms of social organization and/or structures of attachment and being. But to experience and conceptualize difference as primarily cultural is a peculiarly late nineteenth- and twentieth-century phenomenon.[35] What I want to suggest is that this way of conceptualizing culture has analogical connections to (perhaps even genealogical roots in) developments in nineteenth-century social thought and the changing dynamics of late imperial rule. Attending to this period could yield important insights into contemporary conundrums about the relationship between culture and politics—the ways in which politics and political questions are often displaced and circumscribed by cultural forms, and the continuing difficulty of reconciling bounded and static conceptions of culture with transformative accounts of political sovereignty and agency.

ORGANIZATION OF THE BOOK

In elucidating the intellectual and ideological foundations of late empire, the book is organized around an extended analysis of the character and influence of Henry Maine's social and political theory. Maine was a pivotal figure in the transformation of British imperial ideology, in whose work one can trace the most direct, causal connection between the sociotheoretic model of traditional society and the ideology and practice of indirect rule. In this sense, the book aims to reconstruct central features of Maine's work to demonstrate the profound impact of his thought in the practical work of empire in nineteenth century. Maine's intricate analyses of the dynamics of ancient and primitive society are explored less with a view toward assessing their enduring truth value than for understanding the ways in which they articulated and responded to a set of theoretical dilemmas emergent from the imperial experience and, specifically, how Maine's ideas were mobilized to justify definite forms of action in the imperial policy arena.

Contemporary interpretations of Maine's work vary fundamentally depending on the context of intellectual formation and reception in which his work is situated, that is, whether Maine's work is understand in its Indian, British, or European milieus and whether his identity as a legal thinker, social theorist, historian, or political theorist is foregrounded.[36] In terms of Victorian intellectual discourse, Maine's identification of the expansion of the sphere of contract with the apex of civilization offered a conservative, historicist-cultural defense of laissez-faire liberal individualism, a progressivism that could easily be aligned with Victorian evolutionism. Considered from the vantage point of his work on village-communities, however, Maine was also taken up by a variety of advocates of communal property (from agrarian radicals to Indian nationalists) as a sympathetic defender of primitive societies.[37] This particular interpretative paradox—of how Maine came to be seen as simultaneously a defender of both custom *and* contract—is central to the preoccupations of this book. At the theoretical level, there was a crucial ambiguity in Maine's account of custom and precontractual society that lent itself to these divergent readings. While Maine was never a nostalgic champion of the virtues of traditional societies, his methodological approach to the study of primitive societies (the use of historical-comparative methods and the critique of utilitarianism) and his conceptualization of the integrity and rationale of ancient/primitive society worked to historicize and relativize the institutional forms of modern society. Historically, this ambiguity proved to be especially consequential, for despite his own reservations, Maine's account of primitive society would be used to justify the conscious retreat from freedom of contract and the defense of custom under the rubric of indirect rule. This study seeks to explore these interpretative conundrums by expanding the traditional lenses through which Maine's work is analyzed, bringing together his theoretical writings and his policy prescriptions, his lesser-known anthropological work and his jurisprudence, and, most importantly, taking into account the significance of both metropolitan and colonial intellectual arenas in the formation and influence of Maine's social and political theory as a whole.[38]

Chapter one argues that in the latter half of the nineteenth century moral and political justifications of empire, particularly the liberal model of imperialism, receded in significance from the forefront of debates about imperial rule. The chapter charts the transformation of imperial ideologies in the nineteenth century through the analysis of the work of Edmund Burke, James Mill, J. S. Mill, J. F. Stephen, J. R. Seeley, and Henry Maine. Over the course of the century, the central tenets of liberal imperialism were challenged as different forms of rebellion, resistance, and instability in the colonies instigated a more general crisis about the nature and purpose of imperial rule, a crisis that precipitated the waning of ethical justifications of empire. As modes of justification became more tentative in terms of their moral and political aspirations, late imperial ideologies of rule were presented less in ideological than pragmatic terms, as practical responses to and accommodations to the nature of "native society." Under this cover, social, cultural, and racial theories entered through the back door, as it were, to explain and legitimate the existence of empire; they functioned less as justifications than as alibis for the fait accompli of empire. The most important consequence for ideologies of imperial rule was a move away from the commitment to the more transformative ambitions underlying the so-called civilizing mission, a central hallmark of the project of liberal imperialism. In place of the universalist project of civilization, which at its core believed in the possibility of assimilating and modernizing native peoples, a new emphasis on the potentially insurmountable difference between peoples came to the fore.

Chapter two analyzes the relationship between empire and the origins of social theory, with a special focus on the development of a generic, apolitical model of traditional society. In Maine's seminal contribution, traditional society emerged as an integrated social whole that, while contrasted sharply with the imperatives of modern society, was understood to have a logic and rationale of its own. The dichotomy of the modern and the traditional—a central innovation of modern social theory—was constructed upon an intensification of the contrast between ancient and modern society that took place in the aftermath of the French Revolution. This intensification implied a systemic contrast, a move that involved the intermingling of specific methodological and political claims about the functional interdependency of social spheres, the malleability of human nature, the plasticity of social life, and the central determinants of human behavior. In this manner, dominant strands of social theory positioned themselves as critiques of political philosophy and foregrounded the sociological, cultural, and historical conditions that necessarily constrained the domain of political thought and action. The social theoretic model of traditional society exemplified the shift toward a view of human behavior that increasingly emphasized the nonrational bases of sociability, the dominance of social and cultural norms, and the persistence of historical habits and customs, thus intimating the essential features of the modern anthropological definition of culture. Moreover, it was this substantive model of traditional society as an integral whole, held together by reciprocal bonds of custom and structures of kinship, that would provide a theoretical foundation for late imperial ideologies of protection, preservation, and collaboration.

Chapters three and four examine how Maine's model of traditional/ primitive society became elaborated and implicated in two key imperial policy domains—legal reform and land tenure. In both cases, Maine would sharpen his theoretical account of traditional society and propose an innovative sociology of colonialism, demonstrating the ways in which the customary bases of traditional society were undermined through contact with modern institutions. These two domains were not only vital to the structure of imperial rule in South Asia, but the evolutionary history of law and property were also the central themes of Maine's scholarly work. These chapters examine Maine's practical contribution to Indian policy debates as they relate to the general trajectory of his political, historical, and legal thought. Maine was the leading figure of the English school of historical jurisprudence, who made his reputation through his critique of John Austin and the rival claims of utilitarian jurisprudence. Against the Austinian definition of law as "the command of the sovereign," Maine mined ancient and primitive legal sources to elucidate the transformative epochs, such as the era of customary law, through which law was seen to have generally passed before reaching its modern legislative form. Chapter three elaborates the practical and theoretical implications of Maine's jurisprudence by focusing on his intervention in the extended debate on the codification of Indian law. While Maine was a vehement advocate for a uniform civil code, his argument for codification was driven by his direct experience and distinct account of the current, disastrous state of Anglo-Indian law than by any Benthamite zeal for the benefits of enlightened codification. Maine's critical understanding of Anglo-Indian law grew out of his theoretical understanding of the natural trajectory of customary law and the deleterious impact of imperial rule and English law on native law. In this manner, Maine's important work as legal member of the Viceroy's Council is assessed in terms of immediate Indian policy debates as well as in terms of Maine's jurisprudence as a whole.

Chapter four turns to Maine's influential account of the history of property, its decisive role in the nineteenth-century debate on property, and its impact on the controversial debate on land tenure in British India. According to Maine, understanding the origins and evolution of property had been obscured by the dominance of natural law theory (in both its Roman and modern incarnations) that understood dominion in terms of individual modes of natural appropriation. By contrast, Maine offered an alternative sequence in which property was originally held in common and gradually over time becoming divided, breaking down into forms of individual ownership. Maine's thesis about the communal origins of rights in property (and of modern conceptions of rights in general) effectively called into question the historical and logical priority of the unitary conception of individual proprietorship, and imputed alternative communal modes a legitimate historicity. In this way, his evolutionary progressivism and optimism was tempered, perhaps unwittingly, with a historicism that engendered a presumption about the relativity of modern legal and political forms, especially the modern institution of private property in land. In practical terms, the latter made it possible to question the viability and applicability of modern institutions (legal, political, and economic) in societies (like India) considered to have not reached the appropriate stage of social evolution.

Chapter five details how Maine's theoretical portrait of primitive/ancient society, especially his innovative conceptualization of native society in crises, laid the foundation for the theory and practice of indirect rule. Maine argued that modern imperial rule had forced a direct confrontation between modern and traditional institutions, a confrontation that seemed to necessitate the dissolution of native society. Crucially, following

Maine, late imperial policy makers conceived of this dissolution as a major threat to the stability of the imperial order and thus implicated imperial rule in a political logic of protection, preservation, and restoration of traditional society. The chapter examines the specific ways this image of native society in dissolution was mobilized in the context of late imperial policy, first in post-Mutiny India and later in Southeast Asia and colonial Africa. Building upon the work of Maine, administrators such as Alfred Lyall, Lord Cromer, Arthur Gordon, and Lord Lugard, cumulatively elaborated a distinct political theory of indirect rule, institutionally grounded in a policy of decentralization and normatively associated with cosmopolitan pluralism.

Finally, the coda to this study revisits the question of liberalism's past and present relationship to empire and elucidates the theoretical significance, and contemporary political resonances, of this revised account of nineteenth-century imperial ideology. Attending to the origins of late imperial ideology in the crisis of liberal empire, I suggest, focuses critical analysis on a distinct political logic of modern empire—a regressive dynamic marked sequentially by moral idealism, culturalist explanation, and retroactive alibis. I argue that focusing on the political entailments of liberal imperialism, rather than upon its theoretical assumptions alone, offers a distinct (and perhaps more) effective strategy for understanding and criticizing the contemporary revival of liberal arguments for empire.

CHAPTER ONE

THE CRISIS OF LIBERAL IMPERIALISM

IN THE LATTER HALF of the nineteenth century—at the height of British imperial power—moral justifications of empire, paradoxically, receded from the forefront of debates about the nature and purpose of imperial rule. Just as British expansion assumed its greatest geographic reach, an ethically orientated theory of imperial legitimacy, exemplified in the liberal model of imperialism that had become prominent in British imperial discourse since the early nineteenth century, retreated in political significance. Moral justifications of empire were displaced as new sociological understandings of subject societies began to function as alibis for the maintenance of empire.

Since the origins of empire in India in the eighteenth century, major figures of British political thought had struggled not only to make sense of what they considered to be the "strange" and "anomalous" character of British rule in India,[1] but also to construct a politically legitimate and morally justifiable framework for imperial governance. For many, British India was considered to be an unprecedented and contradictory political formation; in Henry Maine's words, it was a "most extraordinary experiment" involving "the virtually despotic government of a dependency by a free people."[2] Thus models of imperial government were forged that could stem the flow of the potentially corrupting influences of despotism on metropolitan political institutions as well as offer a form of rule that was, in principle, beneficial for the subject people. And while there were great debates concerning which models of law and governance best fulfilled these goals, in the writings of Edmund Burke, James Mill, and John Stuart Mill there existed a common attempt to frame these debates in ethical terms, specifically in terms of a standard of moral duty concomitant to the status of the ruling power as a free, civilized people.

The liberal model of imperialism, which tied together a theory of imperial legitimacy with the project of improvement, represented the most fully developed moral justification of empire in nineteenth-century Britain. Liberal imperialism[3] came to embody a coherent ideology marked by an intersecting set of justifications and governing strategies centered on the duty of liberal reform as the primary purpose of imperial rule. In the latter half of the nineteenth century, however, the coherence of this vision as well as the political consensus underlying it began to unravel. The central tenets of liberal imperialism were challenged as various forms of rebellion, resistance, and instability in the colonies precipitated a broad-ranging reassessment of the means and ends appropriate to ruling a disparate and expanding empire.

In particular, the equation of "good government" with the improvement of native society, which was at the core of the discourse of liberal empire, would be subject to mounting skepticism. Influential critics such as James Fitzjames Stephen and Henry Sumner Maine cast doubt upon the philosophical assumptions underlying, and political consequences entailed by, the liberal-imperial idiom of improvement. In contesting the theoretical and practical viability of reshaping subject societies such as India along modern (English) models, late Victorian critics provoked a fundamental transition in imperial ideology.

This chapter explores the origins and consequences of the crisis of liberal imperialism as the fulcrum for understanding the transformation of imperial ideology in nineteenth-century Britain.[4] I seek to demonstrate how this distinct shift in attitudes was enabled, in part, by tensions in the theoretical development of liberal imperialism, tensions that were effectively exploited by liberal empire's sharpest critics. The crisis of liberal imperialism was part and parcel of the waning of moral justifications of empire. As modes of justification became more tentative in terms of their ethical and political aspirations, late imperial ideologies were presented less in normative than pragmatic terms, as practical responses to and accommodations with the nature of "native society." In this context, new sociological and anthropological theories of native society proved particularly effective as alternative modes of imperial legitimation; they functioned less as justifications than as alibis for the fait accompli of empire.

THE MORALITY OF EMPIRE

> . . . at first English power came among them unaccompanied
> by English morality. There was an interval between the
> time at which they became our subjects, and the time at
> which we began to reflect that we were bound to discharge
> towards them the duties of rulers.
> —*T. B. Macaulay*[5]

Determining the moral constraints on imperial power—the conditions under which imperial rule in India could be deemed legitimate—was central to Edmund Burke's agenda in the impeachment trial of Warren Hastings (the first Governor-General of India), the founding political drama of British India.[6] Burke's indictment of early East India Company rule would loom large throughout the nineteenth century and accounts (revisionary and otherwise) of the Hastings trial would be a recurring terrain on which the justification for empire would be debated.[7]

Burke began the impeachment trial by arguing that it was "according to the Judgement that you [the House of Lords] shall pronounce upon the past transactions of India, connected with those principles, that the whole rule, tenure, tendency, and character of our future government in India is to be finally decided."[8] In doing so, Burke construed the Hastings affair to be a verdict on the moral basis of future empire in India. Alongside Burke's charges of violations against "the eternal laws of justice"— in the form of treaty violations, arbitrary and despotic government, and acts of corruption committed by Hastings—was a pressing concern to articulate "some method of governing India *well*, which will not of necessity become the means of governing Great Britain *ill*."[9] In searching for the grounds of good government, Burke's vehement condemnation of Hastings never extended into a wholesale criticism of either the fact of overseas empire or indeed the precarious means by which the East India Company initially came to acquire territorial dominion. Burke famously argued that the legitimacy of government could not depend on the question of the justice of its founding moments. Governments, more often than not, were founded upon unlawful acts of violence, conquest, and usurpation. And, for the sake of stability,

> there is a secret veil to be drawn over the beginnings of all governments. They had their origins, as the beginning of all such things have had, in some matters that had as good be covered in obscurity. . . . But a wise nation, when it has made a revolution itself, and upon its own principles, there rests. The first step in revolution is to give it power; the next good laws, good order, to give it stability.[10]

For Burke, the East India Company wrested sovereign power by extraordinary and unjust means, yet its chief errors lie not in this "revolution" but in its inability to secure stable and lawful governance. Instead, the process of acquisition was followed by yet more revolutions that subverted any semblance of the rule of law; undermined native rights, liberties, and industry; and thus laid to waste a once prospering society. Burke's linking of the question of legitimacy to the securing of sound, lawful institutions set the stage for the succeeding generation of reformist arguments—such as those put forward by philosophic radicals like James Mill and evangelicals like Charles Grant—that likewise rested the moral basis of empire on the possibility of good government. However, the definition of good government, its structure and purpose, varied dramatically between Burke and the liberal reformers to come.

For Burke, to govern India *well* required, firstly, some kind of constitutional reform, that is, the creation of institutional checks to reign in what he saw as the arbitrary and "peculating despotism" of Hastings's rule. The tendency toward despotism was partly based, for Burke, on the fact that the Company acted like a tight-knit corporate entity, composed of young men not yet formed by education and society, and unmoored from any form of social and political restraints; they were "a Republic, a Commonwealth without a people." The problem of this strong esprit de corps among Company officers was that "they consider themselves as having a common interest separated both from the Country that sent them out and from the Country in which they are; and where there is no control by persons who understand their language, who understand their manners, or can apply their conduct to the Laws of the Country."[11] The consequence of which was the exercise of power without anyone to watch over, question, or regulate it. Burke's institutional solution was Fox's East India Bill (1783), which attempted to subject the Company more tightly to Parliamentary oversight and thus render the Company accountable.

Accountability for Burke was the essence of government understood as a *trust*.[12] But a true trust, from which all political power and authority ultimately stemmed, must be oriented toward the welfare of those over whom power is exercised. Hence, the government of India ought to be instituted so as to work for the benefit of the people of India, for their security, protection from oppression, and the preservation of rights and liberties. For Burke, if India could be so governed, Company rule would command a legitimacy based upon the implicit consent of the people governed, an essential feature of the idea of trusteeship. In an early speech on India, Burke elaborated the connection between trust and consent via the question of law. When considering upon which principles—English or Indian—law and legal reform should be based, Burke's answer was unequivocal: "men must be governed by those laws which they love. Where thirty millions are to be governed by a few thousand men, the government must be established by consent, and must be congenial to the feelings and habits of the people."[13] The deference to the customs and habits of the people, moreover, was linked to a normative principle in which the "empire of opinion" and prejudice were not only the grounds of everyday morality but also, for Burke, the key sources of happiness. It was due to this moral conception of the sources of obligation and action, and not just as a matter of stability (as later nineteenth-century imperial policymakers would stress) that Burke argued "that we, if we must govern such a Country, must govern them upon their own principles and maxims and not upon ours, that we must not think to force them to our narrow ideas, but extend ours to take in theirs; because to say that that people shall change their maxims, lives, and opinions, is what cannot be."[14] This was one of Burke's central criticisms against Hastings. Hastings, having ignored this fundamental principle thus undermined the possibility of both stable and moral government.

Burke was certainly mistaken to construe Hastings as a zealous innovator, bent on implementing English ideas and institutions with no regard to native customs and institutions. Hastings was a patron of Oriental learning, instrumental in the establishment of the Asiatic Society of Bengal and the attempted codification of Hindu and Muslim law for integration into Anglo-Indian legal administration. The heated debates of the Hastings trial tend to elide the more fundamental consensus between Burke and Hastings that took as their premise the creation of an imperial regime that was consistent with the "ancient constitution" of India, however differently they may have construed it to be.[15] The most important distinction between Burke and Hastings, in this regard, was in their starkly opposed interpretations of whether Indian polities could be understood under the rubric of "Oriental despotism."

In countering the thesis of Oriental despotism, Burke articulated a reverent image of the ancient laws, customs, and institutions of India, an image that would stand in dramatic contrast to the nineteenth-century view of India's downgraded civilizational status. Throughout the Hastings trial, Burke attempted to "awaken something of sympathy for the unfortunate natives"[16] of India by painting a tableau of India's geographical, social, and political landscape. In doing so Burke hoped to overcome the remoteness of India and what he considered to be the usual tendency to view its people as mere "strangers."[17] But it was by appealing to the antiquity of India, of its laws and religion, that Burke hoped to evoke a humility and appreciation that would deter the instinct toward premature and prejudicial conclusions. Thus Burke warned, "God forbid we should go to pass judgment upon a people who formed their Laws and Institutions prior to our insect origins of yesterday."[18]

It was precisely the reverence for Indian antiquity that James Mill and Charles Grant would target in their influential characterizations of Indian society and history. As Francis Hutchins has aptly shown, these writers sought to undermine the eighteenth-century view of India as a highly developed civilization (as depicted in the work of famed Orientalist William Jones and Scottish philosophical historian William Robertson) and replace it with an account that portrayed Indian society as exhibiting and promoting the most extreme forms of moral degradation. For both, tarnishing the prevailing assessments of India was, paradoxically, the necessary ground upon which to formulate a more expansive and elaborate notion of a "just rule."[19]

James Mill, father of John Stuart Mill and leading figure among radical and utilitarian reformers in early nineteenth-century Britain, was employed by the East India Company from 1819 to 1836. Mill's monumental *The History of British India* signaled a key shift in imperial ideology, and Mill himself, through his various theoretical writings and his prominent institutional position as Chief Examiner, became one of the most important intellectual influences in the shaping of Indian policy.[20] As a radical reassessment of Indian civilization, Mill's *History* was a full-scale assault upon every claim made on behalf of the achievements of Indian arts, science, philosophy, and government. Mill argued that Orientalists like Jones, through long personal contact with India and empathy for the natives, had become partial and thus susceptible to the exaggerated claims of its scholarly and scientific advances. Mill's history would be fundamentally different in that it would be a critical history, that is, "a *judging* history."[21]

The principal task of such a judgment, for Mill, was to accurately ascertain India's position in "a scale of civilization." To do this, one had to form a "joint view of all the circumstances taken together" rather than be misled, as the Orientalists had been, by one or two marks of advancement—such as the grandeur of the Mughal courts, the existence of philosophy, or the intricacies of ancient legal treatises. And with this general view one could then compare and contrast India with past and present societies in "different stages of social progress."[22] Mill used this method to meticulously prove that the so-called accomplishments of Indian thought and practice, if he could not reject them as outright fabrications (as he did in the case of Indian chronology), were consistent with the sorts of institutions and practices prevalent in a "rude and simple" state of society. Although Mill was not as precise as other Scottish historians, the appellation *rude* implied that Indian thought and civilization were the stilted products of a barbarous society, that is, a preagricultural society.[23]

More crucially, for Mill, this reevaluation of Indian society was not merely a scientific endeavor; it was essential for determining the structure and purpose of imperial rule:

> to ascertain the true state of the Hindus in the scale of civilization, is not only an object of curiosity in the history of human nature; but to the people of Great Britain, charged as they are with the government of that great portion of the human species; it is an object of the highest practical importance. No scheme of government can happily conduce to the end of government, unless it is adapted to the state of the people for whose use it is intended. . . . If the mistake in regard to Hindu society, committed by the British nation, and the British government, be very great, if they have conceived the Hindus to be a people of high civilization, while they in reality made but a few of the earliest steps in the progress to civilization, it is impossible that in many of the measures pursued for the government of that people, the mark aimed at should not have been wrong.[24]

Here Mill demonstrates how theories of native society and societal development generate specific strategies of imperial rule. For Mill, to break with the Orientalist philosophy of rule, that is, one that was premised on insinuating itself into existing indigenous traditions, required the rejection of the Orientalist image of Indian civilization. Native society was deemed to be corrupt and corrupting and thus an illegitimate basis upon which to build ideal governmental institutions.

But barbarism in India, while certainly the deep-seated cause of centuries of stagnation, was not, for Mill, a permanent, natural condition.[25] Rather, for Mill, the indolent, mendacious, and superstitious character of the natives was the long-term product of political despotism and religious tyranny. The moral character of the natives as a product of circumstance and social conditioning was, in principle, amenable to transformation, most significantly through the reform of law and government. The underlying image of human nature that sustained Mill's program for reform was intrinsically universal. Mill's obsessive critique of Jones's account of the glories of Indian civilization was meant to argue against viewing India as having a unique and separate historical trajectory. Rather, by insisting that Indian society was comparable to many forms of society in the earlier stages of social progress Mill sought to integrate Indian history into a universal account of the progress of society.[26] And, in doing so, Mill presented the grounds for why India could be deemed capable of improvement as well as a rationale for why Britain, as an advanced civilization, had the necessary knowledge and moral duty to rejuvenate Indian society.

For Mill, in every human society law was the essential mechanism for the transformation of conduct and thus the central tool by which Hindu manners could be freed from the sway of stultifying custom. As Eric Stokes's landmark work has shown, key Indian debates on the nature of governmental reform were made on the terrain of land revenue.[27] The debate on revenue and tax policy highlights the ways in which Mill's argument for rationalizing law was meant not only to promote liberty and rationality in manners but also to cultivate incentives for productive work. Reform would instigate a dual revolution toward both material wealth and the civilization of manners.

While for Mill the engine for moral reform was good government, for evangelicals like Charles Grant it required a more radical change in manners. Grant served with the Company for twenty-two years, from 1768 to 1790, eventually becoming Chairman of the Board of Proprietors. Grant was a key member of the Clapham Sect with close ties to William Wilberforce; he was the crucial figure who turned evangelical energies to the cause of missionization and social reform in India. Like Mill's *History*, Grant's *Observations on the State of Society among the Asiatic Subjects of Great Britain* grounded the project of reform upon the rejection of

Orientalist and Enlightenment histories of India. For Grant, it was the atheistic and anticlerical passion of the philosophical historians, such as Voltaire and Robertson, that sustained their mistaken exaltations of so-called Indian civilization.[28] In Grant's work, like Mill's, all the achievements of Indian society that arguably could be construed as signs of civilized society were ruthlessly condemned. Hindu manners and religion were salaciously portrayed as mired in deep superstition and moral degradation.[29] The source of corruption, and thus the proposed terrain of reform, was religion. For Grant, Hindu religion was despotic in character, maintained by a crafty priestly class determined to suppress all elements of individual autonomy. Good laws and upright administration in themselves would guarantee little, for Grant, if underlying manners fostered venality and indolence. "The true cure of darkness, is the introduction of light,"[30] which for Grant, in the absence of full-scale support for missionary activity, would be sought through the expansion of education, particularly English education.[31] Education in English through the introduction of the use of reason and argument would "silently undermine, and at length subvert, the fabric of error,"[32] without directly assaulting Hindu religion.

The key task for maintaining British rule in India was, for Grant, to determine the "grand moral and political principle, by which we shall henceforth, and in all future generations, govern and deal with our Asiatic subjects: Whether we shall make it our duty to impart to them knowledge, light, and happiness; or under the notion of holding them more quietly in subjection, shall seek to keep them ignorant, corrupt, and mutually injurious, as they are now?"[33] Rather than reconciling government to the nature and traditions of Indian society—rather than to "wink at the stupidity which we deem profitable to us; and as governors, be in effect the conservators of that system which deceives the people,"[34]—the foundation of British rule was to be a policy of assimilation, where Indian society would be reshaped along the lines of British society. For Grant, a policy of assimilation, especially in producing a native class fluent in English and English manners, would build "uniting principles," lasting ties between Britons and Indians that inculcated a native interest in the maintenance of British rule.[35] "This is the noblest species of conquest," argued Grant, "and wherever, we may venture to say, our principles and language are introduced, our commerce will follow."[36] The program of moral reform would lead to both material progress and civilization, developing a mode of intercourse in which both Indians and the British would equally benefit materially from the expansion of trade and commerce. For Grant, duty and self-interest could come together for, as in Macaulay's apt phrase, "to trade with civilised men is infinitely more profitable than to govern savages."[37]

Grant's and Mill's critique of Jones and the sympathetic tendencies of Orientalist scholarship transformed the framework of debates on what constituted a just and morally defensible basis for rule. For both, the Orientalists had become enthralled by the follies and superstition of Brahminical science and religion, and thus rescinded the moral obligation to create a form of government that would work toward the improvement of the subject race. Together they outlined a moral justification for imperial rule based on the prerogative of a liberal project of transformation. For J. R. Seeley, this combined platform of reform (liberal, utilitarian, and evangelical) ushered in the liberal era, in which, at last, Britain had boldly assumed its civilizational role.[38] It would be the dominant ideological idiom in which the British Empire would be understood throughout much of the nineteenth century. And, following an important period of retrenchment in the latter half of the nineteenth century, liberal empire would also significantly reconstitute itself in a developmental guise in the twentieth century.

In orienting the imperial project toward future improvement, rather than in terms of its historical origins, Mill and Grant rendered the foundations of empire *ethical* in a specific sense. The reformist argument for the morality and justness of empire was premised upon a simultaneous disavowal of conquest and force as legitimate sources of imperial authority.[39] This link between the morality of empire and the critique of conquest was elaborated in their portrayals of early Company rule, which was consistently denounced as sheer criminality. In his account of the Hastings trial and its indictment of early Company rule, for example, Mill aligned himself unambiguously with Burke.[40] For Grant, "a great deal was due from us to the people in compensation of the evils which the establishment of our power had introduced among them," and thus he pleaded for a new moral framework for imperial rule as a form of reparation for past misdeeds and the burden of imperial rule.[41] The fulfillment of the British debt owed to the inhabitants of India would be made through the radical reform of native society. This was a moral duty, not only in terms of a duty inherent in power to care for and promote the "civil and social happiness" of subjects, but also to rectify and absolve oneself of the crimes of conquest.[42] If British rule in India could ever be morally defended, it could only be with reference to its future potential rather than its past record.

For these early reformers what was needed to overcome the precarious and illegitimate beginnings of empire in India then was "good government" that is, the creation of a form of rule that would work toward the improvement of the subject race, thereby intertwining the moral defense of empire with a platform of liberal reform. The period of liberal ascendance is usually associated with the tenures of Lords Bentinck (1828–35) and Dalhousie (1848–56). The liberal manifesto of reform included the expansion of education (where missionaries in particular took the lead) and a liberal economic policy (support of laissez-faire and the breaking up of "feudal" tenures). The liberal regime was the most transparently interventionist in its ideals and practices; it was in this period that India became the testing ground for various reformist political, educational, and social experiments.[43] In terms of aspirations the liberal age was the first in which eventual self-government by Indians was first contemplated,[44] for the morality of rule was premised precisely on the grounds that once Britain completed its educative role in improving the morals and habits of the natives, giving them the capacity to exercise their liberty, its paternalist duty would be over. And any argument for the continuation of rule merely for the benefit of English prestige, wealth, or honor would be in principle unjustifiable.

But in tying together the ethical justification of empire with the project of liberal reform, the liberal agenda became susceptible to a variety of critiques that highlighted the theoretical and practical obstacles to improvement. The idea of progressive improvement, that native societies could be radically and rapidly transformed, was sustained by a belief in the infinite malleability of human nature, itself tied to an assumption about the universality of such a view. Both these notions concerning universality and perfectibility would be challenged, even among liberalism's greatest champions, as the claims of culturalism and historicism came to modify its fundamental tenets. And, when the modernizing transformation of native peoples became suspect, as was increasingly the case in the late nineteenth century, empire quickly lost its most salient ethical justification.

JOHN STUART MILL AND THE CRISIS OF LIBERAL IMPERIALISM

A key inheritor of the ethical justification of empire and its liberal idiom of improvement was John Stuart Mill, who, like his father, was a career employee of the East India Company. Mill's most famous formulation of a liberal justification of empire appears in the introduction to *On Liberty* (to be repeated in similar terms in *Considerations on Representative Government* two years later); "despotism is a legitimate mode of government in dealing with barbarians, provided the end be their improvement, and the means justified by actually effecting that end."[45] Mill was adamant that however difficult it was to attain such an ideal, "unless some approach to it is made, the rulers are guilty of a dereliction of the highest moral trust which can devolve upon a nation: and if they do not even aim at it, they are selfish usurpers, on par in criminality with any of those whose ambition and rapacity have sported from age to age with the des-

tiny of masses of mankind."[46] At the same time, while Mill's formulation
is often taken to be the apotheosis of the liberal model of empire, there
were important modifications in Mill's formulation that distanced his position from earlier variants. Indeed, some of the resources for questioning
the viability of the liberal model of improvement could be harnessed from
tensions internal to Mill's theoretical framework, most notably in his account of the necessary historical contrast between barbarism and civilization. In this sense, Mill stands as a crucial transitional figure in the transformation of imperial ideology from its strident belief in the reshaping of
native society toward a more paternalistic deference to the existing state
of native society.[47]

The idea of improvement, or "progress," was even more fundamental to Mill's political philosophy, one that profoundly shaped his theories
of liberty and representative government, and ultimately his argument
for imperial despotism. For Mill, utility as a principle of evaluation must
be understood in "the largest sense, grounded on the permanent interests of man as progressive being."[48] Likewise, a good government
worked to improve the character of its subjects, that is, to create the
proper conditions to support progressive improvement. This theory of
government entailed an intensely reciprocal relationship between political
institutions and a people's character; not only is the institutional compe-
tence of a government dependent on the right character of its subjects—
their virtues and intelligence—but, more importantly, the institutions
themselves had to be so modified as to suit the specific demands that
peoples in various "states of society" and "stages of civilization" required
for improvement.[49]

Mill's account of his own theoretical advance over Bentham's theory
of motivation emphasized the importance of government as one of the
great instruments of forming national character, "of carrying forward the
members of a community towards perfection or preserving them from
degeneracy."[50] One of Bentham's blind spots, according to Mill, was in
never regarding

> political institutions in a higher light, as the principle means of the social
> education of a people. Had he done so, he would have seen that the same
> institutions will no more suit two nations in different stages of civilization,
> than the same lessons will suit two children of different ages.[51]

The central error of Bentham's theory of government was thus its austere
universalism, its tendency to assume "that mankind are alike in all times
and all places,"[52] an error that Mill thought was common to the political
theories "of the last age . . . in which it was customary to claim representative democracy for England and France by arguments which would
equally have proved it the only fit form of government for Bedouins or

Malays." For Mill, what marked "the main point of superiority in the political theories of the present" was the recognition of an important and fundamental truth, that governing "institutions need to be radically different, according to the stage of advancement already reached."[53] This insistence that governing practices and institutions demanded profound alterations depending on the virtues and intelligence of a people, or in his terms the "state of society" or "stage of civilization," was of paramount importance to his defense of imperial despotism. For Mill, liberty was not an unqualified benefit in all times and for all peoples and especially was not appropriate to "any state of things anterior to the time when mankind have become capable of being improved by free and equal discussion."[54] The exercise of liberty to function as a means of improvement, like all principles of government, was dependent on the *antecedent* character of the society in question.

Mill's accounts of the various historical stages of civilization, and the sociological and psychological portraits attached to them, were never carefully elaborated. Although Mill's characterizations were at times loosely reminiscent of the four-stage theory formulated by eighteenth-century Scottish theorists, his portraits not only lacked their precision but also were motivated by very different concerns. Unlike his predecessors, Mill rarely linked the terms *savage* and *barbarian* with specific social structures, property relations, or modes of subsistence.[55] Rather, the portraits were more sociopsychological or culturally oriented, which, when taken in sequence, yielded a precarious, developmental logic that swung between the twin poles of excessive liberty and extreme slavery. Thus savage/barbarian societies were construed as too independent, lacking the ability to obey, whereas barbarian/stationary societies (and former slaves) were seen as suffering from an overdependence on custom and therefore lacking the instincts for spontaneity and self-government.

In an early essay titled "Civilization," Mill distinguished most straightforwardly the central features of savage/barbarian society, and thus obliquely delineated the substantive preconditions for the exercise of liberty. The main features of civilized life were the "direct converse or contrary of rudeness or barbarism." He wrote,

> a savage tribe consists of a handful of individuals, wandering or thinly scattered over a vast tract of country: a dense population, therefore, dwelling in fixed habitations, and largely collected in towns and villages, we term civilized. In savage life there is no commerce, no manufactures, no agriculture: a country rich in the fruits of agriculture: commerce, and manufactures, we call civilized. . . .Wherever, therefore, we find human beings acting together for common purposes in large bodies, and enjoying the pleasures of social intercourse, we term them civilized.[56]

In moving from the sociological to the psychological traits of both forms of social life, Mill deduced the power of social cooperation as the fundamental feature of civilized life. For Mill, what made the life of the savage materially poor and fragile was his inability to compromise, to sacrifice "some portion of individual will, for a common purpose."[57] The savage was pure ego, a selfish will that did not know how to calculate beyond immediate impulses. This portrait would reappear in later writings as one of the principle reasons for why barbarous societies fell outside the community of nations and the norms of international law. As Mill wrote,

> the rules of ordinary international morality imply reciprocity. But barbarians will not reciprocate. They cannot be depended on for observing any rules. Their minds are not capable of so great an effort, nor their will sufficiently under the influence of distant motives.[58]

Thus a savage or barbarous society, unable to either suppress immediate instincts or conceptualize long-term interests, was fundamentally incapable of the organization and discipline necessary for the development of the division of labor, for commerce and manufacture, and for military achievement—in short, for civilization. In such a state, according to Mill, a "vigorous despotism" would be the form of government ideally suited to teach the lesson of obedience.[59] Moreover, discipline, or "perfect cooperation"—the central attribute of civilized society—was deemed something that could only be learned incrementally through practice, for to render discipline into an unconscious habit required an immense length of time, perhaps even centuries.

Although the lesson of obedience was the first and indispensable step toward future improvement and civilization, for Mill, it was also only a partial advance and one that could easily solidify into an unwieldy form of societal stagnation. Even previously progressive societies, such as the civilizations of Egypt, India, and China, fell prey to this kind of immobility, where "the springs of spontaneity" and individuality are emasculated in the vast "despotism of Custom."[60] In this case, however, the governmental form most appropriate to break the bonds of unquestioned obedience was less clear. An ordinary, native despotism would only teach a lesson "only too completely learnt,"[61] and thus the solution must be sought in either the extraordinary appearance of a good despot, in "an Akbar or a Charlemagne, if they are so fortunate to find one"[62] or under the tutelary despotism of an advanced people, who through guidance rather than force can "superinduce from without" the improvement a stationary or slavish people cannot muster themselves.[63] In the age of empire, Mill noted, it was becoming "the universal condition of the more backward populations to be held in direct subjection by the more advanced."[64] Fortunately, an advanced, civilized people, was able, in principle, to provide a constant supply of good despots and could thus counteract the inherent evils of imperial subjection. An advanced people, having already trod the path of civilization, had the foresight to provide knowingly a form of government most conducive to "future permanent improvement."[65]

Mill's reliance on the historical contrast between barbarism and civilization as the central pivot of his defense of imperial despotism exposed a number of internal tensions in Mill's theoretical project, tensions that provided critics the resources for questioning the viability of the project of liberal imperialism itself. In Mill's theoretical framework, the temporal contrast between the civilized and the barbarian functioned to exclude the latter from the benefits of liberty and self-government as well as an equal status in the community of nations. As Mill writes in the introduction to *On Liberty*, the doctrine of liberty

> is meant to apply only to human beings in the maturity of their faculties. We are not speaking of children, or of young persons below the age at which the state may fix as that of manhood or womanhood. Those who are still in a state to require being taken care of by others, must be protected against their own actions as well as against external injury. For the same reason, we may leave out of consideration those backward states of society in which the race itself may be considered as in its nonage.[66]

Conceptually, Mill's recurrent analogy between the immaturity of children and the immaturity of barbarous societies reveals a characteristic vulnerability of liberal universalism. The political exclusion of children is a consistently thorny issue for liberal political theory for it implies what Uday Mehta names a disjuncture or gap between the foundations and actualization of liberal universalism.[67] For Mehta, universalism in liberalism is derived from a minimalist philosophical anthropology, that is, from the articulation of a minimum set of characteristics and capacities taken to be common to all humans. In the liberal tradition, these common, universal, characteristics are often construed as natural freedom, moral equality, and the innate capacity to reason. The political actualization of these universalist premises—for example, to be included in the political constituency of the Lockean social contract or to be capable of permanent improvement in the Millian sense—is nevertheless mediated by the real capacity of the potential citizen to properly exercise their reason. This capacity, what Mill calls intellectual maturity, turns out to be empirically conditioned, and thus not quite or not yet universal. The paradox of the child born free but not yet able to practice liberty is thus particularly revealing of how "behind the universal capacities ascribed [by liberalism] to all human beings exist a thicker set of social credentials that constitute the real bases of political inclusion."[68] Mill projects the paradox of the child onto a scale of civilization and in so doing expands and heightens, in cultural and historical terms, the requirements for political inclusion.

In moving away from Bentham's strict universalism, Mill had already committed himself to a more diversified account of character, one more thoroughly conditioned by custom and society. By tightly binding the benefits of liberty and representative government to civilizational development, Mill further circumscribes the possibility of political liberty with the imperatives of culture and history. In limiting the applicability of liberalism in this manner, Mill's ethical justification of empire displaces the burden of legitimation onto the terrain of empirical (cultural and historical) arguments concerning the nature of subject populations. If the question of how imperial rule ought to be structured is subordinated to a primary and prior question about the nature of native societies, the responsibility for the imperial project becomes inextricably tied to questions about the empirical and theoretical possibility of progress in these societies.

Although Mill's theory of civilization in principle was premised on the inherent potential of all peoples to improve, in his substantive characterization of savage and barbarous states of society, Mill emphasized both the unpredictable, arduous development of civilization, everywhere threatened by potential degeneracy and stagnation, and the potentially limitless time-horizon needed for such advancement. Furthermore, Mill characterized the process of civilization—this training that is the condition of possibility for progress—not only in terms of an incremental process of learning but also one that is collective in nature. In doing so, Mill exposed a deep theoretical tension between the commitment to liberal reform and improvement and the practical impediments for the realization of the progressive transformation of peoples. Thus, the sharp contrast between barbarism and civilization, when grounded in this particular philosophy of history, appeared more and more like a permanent barrier.

In his interest in character formation and improvement as the principle end of governance, Mill emphasized the ways individual character was dependent on and shaped by national character. Indeed, understanding the precise and formative interplay between individual and national character was to be the great theme of his proposed science of "ethology."[69] Although some consider Mill's concern with the diverse forms of national character and his reference to pyschologized portraits of the differences among, for example, Celtic, Anglo-Saxon, and Asiatic characters—and we could add, the savage and the barbarous mind—to be signs of an underlying racism, it is clear that Mill never thought of character as biologically determined. Rather, Mill emphasizes the variability of character within similar states of society and its malleability, impairment, and perfectibility over time. In his famous reply to Carlyle's racist arguments, Mill was clear that any analytical investigation into "laws of the formation of character" would correct "the vulgar error of imputing every difference . . . among human beings to an original difference of nature."[70] At the same time, however, Mill also insisted that the improvement of character, especially "spontaneous" or internally generated improvement was "one of the rarest phenomena in history" and depended on an extraordinary concatenation of accidents and advantages.[71]

But if Mill's concept of character was not a racial one, when conjoined with an emphasis on the group as the bearer of civilizational improvement, it functioned as an analogue of race as a principle of sociological and anthropological explanation. In other words, although Mill objected to racial theories of human diversity, his theory of character formation was meant in part to explain and account for these same, entrenched differences in collective terms. Furthermore, in Mill's reflections on the principle of nationality, collectivities—specifically, the nation—were endowed with a moral character. For Mill, the nation was not only the site for "the growth and development of a people," it was also a form of cultural achievement, equivalent in normative status to civilization. Thus, barbarian societies were not true nations, indeed for them "nationality and independence are either a certain evil, or at best a questionable good."[72] Nationality not only functioned as the means of justifying the exclusion of barbarous societies from the norms of international law; more importantly, it revealed the extent to which, for Mill, civilization and barbarism were only ever features of collectivities.

With the focus on the collective nature of learning and cultivation, Mill's theory of civilization here (as well as Mill's proposed science of ethnology) anticipates the anthropological theory of culture, which also came to emphasize the cultural and historical determination of behavior in the context of ongoing processes of social integration and collective learning. In Mill's characterization of civilization as both precarious and collective in nature, then, we begin to see the turn to culture as a mode of differentiation emerging from within the trajectory of liberal imperialism itself. Mill's ascription of collective characteristics to societies and peoples poses a number of specific challenges to the discourse of liberal empire. On the one hand, it sharpens the contrast between civilization and barbarism in a such a way as to make the eventual transition from the one state to the other seem exceedingly difficult, if not impossible. On the other hand, obstacles to improvement, or failures in achieving this transformation, are effectively redescribed as cultural impediments to the norms and institutions of civilization. A number of these tensions in Mill's portrait of civilization made the liberal project of empire vulnerable to critics who increasingly sought to emphasize the theoretical and practical impediments to improvement. In Mill's work, the basic commitment to an idea of human nature as malleable and infinitely perfectible had lost its purchase when linked to a philosophy of history and a theory of character formation that at the same time emphasized the precarious and incremental development of progressive societies in human history. Critics would emphasize the latter aspect over the former, concluding either that models of perfectibility needed to be abandoned or that moral reform required a great deal more coercion than liberals could countenance.

These criticisms revealingly came to the fore in the most prominent public debates on empire in the late nineteenth century and worked to undermine the political efficacy and salience of the ethical arguments of liberal imperialism. In key imperial scandals of the period, for example, the response to the Indian Mutiny or Rebellion of 1857, the Governor Eyre controversy of 1865, and the Ilbert Bill crisis of 1883, advocates of liberal imperialism found themselves consistently on the losing side of the argument. Here, I begin with the Eyre controversy, not least because Mill himself played a prominent role in this public debate. Moreover, in many of the debates, Millian liberalism would become the avowed target for critics from Carlyle to Stephen, who specifically saw his brand of "sentimental liberalism" as inimical to political stability both at home and abroad.

The public controversy began in 1865 upon news from Jamaica of a "rebellion" in Morant Bay and its suppression by the then Governor of Jamaica, Edward John Eyre.[73] As reports of the extent and brutal nature of the rebellion's suppression came to light, Mill (now a Liberal MP for Westminster) joined the Jamaica committee, which was formed initially to lobby the government for an official inquiry, and then (when it was clear that the government would do no more than dismiss Eyre from his post) to bring criminal charges against Eyre and his deputies. As the Jamaica committee's chair and leading spokesman, Mill made the case for Eyre's criminal prosecution on the grounds that Eyre's abuse of martial law, most egregiously in the military trial and execution of George William Gordon (a well-known mixed-race MP in the Jamaican Assembly), was akin to state-sponsored murder.[74] This amounted to a frontal assault on the rule of law, which for Mill was a principle that necessarily reached across the empire, for it was the duty of advanced, ruling countries to impart this "first necessity of human society"[75] to subject races. If Eyre's actions were excused as the regrettable but understandable excesses of power endemic to a colonial situation (which was the essence of the Royal Inquiry into his actions), the liberal imperial model of benevolent despotism that Mill thought was genuinely possible would be radically undermined. This possibility no doubt fueled Mill's vehement commitment to Eyre's prosecution, which, after three years, came to nothing. Indeed, the vocal public campaign proved to be, in important respects, counterproductive.

The long campaign to publicize Eyre's abuses galvanized an even stronger opposition to the civilizing ideals of liberal imperialism. The widespread opposition to the prosecution of Eyre was, to say the least, multifaceted.[76] Prominent members of the Jamaica committee included John Bright, Charles Darwin, Herbert Spencer, T. H. Huxley, Charles Lyell, and T. H. Green. On the other side, vocal supporters of Eyre included Thomas Carlyle, John Ruskin, A. L. Tennyson, Charles Dickens, and Matthew Arnold. The sharp polarization between the supporters and critics of Eyre intersected with and intimated the growing rift between the proponents and critics of democracy. The Eyre controversy coincided with the public agitation and debate about the Second Reform Bill, and fear of unrest in the empire was necessarily intertwined with anxieties about the growth of popular government and mass democracy. Carlyle and Arnold likened the Hyde Park riots to the events of Morant Bay as evidence of a growing anarchy fanned by liberal sentimentalism, an anarchy that required a strong, decisive show of force.[77] The Eyre crisis would initiate a divide among liberals, between "old" and "new" Liberals, which would culminate in the crisis over Irish Home Rule and the abandonment of the Liberal Party by its more conservative members. In this manner, concerns about liberal imperialism were necessarily implicated in the more general crisis of liberalism, shaping the character and trajectory of nineteenth-century liberalism.[78]

Moreover, the failure of Mill and the Jamaica committee to procure a criminal trial of Eyre portended an important ideological shift in discourses of imperial legitimation and metropolitan attitudes toward subject peoples.[79] The public support for Eyre revealed an increasingly unsympathetic view of subject peoples, in this case toward the ex-slave population of Jamaica. The Morant Bay Rebellion, coming on the heels of the Indian Mutiny/Rebellion of 1857, signaled for many an ingratitude on the part of Jamaicans and Indians for the civilizing character of imperial rule. The fact of rebellion provoked a sense of disillusionment in the progressive ideals of abolition, and the burden of responsibility was placed squarely on the shoulders of freed Jamaican slaves who seemingly failed to take advantage of the benefits of emancipation. Explanations for the "failure" in social and moral improvement, coupled with the drama of revolt, engendered increasingly racialized depictions of the allegedly insolent and irredeemably savage nature of Jamaica's black community.[80] The reform and improvement of native customs and morals seemed not only be limited in effect but also potentially dangerous to the stability of empire. Thus the reactions to the events of Morant Bay, like responses to the Indian Rebellion, heralded a deepening sense of racial and cultural difference between rulers and ruled, on the one hand, and a distancing from the universalist and assimilationist ideals of liberal imperialism, on the other.

IMPERIAL AUTHORITARIANISM BROUGHT HOME: JAMES FITZJAMES STEPHEN AND THE ILBERT BILL CRISIS

Like the public debates unleashed by the Governor Eyre controversy, the Ilbert Bill crisis of 1883 also exemplified central paradoxes in liberal justi-fications of empire. But while the Eyre controversy was instigated by a dramatic episode of violence that shaped the tenor of the debate, the Ilbert Bill crisis was peaked by a relatively minor piece of Indian legislation. Less overdetermined by questions of order, the debate about the Ilbert Bill crisis was framed more explicitly by rival philosophies of imperial rule. The challenge to the ideals of liberal imperialism that was intimated in the Eyre controversy became more openly proclaimed in the defeat of the Ilbert Bill.

In 1883, Courtney Ilbert, as Law Member of the Viceroy's Council, introduced a seemingly innocuous amendment to the Indian Criminal Procedure Code, extending the right to try cases involving Europeans to native magistrates in rural districts.[81] But in attempting to remove this minor "anomaly" to procedural universality, Ilbert unwittingly instigated widespread protest among the nonofficial British population in India and propelled the Government of India into a general crisis.[82] For those British Indians the bill's attempt to equalize the authority of British and native judges also implicitly advocated a philosophy of reform that sought to undermine any special rights, privileges, and protections that the British settlers enjoyed. The bill was clearly grounded in a basic commitment and belief in the legal equality between Indians and Britons, a principle that when insisted upon had also previously provoked resistance.[83] In the face of such vehement opposition, the bill in its original form could not pass the Legislative Council, and instead a watered down version of the bill was finally approved after two years of intense criticism.[84]

As criticism of the bill mounted in both Britain and India, it became increasingly clear that what was at stake was less the status of British Indians per se than the fundamental philosophy of British rule in India. Lord Ripon, the Liberal Viceroy appointed by Gladstone and under whose watch the bill was introduced, articulated the "great question" that was now so openly debated.[85] The question, according to Ripon, was not about the particular provisions supported by the Ilbert Bill, but the principles upon which India is to be governed. Is she to be ruled for the benefit of the Indian people of all races, classes, and creeds, or in the sole interest of a small body of Europeans? Is it England's duty to try to elevate the Indian people, to raise them socially, to train them politically, to promote their progress in material prosperity, in education, and in morality; or is it to be the be all and end all of her rule to maintain a precarious power over what Mr. Branson[86] calls "a subject race with a profound hatred of their subjugators"?[87]

Ripon thus articulated and defended the basic premises of a liberal justification of empire, one in which the purpose of imperial government must be for the moral education and betterment of the subject people, rather than for the benefit of the home country or some faction therein. In practical terms, the aim of the Government of India would be the timely introduction of and expansion of liberal principles in the central institutions of education, law, and government. Through these institutional reforms moral and political education would be ensured. For British and native supporters of the Ilbert Bill, the bill represented the logical fruition of the liberal agenda, because it was due to the success of these policies that native judges qualified for promotion existed at all. The heated contestation of the principle of legal equality that was at stake in the Ilbert Bill thus struck the core of the transformative and educative project of liberal imperialism.

The most eminent spokesman for the opposition was James Fitzjames Stephen, who had previously served as Law Member under Lord Mayo. Stephen opposed the adoption of a similar bill under his tenure and, in the midst of the crisis, published a provocative letter in *The Times* warning that the bill's passage would undermine the foundations of British rule. As Stephen wrote,

if the Government of India have decided on removing all anomalies from India, they ought to remove themselves and their countrymen. Whether or not that mode of expression can be fully justified, there can, I think, be no doubt that it is impossible to imagine any policy more fearfully dangerous and more certain in case of failure to lead to results to which the Mutiny would be child's play, than the policy of shifting the foundations on which the British government of India rests. It is essentially an absolute government, founded, not on consent, but on conquest. It does not represent the native principles of life or of government, and it can never do so until it represents heathenism and barbarism. It represents a belligerent civilization, and no anomaly can be so striking and so dangerous as its administration by men who, being at the head of a Government founded on conquest, implying at every point the superiority of the conquering race, of their ideas, their institutions, their opinions and their principles, and having no justification for its existence except that superiority, shrink from the open, uncompromising, straightforward assertion of it, seek to apologize for their own position, and refuse, from whatever cause, to uphold and support it.[88]

The corollary to the unabashed assertion of superiority, for Stephen, was unapologetic authoritarian rule in the colonies. For Stephen, defenders of liberal empire had confused good government with representative government and, in doing so, assumed that absolute or authoritarian government could only be justified "as a temporary expedient used for the purpose of superseding itself, and as a means of educating those whom it affects into a fitness for parliamentary institutions."[89] But absolute government, argued Stephen, was not the same as arbitrary or despotic rule, and for the purpose of promoting the welfare of native subjects it had "its own merits and conveniences."

Despite the brashness of his rhetoric, Stephen was not merely a jingoistic defender of empire. Stephen thought of himself as articulating a more robust and consistent utilitarian liberalism. Stephen's argument for absolute rule as a form of legitimate and good government was premised on a theoretical account of the necessity of coercion as a mechanism for the improvement of native society. The most important mechanism, in this regard, was the implementation of a sound system of laws based upon English principles that would induce peace and security and thereby effect a change in moral and religious practices. Without law and order, which was Britain's great export, India would dissolve into the chaos and anarchy in which it was supposedly found. For Stephen, coercion was a necessity because Britain's "great and characteristic task is that of imposing on India ways of life and modes of thought which the population regards, to say the least, without sympathy."[90]

This minimal commitment to substitute English civilization for Indian barbarism, however, was not conceived of as a moral duty, less still as a kind of atonement or apology for the sins of conquest. Rather, it was a sign of and the means by which to express England's virtue, honor, and superiority. As such it was in principle a permanent and not temporary enterprise (as the liberal camp proposed) and, for Stephen, ought to have been justified as such. Stephen straightforwardly criticized as dangerous and hypocritical the view of empire as resting upon "a moral duty on the part of the English nation to try to educate the natives in such a way as to lead them to set up a democratic form government administered by representative institutions."[91] While Stephen's argument for vigorous authoritarianism in India overlapped with Mill's emphasis on the need to inculcate habits of discipline in barbarous societies, in criticizing the ethical horizon of liberal empire, Stephen sought to undermine the normative appeal of the goal of self-government more generally. Through the claim that self-government was unfit for India, Stephen hoped to expose its limitations for England as well.

As one of Mill's best-known contemporary critics, Stephen exemplified the ways in which the critique of liberal imperialism coalesced with a more general critique of certain trajectories of liberal thought, especially those of a popular and democratic kind. According to Stephen, the ideas contained in *Liberty, Fraternity, Equality*, his famous polemic against Mill, took shape during his tenure in India. It was his "Indian experience" that confirmed his belief in the dangers of "sentimental" liberalism of the Millian kind for both England and the Empire.[92] *Liberty, Fraternity, Equality* was a wholesale attack on the philosophical basis and sociopolitical consequences of Mill's moral commitment to the idea of liberty, as it was enunciated in *On Liberty*.

For Stephen, Mill's proposition that self-protection could be the only grounds for coercion or compulsion was unsustainable and illustrative of a deeper set of commitments that Stephen found to be philosophically untenable and practically objectionable. Mill's attempt to delineate a sphere of free action, for Stephen, revealed Mill's illegitimate prioritizing of the principle of liberty over that of utility, revealing an absolute and independent commitment to the value of liberty. For Stephen, valuing liberty in this private, individual sense was as amoral as it was incoherent, for it undermined law as well as all systems of morality and religion based upon different forms of coercion deemed illegitimate in Mill's schema. Indeed, for Stephen, what Mill claimed to be the practical effects of liberty in history—that is, the expansion of freedom of speech and discussion and the concomitant shift from compulsion to persuasion as the vehicle of moral improvement—was a misreading of the actual source of moral progress, namely the historical effects of moral and legal coercion. Thus, liberty was only ever a contingent value, subject to the principle of utility and dependent upon the rule of law.

The benevolent despotism of imperial rule, moreover, proved emphatically that liberty was not a necessity for the purpose of good government. For Stephen, man was not by nature a progressive being, but one who was at heart selfish and unruly and therefore needed to be continuously compelled to live peaceably and morally in society. Mill's tenuous distinction between civilized and barbarous societies thus could be easily reversed; what was deemed appropriate for barbarians was equally suitable for civilized society (or at least certain classes therein). Here is a characteristic passage of Stephen's that turns on the inversion of Mill's distinction between barbarism and civilization:

> You admit that children and human beings in "backward states of society" may be coerced for their own good. You would let Charlemagne coerce the Saxons, and Akbar the Hindoos. Why then may not educated men coerce the ignorant? What is there in the character of a very commonplace ignorant peasant or petty shopkeeper in these days which makes him a less fit subject for coercion on Mr. Mill's principle than the Hindoo nobles and princes who were coerced by Akbar?[93]

Stephen pointedly questioned Mill's attribution of the status of civilization and barbarism only to societies and not to individuals therein. And if the collective nature of the classification of stages of civilization were undermined, for Stephen, the principles of imperial government, as a model for moral and legal coercion, could no longer be held at the water's edge; they may indeed be equally well suited for a rapidly democratizing Britain. As Stephen writes, "it seems to me quite impossible to stop short of this principle if compulsion in the case of children and 'backward' races is admitted to be justifiable; for, after all, maturity and civilization are matters of degree."[94]

Stephen's sly critique made apparent the ways in which Mill's criteria of civilization worked to draw the boundaries of the nation in such a way as to include the working classes in the democratic project while sharply excluding the possible extension of these same democratic principles to non-European societies. Stephen's polemic, while certainly sardonic in its concern for "Hindoo nobles," nevertheless called attention to fundamental inconsistencies in Millian liberalism, to the ways in which the commitment to equality as it became evermore tied to collective cultural and historical criteria was necessarily transmuted into a tenuous defense of hierarchy in the imperial realm (a move that threatened the coherence of the original concept of liberal equality itself).[95] Stephen capitalized on Mill's justification of imperial despotism to make a bolder claim for the necessity and even priority of the principle of hierarchy and nonconsensual coercion for all societies, regardless of their supposed place on the civilizational scale.

The muted conclusion of the Eyre controversy and defeat of the Ilbert Bill highlighted persistent cracks in the edifice of liberal justifications of empire, fissures that would be increasingly used by opponents to undermine liberal positions in debates about empire in late Victorian England. As Stephen's arguments exemplify, these debates about empire helped to consolidate a growing illiberal or antiliberal consensus, fueled by domestic fears about the growth of mass democracy. It was not just that conservative views of empire triumphed over liberal views, but that it was on the question of empire that a substantial group of Victorian intellectuals were converted from the liberal to the conservative side.[96] The catastrophic split of the Liberal Party in 1886 was sparked not by a domestic issue but by a dispute about the status of Ireland in the British Empire, specifically about whether the principles of democracy and self-government could be applied to the dependent empire. Self-defined "old Liberals" such as Stephen and Maine had begun to develop a new brand of conservatism that was fundamentally shaped by their experience of empire in India and their critical reappraisal of liberal imperialism.[97]

Stephen and Maine were pivotal conduits for the infusion of authoritarian elements into British political thought, an authoritarianism that was legitimated by their Indian experience and provoked by a fear of popular government. In Stokes's pioneering work, Stephen's thought is seen as the fulfillment of an authoritarian tendency inherent in utilitarianism.[98] However, I would argue that Stephen's authoritarian liberalism, as his critique of liberal modes of imperial legitimation and models of imperial rule demonstrate, instead represented a distinct break with the moral imperatives of the early utilitarian interest and engagement in India. His lifelong association with Maine, who would become the foremost Victorian critic of utilitarianism, attests to the fact that Stephen's conservatism, like Maine's, was cemented by a deep skepticism and disillusionment with utilitarianism in its imperial career, on the one hand, and a profound anxiety about the coming of mass democracy, on the other.

But while the conservative critique of democracy in the end did not stem the tide toward universal suffrage in Britain, this illiberal turn fed the growth of popular imperialism in domestic political discourse and, more crucially for this study, had a profound effect on the transformation of imperial policy in the late Victorian era. The crisis of liberal imperialism signaled a shift in the languages of justification away from ethical frameworks toward racial and cultural premises (as well as a revival of theories of rightful conquest). Yet the transition itself was deeper, for the inefficacy of liberal justifications of empire in the late nineteenth century was symptomatic of a more thoroughgoing transformation of ideologies and practices of imperial rule, transformations that were consciously premised on a critique of previous liberal ideologies of rule.

EMPIRE, NATION, CONQUEST: REVISING THE LANGUAGES OF JUSTIFICATION

... the real Indian question was not whether the English
were justified in staying in the country, but whether they
could find any moral justification for withdrawing from it.
—*Evelyn Baring, Lord Cromer*[99]

The project of liberal imperialism tied its moral justification to a coherent set of ideologies of rule, most notably in outlining a platform of reform based on the transformative goals of the civilizing mission. With the crisis of this overarching vision, both aspects would be subject to critique and revision. Late imperial ideologies and discourses of justification were grounded in a common, conservative opposition to the liberal project. The disavowal of the moral discourse of liberal empire thus functioned alongside and generated alternative strategies for ruling subject peoples. In this section I will focus on the different ways in which the moral vision of liberal imperialism as a discourse of legitimation was criticized, transformed, and revised in the late nineteenth century.

As was noted at the outset, one of the most interesting features of the liberal justification of empire was the way in which it carved out its moral vision through a consistent, often scathing, critique of conquest as a source of imperial legitimacy. The disavowal of conquest was part and parcel of a future-oriented view in which the purpose of empire was tied to the realization of a particular moral project. Thus, revising the accepted narrative about the early history of Company rule, constituted by the critical writings of Burke, James Mill, and Macaulay, was a prominent and revealing feature of late Victorian imperial writing.

In one of Stephen's last works, *The Story of Nuncomar and the Impeachment of Sir Elijah Impey*, Stephen revisited the original "crimes" of British India and the impeachment trial of Warren Hastings.[100] Ever since Burke's famous prosecution of Hastings at the end of the eighteenth century, the question of the legitimacy of British rule in India was intimately tied to one's position vis-à-vis this originary moment.[101] For liberals like James Mill and Macaulay the disavowal of conquest and the critique of early Company rule was the necessary first step in arguing for a new, firmer, and more moral, basis for imperial rule. Thus for Stephen the return to the trial was a way to sever the link between the morality of empire and the critique of conquest. In rehabilitating the notorious figure of Impey,[102] Stephen tried instead to argue that the so-called crimes of conquest were exaggerated if not entirely fabricated. In this way, conquest, now devoid of its associations with criminality, could emerge as legitimate on its own terms. And as was clear in *Liberty, Equality, Fraternity*, for Stephen, power and force were legitimate and primary sources of authority in both domestic and imperial arenas.

Stephen's revisionary history of the Hastings's era, with its audacious defense of the legitimacy of conquest and force, struck at the heart of an earlier liberal consensus. For Stephen, imperialism had no moral component except as a sign of a kind of superiority that was both expressed by and justified an inherent right to rule. Of course an authoritarian form of imperial rule was conceived of as a model of good government in terms of stability and for providing some form of coercive moral education. But imperial rule was never to be conceived of as primarily an educative project, especially one with a limited temporal horizon. The right to rule severed from the fulfillment of any particular vision or purpose merely held a self-referential, expressive function.

Stephen's reformulation, however, was avowedly critical of liberal imperialism and represents the reversal of its tenets in the starkest of terms. Other liberals responded more ambivalently, and this is nowhere more evident that in relation to the theme of conquest. In J. R. Seeley's great work, *The Expansion of England*,[103] the fact of conquest is consistently raised only to be disavowed as a proper characterization of either the mode by which England acquired its Indian empire or as a justification of India's present status as a dependency. What is significant in Seeley's attempt to cleanse empire of its unsavory associations with conquest is that it is also severed from any distinct moral project or aim. These two aspects, I would argue, are not unrelated, for what lent the liberal project its peculiar ethical weight was its ability to frame and judge the history of empire in moral terms. As we shall see, in rendering the moral grounds of empire in more ambivalent terms, empire itself lost a straightforward purpose or substantive agenda.

Seeley's ambivalence can be seen in the ways in which he mobilized traditional liberal arguments and motifs but also reoriented them in important ways. Like the earlier liberal project, Seeley conceived of empire as essentially a temporary enterprise, whose ultimate telos, in principle, was Indian independence. Yet, the criteria for when India would be deemed capable of self-government are conceived of in new terms. Moreover, like Grant and James Mill, there is throughout Seeley's work a sense in which England must bear some responsibility for the current state of Indian society. Seeley's account of this responsibility had less to do with a kind of moral atonement (as Grant's evangelical language implied) and it was paradoxically both more hesitant and more triumphalist. Seeley claimed that in the founding of empire, there were "some deeds which, though they had been better not done, cannot be undone."[104] Through the recounting of the lawlessness and violence of acquisition, on the one hand, and a more subtle picture of the ways in which the introduction of English education and science undermined traditional beliefs and authority structures, on the other, Seeley accepted that keeping India within the fold of empire imposed serious and difficult responsibilities. Yet, at the same time, Seeley also construed these responsibilities in the narrowest of terms. In doing so, Seeley's portrayal is guided by a spirit of triumphalism; imperial rule from the moment of conquest was construed as a success, as already a better alternative to leaving India in its natural trajectory toward disintegration.

In Seeley's account, "conquest" was declared a misnomer as a description of the acquisition of the Indian empire. English rule was the natural fulfillment of a purely *internal* tendency of Indian political history. The eighteenth-century machinations of rival Indian principalities in alliance with competing European powers in the subcontinent, was, for Seeley, a time when "the distinction of national and foreign seems to be lost." And thus, "India can hardly be said to have been conquered at all by foreigners; she has rather conquered herself."[105] Since mercenary Indian armies were fighting to wrest control from rival powers, the ascendancy of the British was less a foreign conquest than a coup d'état: "to term the event a conquest is thoroughly misleading. It is not a foreign conquest, but rather an internal revolution."[106] If there was no conquest, there was nothing for which the British needed to atone. For Seeley, since British rule brought stability and government, it was always already an advance upon the supposed anarchy that had ensued in the wake of the disintegration of the Mughal Empire. Moreover, the term *conquest* was misleading because, for Seeley, it implied a *foreign* conquest. And in suggestively arguing that terms such as *national* and *foreign* had no meaning in the context of eighteenth-century India, Seeley was in fact putting forward a far bolder claim, namely, that in India there was and is no sense of nationality. Conquest could only be conceived of as a political affront if the subjected population formed a recognizable community, because "it is upon the assumption of such a homogenous community that all our ideas of patriotism and public virtue depend."[107]

The use of the moral discourse around the nation and nationality as a justification of imperial rule became more insistent in the late nineteenth century, even as the discourse around the so-called civilizing mission waned. While, for Mill, the claim that barbarians could not form true nations was certainly meant to legitimate imperial subjection (and perhaps even outright conquest), it was subordinated to the purpose of civilizing. The primary reason for withholding the status of nationhood from barbarous societies was that for these societies "nationality and independence are either a certain evil, or at best a questionable good."[108] In other words, for Mill, nationality (especially as it relates to so-called barbarians) is conceptualized more in normative rather than sociological terms as an equivalent for self-government and thus subject to the same moral and civilizational requirements.

Later liberal theorists of empire tended to mobilize and prioritize the sociological analysis of nationality, severed from any strict or elaborate scale of civilization, as the linchpin to justify imperial rule. For Seeley, here originating a highly influential view of India's internal divisions to be circulated by prominent imperial observers of the time,[109] India lacked uniting forces; there was no community of race or religion out of which a feeling or belief in nationality could develop. As Seeley writes, "it appears then that India is not a political name, but only a geographical expression like Europe or Africa,"[110] and in its history if it displayed any semblance of a unified state it only did so because of the unity that British power has bestowed upon it after a century of rule. But if India were to ever show signs of a love of independence, of acting in concert as "the expression of a universal feeling of nationality, at that moment all hope is at an end, as all desire ought to be at an end, of preserving our Empire."[111] If the hallmark of liberal imperialism was the implicit belief in the temporary, benevolent nature of British rule in India, liberals like Seeley transferred the criteria of future self-government from the strict model of improvement or assimilation to English manners to the question of nationality. The fact that India was not yet a nation, however, was the descriptive, sociological basis upon which the continuity of imperial rule rested. What was implicit in the denial of nationality was a belief in a "natural" tendency of Indian society to devolve into anarchy and/or communal divisions. British rule was justified less in ambitious moral and political terms than as the lesser evil compared to leaving India to disintegrate on her own. Tied less to the specific project of transformation (even for making India a "nation"), sociological theories instead legitimated Britain's continued presence as a political necessity emergent from the fraught inner dynamics of Indian society.

REVERSING THE CIVILIZING MISSION: MAINE
AND THE LESSONS OF 1857

> The thinker or scholar who approaches it [India] in a serious
> spirit finds it pregnant with difficult questions, not to be
> disentangled without prodigious pains, not to be solved
> indeed unless the observer goes through a process at all
> times most distasteful to an Englishman, and (I will not say)
> reverses his accustomed political maxims, but revises
> them, and admits that they may be qualified under the
> influence of circumstance and time.
> —Henry Maine[112]

The crisis of liberal imperialism generated alternative modes of imperial legitimation, ones that openly disavowed the moral discourse of liberal empire—the language of a civilizing rule and the goal of self-government. Late imperial administrators such as A. C. Lyall and Lord Cromer not only rejected the slow introduction of representative institutions in Eastern dependencies but also came to insist that the mere attempt to ground empire in a language of moral legitimacy was misplaced and dangerous to the stability of the imperial order.[113] This repudiation occasioned new and distinct governing practices specifically premised upon the critique of previous liberal strategies of rule. Sociological and anthropological theories of native society, in rejecting the theoretical and practical assumptions of policies of assimilation and modernization, provided novel rationales and practical models for the protection and preservation of native society.

Historically, one of the key events that occasioned this shift in imperial governing strategies was the Indian Rebellion of 1857. In response to the rebellion, the Crown assumed direct responsibility over the Company's former Indian territories and in its first official act explicitly put forth a doctrine of nonintervention as the directive principle of British rule:

> We declare it to be our royal will and pleasure that none be in anywise favoured, none molested or disquieted, by reason of their religious faith or observances, but that all shall alike enjoy the equal and impartial protection of the law; and we do strictly charge to enjoin all those who may be in authority under us that they abstain from all interference with the religious belief or worship of any of our subjects on pain of our highest displeasure.[114]

Moreover, "we will that generally, in framing and administration of law, due regard be paid to the ancient rights, usages and customs of India."[115] The significance of the 1858 Proclamation rests as much on this endorsement of noninterference as on the timing and context of the pronouncement. Propositions about noninterference *after* 1857 were necessarily imbued with reflections upon the causes of the rebellion, implying a critique of previous strategies of governance that were seen to have precipitated revolt.

Numerous explanations were proposed and debated as the "lessons of 1857" rippled through imperial policy circles for decades to come.[116] Victoria's Proclamation, like many prominent explanations circulated at the time, emphasized the religious aspects of revolt, a perspective that continues to dominate the popular historiography of 1857. Religious explanations functioned at many levels, most evocatively at locating the proximate cause of the mutiny of the Bengal army. In this account, the emphasis is placed on how the mutiny began in response to a rumor that the newly issued cartridges for Minié/Enfield rifles were greased with pork and beef fats, thus offending both Muslim and Hindu sentiments. Henry Maine concurred with this account and deemed "terrified fanaticism" as the true, and not merely incidental, spark of revolt.[117]

According to Maine, the mutiny was a shock to the English mind, not only because of the unprecedented speed and scale of the mutiny's expansion into insurrection but also because it seemingly sprung from such inscrutable sentiments.[118] Maine argued that the persistence and strength of Indian social and religious sentiments, specifically "caste sentiments," had eluded British policymakers and especially liberal reformers because they assumed that the relevance of caste and religion would weaken with the modernization of Indian society. In Maine, the Rebellion was therefore interpreted as an epistemic failure; it was a symptom of a fundamental "defect of knowledge."[119] He wrote, "I am not making any confident assertion on a subject so vast and so superficially examined as the character of native Indian religious and social belief. But I insist on the necessity of having some accurate ideas about it, and on the fact that a mistake about it caused the Sepoy Mutiny."[120]

In this manner, questions about the nature of native society became inextricably linked to the practical demands of imperial rule. And in his plea for more precise and trustworthy knowledge of native beliefs and customs, Maine sought to redefine what constituted appropriate knowledge of India. Through his methodological innovations in relation to the study of Indian society, Maine initiated an important anthropological reconceptualization of native society, one that, in the context of imperial policy, provoked a profound change in attitudes regarding the scientific and practical basis of liberal ideologies of rule. For Maine, previous European accounts of Indian society suffered from a number of drawbacks. On the one hand, Orientalist scholarship, from an overreliance on Sanskritic textual sources and the opinions of Brahmin native informants, had mistakenly imputed an empirical dominance to Brahminical norms and practices. The logic of native institutions, Maine argued, was to be found instead in local customs and traditions and thus could not be derived from the study of Sanskrit texts alone. Rather, the colonial administrative archive, as the site of ethnographic knowledge, was to be the locus of evidential truth about India's living customs.[121] On the other hand, Maine suspected that eighteenth-century European philosophical accounts of India (such as Raynal's and Diderot's *Histoire des deux Indes*) as well as those of English colonial officers, were primarily based on contact with more urbanized and secularized coastal Indian cultures, which they took to be representative of all of India. Without access to India's "vast interior mass" made up of self-governing, agricultural village-communities, they overestimated the possibility of reforming native belief along Western lines—that is, they believed "that Indians required nothing but School Boards and Normal Schools to turn them into Englishmen."[122] Maine argued that a similarly mistaken view of Indian society was also inherent in utilitarianism, which had had an enormous impact in shaping the liberal agenda of colonial reform.

In *Ancient Law* and *Village-Communities in the East and West*, Maine famously criticized the abstract methods of utilitarianism, arguing that analytical conceptions of law and political economy were inapplicable to primitive or ancient societies, of which India was the prime example. India was "the great repository of verifiable phenomena of ancient usage and ancient juridical thought,"[123] and thus its study would shed light on the historical and evolutionary development of law and society. India and England also shared an Indo-European heritage and thus a common institutional history. But while this filiation grounded India's epistemological centrality for the comparative study of institutions, it also construed India as representing the "living past" of Europe. The study of contemporary Indian social and political institutions, especially the customs of village-communities, casts light upon the evolutionary history of Aryan societies and peoples precisely because Indian society was assumed to have stagnated, arresting development of institutions at an early stage, and, thus, preserving their ancient character. Therefore, alongside the claim to a deep affinity, Maine asserted the radical difference between Indian and English institutions. With the assertion of difference, however, also came a stress on understanding the unique logic of primitive society. Thus Maine's historicism was accompanied by an anthropological sense that viewed native society as functional wholes, ordered by the dictates of primitive custom.[124]

Whereas Stephen's Indian experience led to a frontal attack on liberalism's central tenets, Maine's critique of popular government took a more circuitous route through his scholarly work on primitive societies. The study of close-knit kin communities, such as those prevalent in India, demonstrated for Maine that the natural condition of mankind was *immobility* and a resistance to radical change. In the slow, evolutionary transition from small-scale patriarchal communities to a modern society of individuals, the individual is steadily freed from the strictures of primitive law and custom, culminating in the establishment of freedom of contract and private property. In *Popular Government*, Maine contended that the new ascendancy of mass democracy threatened the stability of this liberal achievement. By emphasizing the a priori superiority of popular government, proponents of democracy not only seemed to overestimate mankind's ability and interest in perfection and innovation, but also promoted a form of government that was inherently unstable, one that naturally tended in its dissolution toward despotism.

Maine's reconstitution of the appropriate foundation of knowledge and his revised account of the customary basis of native society served as an enormous stimulus for "official anthropology" and its influence in crafting imperial policy.[125] It directly spurred, in some quarters, a wholesale rejection of the liberal agenda of reform in favor of policies that sought the rehabilitation and protection of native customs and institutions. For some, protecting native "traditions" was a normative priority and, for them, Maine's evocative account of native society, where primitive custom rationally ordered social, political, and economic life, was particularly appealing. Most, however, argued for a policy of protection and/or rehabilitation as a safeguard against instability, unrest, and rebellion. One of the central lessons of 1857 was that if certain forms of native beliefs, such as the belief in caste, "continues unimpaired or but slightly decayed, some paths of legislation and of executive action are seriously unsafe."[126] In reading 1857 in primarily cultural terms, as rooted in cultural intransigence and resistance to imposed modernization, recognition of native custom became an important strategic imperative.

Maine supplied additional credence to the strategic argument for a presumptive deference to native custom through a provocative account of the structural impact of modern empire on native society. The transition from status to contract, Maine's thematic framing of the historical evolution from ancient to modern society, had been dramatically hastened in India with the coming of British rule. That is, despite the internal coherence of native society, its structural integrity was construed as increasingly undermined through contact with modern institutions. The vitality and customary basis of the Indian village-community, for example, were quickly dissolving with the intrusion of modern notions of legal right, absolute property, and freedom of contract. In practical terms, the rapidity of the process of disintegration, for Maine, engendered grave consequences for the stability of imperial rule.[127]

In prioritizing the maintenance of order, liberal models of education, economy, and politics would all be limited because they were now considered to inherently bear disintegrative effects on native/traditional society. Unlike liberal ruling strategies that construed "traditional" social structures, customs, and identities, such as those relating to caste and religion, as impediments to the project of improvement and thus good and moral governance, the new strategies of rule stressed the need for reconciliation with native institutions and structures of authority. In practical terms this entailed a more conciliatory relation to the princely states, now seen both as bulwarks against radicalism and as authorities that commanded "natural" obedience.[128] There was also a shift away from the institution of the principles of laissez-faire and private property rights for the sake of protecting the "traditional" foundations of agrarian society, such as caste and the village-community.[129]

The lessons of 1857 prioritized a practical and strategic concern for questions of law and order over issues of imperial legitimacy and moral purpose. The noninterference principle precisely expressed the difficulty of reforming the native and indeed the political danger that attempts at transformation could entail. In construing the rebellion as an example of the failure of liberal reform to either transform native habits and customs or lend security to the imperial enterprise, reflections on 1857 also spurred ethnographic and sociological investigations into the nature of native society—accounts that would mirror and account for the newly understood rigidity of native customs and traditions. In attributing to native society a new kind of stability and intransigence to reform, anthropological and sociological accounts of native society buttressed methods of rule that sought to harness and incorporate these native energies to ensure order and stability. In doing so, subject societies began to function as the displaced site of imperial legitimation, whose immanent logic and crises necessitated continued imperial rule and protection.

FROM ANOMALY TO EXEMPLAR: BRITISH INDIA AND LATE IMPERIAL IDEOLOGY

"Our Indian Empire," according to Seeley, produced "bewilderment," for the "English public does not know what to make of it, but looks with blank indignation and despair upon a Government which seems utterly un-English, which is bureaucratic and in the hands of the ruling race, which rests mainly on military force, which raises its revenue, not in the European fashion, but by monopolies of salt and opium and by taking the place of a universal landlord, and in a hundred other ways departs from the traditions of England."[130] For Seeley, what made this state of affairs particularly anomalous was that in seemingly contradicting English principles of government it also departed from the normal model of British imperial expansion. Expansion, as Seeley strikingly noted, "is the great fact of modern English history,"[131] but it had developed along two markedly distinct trajectories. On the one hand, in the colonies of North America, South Africa, and Australia, emigrants set forth to create political communities in which governments and institutions were "ultra-English."[132] The colonies, according to Seeley, were intimately connected to England by ties of race, religion, and interest. Indeed, the British Empire in relation to these colonies was not an empire in the true sense; rather, it held within itself the potential seeds of a new kind of federative union. The great exception that lay outside the imaginative forging of a "Greater Britain" was India. For Seeley, "our Indian Empire . . . is so different in kind from both England itself and from the Colonial Empire that it requires wholly different principles of policy."[133] And it was this rather sharp deviation in the principles of rule between Britain and the colonies, on the one hand, and India, on the other, that constituted that strange, unprecedented political entity known as British India.

Seeley's sharp differentiation between the colonial empire—the colonies of white settlement—and India served to sanction as pregiven a distinction that was in fact the historical product of the development of the British Empire throughout the nineteenth century. From the Durham Report (1839), which granted Canadian colonies some measure of autonomy, settler colonies such as Australia, New Zealand, and South Africa had been placed on a reformist path of increasing self-government. At the same time, for colonies with overwhelmingly nonwhite populations, the opposite trajectory—the permanent delay or denial of representative institutions—was developing into the accepted norm. One of the fateful moments that seemingly cemented this constitutional division within the Empire was the decision of the Jamaican Assembly, in the wake of the Morant Bay Rebellion, to voluntary dissolve and assume the status of a dependent Crown Colony.

Despite Seeley's ideological investment in a "natural" division between colony and dependency, there was some truth to the distinction; the fashioning of empire in India differed in important ways from prior British experience. Unlike the colonization of North America, South Africa, and Australia, conquests in the East were never premised on programs of settlement. In North America, South Africa, and Australia, where native populations were eradicated and/or radically marginalized, the legal and political institutions of the colonies were derived in large part from their British counterparts. Where the prospects of settlement were absent, formulating strategies for ruling over native subjects became a necessity. And it was in the long process of political and administrative innovation in response to the dilemmas of ruling alien subjects that British rule in India took on a unique and experimental character.

Since its inception, empire in India had been subject to a vigorous debate concerning the principles and purposes of imperial rule, with the liberal commitment to the improvement of native society becoming a salient ideology in the early nineteenth century. As D. A. Low has argued, the prominence of the liberal view, and in a sense the debate itself, came to an abrupt end in the wake of the 1857 Rebellion, with the consolidation of a new consensus that prioritized questions of security and order over modernization. This consensus, what Low terms "the settled view," initiated in India a more overtly authoritarian insistence on efficiency and stability as the watchwords of imperial policy, and also a reversal of liberal efforts at civilizing and creative reform in favor of protecting and conserving native society. And with the expansion of direct British rule to Africa and Southeast Asia, "the settled view" would become institutionalized as the basic framework of British imperial policy.[134] British rule in India served to be a testing ground for methods of rule that were to become, in the period of high empire, transportable in many key respects.

Rather than the "anomalous" and "exceptional" experiment that British India seemed to be, by the end of the century, empire in India furnished a set of exemplary models for the rule over non-European peoples.

Low's "the settled view" is, I would argue, another name for the underlying ideological structure of the theory and practice of *indirect rule*. Indirect rule, the rule through native institutions, would be hailed as the unique and defining principle of British imperial rule in Asia and Africa. As a distinct mode of imperial legitimation—as an alibi of empire—indirect rule often disclaimed having any overt ideological or moral agenda, professing itself to be merely a strategic or administrative necessity. The language of pure expediency marked the cumulative diminution of the moral agenda of liberal empire, and the burden of imperial legitimation conclusively came to rest on native society alone.

── CHAPTER TWO ──

INVENTING TRADITIONAL SOCIETY:
EMPIRE AND THE ORIGINS OF SOCIAL THEORY

> When in truth we have to some extent succeeded in freeing
> ourselves from that limited conception of the world and
> mankind, beyond which the most civilized societies and
> (I will add) some of the greatest thinkers do not always rise;
> when we gain something like an adequate idea of the
> vastness and variety of the phenomena of human society;
> when in particular we have learned not to exclude from our
> view of the earth and man those great and unexplored
> regions which we vaguely term the East, we find it to be
> wholly a conceit or a paradox to say that the distinction
> between the Present and the Past disappears. Sometimes the
> Past is the Present; much more often it is removed from it by
> varying distances, which however, cannot be estimated or
> expressed chronologically.
> —*Henry Maine*[1]

> The great question facing civilized man for three centuries
> would be knowing where the savage began and ended, and
> which of the two events was the worthier.
> —*Raymond Schwab*[2]

THE TRANSFORMATION of imperial ideology from moral justifications to retroactive alibis was in part effected by the reassessment of past imperial policy failures, itself occasioned by various forms of native unrest and resistance. As reassessments sought to make sense of native disenchantment as well as the inability of past policy to successfully "civilize" native society, they gave credence to new imperial alibis that construed imperial rule as necessitated by, and in need of accommodation with, the "nature" of native society. This ideological reorientation was closely tied to the development of anthropological and sociological theories of native society, accounts that gave sustenance to the newly understood rigidity of native customs and traditions. In this sense, the intellectual roots of late imperial ideology lay in the emergence of an ideal-typical model of *traditional society*, a central innovation of nineteenth-century social theory.

This chapter seeks to frame this reciprocal relationship between empire and social theory with a special focus on the development of this new model of traditional society. With the expansion of European empires in the nineteenth century, historical and ethnographic research in and on the non-European world was also subject to an extraordinary enlargement and crystallization, with profound consequences for the development of modern social science. In addition to the work of scientist-explorers, official information by administrators, missionaries, and merchants who had sustained contact with native cultures in areas under European control not only grew in breadth but also became more systematic in character as it was increasingly tied to the dynamics of imperial governance.

Expanding colonial knowledge brought to light a variety of new facts to be confronted and comprehended, generating new modes of comparison—new methodologies by which unfamiliar cultures and practices would be made scientifically (and morally) comprehensible. The nineteenth century was marked by the widespread enthusiasm for comparative methodologies; "the comparative method" became a subject for philosophical elucidation as well as a privileged model for attaining scientific certainty with a universal scope. Nineteenth-century social theory and evolutionary anthropology represent two of the most ambitious comparative endeavors that recognized and sought to make of sense of the radically expanded framework of global diversity.[3] In an important sense, it was a unified field of research with a common enterprise, to comprehend non-European social formations in relation to the prehistory (and future) of European man and society. The nineteenth-century project of universal comparison, framed and limited by the attempt to chart the unique trajectory of Western modernity, shaped a new vision of the relationship between past and present and thereby contributed to a fundamental rethinking of the idea of the primitive.

Henry Maine was a central figure in this new intellectual constellation, and his work shaped the development of the modern disciplines of sociology and anthropology.[4] Maine's contrast between the communal and corporate nature of ancient/primitive society versus the individualist focus of modern society was representative of the binary construction of traditional and modern societies typical of nineteenth-century social theory. For anthropology, Maine was among the earliest to theorize kinship as the structuring principle of social interaction, as a cornerstone of a holistic model of society. In Maine's seminal contribution, traditional society emerged as an integrated social whole that, while contrasted sharply with the imperatives of modern society, was understood to have a logic and rationale of its own. This model of native society as an integral whole, held together by reciprocal bonds of custom and structures of kinship, would provide a theoretical foundation for late imperial ideologies of protection, preservation, and collaboration.

In contrast to the dynamism of modern society, traditional society in social theory was often construed as fundamentally apolitical, dominated by nonrational—customary and kin-based—norms of politics and economics. This conceptualization of traditional society, in the work of some of its key proponents, was shaped by a self-conscious critique of political models of social cohesion and transformation. The social theoretic model of traditional society exemplified a shift toward a view of human behavior that increasingly emphasized the nonrational bases of sociability, the dominance of social and cultural norms, and the persistence of historical habits and customs. Social theory came to stress the primacy of the "social" for understanding and explaining the nature and dynamics of society in general. By positing the social as primary in both a substantive and a methodological sense, social theory contested the priority that had been traditionally accorded to politics as the organizing force of society, the source of social unity and definition. This concept of *society* in sociology functioned analogously to the concept of *culture* in anthropology, namely a quasi-autonomous sphere that shapes and even determines the character of social, political, and economic institutions. With the rise of social theory, the question of politics was reframed in a context that increasingly emphasized the limits of political thought and action in relation to social, cultural, and historical imperatives.

THE ANCIENT AND THE MODERN: THE ORIGINS OF SOCIAL THEORY

One of the characteristic features of nineteenth-century social theory was its tendency to view the historical trajectory of society in binary terms, the modern/tradition dichotomy encapsulating the essence of a number of other prominent distinctions such as status/contract (Maine), *Gemeinschaft/Gesellschaft* (Tönnies), mechanical/organic (Durkheim), militant/industrial (Spencer), and *societas/civitas* (Gierke).[5] In some formulations this model functioned as an ideal-typical contrast between two types of sociality, while in others it was a contrast that was embedded in a larger narrative of transition from one historical form of society to the other. This austere mode of classification differed markedly from the most prominent, early-modern conceptual schemas for understanding the growth of human societies. Ever since Europe's dramatic encounter with the Americas, the tendency in modern comparative ethnologies and historical theories had been toward multiplying and diversifying the stages of social development, reaching a culmination of sorts in the sophisticated uses of a four-stage or *stadial* model of human progress in the eighteenth century.[6]

The stadial theory posited a distinct relationship among modes of subsistence, types of property, and forms of government that defined particular stages of societal development. These stages were often understood to stand as a series of successive epochs from a savage stage linked to hunting-gathering societies, barbarian society of pastoral and shepherding peoples, to agricultural society, finally culminating in modern commercial society. These theories were put to a variety of uses, from analyzing the dynamics of socioeconomic development, to complex historical accounts of the demise of the Roman Empire, the origins of feudalism, the development of modern constitutional government, and the rise of commercial society. The four-stage theory would also serve as a prime referent with which to comprehend the unprecedented dynamics of contact, settlement, and colonization as they were unfolding with the global expansion of European empires.[7]

And yet, despite the prominence of the model among eighteenth-century thinkers, the stadial theory seems not to have made a seminal impact on the shape of classical social theory of the nineteenth century. Neither Maine, Durkheim, nor Spencer (and the same could be said of Tönnies and Weber) directly referenced stadial theories of development, and in some instances consciously distanced themselves from the standard terms of the debate about the interlinked nature of forms of government, property, and society. Even political thinkers who were direct heirs of the Scottish enlightenment, such as James and John Stuart Mill, tended to use the terms *savage* and *barbarian* more loosely, most often devoid of the historical and sociological specificity that had been the bedrock of the original model. There were, of course, important exceptions such as Hegel and Marx in their conceptualization of civil society, and in the evolutionary anthropology of Morgan and McLennan. But, notably, in both these streams, the historical models at work rarely were contained within a strict and elemental binary contrast.

Thus, while eighteenth-century theorists of social development were precursors of important aspects of nineteenth-century social theory's account of modernity, the roots of its stylized binary between modern and traditional society seemingly lay elsewhere. In this respect, I argue for the seminal importance of a series of debates about ancient politics and society that took shape in the aftermath of the French Revolution and continued throughout the nineteenth century. These debates initiated a fundamental reevaluation of ancient society that was now argued to be so different from modern society that any attempt to revive "ancient politics" could only lead to the kind of calamities witnessed in the decades after 1789. Moreover, in treating the foundations of Greco-Roman societies as radically opposed to those of modern society, this debate was decisive for the development of holistic conceptions of kinship, culture, and society. For it was on the terrain of ancient history, and through the influence of new critical approaches to the study of ancient society, that the anthropological theory of kinship was first formulated. In other words, the legacy of the French Revolution was to inaugurate a new kind of quarrel between the ancients and the moderns, which was a central factor in the origins of modern social theory.[8]

Benjamin Constant's 1819 speech comparing ancient and modern liberty indicates some of the directions postrevolutionary reevaluations of the ancient world would take in the nineteenth century.[9] Constant's distinction between the collective political liberty of the ancient republics and the individual liberty of the moderns was put forward in the context of a defense of representative government, and thus, in important ways, resuming a central eighteenth-century debate about the form of government most appropriate to modern commercial society. Many eighteenth-century thinkers had questioned the viability of ancient city-state or republican politics in an age of commerce, and had sought to defend specifically modern forms of representative and constitutional government. Likewise, Constant considered ancient liberty to be intimately tied to a distinctive set of historical institutions—slavery, structure of war and the citizen army, lack of commerce—that may be both impossible and undesirable to reproduce in modern times. For Constant, however, not only was achieving ancient liberty something impracticable, it was also a form of liberty that was far from ideal; it was in essence a *collective* freedom, one that demanded sacrifices of individual freedom. The fact that in Rome "the individual, almost always sovereign in public affairs, was a slave in all his private relations"[10] demonstrated, for Constant, that the ancients "had no notion of individual rights."[11] It was a society in which the law regulated the minutest customs and private lives were always under strict surveillance. "Their social organization led them to desire an entirely different freedom," one that was compatible with "the complete subjection of the individual to the authority of the community."[12] Thus, ancient society was seen to harbor the seeds of despotism.

The important nineteenth-century twist that Constant gave to this more standard debate about the relative merits of ancient versus modern politics was the idea that it was in fact the experience of the French Revolution, its extravagances and disappointments, that demonstrated most forcibly the practical dangers of trying to recreate "ancient politics." For Constant, the revolutionaries, "steeped in ancient views," had derived sanction for their unmixed admiration of ancient politics from philosophers such as Rousseau (and de Mably) "who had themselves failed to recognize the changes brought by two thousand years in the dispositions of mankind."[13] Instead, "by transposing into our modern age an extent of social power, of collective sovereignty, which belonged to other centuries, this sublime genius, animated by the purest love of liberty, has nevertheless furnished deadly pretexts for more than one kind of tyranny."[14] The less discriminating of Rousseau's revolutionary successors, in their desire to reorder political life along the maxims of ancient liberty, insisted "that the citizens should be entirely subjected in order for the nation to be sovereign, and that the individual should be enslaved for the people to be free," thus enabling the many injustices of the Revolution.[15]

The notion that advocates of the French Revolution had made a disastrous political error in attempting to recreate ancient institutions in modern times was to be repeated throughout the nineteenth century.[16] The claim would, in the context of the study of ancient society, be closely tied to an argument that what had in fact laid the grounds for these political misadventures was a false picture of ancient society and politics. Thus, to correct their mistaken view of ancient society was to undo the appeal of ancient politics. While there were intimations of this line of reasoning in Constant, especially in the claim that ancient social organization was so profoundly regulated by communal power that men "were merely machines,"[17] there was a difference between Constant's standpoint and the later theorists of ancient society. Most obviously, Constant's argument was foremost a political one, made in defense of modern liberty and the form of representative government he thought would sustain it (and not primarily a methodological question about how to understand the nature of ancient society). Moreover, for Constant though the distinction between the ancients and the moderns was linked to a difference in ethos, and not just a difference of forms of government in a purely institutional sense, the values and virtues of the ancients were not seen as entirely irretrievable. Rather, enthusiasm for ancient liberty had to be tempered by a more balanced assessment of its limitations, paving the way for a potential optimal melding of both ancient and modern forms of liberty.

Whereas Constant could continue to admire aspects of ancient political liberty (its connection to virtue and self-development), later histories would present Roman life as so foreign and indeed so primitive as to be inimitable in any form. By midcentury, in the more conservative vision of Maine and Fustel de Coulanges, a new interpretation of Greco-Roman societies highlighted those aspects that most differentiated ancient from modern society and, in the process, thoroughly "ethnologized" the ancients. Even as these latter contributions were more substantively concerned with questions about how to conceptualize the nature of ancient society, the long shadow of the Revolution continued to form the political backdrop to nineteenth-century social thought.

Barthold Georg Niebuhr's *History of Rome*, covering the earliest periods of Roman prehistory, provided the nineteenth-century's most influential historical-ethnological account of the origins of Roman political institutions.[18] In Arnaldo Momigliano's words, Neibuhr "virtually created the modern study of Roman history."[19] Niebuhr was an exponent of a new kind of empirical history that aspired to scientific rigor and precision, but consciously did not limit itself to strict philological and textual analysis. Niebuhr provocatively used comparative methodology to illuminate and speculate on the more obscure and controversial aspects of ancient history. The central issue that spurred Niebuhr's interest in early Roman society (and which he considered his greatest achievement) was clarifying Roman agrarian history and landownership, specifically in relation to the much-disputed *agrarian law*. Niebuhr himself was intimately concerned with various debates about Prussian land reform, the abolition of serfdom, and the kinds of protection needed to offset agrarian unrest. What Niebuhr feared most was a renewal in Prussia of the revolutionary fervor for land redistribution of the kind witnessed during the French Revolution. Niebuhr's studies were sparked by a political concern to stem the revolutionary idea of limiting property, especially as made by communist factions that justified state enforced equalization of property with ancient examples. The most egregious and dangerous example of this political use of ancient history was epitomized, for Niebuhr, by "Gracchus" Babeuf and his followers in their call to implement the so-called agrarian law in revolutionary France. To contest the radical implications that the support for the agrarian law entailed, Niebuhr turned to the historical study of the nature of these laws in ancient Rome. In doing so, Niebuhr proposed a fundamental reinterpretation of the nature and function of the agrarian law, one that overturned the account that had attained widespread acceptance, especially in republican political thought since the Renaissance.[20]

Niebuhr's strategy in contesting the revolutionary interpretation of Roman politics was to emphasize the radical gulf between the ideas that animated Roman institutions and those of their modern imitators. "The ideas on which the institutions of the Roman state and its administration were founded," argued Niebuhr, were "no less different from ours, than Roman dwellings, clothing, and food."[21] Clear and accurate knowledge of the distinctiveness of ancient institutions would thus serve to preclude "the silly desire of transferring out of ages totally different in character what would now be altogether inapplicable."[22] The most distinctive and fundamental institution of ancient society, for Niebuhr, was its *gentile* organization; it was the key to understanding the nature of the ancient state. For Niebuhr, all nations of antiquity lived in fixed forms, and their civil relations were always marked by specific kinds of divisions and subdivisions. "When cities raise themselves to the rank of nations," argued Niebuhr, "we always find a division at first into tribes."[23] The Roman tribe was comprised of *curiae* (in Greece, the *phratry*), which in turn were comprised of several *gentes*. The *gens* was a patrilineal community, comprised of all persons who could trace their descent to a common ancestor through the male line, that is, agnatically. Membership of the *gens* was ostensibly given by birth, and its elemental unit was the patriarchal family. The *gentes*, however, were not, for Niebuhr, families in any simple sense, but free corporations or self-regulating associations, each of which consisted of several families, "united by a common chapel and a common hero."[24] These associations had their own assemblies, courts, religious rights, and laws of inheritance. The *gens* was thus simultaneously a social, religious, and political institution. Not only did each *gens* have its own *gentilician sacra*, membership of a *gens* (and in its larger aggregation the *curiae*) defined both religious and political privileges, such as the right of voting in popular assemblies; for Niebuhr, the ancients did not vote as individuals, but as corporations.[25]

Most importantly, then, membership in a specific *gens* defined one's rights and duties as a citizen, it was the basis of "the relation in which individuals stood to the state."[26] For Niebuhr, unlike modern states, which in their forms of administration and representation are organized with reference to territory (such as the district, ward, province), "the ancients viewed the soil only as the *substratum* of the state."[27] The ancient state, rather, rested upon individuals defined as members of gentile associations, whose status as members was linked to birth regardless of where one lived. With this new understanding of the ancient state, the classic dynamics of ancient politics were reinterpreted by Niebuhr as modes of contestation around membership in the *gentes*. The *gens*, while not entirely closed (it allowed for the incorporation through adoption), was by definition exclusive. And as citizenship was derivative of gentile membership, for Niebuhr, the central contest between plebeians and patricians was in effect a contest for inclusion into the gentile system. The distinction between plebian and patrician was not one between the rich and the poor but a difference between original citizens and those outsiders who either had lost connection to their *gens* or were members of a *gens* that had no access to citizenship.[28] The plebeians therefore had a precarious and liminal status; they were a necessary part of the state but had no stable rights as citizens, rights that could only be gained via gentile privileges. In this reinterpretation of the structure, power, and nature of gentile organization, Niebuhr effectively recast the central drama of ancient politics—the conflict of the orders—in part in ethnological terms.

As the *gens* was in essence a self-regulating society—for Niebuhr, it was a state within in a state—the ancient state had little power to regularly intervene in the *gens'* rules of self-constitution. But, the ancient state in extraordinary historical moments did reorder the *gentes*/tribes/*curiae*, such as the famous reforms of Servius Tullius. These were revolutionary moments in Roman constitutional history, for in changing the constitution of the *gens*, the entire character of the state would be altered. More generally, Niebuhr intimated that the key to the transition from ancient to modern politics could be found in the transformation from genealogically ordered houses/*gens* into local, territorial groupings, which in Rome was associated with the reforms of Tullius, and in Greece with those of Cleisthenes.[29] Hence, in Niebuhr's work we glimpse the origins of the idea of a world-historical transition from kinship to locality as the basis of the state and political obligation that would be subsequently elaborated in the work of Maine, Morgan, and Marx and Engels.

Niebuhr's conception of the Roman *gens* as the basis upon which political communities were first built would prove to be immensely influential.[30] For Niebuhr, the *gens* was the exact counterpart of the Greek "genos" and could also be likened to clan formation of the Scottish highlanders, the tribes of Arabia, and the *Geschlechter* of the medieval Germans.[31] As was noted, these social groups were not families in any simple sense, but common (real or fictive) lineage was a key defining feature. Houses were not only small self-regulating societies with their own distinct social laws and customs, but were also political associations that acted collectively in the context of ancient politics. The discovery of gentile organization, organized by lineage and aggregated into larger groups such as the Grecian phratry or the Roman *curiae*, now understood as the earliest form of society, had a profound impact upon all of the original studies of kinship, from Maine's *Ancient Law* (1861) to Morgan's *Ancient Society* (1877).[32] Between these two publications appeared all the classic studies of kinship: Bachofen's *Das Mutterrecht* (1861), Fustel de Coulanges's *La cité antique* (1864), McLennan's *Primitive Marriage* (1865), and Morgan's *Systems of Consanguinity and Affinity of the Human Family* (1871). Taken together, these works, all authored by lawyers/legal historians, initiated the first sustained theoretical discussion of kinship, thus constituting the central concept of modern anthropology.[33] The fact that kinship was "discovered" through the lens of studies of antiquity attests to the significance of postrevolutionary legal histories of Rome and Greece as the basis for systematic comparison across societies. For these later works, sustained analyses of the origins and functions of the *gens* would not only help to explain certain peculiarities of ancient law and politics (such as the nature of inheritance and the origin of the plebs), but it would also serve as a way to conceptualize the early history of man—primitive societies—more generally. In other words, by designating the *gens* as the foundation of the ancient city-state, these works came to view (and sought to demonstrate) that kinship structures—patterns of descent and lineage—were systematically bound up with the ideas and institutions of primitive society, especially the nature of hierarchy/power, property rights, and primitive religion.

Fustel de Coulanges's *La cité antique* and Maine's *Ancient Law* were two seminal works in this vein. Both offered systematic theories about the origins and function of gentile organization in ancient society, which significantly pointed toward a more general sociological categorization.[34] Part of this drive for generalization was given in their conscious application of the comparative method to the study of antiquity, in which the idea of a unity of Aryan peoples enabled the use of ancient Indian material to speculate on the remotest origins and more obscure aspects of Greco-Roman institutions. Moreover, both Fustel de Coulanges and Maine, like Niebuhr, oriented their work against radical interpretations of ancient Rome and thus also contra the political implications of the French Revolution.

Partisans of the Revolution "having imperfectly observed the institutions of the ancient city," argued Fustel,

> have dreamed of reviving them among us. They have deceived themselves about the liberty of the ancients, and on this very account liberty among the moderns has been put in peril. The last eighty years have clearly shown that one of the great difficulties which impede the march of modern society is the habit which it has of always keeping Greek and Roman antiquity before its eyes.[35]

For Fustel, there were "radical" and "essential" differences between ancient and modern peoples. When objectively observed, Greece and Rome should appear as foreign to us as "ancient India or Arabia," and thus, "in a character absolutely inimitable; nothing in modern times resembles them; nothing in the future can resemble. We shall attempt to show by what rules these societies were regulated, and it will be freely admitted that the same rules can never govern humanity again."[36]

The "rules" of Greco-Roman society were fundamentally linked to the structure of the *gens*, or the ancient family. The *gens* was the agnatic family of Roman law, a community of persons linked by descent in the male line. As such it was a much larger entity than the nuclear family and not strictly defined by blood. On the one hand, an entire set of biologically close relations (cognates) would be excluded from this community, and, on the other, dependents (such as slaves and clients) with no blood relations would be included, albeit in a subordinate way. But if ancient kinship was not strictly based upon blood, and thus not strictly a "natural" association, what could account for its origins and maintenance? For Fustel, the *gens* was emphatically not a natural association, nor could it have been established and maintained by sheer force or power. Rather, an institution as pervasive enough as to shape the entire range of ancient social and political relations had to be grounded in a more foundational set of ideas and beliefs, which for Fustel was to be found in ancient religion. Ancient kinship marked out a community of worship, which in turn set the rules for marriage, laws of property and inheritance, as well as political institutions. This religion was the primeval cult of ancestors common to the Aryan family. Private property, *patria potestas*, and primogeniture were all institutions that, for Fustel, had their origins in the protection and worship of ancestors.[37]

The focus on primitive religion and the centrality of its rites and beliefs to Roman life lent Fustel's vision a conservative hue, one that was consciously worded to challenge constitutional and secular interpretations of the origin of Roman institutions. The conservatism went further in the sense that, for Fustel, ancient religion was so imbricated in the foundation and maintenance of state institutions that "these two powers, associated and confounded, formed a power almost superhuman, to which the soul and body were equally enslaved."[38] In other words, following upon Constant's suggestion, Fustel argued that the ancients "knew nothing of Individual Liberty";[39] all thought and action were seen to be deeply circumscribed by law. The imperative was always toward strict conformity with communal, religious norms.

The ethnologizing of Rome in Maine's work also sought to stem the radical political implications that eighteenth-century invocations of republican Rome held. Whereas Fustel emphasized ancient religious rites and beliefs to mark the radical difference between ancient and modern society, Maine focused instead on the structure of the patriarchal family itself. As opposed to liberty, Maine's Rome was defined by the oppressive strictures of *patria potestas* and submission to the patriarchal head of the ancient family. What Rousseau had idealized as primitive, natural liberty—and what the Revolutionaries had tried to recreate—stemmed, Maine argued, from a fundamental misconception of the individuality, equality, and uniformity of man in a supposed state of nature.

Deducing the origin of society from individual motivation in the natural state was premised upon a basic misconception of the historical process as well as the actual nature of ancient society. In Maine's view, "Ancient Law knows next to nothing of Individuals";[40] rights and duties are exclusively conferred upon family units, not individual citizens. The ancient patriarchal family was a corporate group (the unit of Niebuhr's gentile organization), organized under the archaic jurisdiction of *patria potestas*, the despotic power of the patriarch over dependent persons and property. Ancient society, then, was an aggregation of families, modern society a collection of individuals. For Maine, "this contrast is most forcibly expressed by saying that the *unit* of an ancient society was the Family, of modern society the Individual."[41] And, it was the *corporate* character of the ancient family that stamped itself on all areas of law in early jurisprudence.

In Maine's work, kinship signified an essentially political relationship; all individuals who were subject to *patria potestas*, who fell under the archaic jurisdiction of a common patriarchal head, were considered kin. This political reading of kinship also served to tie the concepts of property, contract, and right together. In the patriarchal family, where the space of "kinship" was equivalent to the space of power; the Law of Persons contained and confounded all other rights and duties (such as those relating to property). In the transition from status to contract, then, the paring down of kinship ties, the division of communal property, the expansion of freedom of contract, and the progress of individual right were all parallel processes. Transformations in one sphere were necessarily linked to changes in another, thus intimating a holistic understanding of the interplay of ideas and institutions, as animating forces defining social formations.

In these original studies, *kinship* was conceived of as a key structural and comparative concept, a holistic marker signifying the unity and interdependence of social, political, legal, and domestic relations. Whether the kinship structure of gentile organization was ultimately derived from political power (as in Maine), primitive religious rites (Fustel), marriage classes (Morgan), or social structure (Durkheim), it was a unifying concept, one that was mirrored in every other major societal institution.[42] In this way, Maine and Fustel clearly stand in line with the burgeoning of modern social theory and a functionalist sociology that took as their methodological starting point the internal unity of social structure. And importantly, this recognition of the differences in social structure, in the internal rhythms of society, was dissolved into a dichotomous schema of radical opposites, the ancient versus the modern.

THE "SOCIAL" AND THE LIMITS OF POLITICS

The origin of social theory is often portrayed as primarily a methodological revolution, linked to the discovery of *society* as an organic and independent entity, whose inner lawlike dynamics can be discerned through scientific analysis. The methodological innovation appears as a break from the idealism and individualism implicit in previous approaches to the study of society, especially as embodied in traditions of political philosophy. But to construe the specificity of social theory wholly in methodological terms would be to miss its substantive critique of political philosophy, especially of eighteenth-century political thought and the distinctive politics that it had spawned. Implicit in the logical priority claimed for the "social" was a substantive claim for preeminence as well. In conceptualizing the social in a way that revealed its pervasive role in the constitution of human action (and a central place as an explanation of action), political institutions and structures of authority were seen to express, rather than constitute, underlying social relations. Further, the "individual" was conceived of as produced, and even constrained, by social structures, thus implying a number of substantive theoretical claims about the malleability of human nature, the plasticity of social life, and the central determinants of human behavior. More specifically, notable strands of nineteenth-century social thought arose in opposition to, and as a critique of, the kind of political thinking that was considered to have nurtured the radicalism of the French Revolution. For what eighteenth-century revolutionary politics proposed, especially in the attempt to revive "ancient politics," was a view of the social world as eminently transformable and, indeed, perfectible through the agency of politics.

Thinkers like Maine and Durkheim conflated methodological and substantive claims about the nature of society, the sociocultural determination of action, and the functional interdependence of social spheres. While many social theorists proffered their critiques of political philosophy in the name of scientific rigor, thinkers like Maine also contended that methodological claims about, for example, natural equality necessarily carried normative implications, and thus were especially keen to undermine their empirical validity. Alongside the rejection of the supposed idealism and utopianism of political philosophy was a more substantive, empirical questioning of the specific political philosophical claims, namely, (liberal) assumptions of, especially, social contract theory and utilitarianism.

A number of political theorists from Hannah Arendt, Leo Strauss, to Sheldon Wolin have construed the rise of the "social" and social science in the nineteenth century as a threat to the "political." Wolin's discussion in *Politics and Vision* comes closest to the analysis presented here.[43] The conception of the political in Arendt and Strauss, in contrast, often defines politics as a certain kind of activity—in Strauss, a certain kind of philosophical activity—that has its roots in ancient politics.[44] However, the notion of politics and political philosophy that I argue nineteenth-century social theory challenged, was much more specific and more modern, defined in large part by the priority given to the state and political institutions as formative influences on society (and a view arguably traceable to Hobbes). It was a view in which politics could be an independent agent of change and creative reform, one that positively accepts the possibility of a rational, willed transformation of society. The underlying, universal assumption about the character of social actors, especially as objects of change, was therefore one that emphasized equality, mutability, and perfectibility.

The reevaluation of Rome following the Revolution demonstrates forcefully two characteristic propositions of modern social theory, both of which were simultaneously methodological and substantive theses. The distinctive features of ancient life were contrasted to the modern as another world in its entirety; it was not just one or two institutions of ancient life (such as slavery) that were singled out as foreign to modern sensibilities, but ancient culture—its fundamental ideas and institutions—was construed as opposed to the very premises of modern society. Furthermore, this radical difference was not only conceived of as systemic but was also depoliticized. In a fundamental sense, the primacy of political institutions—forms of government or regime type—as having a seminal power to shape social life was contested. Whereas in the work of Montesquieu, a century before, Roman law and *patria potestas* were ultimately related to the principle of government, namely republican government;[45] for Fustel political ideas and institutions were seen as derivative of an elemental religious orientation. Likewise, even in Maine's more political characterization of ancient law and kinship, the autonomy of political life and imagination was precluded by being strictly intertwined with social-structural imperatives.

It was a difference in the nature of *society* that could explain the irreconcilable differences between the ancient and the modern worlds. The study of kinship, by unveiling a deep, even causal, logic to social organization, provided a substantive basis to the concept of the *social* as it came to be theoretically elaborated in classical sociology. Durkheim in an early dissertation on Montesquieu and the foundation of social science—a thesis that was supervised by and dedicated to Fustel—explicitly argued that the proper recognition of "society" as a real, natural "thing" went hand in hand with a rejection of the claims of political philosophy. For Durkheim, political philosophers before Montesquieu tended to view aspects of social life, for example laws, customs, and religion, as products of human will and thus as amenable to alteration and perfection. The defining features of social life—those features that distinguished one society from another—were ultimately associated with and categorized according to regime type. In this way, both the central agencies of transformation and the most formative institutions were primarily political. Durkheim's argument, in part, was a methodological one, one that associated the emphasis on the human will with the priority given to normative theorizing over scientific explanation. In his terms, political science was seen as an "art" and not a science; rather than "knowing" society, it sought to correct and transform society according to an ideal.[46]

But this methodological argument was grounded upon a substantive claim; for Durkheim, what social science or sociology truly lacked was less a clear method than a distinctive object of study. In positing the social or society as a subject matter worthy of science, one had to recognize that social phenomena were "natural" things that, "like all other things in nature, which have their particular characteristics," do not "depend upon the human will."[47] For Durkheim, it was Montesquieu's great innovation to have realized that forms of government had some necessary connection to particular types of society. And while his classification was formulated according to regime type in the traditional manner (that is, with respect to republics, monarchies, and despotisms), Durkheim contended that it was in fact a classification of societies (not forms of government) and thus a view that first recognized the causal priority of society in understanding the nature of a regime. Forms of government in themselves, while reflective of social arrangements, were, for Durkheim, epiphenomenal at best, and purely contingent at worst—either way, they held little importance in understanding the nature of society or in actually shaping social phenomena.[48] In short, political philosophy (with the partial exception of Montesquieu) in its preoccupation with imagining ideal political arrangements obscured the immanent harmony and cohesiveness of social phenomena. This harmony was independent of the nature of political authority, the willed actions of citizens, or the contingent art of the (mythic) legislator. Social science began at precisely that moment when the traditional project of political philosophy was abandoned, for "if social [political] science is really to exist, societies must be assumed to have a certain nature which results from the nature and arrangement of the elements composing them, and which is the source of social phenomena. Once the existence of such elements is granted, our lawgiver vanishes and his legend with him."[49]

Maine, like Durkheim, praised Montesquieu as a founder of modern social science, and especially of historical and comparative methods. Maine argued that Montesquieu was especially important because he was attentive to the great historical and anthropological variation in social customs and attitudes. Yet, both Durkheim and Maine faulted Montesquieu for mistaking this variation for instability and thus exaggerating the plasticity of human nature. To accept a more radical account of the artificial or constructivist origins of social institutions would be to assume that at bottom men "are always and everywhere the same"[50] and thus open the way for the Enlightenment view of the social world as eminently transformable and, indeed, perfectible through the agency of politics.

The view of human behavior enunciated by these variants of nineteenth-century social theory implied a specific combination of stability and variation. While the individual, in terms of behavior as well as beliefs, was conceived of as a product of social structure and thus was by nature both diverse and in principle subject to profound variation, the idea that human nature could be radically and rapidly changed by deliberate institutional transformation was foreclosed. Maine articulated this sentiment in quite precise terms when he argued that Montesquieu's greatness was tempered by his

> unwillingness to break quite openly with the views hitherto popular. . . . Montesquieu seems . . . to have looked on the nature of man as entirely plastic, as passively reproducing the impressions, and submitting implicitly to the impulses which he receives from without. And here no doubt lies the error which vitiates his system as a system. He greatly underrates the stability of human nature. He pays little or no regard to the inherited qualities of the race, those qualities which each generation receives from its predecessors, and transmits but slightly altered to the generation which follows it. . . . Many of the anomalies he parades . . . prove the permanence rather than the variableness of man's nature, since they are relics of older stages of the race which have obstinately defied the influences that have elsewhere had effect. The truth is that the stable part of our mental, moral, and physical constitution is the largest part of it, and the resistance it opposes to change is such that, though the variations of human society in a portion of the world are plain enough, they are neither so rapid nor so extensive that their amount, character, and general direction cannot be ascertained.[51]

What was implied in this view of human behavior was that social institutions do shape (and are shaped by) the variety of impulses and habits that constitute human nature, and thus it is the differences of customs, history, and manners that account for a certain diversity and variability among social institutions. At the same time, human nature, while variable, exhibits a kind of stability because of this reciprocal dependence on social structure and thus is resistant to rapid and radical transformation.

Liberal political thinkers of the nineteenth century put forward a similar view of the interdependence of mores, customs, and character and political institutions, with the implication that political institutions alone could not guarantee good government. As was suggested in the previous chapter, like the social theorists, Mill displayed a suspicion of the universality of political institutions—that there is one ideal form of government for all societies—that was partly based on the skepticism about the role of government in determining the shape of human affairs. This skepticism was premised on a rejection of the strict egalitarianism that assumed "that mankind are alike in all times and all places"; an error that Mill thought was common to the political theories "of the last age . . . in which it was customary to claim representative democracy for England and France by arguments which would equally have proved it the only fit form of government for Bedouins or Malays."[52]

Durkheim and Maine were equally adamant in their denial of the existence of ideal political types "supposedly transcending all considerations of place or time and suitable to all mankind."[53] Indeed, Maine considered the Revolution to be born of Rousseau's mistaken insistence that "a perfect social order could be evolved . . . irrespective of the actual condition of the world and wholly unlike it."[54] To rationalize ideal political arrangements through a logical deduction from individual motivation in a supposed state of nature was to risk radical political conclusions at the expense of historical judgment. What made the attention to history so necessary was the underlying claim that man as such was a historical animal, a creature of habit and custom whose mode of being was the achievement of the long institutional history of civilization. Contract as the *precarious* accomplishment of progressive societies was not a logically given fact of human nature.[55] Since the plasticity of social life underwrote earlier invocations of the ancient polis as a model for modern politics, the autonomy of political will is thus consciously criticized.

This critique of the priority of politics as the vehicle for the radical reconstitution of society resonated with a number of earlier eighteenth-century arguments about the complexity of society, especially in the Montesquieuian tradition that emphasized the importance of the intricate play of manners and customs in the making of human sociability. This is also often echoed in a general Aristotelian line of thinking that likewise emphasizes the need for forms of government to be adjusted to suit some basic sociological features of any given society. The distinctiveness of the nineteenth-century critique, I would argue, stems in part from a more rigid account of manners and custom, on the one hand, and a more holistic account of the social, on the other. The tendency of nineteenth-century social theory was to insist on a great deal of systematicity to the social; society here emerges as tight-knit, functional system. In Durkheim, the sui generis status of society implied that politics and forms of government were only ever epiphenomenal and/or merely contingently tied to social life; they were never constitutive of society. Maine, while more attentive to the dynamic interplay between externally imposed change and social progress, nevertheless viewed societies as having an internal coherence and logic that was prior to and independent of politics.

By the late nineteenth century not only was recreating Roman society seen as politically undesirable (as in Constant), it was also now conceived of as impossible because man was considered to be much more compelled by history and culture. The autonomy of politics was eclipsed as it was reduced to a derivative reflex of the more essential nature of society, however conceived. In contesting the eighteenth-century (Enlightenment) view of the political world and man's nature as essentially perfectible, social theory in these conservative strands implied a general theory of society in which both ancient and modern man were seen to be much more inhibited in the field of political imagination and action by their societal formations. In Durkheim's famous rendering of the distinctiveness of modern social theory, social phenomena are "natural" things that, "like all other things in nature, which have their particular characteristics," do not "depend upon the human will."[56] Societies are natural equilibria and politics and political will no longer figure as determining elements, and, one may add, are no longer free to imagine a world beyond these imposed constraints. The *social* thus emerges to mark the limits of politics.

THE MODERN AND THE TRADITIONAL: MAINE AND THE COMPARATIVE IMAGINATION

The vivid account of the singular nature of ancient society initiated a generalized structure of contrast that would become foundational to the comparative imagination of modern social theory. In highlighting its difference from the dynamics of modern society, the newly "ethnologized" ancient world would be bracketed together with primitive, feudal-medieval, and Eastern social forms as *traditional* societies defined through a common opposition to the unique trajectory of industrializing societies of the West.

The impulse toward universal schemes of classification was bolstered by the ubiquitous enthusiasm for comparative methodologies in the nineteenth century. One of the key sources for this enthusiasm lay in the success of comparative philology and the dramatic impact of its proposition of an Indo-European language family linking Sanskrit to Greek and Latin.[57] The remapping of the historical relationship between languages and nations heralded by this discovery radically altered the context for the study of Greco-Roman antiquity, now firmly oriented eastward with India as the privileged site of comparison. The conceptual boldness of Fustel's and Maine's reformulations of ancient society stemmed in part from their systematic (and unprecedented) use of Indian evidence to make sense of ambiguous or unintelligible practices and beliefs of early antiquity. On the one hand, the Indo-European or Aryan idea functioned as an incorporative framework, used to extend the grounds of comparison globally; linguistic affinity could demonstrate institutional filiations between East and West and thereby elucidate what are taken to be general tendencies in human history. On the other hand, a radical difference was also imputed to ancient customs, ideas, and institutions (especially Indian institutions); a difference both subsumed and (chronologically) particularized in terms of a relegation to the "early history of society." In Maine's work, it was at first the ancient patriarchal family and then the agricultural village-community that were singled out as universal institutions that both bridge *and* entrench the divide between East and West, ancient and modern.

Comparative philology was the acknowledged model for Maine's project of "comparative jurisprudence."[58] The great achievement of comparative philology was the discovery of the Indo-European language family that "suggested a grouping of peoples quite unlike anything that had been thought of before."[59] This revolution in the understanding of the ethnological relationship among peoples underpinned India's epistemological centrality as "the great repository of verifiable phenomena of ancient usage and ancient juridical thought."[60] Primitive legal ideas "are to the jurist what the primary crusts of the earth are to the geologist. They contain, potentially, all the forms in which law has subsequently exhibited itself."[61] As such they are the "germs out of which has assuredly been unfolded every form of moral restraint which controls our actions and shapes our conduct at the present moment."[62] Thus, while the social state of India is "barbarism," it is a "barbarism which contains a great part of our own civilization, with its elements as yet inseparate and not yet unfolded."[63]

Maine's notion of comparison was predicated upon a specifically *anthropological* timescale, one in which differences in place and customs are represented as differences in time.[64] To compare was to "take a number of contemporary facts, ideas, and customs, and . . . infer the past form of those facts, ideas, and customs not only from historical records of that past form, but from examples of it which have not yet died out of the world." This would entail examining "parallel phenomena," data that are contemporaneous in time, "with a view of establishing, if possible, that some of them are related to one another in the order of historical succession."[65] In practical terms, this meant that ethnological data of extant "primitive" societies such as India provided a crucial link in the attempted reconstruction of a universal history of civilization, with Western society as its apex. The Aryan or Indo-European idea implicated India, ancient Rome, and feudal and modern Europe in a singular (evolutionary) history of institutional development and, thus, became a vehicle through which universal history could be imagined.[66]

Comparative philology, however, proved to be more of an inspirational analogy for Maine's investigations and less a strict methodological model. While Maine was attentive to linguistic affinities among legal terms in various systems of archaic law, this was not his primary mode of investigation (which was historical and ethnographic). Moreover, comparative jurisprudence was considered to be a more ambitious project by nature and thus also likely to produce more tentative generalizations than comparative philology. Jurisprudence took as it object the entire "phenomena of human society" and "laws and legal ideas, opinions and usages, are vastly more affected by external circumstances than language. They are much more at the mercy of individual volition, and consequently much more subject to change effected deliberately from without."[67] The fact of deliberate social change, which for Maine was even more exaggerated in the history of "progressive" societies, was considered to be one of the central factors that had "done most to obscure the oldest institutions of the portion of the human race to which we belong."[68] The two most important historical manifestations of this were, firstly, the specific influence of the Roman Empire (and through it, Roman law) and, secondly, the general impact of centralizing state power and legislation (of which Rome was also the key example). It was in those very areas of the world—such as India and Ireland—where the impact of these two great historical forces was thought to have been most dimly felt, that one could ascertain the autochthonous nature and logic of primitive institutions.

This was another reason why India remained a privileged point of entry for the discussion of primitive law and society—it represented the "living past" of Europe. For Maine, "there is no country, probably, in which Custom is so stable as it is in India."[69] The study of contemporary Indian social and political institutions thus cast light upon the past history of Aryan societies and peoples precisely because Indian society was assumed to have stagnated, arresting development of institutions at an early stage, and, thus, preserving their ancient character. India "includes a whole world of Aryan institutions, Aryan customs, Aryan laws, Aryan ideas, Aryan beliefs, in a far earlier stage of growth and development than any which survive beyond its borders."[70] Scientific observation of Indian institutions and practices could serve to fill in numerous gaps, as it were, in the existing historical record. As history itself was understood to have a definite direction, a proper characterization of the point of origin—what the term *ancient* served to designate—was fundamental.

From his earliest work, Maine's interest in history was always theoretically oriented. Throughout his corpus, he attempted to reconstruct the historical origins, logic, and development of institutions, especially the *ideas* that formed and sustained them, in the service of substantiating generalizations about the evolutionary logic of history. The basic theoretical formulation of that historical logic—summed up in Maine's most famous maxim, "from Status to Contract"—was first proposed in *Ancient Law* (his earliest work) and dominated the theoretical horizon of all later works with remarkably little hesitation or alteration. Maine's theoretical confidence and consistency was not that of a philosophical historian; he presented his theoretical conclusions as inductively formed from a close reading of historical and ethnographic evidence and never as hypotheses derived from abstract reflections on man's nature or first principles. At the same time, the status/contract contrast arguably proposed an equally abstract and stylized historical narrative in which modern society gradually developed out of an ancient/primitive society that is conceived as its radical inverse.

In *Ancient Law* Maine introduces the dictum "from Status to Contract" as a "law of progress" in which the "individual is steadily substituted for the Family, as the unit of which civil laws take account." And "the tie between man and man which replaces by degrees those forms of reciprocity in rights and duties which have their origin in the Family . . . is Contract."[71] The "Family" from which Maine believed our modern conceptions of rights and duties were distilled, or more precisely *disentangled*, was not the "natural" nuclear family, but rather the particular constellation of kinship and power embodied in the ancient patriarchal family. Comparative jurisprudence, again undergirded by the highly generative idea of an Indo-European language family, had demonstrated the widespread (perhaps even universal) existence of the ancient patriarchal family as the "the primeval condition of the human race."[72] While the clearest delineation of the ancient family as a legal institution would be traced in Roman law, in later works, Maine attempted to establish its generality and its varied articulation in institutions from the Hindu Joint Family, the East European (Slavic) House-Community, to its final transitional form in the Germanic (medieval) and Indian village-community. In proposing the patriarchal family as the original sociopolitical form of the (Indo-European) civilized world Maine argued for the theoretical primacy of kinship as the ideological and institutional basis of early society. Modern society, then, begins to take shape in the interstices of the dissolution of the ancient family, leading to the emergence of the individual (as opposed to the corporate family) as the primary legal unit of society, and of territory (and opposed to kinship) and the primary grounds of political obligation.

The ancient patriarchal family in all its forms was most importantly a corporate group, organized under something akin to the archaic jurisdiction of *patria potestas*—the absolute power of the patriarch over dependent persons and property.[73] It was a patriarchal or patrilineal aggregate in that it is defined by agnatic consanguinity, its unity given by common obedience to the eldest male ascendant. The authority of the patriarch was supreme over "the life and death" of a whole host of dependents— mothers, siblings, wives, children, clients, slaves—and extended to (their) possessions he held in what Maine termed a "representative rather than in a proprietary character."[74] In Roman civil law, the patriarchal family had a specific legal character and identity; it was a corporation perpetuating itself intergenerationally as a single unit identifiable through patronymic and gentile nomenclature. In terms of property and succession the "family" was inherited as whole, and in terms of liability it was collectively responsible for reparations. For Maine, it is this *corporate* character of the ancient family that stamped itself on all areas of law in early jurisprudence. In technical terms, it meant that in archaic law the law of persons would confound all other spheres of law. The transition from ancient to modern law would therefore entail the continual restriction of the law of persons, that is, "the gradual dissolution of family dependency and the growth of individual obligation in its place." In this particular narrative of legal development, modern society reaches its telos in "a phase of social order in which all these relations arise from the free agreement of individuals."[75]

The severity of the domestic despotism in the ancient family was a specific feature of private law and thus coexisted with public principles of liberty and equality (especially between father and son) in the realm of ancient citizenship.[76] Ancient law, especially as embodied in the primitive codes such as the Twelve Tables and Laws of Manu, Maine argued, displayed a paradoxical blend of scantiness and fine detail. While the rigid formalism of private law, especially laws relating to the family, would abound in minute formulations of proper procedure and ceremony, whole spheres of public law would be absent. Even after state or public law comes into being, it was still the case that its ordinances have limited application, rarely penetrating into the jurisdiction of the ancient family. It was in respect to the unity and independence of the ancient family that Maine insisted that ancient society, in a fundamental sense, was *imperium in imperio*, a society of commonwealths, an aggregation of families in contrast to the collection of individuals that comprises modern society. The closest modern analogy to archaic public law therefore was international law, where a minimal set of rights and duties extended only to the head of family, who was sovereign in his own domestic domain.[77] Although Maine deliberately invoked Robert Filmer in arguing for the primary fact of the patriarchal family in the history of society, his own account of the relation between original patriarchy and the development of sovereignty ran in the opposite direction.[78] In Filmer's patriarchal theory, the relations within the patriarchal family mirrored the sovereign's relation to his citizens. By contrast, rather than as a model of sovereignty expanding outward from the pattern of rule within the family, in Maine's account, households were instead construed as kingdoms/sovereignties in miniature.[79] The trajectory from ancient to modern society, then, was one in which patriarchal power gradually lost its hold over dependents, becoming more and more circumscribed by a civil/public law that tended to enlarge itself, and finally independence conferred the entire set of rights of duties of the family onto individual persons. Whereas ancient law consisted of a system of rights and duties among sovereigns understood as families, in modern law, individuals relate to one another as little sovereigns.

The ancient family was the essential starting point for understanding the dynamic of legal progress, for "a great part of the legal ideas of civilised races may be traced to this conception," and, "the history of their development is the history of its slow unwinding."[80] In the specific account of the hierarchical, despotic basis of the ancient family and the highly circumscribed modes of action instituted in that social system, Maine offered a novel portrait of primitive life. If stadial theories of human society tended to view the savage as highly individualistic— in Mill's account the savage was pure ego motivated by uncontainable desire—Maine's work depicted primitive society as a way of life that was deeply marked by ritualized forms of thinking and action. The development of civilization lies not in a growing sense of social coordination and orientation toward the public but rather in the freeing of the individual from the constraints of communal obligation via the steady amelioration of the rigidity of ancient law. At the same time, in focusing on patriarchal power as the nexus around which the ancient family took shape, Maine also sought to demonstrate the centrality of kinship as the primary basis of ancient society. Kinship, however, was far from a "natural" relationship; it was a highly artificial, fictive set of relationships, thoroughly imbued with and constituted by structures of power.[81]

The simplest illustration of the ideological constructedness of the agnatic family was the way it privileged one side of the family tree and excluded another equally proximate set of familial ties (cognates). Also, through the widespread practice of adoption, a feature Maine argued was a universal and essential feature of archaic social systems, "strangers" could be legally recognized as kin. Kinship as an institution was not the reflection of "natural" social ties, but rather, Maine argued, was best understood as a political institution marking subjection to a common authority. Kinship was a primitive ideological marker or name for essentially political relationships and configurations of power. By contrast, Morgan and McLennan regarded lineage systems as emergent from and proof of distinct evolutionary stages in the institution of marriage (specifically the creation of marriage classes via rules of exogamy and endogamy). Fustel de Coulanges derived agnatic consanguinity and the patriarchal family from a prior religious orientation, namely the structure of ancestor worship and the constitution of classes of persons who were authorized to perform the appropriate sacred rites. Durkheim famously conceived of social structure itself as the primary or a priori source of primitive systems of classification (the origin of the logical categories of understanding).

In Maine's model, however, power and kinship are always blended in such a way that power is considered to be the original source and "formative cause" of the coming together of people (and the continuing force that binds groups).[82] Thus kinship as a social institution was not merely derivable from biological (or cultural) theories of sex and marriage, religious sentiment, or social structure, although it would almost certainly insinuate itself into and even structure these other spheres. Rather, kinship is the central conceptual device of primitive political theory; it functions primarily as a way of *naming* (and thus comprehending and masking) political relations. According to Maine, "societies still under the influence of primitive thought labour under a certain incapacity for regarding men, grouped together by virtue of any institutions whatsoever, as connected otherwise than through blood-relationship."[83] In Maine's view, society begins from the family at its nucleus and extends outward, in concentric circles, to include the *gens* (an aggregation of families), the tribe (an aggregation of *gentes*), and finally the commonwealth. And each extension of kinship bears within it a particular set of mutual rights and responsibilities. Kinship, when it moves beyond the confines of the natural family (as it does in the ancient patriarchal family) to include gentile and tribal groupings is in reality an artificial, imagined, or fictive relation, one whose ideological function is to veil the transformations involved in the slow transition to large-scale, territorially based political communities.

"The history of political ideas begins," argued Maine, "with the assumption that kinship in blood is the sole possible ground of community in political functions."[84] While empirically a legal fiction, since no families (or tribes, or nations, for that matter) were ever descended unmixed from some known ancestor, it was a fiction that made possible the growth of political communities. Ancient polities, like all existing political communities, were born of war, conquest, and absorption, yet despite this, they were continually (re)constituted and ordered on the model of an association of kindred and "all thought, language, and law adjusted themselves to this assumption."[85] The efficiency and elasticity of this legal fiction explains the breadth and endurance of the ideology of kinship as the name for connective bonds among people in traditional society. And its displacement by a rival principle of political association, namely locality or territoriality, was nothing if not a world-historical revolution. Nothing in the history of political ideology was "so startling and so complete as the change which is accomplished when . . . *local contiguity* . . . establishes itself for the first time as the basis of common political action."[86]

Although this remarkable transition was indeed a revolution, it was, for Maine, a historical development that transpired extremely slowly, gradually taking shape in parallel forms in scales both large and small. The large-scale shift from kinship to locality marked the transformation from tribal sovereignty to the territorial sovereignty of the modern nation-state. Maine offered the changing nomenclature of European monarchs as evidence of this shift, that is, the alteration in titles from King of *the Franks* to King of *France*.[87] The former represented a relation of authority over a specific group of people, while the latter, a relation of dominion over a definite piece of land. The shift presumes the prior development of exclusive ownership or proprietorship over land. The doubling of sovereignty and dominion was, for Maine, a specific outgrowth of the process of feudalization in Europe. The importance of dominion to the principle of territorial sovereignty was confirmed and legitimated in the tenets of modern international law, particularly those aspects of it that were imported from Roman law. For Maine, the ways in which sovereign states were conceptualized in modern international law seemed to be modeled on Roman civil law; sovereigns thus related to one another like individual Roman proprietors (especially in laws relating to questions of use, occupancy, and dominion).[88]

On a smaller scale, this transition from kinship to locality as the source of communal affiliation and obligation began when primitive lineage groups become (primarily) agricultural communities, that is, when tribal communities "settled down upon a definite piece of land." In this process, "the Land begins to be the basis of society . . . at the expense of Kinship, ever more vaguely conceived."[89] The central example of this transition was the agricultural village-community, which Maine argued was the essential social form of both Eastern and Western societies. The study of the village-community dominated Maine's later works, for as he conjectured at the end of *Ancient Law*, in its historical development one could chart the breakdown of the ideological hold of kinship, the dissolution of family dependency, and the concomitant growth of individualism, which in this context ended in the development of private property in land. In Maine's words, "our studies in the Law of Persons seemed to show us the Family expanding into the Agnatic group of kinsmen, then the Agnatic group dissolving into separate households; lastly, the household supplanted by the individual; and it is now suggested that each step in the change corresponds to an analogous alteration in the nature of Ownership."[90] Private property, "in the shape in which we know it, was chiefly formed by the gradual disentanglement of the separate rights of individuals from the blended rights of a community."[91]

Maine's precise account of the emergence of private property in land will be taken up more directly in chapter four. For now, I want to focus on what Maine's characterization of village-communities was meant to reveal about the nature of traditional societies. Village-communities represented a midway point, as it were, between kinship and locality. In effect, they marked the pure doubling of kinship and locality; the "Village-Community of India is at once an organised patriarchal society and an assemblage of co-proprietors. Personal relationships are confounded with proprietary rights."[92] In later writings, Maine would emphasize the ways in which the inner trajectory of village-communities continually tended toward the displacement of their self-identification as a body of kinsmen by a more abstract notion of community held together by mutual rights and obligations in relation to land. Significantly, the move to locality as the primary source of identification was still structured by communal obligations, and as such the village-community was still far removed from the free rein of individualism embodied in a society based upon contract. The shift from kinship to locality, while fundamental to the dilution of the ideological basis of ancient society, remained a transitional phase in the coming of contractual society.

Maine's contrast between status and contract, which, in *Ancient Law,* was a formulation about the historical trajectory of Roman law (and analogously the development of Western legal systems), initiated a general classificatory framework, as the ancient was equated with other social systems in common opposition to the modern. The ancient family and, even more crucially, the village-community became nodal points of comparison through which Maine would weave together the histories of the various branches of the Aryan tree (India, Ireland, Rome, and Germany) into a continuous institutional history of the progressive development of private property, freedom of contract, and individual right. Maine's use of the comparative method, despite its expansive historical and geographical imagination, tended to reinforce the conceptual contrast between status and contract as structuring principles of radically opposed social formations. Although Maine utilized a wide array of historical sources (extending from the Germanic, Indian, and Roman to the Slavic, Russian, and Irish) this diversity was circumscribed and contained within this elementary contrast of status or contract. Status (or custom) and contract not only defined the two endpoints of historical development but also determined the nature of all the intermediate stages, which exhibited no distinct internal principle of organization not derived from the elementary construction of status or contract. For example, in Maine's account of the various kinds of village-communities in Europe and India, especially of those forms which have developed most in the direction of feudalism, Maine examined many historical and contemporary examples of land law where customary and contractual principles were intermingled. But rather than searching for a unique definition of this vast set of "mixed" cases, Maine tended to see them as various midway points in the larger transition from status to contract. Contemporary evidence of customary or communal principles was characterized as "traces" or "survivals" of the ancient type. Thus, less than differentiating and classifying a number of distinct evolutionary stages in history, status and contract worked to describe opposed ideal-typical formulations of ancient and modern societies.

This contrast was further accentuated by the temporal horizon of the comparative method, which tended to conceptualize differences in social forms as differences in developmental states, that is, as differences in time. Maine's study of village-communities, for example, was premised upon and reinforced this kind of temporal and spatial contrast, especially along the lines of an East/West and traditional/modern dichotomy. The patriarchal village-community, characterized by the communal ownership of property, was the prime nexus around which English, Teutonic (German), and Indian (extending to Russian, Slavic, and Irish) agrarian and legal histories were woven into a common theoretical framework. In establishing these historical affinities, the framework however produced a temporal equivalence between the institutions of the medieval West and contemporary Eastern phenomena, a process of comparison in which what laid *beyond* Europe was always already *before* Europe.[93]

Moreover, the commonality established between the *contemporary* East and the *premodern* West was not only built upon a temporal distancing but, more crucially, was also construed in such a away as to reinforce a unified concept of status-oriented or *traditional* societies in opposition to the uniqueness of modernity in the West. The ancient, medieval, and primitive are collapsed and subsumed under the generalizable category of *tradition*, poised in common opposition to the uniqueness of the modern West. The particularity of Western modernity was, thus, constructed through both an anthropological time frame and the consolidation of a unified and generalized category of *tradition* as *pre*modern.

TOWARD HOLISTIC MODELS OF CULTURE AND SOCIETY

The way Maine utilized the temporal axis of comparison to stress the dichotomous account of status and contract, or tradition and modernity, demonstrates a central feature of his work, a feature that undercuts a wholesale identification of Maine with mainstream Victorian evolutionary theory. Unlike evolutionary anthropologists, many of whom (such as Morgan) retained the eighteenth-century triad of savagery-barbarism-civilization and sought to demarcate strict hierarchal stages in the evolution of civilization, Maine tended to rely on a binary mode for the classification of societies. As we have seen, the status-contract dichotomy was the metaframe for a whole series of more detailed investigations of the historical conjunctures and social forms, such as the rise and demise of village-communities and the process of feudalization, that occupied the space between both extremes. Despite the temporal logic implicit in his comparative method and the generalizations about the progressive direction of history—both of which resonated with the contours of Victorian evolutionism—Maine is more appropriately understood as fundamentally a dichotomist.[94] It is in its difference from classical social evolutionism that one can best understand the resonance of Maine's work both for social theory and (twentieth-century) anthropology. In terms of the former, the status/contract dichotomy provided a particularly evocative classificatory scheme and also a systematic concept of social structure. While for the latter, Maine's account of traditional society (in particular) gave substance to the systematicity of the *social* and, at the same time, anticipated a model of culture that would become its defining concept.

The model of opposing ideal-typical societies imbued Maine's conceptualization of society with a new form of spatialization; status and contract were part of a deeply synchronic account of social formations. Status and contract were principles that rationally ordered and defined the internal relations that governed ideas, institutions, and practices. In this way, societies whether defined through status or contract relations were conceived of as functionally ordered, structured totalities, holistic societies where central principles animated and connected the different sets of relations and institutions. The larger picture produced, then, is less a ladder of civilization upon which all societies are placed hierarchically than a spatial frontier where bounded societies live side by side, yet, significantly, in different temporalities.[95]

In a substantive sense, both the ancient family and the village-community were traditional social forms that were defined by their corporate or communal character. The family as a legal construct was explicitly modeled along the lines of a corporation sole, where the paterfamilias acted as the representative trustee of a unit that was succeeded to universally and retained its personality intergenerationally. Kinship was its foundation; kinship rules allocated legal/civil ranks and determined the status relations between persons. Importantly, kinship and kinship terminology were not just assemblages of customs and usages; they could not be reduced to a mere system of naming, a purely psychological guide to familial ties, or epiphenomenal residues of material relations, religious concepts, or biological drives. Rather, kinship rules were *constitutive* of social relations and thus of the social order; it was kinship that gave systematicity to social relations. This systemic aspect is what later twentieth-century theorists of kinship would call the structural or synchronic analysis of kinship, the core of which many argued could be derived from Maine's original insights.[96]

As a model of traditional society, the village-community also embodied a communal social form that was deemed to be self-sufficient in important ways. The village-community not only retained traces of the bonds of kinship in the form of communal limitations on ways in which land can be cultivated, distributed, and alienated but was also characterized by an adaptive feature variously noted as the capacity for "self-acting," "self-governing," and "self-organizing." The village-community, in this sense, was thought to be independent and complete unto itself; it "contains within itself the means of following its occupation without help from the outside."[97] It was a functional whole, whose self-sustaining capacity allows it to order various social, political, legal, and economic spheres toward a communal purpose.

With the emphasis on the synchronic interdependency of social spheres, a feature especially prominent in but, importantly, not limited to Maine's stress on communal integration in traditional societies, Maine's work exhibited simultaneously a substantive and methodological stress on viewing societies as rational, functional wholes. This feature was further accentuated in Maine's sociology of colonialism (which I will discuss more fully in chapter five) in which the bases of traditional society were seen as increasingly undermined by contact with the modern. The collapse of traditional society was conceived of in terms of disruptions to a delicate social and cultural equilibrium, which cascade into eventual disintegration. The dissolution of the Indian village-community under the rubric of British imperialism was a vivid example of the ways in which the colonizing process set traditional and modern societies into a dramatic, living (and potentially devastating) opposition.

Conceptualizing societies as systemic wholes, a development that was also at the core of the sociologies of Comte, Durkheim, and Spencer, was a central feature of structural-functionalism in twentieth-century sociology and social anthropology as well as of the anthropological conception of culture as it came to be consolidated in the work of Franz Boas in the early decades of the twentieth century.[98] By contrast, *culture* in evolutionary anthropology, for example in E. B. Tylor's seminal contribution *Primitive Culture*, more often signified a psychological state of humanistic cultivation, linked to the development of the arts and akin to and often used interchangeably with the concept of civilization.[99] In Tylor's work, while aspects of culture (such as religion and philosophy) were analyzed in terms of developmental stages, these features were never conceptualized as bearing or expressing the nature of their respective societies. They were not conceived of as distinctive of social *systems* as opposed to psychological states. The evolution of culture (a singular and not plural notion) revealed less about the structure of primitive societies than about the nature of the primitive mind (especially those tendencies it shared with civilized man, such as rationality and inventiveness). In this line of thinking, culture was not associated with tradition, in the sense of something that constrains and limits human action and imagination.

In contrast to this perfectionist and progressive notion of culture, the modern anthropological concept of culture stressed the historicity, plurality, integrative capacity, and relativity of cultures understood as bounded wholes, one that saw culture as a determinative shaper of human behavior.[100] This concept of culture, arguably the central and defining concept of twentieth-century anthropology, was built upon the critique of the racial and evolutionary basis of much Victorian anthropology. It was a critique mounted by the cultural and structural-functional schools of anthropology. On the one hand, Boas and the cultural school had inaugurated a successful critique of the comparative method and the evolutionary differences it had claimed to unearth and schematize. For Boas, similar phenomena, that is, similar customary practices, could be the product of diffusion and imitation rather then evolution; they need not have common origins or common causes, making it impossible to distinguish some practices as "early" or "primitive" as opposed to "advanced" or "developed." Moreover, by emphasizing the historical conditions of diffusion, Boas contested the explanatory value of race (biological differences) as a standard of valuation as well as an explanation for the persistence of differences in customs and practices.[101] As race's explanatory potency was undermined, however, the fact of deep-seated cultural traditions was paradoxically reinforced. Culture, now conceived as a singular, unique phenomenon, present in all peoples, still functioned as determinative of behavior. The pervasiveness of cultural determination—of societies conceived as primarily cultural wholes—is what grounded the plurality and relativity of cultures, no longer tied to any overarching, external standards of racial or civilizational progress.

The structural-functional school of social anthropology, likewise, contested the evolutionary and stagist conception of social progress, for example, by denying the claim that forms of marriage and kinship structure could be seen to develop in sequential stages from primitive promiscuity, then matriarchy, to patriarchy and the modern nuclear family.[102] At the same time, the functionalist critique of evolutionism generated a revival of interest in the structural analysis of kinship, as the sui generis foundation of the social structure of (especially) tribal societies. In severing the ties to speculative stages in kinship structure, structural-functional theories of kinship also reinforced the synchronic coherence and boundedness of social structure, in which customs and usages were internally constituted (again, deeming a universal comparative method inappropriate for the study of discrete cultural-social wholes). It was in this tradition of British social anthropology that Maine's legal model of kinship was substantially revived.[103] While structural-functionalism and the cultural school developed concepts of the *social* and of *culture* that were methodologically invested in concepts of relativity, boundedness, and holism, they were (as in Maine) also premised upon substantive theses about the nature of traditional society, an intermingling that tended to reinforce at both levels assumptions about the internal cohesiveness and communal orientation of traditional societies, the cultural and social determination of individual action and behavior, and thus to de-emphasize (political) conflict, change, and agency.[104]

If we return to Maine's substantive characterization of traditional society and its implicit view of agency we can see how the doubling of methodological and substantive imperatives produces a particular view of agency. In Maine's rendering of the limited theoretical imagination of primitive man, as well as the implied psychological resistance to change, emerged an account of human action and behavior that was profoundly shaped and limited by cultural and social norms. Maine's discussion of kinship as the central organizing principle of primitive society demonstrates his more general insistence on the slow and incremental generation of new legal ideas and practices. For Maine, society was always "in advance" of the law (especially in progressive societies). Legal transformation was thus a process of harmonizing essentially rigid and technical categories to new social relations.[105] Yet, while Eastern ideas "move always within a distinctly drawn circle of unchanging notions," Maine saw the difference between East and West as "really only a difference of degree." Even in the most progressive of Western societies, "there are more natural limitations on the fertility of the intellect than we always admit to ourselves."[106] A fundamental fact of man, primitive as well as modern, was his inherent psychological resistance to change and innovation.[107] In this last conjecture, Maine took a psychological predisposition supposedly characteristic of primitive society and promotes it to a general feature of humankind.

This deterministic account of behavior was thus not only characteristic of primitive or premodern societies, but had implications for the general theory of human sociability. While for Spencer, for example, the "tyranny of custom" was peculiar to the early stages of society, Maine elevated it to the status of a sociological constant or maxim about human nature as such. Human behavior was construed to be a product of social learning, institutional conditioning, and historically and culturally informed custom. By the end of the nineteenth century, these elements came to constitute the core of the modern anthropological definition of culture. And as Margaret Archer has argued, this generalization also produced a kind of inversion of the modern/tradition dichotomy, where the anthropological study of traditional society inaugurated a view of culture that was then imported back into the sociological tradition as a general account of social integration and structural interdependency. The important methodological implication of this translation is how the structure/agency problem characteristic of modern social theory represents a doubling of and mirrors the culture/agency problem.[108]

ANTHROPOLOGY AND COLONIALISM

Maine's theoretical affinity to later anthropological models of culture was one of the features that distinguished his work from his contemporary social evolutionists. Moreover, his status as an outlier of sorts to that tradition was also what rendered his work more resonant with imperial policy. In the late nineteenth century, evolutionary anthropology's attention was focused on the absolute origins of civilization. Substantively, this entailed a primary interest in "prehistorical" and "savage" societies and, methodologically, a turn to Darwinian-inspired speculative theories of evolution. In this context, Maine's patriarchal theory was consistently challenged and ultimately abandoned. But while evolutionary anthropology, especially in its more racialized models, informed and justified the general ideological framework of empire, its insinuation into the modalities of colonial rule was arguably more eclectic.[109]

The enthusiasm in imperial administrative circles for Maine's work, as opposed to, for example, that of Lubbock, McLennan, or Tylor, in part, stemmed from the fact that Maine focused on issues such as land tenure, legal transformation, and village society, issues that were seen to be central to the immediate administrative concerns of imperial rule.[110] But there was a deeper theoretical affinity between Maine's approach to traditional society and the exigencies of colonial governance. This deep affinity is attested to in the ways in which Maine's work was revived in twentieth-century anthropology, in the wake of the critique of evolutionary models. Maine's work was directly taken up in and shaped the tradition of British structural-functional anthropology inaugurated by Radcliffe-Brown. Maine's "jural" model of culture and kinship, as mutual sets of rights and duties, was consciously adopted by Fortes and Gluckman in their respective work on African political and legal systems.[111] But what is most telling in this appropriation is that Maine's work appeared exceptionally relevant in the context of the anthropological study of colonial societies, one that was deeply implicated in the theory and practice of indirect rule in Africa. Like Maine's understanding of traditional societies, these works also assumed a holistic essence to native societies, in this case tribal society, in which questions of politics and power were displaced by a stress on the normative and social cohesiveness of African polities.[112] It was in this sense that the anthropological model of culture and structural-functional analysis of traditional societies inaugurated in Maine's work bears a specific and intimate, as opposed to an incidental, relationship to the dynamics of colonial power and late imperial ideology.

CHAPTER THREE

CODIFICATION IN THE EAST AND WEST

THE INVENTION OF TRADITIONAL SOCIETY was one of the key conceptual preconditions for the theory and practice of indirect rule. Maine's seminal contribution to its theorization was to have a direct role in the shaping of late imperial ideology (which will be taken up more directly in chapter five). The next two chapters will examine the specific ways in which Maine's model of traditional society became elaborated and implicated in two vital imperial policy domains—legal reform and land tenure. The codification of law and the administration of land revenue were intricately connected to the ideological and practical basis of the British Empire in South Asia.[1] They were the arenas in which imperial governance most directly intervened in and confronted the basic institutions of everyday life, and thus central domains in which ideas of "Indian society" were constituted and employed. Moreover, for the liberal-imperial agenda, in addition to educational reform, legal codification and revising land tenure were seen to be elemental to any project of modernizing improvement.

Retracing the early history and evolutionary trajectory of law and property was, moreover, the central preoccupation of Maine's scholarly endeavors; it was the agenda that most shaped his contemporary reputation and, given its intimate connection to the concerns of imperial administration, accounted for Maine's prominence in imperial policy debates. Chapters three and four will focus in turn on these two broad questions—law and property—and examine Maine's practical contribution to Indian policy debates in light of the theoretical agenda put forward in his historical, legal, and political thought.

In terms of his approach to the study of Indian society, commentators often portray Maine as applying preformed theories of ancient society to India and thus underemphasize the ways in which Maine's seven-year tenure in India substantially shaped his conceptualization of primitive societies (and his social theory more generally). In relation to imperial politics, not only would Maine sharpen his account of the dynamics of traditional society, but he also formulated a distinct sociology of colonialism in which native societies were seen to be increasingly endangered through contact with modern ideas and institutions. In relation to both the question of legal reform and land tenure policy, Maine would bring to light the myriad ways in which the customary basis of native society had been dramatically undermined with the imposition of imperial rule.

Maine's understanding of the structural conditions of native society, and how these were altered with the coming of imperial rule, revised the terms of debate about imperial reform and stability.

In arguing for the necessity of understanding law not in its abstract and idealized form, but rather in terms of the various stages of its historical development, Maine became the leading figure in England of historical jurisprudence, inspired in part by the work of Savigny and the German Historical School. Maine's reputation as a legal theorist was shaped by his criticism of the rival school of utilitarian and "analytical jurisprudence" as expressed in the work of John Austin. Against the Austinian definition of law as "the command of the sovereign," Maine took the example of Roman legal development to elucidate the transformative epochs, such as the era of customary law, through which law was seen to have generally passed before reaching its modern legislative form. In this chapter, I elaborate the practical and theoretical implications of Maine's distinct brand of historical jurisprudence by focusing on his views on the contentious question of codification, and specifically his intervention in the extended debate on the codification of Indian law. I argue that Maine's proposal for a uniform civil code was premised less upon a Benthamite belief in the inherent superiority of enlightened codification than upon a distinct account of the practical constraints emergent from the current, disordered state of Anglo-Indian law. This account was linked to his theoretical insights into the natural trajectory of customary law and the deleterious impact of imperial rule on native law, both of which were informed by his understanding of the intimate connection among legal change, legal practice, and social transformation. In this way, Maine's important work as Law Member in the Viceroy's Council is assessed in terms of immediate Indian policy debates as well as in terms of Maine's jurisprudence as a whole.

CODIFICATION IN THE EAST: FROM MACAULAY TO MAINE

As major intellectuals of nineteenth-century Britain came to puzzle over the intricacies of British rule in India, one prominent issue that was especially subject to energetic theoretical and practical debate was the case of law and legal reform, particularly, what kind of law was best suited for British India. From Macaulay's inaugural tenure to those of Henry Maine and James Fitzjames Stephen in the 1860s and 1870s, the position of Law Member in the Government of India[2] was occupied in turn by several of the leading figures (and representatives of the main schools of) nineteenth-century jurisprudence. At one level, the rule of law had become, by the end of the century, a de facto byword for the justification of British rule;

its establishment in India was deemed to be the supreme gift imparted by imperial rule. Law, in Stephen's words, was nothing less than "the gospel of the English," the linchpin of the "moral conquest" of India.[3] At the same time, throughout the century, the question of importing English law to India was complicated not only by questions about whether imperial rule should aim at transforming native customs and practices but also a general unease, especially prominent among legal reformers and jurists, about the current state of the common law in England. In this context, the debate concerning legal reform and legal codification in India necessarily intersected with the concurrent debate about the present and future shape of English common law, and, thus, proved to be an important conduit for experimenting with models of reform that could be reimported, as it were, to England.

For later Victorians, in respect to the question of codification especially, there was a sense that Indian legal reform had generally outpaced English reform efforts. The Indian Penal Code (1861) was not only seen as the landmark achievement of the Government of India but, in its formulation and enactment, was also practical proof of the possibility of scientific juris-prudence, of building effective codes of substantive law built upon ratio-nal, deductive principles. The movement for scientific codification, which had its roots in enlightened jurisprudence, was given an enormous fillip with the adoption of the French Civil Code, or *Code Napoléon*, in 1804. Yet, as the nineteenth-century movement for codification had assumed global dimensions—from the famous debate between Thibaut and Savi-gny in Prussia about the adoption of the Code Napoléon, the codification projects by the State of New York, to the final enactment of the German Civil Code (*Bürgerliches Gesetzbuch*) in 1900—resistance to it became ever more acute, especially in countries with a tradition of common law. In England, the movement for codification, especially in its purest Ben-thamite hue, had been a notable failure, despite the appointment of numer-ous law commissions to digest and/or codify aspects of the common law.[4]

In this context, the success of Indian codification stands out as a pecu-liar anomaly. The Indian Penal Code was the earliest penal code, perhaps even the earliest code of any kind, adopted in a common law country. A number of American states and British colonies subsequently adopted a penal code: New York in 1881, Canada in 1892, New Zealand in 1893.[5] England has yet to adopt a criminal code after major attempts in the 1830s, again under Stephen in 1880s, and most recently attempted in 1989 when the law commission published a draft penal code for England and Wales.[6] Moreover, the Indian Penal Code, unlike later substantive codes, was not a work of consolidation or digest, that is, it did not take current English law and systematize, simplify, and rationalize it. Rather, it was a self-conscious attempt to construct a code de novo, based upon first principles, taking inspiration from other systematic codes, notably the French *Code Pénal* and Livingston's code for Louisiana. In this respect, the Indian Penal Code may be the closest to anything like a pure philosophical code to be enacted in the nineteenth century.[7]

The Indian Penal Code was adopted amid a flurry of Indian legislation; it was preceded by the adoption of the Code of Civil Procedure in 1860 (revised in 1882) and was followed by the subsequent adoption of the Code of Criminal Procedure in 1862 (revised in 1872 and 1882), the Evidence Act of 1872, and number of substantive acts on succession, contract, and commercial law.[8] The pace of codification was such that Stephen could confidently say that in this period, "the law of India may be said, without exaggeration, to have been all but completely codified,"[9] despite the glaring absence of a uniform civil code. A number of conundrums arise when explaining the success of codification in British India. Given the almost total failure of the codification of substantive law in England, why was the project of Indian codification propelled by its most eminent jurists late into the nineteenth century, that is, well after the tide of Benthamism had waned in both contexts? Moreover, the period of rapid codification in India sits uneasily with the post-Mutiny distancing from ambitious projects for the modernization and assimilation of Indian society. Maine and Stephen, who not only oversaw these legislative enactments but also continued to advocate for the ill-fated codification of civil law, were highly skeptical of "speculative" jurisprudence. Maine's reputation in England (and India) had been built upon a critique of analytical jurisprudence associated with the work of Bentham and John Austin, and he was considered to be the leading figure of a rival historical school.

Maine's antipathy to what he considered the more extravagant claims of analytical jurisprudence should not belie his measured admiration for Bentham's and Austin's approach to jurisprudence. While in no sense a utilitarian, Maine's critique of the analytical school was notably less vociferous than his critique of the modern school of natural law. Furthermore, his innovative defense of codification in India, one that is uniquely situated against both a purely rationalist argument for scientific codification and a conservative, historicist critique of legislation, allows one to gain leverage on the practical implications and normative underpinnings of Maine's more methodological writings. In this light, Maine's jurisprudence emerges as a complicated, conservative defense of liberal reform, one that seeks to preserve the historical achievements of the precarious, progressive logic of modernity.

"Scientific jurisprudence," according to Frederic Harrison, was "not an intellectual luxury, but a practical necessity for an English lawyer."[10] The practical demands of fashioning law for a diversified and expanding empire necessitated a more abstract approach to law than might have readily come forth from the insular common lawyer. Because England could not just send "our bench or bar" overseas—that is, the two institutions commonly taken to be necessary checks on uncertainty or arbitrariness in adjudicating common law—it had to devise ways of making English law accessible and easy to administer by imperial magistrates and political officers who lacked legal training. Harrison argued that the practical demands of simplifying and making sense of English law, as well as making it suitable for an alien population, necessarily propelled the jurist to make English law more systematic and methodical. With the Indian codes being the exemplary model—even the basis of a future "English Corpus Juris"—empire was the curious route through which English common law could be transmuted into a "scientific and more modern form."[11]

Harrison's comments alert us not only to the optimism with which Indian codification was viewed but also to the unique opportunities afforded by the peculiar conditions under which Anglo-Indian law would be fashioned, an imperial predicament that both required and made possible innovative legislative responses. The anomalous structure that defined British rule in India was often argued to be the supreme political fact that occasioned bold jurisprudential experiments. The most ambitious imperial legislators, such Macaulay and Stephen, considered absolute government to be uniquely suited to the purposes of systematic codification. During the Commons debate on the renewal of the Company's charter in 1833, Macaulay forcefully argued that

> as I believe that India stands more in need of a code than any other country in the world, I believe also that there is no country on which that great benefit can more easily be conferred. A code is almost the only blessing, perhaps is the only blessing, which absolute governments are better fitted to confer on a nation than popular governments. . . . It is a work which cannot be well performed in an age of barbarism, which cannot without great difficulty be performed in an age of freedom. It is a work which especially belongs to a government like that of India, to an enlightened and paternal despotism.[12]

Too riven by faction and too deferential to the established power of the bar and the bench, popular assemblies like Parliament, for Macaulay, had yet to prove themselves suitable to the task of codification. But the absence of these key institutions in India also meant that a simple transfer of existing English law to India would only confound the problem. For Macaulay, conditions in India had exacerbated the defects of common law jurisprudence; the uncertainty inherent in "judge-made law," without the mitigating effects of informed legal and public opinion, had produced a system that was "not law, but a kind of rude and capricious equity."[13] Judge-made law coupled with an absolute government was, for Macaulay, "a curse and a scandal not to be endured."[14]

Macaulay's solution was for the immediate formulation and adoption of "a complete written code of laws."[15] Macaulay's understanding of the necessity for codification would become foundational; its basic contours would be repeated by advocates of codification throughout the century. Macaulay's understanding of the necessity of codification, as well as his notion of what codification actually entailed, was of a distinctive kind, shaped by the political tenor of the 1833 charter debates and its spirit of reform (and the general interest in codification in England as well). The 1833 Charter Act established, for the first time, a legislative instrument for India in the form of the Governor-General's Council in Calcutta that would formulate laws for the whole of British India. For matters of legislation, the act established the position of Law Member to sit with Council when questions of legislation arose and also founded an Indian Law Commission with the express job of formulating codes of statute law. James Mill had envisaged the role of legal member in grandiose terms, as a kind of philosopher-legislator for India; institutionally the legal member was to be a civilian (a non-Company employee). Macaulay as the first Law Member and head of the Law Commission relished his role as India's first modern lawgiver.[16]

The Indian Penal Code, of which Macaulay was the prime author, was the first and most significant achievement of this new era confident of the broad-ranging benefits of codification. Law was understood as an interdependent system, the systematization of the penal law was to be just the first part of an attempt at total uniformity, with its pinnacle in the creation of a full substantive, civil code. Macaulay had explicitly directed the Law Commission to understand its work as one of reform-oriented codification, and not just the mere consolidation of existing law. The code would not be adopted officially until 1860, but its ambition was marked. Macaulay considered it to be a scientific code in the truest sense; it was "not a digest of any existing system" since "no existing system has furnished us even with a groundwork."[17] While aspects from the "most celebrated systems of Western jurisprudence," such as the French Code and the Code of Louisiana, were consulted, the style and substance of the code were understood to be charting their own path.[18]

Despite Macaulay's well-known critique of utilitarian ethics, the code was his most Benthamite endeavor. With reference to drafting of the code, Macaulay remarked that in matters of jurisprudence, no one had surpassed Bentham.[19] Like Bentham, Macaulay sought to formulate a code that would be simple and complete, accessible and efficient, premised upon a rationalistic view of punishment and deterrence. Codification was tied to a model of the law in which legislation was viewed as the only appropriate instrument of law making, and thus Macaulay was consciously critical of the form and practice of the common law. Like Bentham, Macaulay considered the looseness of "judge-made" law to be ripe for arbitrariness and corruption. It was also a system that necessarily left rights and duties in flux. One of his stylistic innovations, wholly unique in terms of practical legislation, was the use of "Illustrations" in conjunction with each provision, like a geometric application following a theorem. Macaulay explicitly sought to distinguish these illustrative cases from any analogy with English case law. They were to "make nothing law which would not be law without them."[20] Rather, they were hypothetical applications—more on the model of Roman imperial rescripts—whose purpose was to greatly limit the power of judges to interpret the law. The cases, like the laws, were to be made as specific as possible. And both were to be regarded as subject solely to legislative interpretation and reenactment, again, wresting away any power from the Courts of Justice to make new law through processes of adjudication.

Macaulay's most Benthamite moment in many ways was an exemplary one in the relatively brief triumph of Benthamism in India. The argument for codification in this era could easily align itself with the spirit of innovation and reform, which, in this case, rightly saw that India was a kind of political blank slate, and thus could be the testing ground for a whole series of institutional reforms. Reformers in India had a free hand since India lacked those entrenched interests that would undo the progress of codification in England.[21] Moreover, Macaulay's defense of codification was closely tied to a liberal justification of imperial rule. Codification was construed to bring forth the universal benefits of uniformity and certainty in the law, and also guarantee equality between European and native subjects.

The question of equality, for Macaulay, had attained a new political urgency as the Charter Act of 1833 had lifted all previous restrictions on the admission of Europeans to India.[22] Formerly under tight regulation by the government, and in practice restricted to Presidency towns, the new policy augured the rapid settlement of Europeans in the interiors of the subcontinent. For Macaulay, while these new conditions of social intercourse and intellectual exposure to Europeans could be supremely beneficial for the natives of India, in practice, there was the ever-present danger that a new class of oppressors would emerge. Uniformity in law and judicial administration was equally urgent to constrain these new subjects and place them on a level of legal equality with natives. Macaulay's other great success during his tenure in India was the passage of the infamous Black Act of 1836, so-called because of the furor raised by European residents in opposition to it. The Black Act, especially in the nature of opposition to it, was a precursor to the Ilbert Bill controversy in the 1880s. Macaulay's act sought to institutionalize equality between Europeans and natives in civil jurisdictions by making European residents outside Calcutta immediately subject to the jurisdiction of Company courts in civil cases (and depriving them of the right to appeal directly to the Supreme Court). While Macaulay often placated his critics by arguing that the act was only correcting a jurisdictional anomaly, he was never shy from defending the principle of equality on moral grounds:

> I am not desirous to exempt the English settler from any evil under which his Hindu neighbor suffers. I am sorry that there should be such evils, but, whilst they exist, I wish that they should be felt, not only by the mute, the effeminate, the helpless, but by the noisy, the bold and the powerful.[23]

While Macaulay did not view law, as James Mill had, as the primary mode for improvement, legal uniformity and equality were essential to protect subjects from abuses of power and thus for the long-term cultivation of practices of political liberty. Coupled with liberal education and the inclusion of natives in governing institutions, legal equality would be the cornerstone of Macaulay's liberal model of empire, with self-government as its avowed goal.[24]

The Indian Penal Code, the most philosophical of all the Indian codes, ironically came into force in 1861 in a period that saw the official abandonment of the goal of a complete codification of native law. The Mutiny had dampened the ambition for major legislative reform, especially those with the potential to intrude on native practices and beliefs. At the same time the post-Mutiny period also witnessed the most widespread codification, with the passage of the Penal Code and codes of civil and criminal procedures (in addition to various aspects of commercial law). These latter codes, however, were more akin to digests of existing English law. The Benthamite hue of Macaulay's Code would be an anomaly, as later codifiers demurred from the style of "speculative" legislation.

Maine assumed the position of Law Member in the Viceroy's Council in these crucial years of post-Mutiny consolidation. His tenure would last seven years, between 1862 and 1869, the longest of any legal member in the nineteenth century. Current assessments of Maine's tenure emphasize two opposing tendencies of his legislative work. On the one hand, Maine is often characterized as practically oriented and, thus, a tepid legislator, whose good political sense was wary of radical innovation.[25] On the other hand, citing over two hundred pieces of legislation passed under Maine's supervision, there is another view of Maine as an undaunted advocate of complete codification, confident of the ultimate benefits of introducing Western law wholesale into India. The ambivalent assessment betrays something of the complicated nature of Maine's tenure and the conflicting agendas at work in this period. Contemporary critics of Maine's tenure also veered between the accusations of inaction and "overlegislation."

The often-contradictory assessments of Maine also offer a clue as to the complexity of his position on legislation and codification. Maine's experience of the peculiarities of Indian law invigorated a broad commitment to codification, but it was a commitment consciously critical of codification understood on a Benthamite model. For Maine, the idea that India could be taken as a blank slate for speculative legislative experimentation was a recipe for political disaster. Yet the state of Anglo-Indian law was such that the worst aspects of English common law were continually, and haphazardly, introduced into an already indeterminate system of native law set upon a weak institutional frame. Additionally, the push for any kind of institutionalization of law was resisted by a ruling elite that increasingly came to view unrestrained paternal despotism as the best form of rule for post-Mutiny India.

Maine's solution was to offer a distinctive argument for codification, one that emphasized the historical and practical conditions in which codification was both desirable and realizable. In his investigations into the history of codification, especially in *Ancient Law*, and in his contemporary commentary on its potential in England, Maine held a more favorable attitude toward codification than his affiliation with historical jurisprudence at first sight commends. For Maine, when codification could be achieved properly it carried the prospect of harmonizing law with the new demands created by modernizing societies. In India's present condition, while far from the historical stage with which one associated modern codification, the peculiarities of the imperial predicament left codification as the only viable solution to its many legal dilemmas. In this regard, Maine's Indian jurisprudence built upon his considered views of codification, but modified them, paradoxically at times, in a more *universalist* direction. That is, despite his continued opposition to analytical jurisprudence, the Indian experience pushed Maine's advocacy of complete codification in terms that at times echoed his Benthamite predecessors. This was due partly to ways in which the encounter with the actual workings of the common law in India had deepened Maine's skepticism toward the common law and its traditionalist defenders. The fact that Maine became a more vehement advocate of codification and a greater critic of the common law during his Indian experience also lends some insight into why conservative Indian legislators continued the argument for codification well into the closing decades of the nineteenth century, at a time in England when common law advocates had waged a successful defense against the radical reformers. In laying out Maine's theoretical position on codification and its transformations through his Indian experience, one can garner a more precise sense of the nature and legacy of Maine's jurisprudence.

CODIFICATION AND HISTORICAL JURISPRUDENCE:
THE LESSONS OF ROMAN LAW

In 1814, in the aftermath of Napoleon's defeat, Karl Friedrich von Savigny, leader of the German Historical School, published a famous pamphlet against universal codification, titled "Of the Vocation in Our Age for Legislation and Jurisprudence."[26] Savigny's critique of proposals for a uniform civil code for Germany, which was translated into English in the 1830s, defined the broad philosophical lines of the nineteenth-century debate on codification. For Savigny, the modern idea of codification, and its most famous example, the Code Napoléon, had its intellectual origins in the spirit of the eighteenth century. During this period, argued Savigny,

> the whole of Europe was actuated by a blind rage for improvement. All sense and feeling of the greatness by which other times were characterized, as also of the natural development of communities and institutions, all, consequently, that is wholesome and profitable in history, was lost; its place was supplied by the most extravagant anticipations of the present age, which was believed to be destined to nothing less than to the [*sic*] being a picture of absolute perfection.[27]

In the legal realm, the pretense toward perfectibility expressed itself in the call for complete codification as a way to overcome imprecision and arbitrariness in the formulation and application of the law. For Savigny this was a fantasy, a longing for pure abstract universality, for a code that was in principle applicable to "all nations and all times."[28]

Politically, codification in the modern sense was integrally connected to uniform sovereignty. For Savigny, codification in overriding existing provincial and town laws threatened the local authorities that were the cornerstone of people's identification. On the authority of Montesquieu, Savigny raised a corporatist argument defending freedom and the sanctity of mores that unmediated sovereignty was seen to threaten.[29] Moreover, in attempting to fix a code that would be complete in principle, that is, one that would anticipate a decision in every case, one had to presume that the modern age has reached such an advanced stage of legal knowledge and science, surpassing all previous epochs, as to be able to both dissect existing laws and frame new laws. This requires the existence of persons possessing the ability to grasp and comprehend the extraordinary diversity of current legal practices as well as the technical capacity to distill and form legal principles and axioms. For Savigny, however fantastical and politically dangerous an idea of a truly complete code was, in practical terms, the burgeoning new science of jurisprudence was decidedly not up to the task.

In an early essay, "Roman Law and Legal Education," Maine engaged the question of codification directly. For Maine, English common law in particular could profit greatly from some form of rational consolidation as a way of removing the ambiguities and contradictions that seemed to him inherent in a system based upon judicial legislation, legal precedent, and case law. Yet, in a manner akin to Savigny, Maine expressed skepticism about the practical possibilities of producing a well-written code in England. "Can any body of men be collected," Maine asked, "which shall join accurate knowledge of the existing law to a complete command of legislative expression and an intimate familiarity with the principles of legal classification?"[30] In 1856, Maine's answer was decidedly negative. Maine concurred with Savigny on the impossibility of producing a code that could be so complete as to anticipate all future cases or not be altered by judicial interpretation. The danger of judicial legislation—especially ripe as a source of ambiguity in the common law—was, for Maine, a permanent possibility, one that contra Bentham codification could never eliminate but only narrow in scope. But Maine's skepticism, while shaped in part by a general suspicion of the more abstract arguments made in favor of codification, was directed more pointedly at the current state of English law, and especially, English jurisprudence. It was English jurisprudence and its distinctive mode of developing law through cases that had stymied the emergence of technical skills in legal reasoning and clarity that the modern project of codification demanded.

This lacuna recommended the serious study of Roman law as a central part of Victorian legal education.[31] The study of Roman legal development could furnish English lawyers that which its jurisprudence was precisely lacking, namely a mode of reasoning and technical language with which to frame general legal principles. Maine strikingly argued that

> it is not because our own jurisprudence and that of Rome were *once* alike that they ought to be studied together—it is because they *will be* alike. It is because all laws, however dissimilar in their infancy, tend to resemble each other in maturity; and because we in England are slowly, and perhaps unconsciously or unwittingly, but still steadily and certainly accustoming ourselves to the same modes of legal thought and to the same conceptions of legal principle to which the Roman jurisconsults had attained after centuries of accumulated experience and unwearied cultivation.[32]

The most important practical lessons that the study of Roman law could teach the Victorian lawyer were not substantive but formal and historical. Unlike Continental legal systems, the development of English common law was little affected by the infiltration of Roman law after its revival in the twelfth century. While Maine denied the view that the *Corpus Juris*, the compendium of Roman law issued under Emperor Justinian in the sixth century and whose study and dissemination was revived in the twelfth century, ought to be strictly construed as *ratio scripta* (as the abstract embodiment of reason), he thought Roman law in its historical development came to be "distinguished above all others for its symmetry and its close correspondence with fundamental rules."[33] Roman law thus could serve as the archetype or paradigm for mature jurisprudence.

That Roman civil law could be seen as the source of principles and jurisprudence for English law did not originate in Maine, but was, rather, a widespread view especially prominent among reformers of the common law. Blackstone had attempted to reformulate the common law on a Roman law structure, stressing the unity of law by showing how it could be restated according to the principles of natural law.[34] Although Bentham jettisoned his own project of rationally reconstructing common law in favor of a purely deductive code, Austin saw the value of Roman law in the manner in which its expositors have "seized its general principles with great clearness and penetration, have applied these principles with admirable logic to the explanation of details, and have thus reduced this positive system of law to a compact and coherent whole."[35] While Maine clearly shared this admiration for the systematicity of Roman law, he did not view it as a model from which a universal jurisprudence could be simply derived. Rather, it was in its *historical development* that lessons were to be sought.

In this respect, the influence of German historical jurisprudence, especially of Savigny, was pivotal. While Maine was more sanguine about the ultimate benefits of codification in the age of legislation, there was much in Savigny's attack on codification and his seminal studies in the history of Roman law that shaped Maine's understanding of the lessons of Roman law for modern jurisprudence. Maine's essay, and later *Ancient Law*, would mimic one key rhetorical and methodological feature of Savigny's famous pamphlet, namely, structuring its theoretical and normative claims through a meditation on the meaning and value of the historical study of Roman law. More substantively, Maine would appropriate and develop Savigny's argument for why Roman jurisprudence, in its long history of uninterrupted development, served as a model for legal reasoning. For both Maine and Savigny, it furnished the necessary tools for the perfection of the *technical* element of law.[36]

In Savigny's account of legal development, law, in its most primitive form, was integrally linked to the life of a nation. Its expression and growth were organically connected to the whole, analogous to the language and mores of a people. But the intellectual world of nations in their "youth" was limited; there was little progress in terms of the general expression of principles. Rather, law was articulated in formal and ritual acts, whose authority was not consciously connected to rules. And while codes often appear in this age, they are of little use as models to revive.[37] What they lacked most was exactly the precision and clarity sought in the modern call for codification. As nations progress this technical element develops, usually under the guardianship of a specialized class of legal scholars; in Rome this was the distinctive role of the jurisconsults. Maine was also keen to highlight the seminal importance of this mode of legal evolution as a corrective contrast to the development of English common law.

Common law's strict adherence to legal precedent and the authority of case law had fostered a distrust of generalization that led to both the deterioration of technical terminology and its displacement by popular, and imprecise, modes of legal expression (exemplified for Maine in the length and language of the Law Reports). This was the same conundrum that Bentham was responding to with his critique of fictions in the common law and his argument for codification. The priority given to actual cases as the only means by which legal principles could be evinced was, for Maine, the primary reason for the inability of English law to engender rational, generalizable legal principles. By contrast, Roman legal development unfolded in the writings of its jurisconsults, in commentaries that were not constrained by the exact conditions of any particular case. Thus, Roman jurisprudence freed from these limitations could invent new questions and hypothetical cases and thereby facilitated the evolution of general rules.[38]

What was crucial in the example of Roman law, especially as a practical lesson for English law, was not only its refined systematization and technical clarity, but also "because it shows, by the history of the Institutional Treatises, in what way an undergrowth of new technical language may be constantly reared to furnish the means of expression to new legal conceptions, and to supply the place of older technicalities as they fall into desuetude."[39] In this respect, what Maine was keen to expose and recommend from the Roman tradition was a method of systematization—of codification—that would avoid the twin dangers of stagnation and radical overturning. It would be one of the central tasks of Maine's *Ancient Law* to elicit from the millennial history of Roman legal development a prescriptive theory about the relationship between legal evolution and social progress, one in which the question of proper codification was vital.

In one crucial respect Maine parted ways with Savigny. For Savigny, codification was only ever a product of either immaturity or decline, emerging in those historical junctures when the foundations and sources of law were most precarious. At the peak age of a nation's flourishing, when its legal science was at its most effective, for example in the classical period of Roman law under the Antonine Caesers, the need for codification was not felt. By contrast, the *Corpus Juris* was the product of decadence, trying its best to recover and revive the lost legal science of the classical age.[40] For Maine, however, not only was codification "one of the highest and worthiest objects of human endeavour,"[41] but, as evidenced by the history of Roman law, it was also fundamental to legal progress. The awesome task of codification, as Maine's account of its many historical articulations in *Ancient Law* would seek to demonstrate, required a judicious sense of humility in the face of history. Successful codification was a rare historical event; for the precocious Greeks it was attempted too early, while for the Hindus, it came too late, burdened by (religious) formalities. Roman codification was a unique achievement because of its ability to mix innovation and tradition. Thus, by contrast to Savigny's account of Roman law as a cyclical, organic tale of birth, flowering, and eventual decay, in Maine's progressivist rendering, codification was the great achievement that set the stage for Rome's historical flourishing. Despite their differing characterizations of the important moments in Roman legal development, Maine and Savigny shared the view of Rome as the central historical model with which all attempts at scientific jurisprudence must reckon. For Savigny, despite its eventual decline, the jurisconsults of Rome were exemplars of proper juridical method, one that sensibly mixed a reverence for past with the foresight and ability to innovate according to principles. And finally, for both Savigny and Maine the example of Roman law demonstrated the importance of history itself to temper the claims of a modern jurisprudence that sought to remake society anew.

"The most celebrated system of jurisprudence known to the world begins, as it ends, with a Code."[42] The opening sentence of Maine's best-known work, *Ancient Law* (1861) strikingly posits the centrality of codification to the evolution of law, signifying his unique defense of codification as well as his distinct account of the historical grounds of legal progress. *Ancient Law*'s key introductory chapters presented an account of the stages of legal development in which codification punctuates and defines two vital cycles in the evolution of law. Codification for Maine had two distinct meanings and performed two different historical functions. In its more primitive or ancient form codification marked the transition from unwritten to written law and thus signaled the end of the "spontaneous" or natural development of law. The second, more advanced form of codification, linked to the age of legislation, was construed as the last and most scientific instrument for legal change. In both senses, the structure and timing of codification had enormous consequences for the shape of legal and social progress.

In elucidating the stages of legal development and the historical function of codification, as exemplified most clearly in the millennial history of Roman law, Maine sought to challenge the abstract characterization of law put forward by the so-called analytical jurists.[43] For Austin, positive law involved a definite and logically necessary structure; positive law was defined by the issuing of a general *command* by a sovereign agent and the correlative imposition of an *obligation* or duty to obey, both of which were premised upon the threat of force or *sanction* for disobedience.[44] Maine considered this conception of law to be apt as a characterization of modern law in its highest stage of legal development, that is, in the age of legislation. In this respect, utilitarian jurisprudence, with its attempt at scientific systematization, furnished the study of jurisprudence and morals with "a rigidly consistent terminology,"[45] and thus could be credited with bringing much-needed clarity to English legal concepts. Yet understanding the early history of legal forms could not begin with the same kind of analysis, for "the farther we penetrate into the primitive history of thought, the farther we find ourselves from a conception of law which at all resembles a compound of the elements which Bentham determined."[46] For Maine, the terms of Austinian jurisprudence assumed the prior historical establishment of the institutional conditions of modern legal universality, that is, the development of a centralized state and the principle of territorial sovereignty. One of Maine's most salient objections to utilitarian thought (and this applies equally to his critique of political economy) was less its approach to modern law than its pretense to universality, a pretense that necessarily obscured the very different principles upon which alternative legal systems were based.

According to Maine, in contrast to the generality that modern law evokes, ancient law commenced with particular decrees, which slowly expanded into sets of customary observances. While the first stage of law began with the commands of a ruler, these commands were "arbitrary" in the sense that their legitimacy was without reference to universal norms. These commands, rather than laws per se, were better construed as a series of isolated judgments, held together by the nature of the dispensing agency (that is, divine kingship) than by any internal principles. The next era, the epoch of customary law, took shape as an aristocratic class emerged and monopolized knowledge of traditional rules; these rules still only embodied accumulated sets of practices and were not constructed around any principle of legitimacy except tradition and precedent. Customary laws, in their earliest forms, tended to resemble rules of conduct; they were highly ritualistic and formal in character. True customary law was unwritten law. When customary rules were first written and publicized in the form of ancient codes, the transformation of custom was frozen into a set of prescriptions, thus ending the spontaneous development of law. The manner and timing in which societies realized these ancient codes, "at what stage of their social progress, they should have their laws put into writing,"[47] profoundly affected the possibility of subsequent legal progress; successful codification, then, was the criterion that initially divided the world into "progressive" and "stationary" societies.[48]

This natural history of law, the first cycle of legal evolution, was not a purely immanent development, but was intimately connected to political transformations. The transition from law as mere command to customary practice was associated in Maine with a political revolution from (divine) kinship to the rise of aristocracies, which came to function as both depositories and administrators of the law. And depending on whether these aristocracies were primarily civil, military, or religious in character, the law exhibited a different emphasis. Likewise, while the initial move to codification was spurred by the technical invention of writing, political forms again shaped codified law. In Maine's view, early law was especially suspect to two dangers, excessive rigidity and loss of all formality, both associated with the *timing* of codification. In the first case, unwritten custom always threatened to become superstition, that is, practices and usages that were once preserved for their expediency over time garnered a reverence and justification that was wholly at odds with their original flourishing and their present usefulness. The precarious nature of codification, and in some sense all legal development, stemmed from the fact that legal norms, in this case unwritten custom, ought ideally to be codified when the usages and practices upon which they are based were still wholesome and expedient.[49] For Maine, Hindu law was the key example of codification coming too late. It represented a model of distorted and arrested development, in which a religious aristocracy so tenaciously maintained a monopoly of the traditional, customary order that when codification took place the rational core of Hindu law had already been overlaid with ritual formalities and a superstitious attachment to religious texts. The Laws of Manu thus embodied less a snapshot of the actual state of Hindu law at the time of compilation, but more "an ideal picture of that which, in the view of the Brahmins, *ought* to be law."[50] It was thus fully severed from actual practice, free to justify the preservation of outmoded practices and invent new norms (for Maine, irrational and absurd ones like caste) merely from a theological mandate.

It was in this sense that Maine would argue that the "fate of the Hindoo law is, in fact, the measure of the value of the Roman Code."[51] Not only was the Roman legal order the property of a civil (and not religious) oligarchy, codification itself was the outcome of a successful challenge to this order by the popular and plebian element. This challenge not only allowed for an earlier codification in the West, but also allowed codes to function as both a public check on oligarchic power and a formal mode by which institutions could be solidified and developed. If late codification was linked to a persistent rigidity of law, then the problem of precocious codification threatened the formality of law itself. Here, Maine cited the

Greeks as embarking on a path of overly rapid legal development, spurred by early codification. In this case, written rules and technicalities were increasingly held suspect when they came into conflict with popular notions of justice. The "nobility and the elasticity"[52] of the Greek mind, coupled with the institutional strength of the popular courts of justice, did not hesitate to relax the rule of law for the sake of a more just decision. In the long run this tendency necessarily undermined all reverence for the rule of law as such, and the institutional stability required for legal development.[53]

The dangers of excessive rigidity and complete loss of formality continued to haunt legal evolution even after the initial challenge of codification was successfully met. Once the internal, spontaneous development of law came to an end with the publication of the ancient codes, legal evolution began a new cycle in progressive societies in which law was modified by deliberate attempts at reform "from without." Here, Maine introduced his famous triad of legal fictions, equity, and legislation as successive agencies of legal change by which codes were adapted to meet changing societal needs.[54] In progressive societies, social progress and social opinion "are always more or less in advance of Law."[55] To sustain progress, law, which necessarily tended toward fixity, needed to be harmonized with the state of society. These agencies of legal change functioned to ameliorate and bridge the ever-present gap between law and society. And, again, it was the millennial history of Roman law that typified the wisest course of development, one in which innovation was always tethered to a respect for tradition.

Fictions, the most primitive instruments of legal change, were expansively defined by Maine as "any assumption which conceals, or affects to conceal, the fact that a rule of law has undergone alteration."[56] They were invaluable instruments in the early development of law because they provided a mechanism for improvement, a way to overcome the rigidity of law without overtly contradicting the law or offending superstition. In ancient Indo-European law the most prominent and historically crucial one had been the legal fiction of adoption, which allowed for the continuity, development, and expansion of its central social institution, the ancient family. The dynamics of case law in the common law was another key example of legal fictions at work. But while fictions, for Maine, had played a key role in the historical development of law, their continued use in more mature systems of law was an anachronism. While Maine thought Bentham's critique of fictions in the common law was too one-sided, and thus ignorant of their progressive role in early law, he agreed with Bentham that modern English law ought to "prune away" its legal fictions, as they only served as obstacles to scientific classification, simplicity, and orderly distribution.

If fictions functioned only insofar as they concealed the mode by which they transformed the law, equity jurisprudence developed as a distinct system of rules or principles, separate from the civil law that could openly supersede the civil law.[57] In Roman law, equity was formed through the institutional development of the Praetor's Edict and the commentaries on it, which imported the originally Greek theory of natural law as a mode by which to formulate a set of principles that could direct legal reform. The enthusiastic reception of the law of nature by Roman jurisconsults, for Maine, enormously stimulated the rationalization of its law, guided by principles of simplicity, generalization, symmetry, and intelligibility. Natural law had historically saved Roman law from the stagnation of Hindu law; it allowed it to formulate a norm to direct legal reform. At the same time, it never came to serve as a complete system of ethics that necessarily overrode or entirely superseded existing law. Equity jurisprudence thus functioned to build upon the existing foundation of Roman law, it was always remedial rather than revolutionary, solidifying the law rather than undermining it. Maine speculated that "Benthamism" had perhaps played an equivalent productive role in the modern reform of the common law, with the principle of expediency providing a norm by which irregularities could be removed and simplicity attained.[58] Modern natural law, especially as it had developed in France, had however become an "undirected" and thus unconstrained norm, one that functioned more as "an article of speculative faith as opposed to a theory which guided practice."[59]

Equity jurisprudence, like all agencies of legal change in Maine's work, had its appropriate time and place. With the increasing systemization of law and development of centralized states, rival systems of jurisprudence needed to be harmonized in a more permanent manner. The eventual institutional fusion of equity and law heralded the coming of the age of legislation, where legal change was instituted by the unparalleled authority of the state. Unlike equity, whose authority to intervene in law rested in the special sanctity of its rules, legislation derived its authority purely from an external political body, usually an institution assumed to be the representative organ of society. The obligatory force of legislation was now entirely severed from the sanction of tradition or the internal principles it embodied. The era of legislation was thus the era of scientific systematization, that is, the era of modern codification. While modern legislation, freed from all constraints, had the potential to better meet the complex legal demands of commercial society, it also contained nothing that could "prevent its legislating in the wantonness of caprice."[60] Indeed, in his pessimistic late work, *Popular Government*, Maine explicitly worried that the conjunction of legislation with the instability of democratic politics threatened to undo the precarious achievements of legal evolution.

At one level, Maine's elaboration of the historical evolution of law strove to complicate Bentham's alleged reduction of all forms of law to the model of legislation. While legislation, and thus modern codification, represented the pinnacle of legal progress, deriving the entirety of the meaning and function of law from this unique historical form meant ignoring the complex interaction of law and society in history. Recovering the historical variety of mechanisms of legal change was not only meant as a scholarly corrective, but also endeavored to specify the particular challenges that the ever-present gap between law and social progress poses for legal reformers, past and present.[61] Some of the practical lessons of Maine's jurisprudence come to light when we turn again to his more specific views on the debate on codification in India.

THE TRANSFORMATION OF INDIAN LAW AND CUSTOM UNDER BRITISH RULE

If in the 1850s Maine held the prospects of successful codification in England to be relatively bleak, his Indian experience made him more confident of the prospects of codification in both contexts. His critical assessment of the current state of Anglo-Indian law confirmed his view that good laws had to be connected to social practices. In India, however, the question was not only one of harmonizing law to the existing state of social progress, for imperial rule had fundamentally disrupted the natural evolution of both codified Hindu law and customary law. Native law had either been made more rigid or had been displaced by maxims of the common law that were indiscriminately introduced through the Courts of Justice. This system of law was considered by Maine to be so irreparable on its own terms that it necessitated a radical solution: "the cure can only consist in the enactment of uniform, simple, codified law, formed for the most part upon the best European models."[62] In this endeavor, Maine was more confident of the existence of a body of experts who could face the challenge of codification, namely the small circle of legal scholars like himself who combined scientific knowledge of jurisprudence with practical knowledge of Indian law and politics.

In Maine's view, even before the 1833 Charter Act established formal legislative machinery, Indian law had been fundamentally transformed by the introduction and growth of English Courts of Justice, a process that had begun from the inception of Company rule.[63] While Company policy, especially in its early days, had meant for the settlement of disputes to be made with strict reference to native customs and usages, for Maine, the very process of integrating native law into the court system had had profound effects. On the one hand, in order to administer native law, judges and court officers had to determine what native law was and where it could be authoritatively located. In this process, one of the most significant errors made by British courts and officers, according to Maine, was in assuming native custom to be closely tied to the ancient legal texts of Hinduism, which many administrator-scholars and their Brahminical interpreters had assigned as the codified law for the whole of India. Indeed, some of the earliest compilers of Hindu law for administrative use were also famed Orientalists.[64] The resulting application of "native" law had the curious effect that with British dominion the scope, power, and influence of Brahminical law actually increased, overriding the authority of local custom.[65] In Maine's view, Company magistrates, many of whom had little formal legal training,, "acted as if they believed in native law more than its native inhabitants and much Brahminical ritual and not a little doctrine became the subject of decision."[66] As historians of colonial law have argued, here echoing Maine, in the compilation and administering of Hindu law, the British legal administration tended to privilege notions of purity that coincided with the most ancient interpretations of the code, thus overemphasizing the religious and scriptural character of Hindu law.[67]

Maine contended that the interaction of English legal procedure and Hindu law also had a rigidifying effect on Hindu law. On the eve of conquest, Hindu jurisprudence, like all ancient legal systems, was based upon commentaries. Commentaries were vital instruments in the history of legal development; they were on the whole a liberalizing influence, allowing codified laws to adjust to the changing needs of a society.[68] But the imposition of English systems of interpretation, that is, the mode of developing bodies of law through decided cases, tended to arrest the natural, flexible development and improvement of Hindu law. In the process, "native rules hardened, and contracted a rigidity which they never had in real native practice."[69]

If the codified law of India could not withstand the penetration of English modes of legal thought and practice, unwritten customary laws and usages were even more susceptible to the "contagion, so to speak, of the English system of law."[70] According to Maine, what had come to light, most importantly with the settlement of the Northwest Frontier, was the existence of large bodies of customary usages that had historically developed independently of written law. And from 1857 onward, these "unwritten usages, probably older and purer than Brahminical written law are now having their authority acknowledged even by the Indian Courts, once the jealous conservators of the integrity of the sacerdotal system."[71] But, even with this official recognition and endorsement, more than the prejudices or conservatism of English lawyers, in the lower jurisdictions it was the "mere establishment of local courts" that upon contact with native usage functioned to undermine the social and political bases of the system of archaic jurisprudence. In a striking dramatization of the effects of colonial legal intrusion at the village level, Maine narrated the effect of British dominion as not only rigidifying native custom but also instantiating a legal revolution; customary practices

> are generally collected from the testimony of village elders; but when these elders are once called upon to give evidence, they necessarily lose their old position. They are no longer a half-judicial, half-legislative council. That which they have affirmed to be the custom is henceforward sought from the decisions of the Courts of Justice, or from official documents which those courts receive as evidence. . . . Usage, once recorded upon evidence given, immediately becomes written and fixed law. Nor is it any longer obeyed as usage. It is henceforth obeyed as the law administered by a British Court, and has thus really the command of the sovereign. The next thing is that the vague sanctions of customary law disappear. The local courts have of course power to order and guide the execution of their decrees, and thus we have at once the sanction or penalty following disobedience of the command. And, with the command and with the sanction, come the conceptions of legal right and duty.[72]

The effect of British dominion, then, was to reground law in India upon Austinian principles of command, sovereignty, sanction, and right, but in a manner that transmutes custom beyond recognition.

The presence of the English legal system initiated a cascading process whereby continuous legal interventions were made necessary by this initial transformation of custom into written law. The essence of unwritten customary law, and indeed the feature that accounted for its longevity, was its inherent flexibility. The tribal assembly or village council, or whatever body was charged with its supervision, functioned both as a legislative and judicial body, with the ability to reshape usage in the face of changing circumstances, through the tacit invention of new rules.[73] Once customary practice was set into writing, however, the invention of new rules became impossible, for customary law could offer no other explicit principle upon which to base legal reform, except in reference to the authority of tradition or ancient usage. Without explicit principles, the courts, when confronted with ever-increasing disputes of a modern kind that could not be resolved within the terms of newly codified custom, inevitably augmented these laws with "wholesale and indiscriminate borrowing from English law."[74] The unfortunate result was a motley amalgamation of unreconstructed native custom alongside a haphazard set of substantive English law.

According to Maine, primitive customary law, like ancient law more generally, had a double peculiarity; it was extremely scanty in some departments, while overly detailed in other respects. But those departments in which it had an excess supply of rules were precisely those areas of law that became less and less important as society became more modern. Moreover, the transition to written law via the English mode of deciding cases had had a particularly conservative effect, tending to "stereotype" custom and halting avenues of improvement and change. Thus, the structural transformations wrought by British rule neither improved nor corrected native customs, but rather confirmed them in their most abstracted and archaic forms. So even though Maine considered custom to be a legitimate and rational principle for the organization of native law, the impact of the institutions and procedures of British law had had a deleterious and arresting effect on the developmental mechanisms of customary law. The combined effect was that customary law became increasingly detached from practice, increasingly subject to amalgamation and distortion from outside. In this context, to think one could renovate traditional law from within, that is, that customary law could be reformed in such a way as to respond to modern legal demands, would be an absurd solution for it would be asking traditional law "to solve some of the most complicated problems of modern society, problems produced by the collapse of the very social system which is assumed to have in itself their secret."[75] Customary law in a modern society was a pure anachronism; rather that encumbering traditional law with technicalities and rules it could not absorb, the only solution would be a wholly modern one, the consolidation and systemization of law in a written code.

During Maine's tenure as Law Member from 1862 to 1869, he oversaw the passage of over two hundred legislative acts. Yet few of these would be considered to have come close to answering his call for a complete codification of Indian law. The real flurry of codification was effected by Maine's successor Stephen, who in a mere two and half years steered the passage of the Evidence Act, the Contract Act, and a revised Code of Criminal Procedure. While Stephen is rightly regarded, on a par with Macaulay, as one of the most important legislators of nineteenth-century India, Maine always thought Stephen had not fully acknowledged his debt to the preparatory work Maine and his Legislative Department had done to pave the way for Stephen's later achievements. The most lasting legacy of Maine's tenure was the Native Marriages Act (1872); while initially formulated in response to calls from Hindu reformers for the sanctioning of marriage outside the purview of Hindu personal law, Maine in effect formulated a general law for civil marriage that remains in force in India today.[76] Maine was also involved in a failed but ambitious attempt to pass a general Contract Law. Like the Marriage Act, and the concurrent

Succession Act, the Contract Act was significant in that it was the first major legislation that would have substantially affected native civil law and practice (the only other substantive intervention being the Penal Code). But the passage of the Contract Act was stalled, in part due to Maine's own resistance to specific provisions that stipulated breaches of contract in criminal rather than in civil terms. In defending his resistance to the contract law, Maine criticized the Law Commission for being under the sway of an older ethos of legal reform, such as that embodied in the writings of Macaulay, which "give an impression that India is a field for the application of a diluted Benthamism." For Maine, "if ever India was a perfectly ductile & plastic body under the hand of the Legislator, it has ceased to be so now." The great hope for India would be codification understood as the consolidation and reduction of existing law, a redaction of law "rather than an effort to attain theoretical perfection."[77]

As opposed to the Law Commission now seated in England, the immediate resistance in India to the sort of legislation envisioned by Maine came less from Benthamite quarters than from a political-administrative ethos that distrusted the expansion of any form of legal institutionalization. Maine and his successor Stephen were often charged with "overlegislating." Maine's critics argued that the expansion of codified legislation was unnecessarily introducing an overly technical legal language in the administration of law, which was unsuitable to the needs and comprehension of India's peasant majority, on the one hand, and had the effect of further slowing down an already overburdened and inefficient legal system, on the other. Maine entirely concurred with the objective of simplifying and hastening the legal process, but considered the critique partially disingenuous. What many critics sought in limiting legislation was a widened sphere of executive authority and the consolidation of a kind of patriarchal despotism as the best model of imperial rule, a view that was especially popular in the aftermath of the Mutiny and the successful settlement effected by the authoritarian-leaning Punjab school of administration. Maine was highly critical of this defense of discretionary power, considering it only appropriate to extraordinary situations and untenable as a general model for British India, which had always tended toward conforming political rule to the structure of law. To turn back this long-standing tendency would be politically disastrous, inciting resentment by the most advanced native classes, and unprincipled, as all civilized rule was necessarily tied to the rule of law.[78]

Maine considered the view that the growing intricacy and technicality of Indian law could be simply obviated by halting formal legislation tenuous in the extreme. Even if the Indian legislature were abolished, legislation as such would hardly end. The most revolutionary and active arena of lawmaking in India, Maine argued, were the Courts of Justice, who

since their establishment were chiefly responsible for producing the confused state of Anglo-Indian law. But, legislation by Indian judges "has all
the drawbacks of judicial legislation elsewhere, and a great many more."[79]
While Maine's critique of judicial legislation was certainly less severe than
that of Bentham, who saw it as nothing more than "dog law" that functioned by issuing the law ex post facto, Maine thought that as a process
of lawmaking it was "haphazard, inordinately dilatory, and expensive."[80]
Judicial legislation was, for Maine, one of the central drawbacks of common law jurisprudence. In India, the low level of legal training among
Company judges worsened this situation. While Supreme Court justices,
when confronted with the absence of any clear legal rule, may be diligent
enough to rule by referring to principles of "justice, equity, and good
conscience," judges in the lower courts, lacking access to law libraries for
guidance, tended to refer to half-remembered maxims of English law and
vulgarized, popular notions sifted from legal textbooks, thus casually incorporating "undigested masses of English law."[81] On top of this chaos
in the civil law, "in which fragments of English law joust against shreds
of native custom,"[82] a whole series of procedural technicalities were incorporated that increasingly made the law the province of experts, and thus
further severed from native practice and comprehension. Finally, "in India
judicial legislation is, besides, in the long run, legislation by foreigners,
who are under the thraldom of precedents and analogies belonging to a
foreign law, developed thousands of miles away, under a different climate,
and for a different civilization."[83]

   It was for these reasons that Maine could never see the mere importation of unreformed English law and its court system as a solution for
India's legal needs. But if "the true remedy" could only be sought in "the
development of clearly written Statute law, and the introduction of a code
or substantive body of fundamental rules,"[84] Maine's commitment to
codification was very different from earlier Benthamite arguments for
Indian codification. Maine's call was premised less upon a commitment to
the universal superiority of enlightened codification or indeed of English
common law than upon a recognition that with the disintegration of any
native alternative, legal codes based on rational principles were the better
option than the existing state in which English common law was arbi-
trarily and haphazardly introduced through judicial legislation. It is as
mistaken to see Maine simply as one more undifferentiated figure in a
long list of legal modernizers and codifiers as is it to characterize his
Indian jurisprudence as merely practical in orientation. Not only was
Maine's distinct analysis of the state of Indian law and the sorts of reform
it necessitated informed by his critical views of English common law,
more importantly, it was shaped by his theoretical understanding of the
natural trajectory of customary law, the impact of imperial rule upon it,

and the intimate connection among legal change, legal practice, and social transformation.

Maine's insistence on the necessity of codification, extending even to the contested terrain of civil law, was a commitment that seemed to become firmer throughout his life. Upon his return to England, Maine was at pains to repeat his arguments concerning the importance of codification throughout his membership in the Council of India. In these late interventions, Maine had clearly moved far beyond the somewhat reluctant endorsement of codification embodied in his early essays. Not only was there a general sense that the Indian codes were an enormous achievement, they were seen to be important jurisprudential models for any future codification of English law. While Maine was never again actively involved in debates about the future of English codification, he had (naively) concluded that given the success of codification in Europe and India, contemporary objections to codification in England were anachronistic and transitory.

SOVEREIGNTY AND THE FORCE OF LAW

While the debate on codification exemplifies some of the distinctive implications of Maine's theory of law in practice, it only partially reveals the significant, and far more enduring, relevance of his work as a critic of utilitarianism, especially its underlying conception of sovereignty. Like his views of modern codification, there was a certain ambiguity to Maine's assessment of utilitarianism. Alongside Maine's insistent criticisms of the abstract and ahistorical bent of both utilitarian jurisprudence and political economy, there was also sometimes a measured respect for its scientific ambition and logical rigor. While Maine was convinced that utilitarianism had little to offer, and did much to confuse, historical investigations into the nature of primitive and ancient society, he was more sanguine about the appropriateness of utilitarianism for understanding the dynamics of modern society. At this level, his most important disagreements with utilitarianism could be construed as largely methodological. At the same time, to view Maine's achievement in this regard wholly in methodological terms tends to downplay his substantive theoretical contributions. As I have emphasized in this chapter, Maine's jurisprudence may also been seen as harboring a distinct, alternative account of the relationship between law and society, uncovered through a close analysis of evolution of law in history. Furthermore, despite Maine's insistence on the variability of the meaning and character of law in different ages and times, in his later works, his view of law seems to harbor deeper philosophical and normative underpinnings.[85]

The utilitarian theory of law, in which law was understood as a positive command issued from an identifiable sovereign, where the duty to obey was backed by the threat of sanction or force, for Maine, held little value for understanding the historical and anthropological diversity of law. What was for Austin law's logical and necessary structure, while possibly suitable for the analysis of the structure of legislation in modern society, was especially difficult to apply to the logic of primitive legal forms. In *Ancient Law*, as we have seen, Maine offered a theoretical account of the evolution of law, which expressly demurred from viewing law in an abstract and idealized form and rather sought to outline the various stages of its historical development. In this account Maine emphasized the ways in which, with the evolution of law, the process of law-making, the agents involved in its creation and transformation, and the ideas and institutions that grounded its authority, all went through profound alterations and thereby also altered the meaning and character of law as such. After *Ancient Law*, Maine increasingly turned to anthropological and historical evidence from Indian village-communities, the Germanic *Markgenossenschaft*, and ancient Irish law to substantiate his view of the alternative sources of legal authority and obligation in primitive society and to contest the universality and the political assumptions of the Austinian definition of law and sovereignty.

In contrast to *Ancient Law*, where a whole variety of legal orders are elucidated, later work on village-communities tended to offer a sharpened contrast between an enlarged era of customary law and modern legislation, indeed Maine increasingly refers to these systems of law as ordered by two distinct types of political society.[86] The more ancient order was one in which "the great bulk of men derive their rules of life from customs of their village or city."[87] Village-communities were understood to be independent, self-acting, self-organized social groups, where social and political life was maintained by adherence to sets of customs seen to represent inherited traditions. The council of village elders, or assembly of co-proprietors, was both a quasi-judicial and quasi-legislative body; while obstinate conservators of traditional rules, it also continuously modified customs by tacitly inventing new rules, and in this way tradition was kept in line with new practices. The village council was viewed as more akin to a judicial rather than a legislative organ. In processes of adjudication and lawmaking, the council never claimed to issue universal commands; it merely declared the ancient practices that had always been. Antiquity and precedent, rather than divine or political authority, legitimated usage. There were no concepts strictly analogous to individual right or duty, and sanctions, if they existed at all, appeared in the form of universal disapprobation, without any threat of force.[88] Additionally, penal sanctions were based upon opinion and superstition, even "blind and unconscious"[89] instinct, rather than a concern about coercive force. Duties often emerged and appeared as duties of kinship, legitimated by patriarchal authority, where sanctions were less focused on punishment than on reconciling litigants to the communal order.

Austin purposively denied that customary law of this kind (if it ever existed in this ideal form) would fit under his specific definition of positive law. It would instead be a case of "positive morality," that is, a set of rules spontaneously adopted by the governed and sanctioned or enforced morally.[90] To be considered true law, these customs had to have obligatory force, which for Austin could only stem from sovereign authorization. Austin argued specifically against "admirers of customary laws" (especially German admirers) who sought to ground the authority of custom directly in the opinions and practices of the people, rather than in the superior political authority which, for Austin, was the true source of their obligation and force. Even if customary laws originally emerged from popular practices and opinions, as soon as they are "adopted as such by the courts of justice, and when the judicial decisions fashioned upon are enforced by power of the state"[91] custom is transmuted into positive law.

At one level, Maine's critique of Austin amounted to a quarrel over definition. What Austin defined as "positive morality" Maine sought to christen as a distinctive form of law. As defenders of Austin have argued, Austin was aware that what he defined as law was only applicable under centralized political orders of a relatively modern kind, thus forestalling Maine's claim that Austin was unjustly universalizing a historically specific form of legal order.[92] The issue at stake was not one of definition only, but a more substantive dispute about the ultimate source of legal authority and obligation. For Maine, the sharp distinction in Austin between law and morality, resting upon a strict Hobbesian conception of sovereignty, was "perfectly defensible as a theory, but its practical value and the degree in which it approximates to truth differs greatly in different ages and countries."[93]

It was Hobbes, Maine argued, who was the true founder of the modern theory of sovereignty, its greatest theoretician and most powerful advocate. In this respect, Austin added little in terms of the conceptualization of sovereignty, focusing more on its implications for legal concepts and jurisprudence. Not surprisingly Maine objected to Hobbes's specific characterization of the state of nature as a state of war, since for him "ultra-legality" not anarchy was the norm of early societies. Nevertheless Maine considered Hobbes's *Leviathan* to be a powerful rendering of the historically specific condition of modern state-formation, and unlike his later theoretical successors, more frank in its political commitments. Hobbes was acutely aware of, and indeed positively advocated, the political process associated with the development of modern sovereignty, that is, the constitution of "highly centralized, actively legislating, States"[94] which necessitated the breaking-up of local life beneath them. In other words, what Austin had described as an analytical distinction between law and morality was in fact a historical distinction between two distinct but unequal forms of political societies in which the emergence of one led to the decay of the other.

Thus analytical jurisprudence constructed a philosophy of law well suited to an age of legislation; indeed it worked to legitimate the normative underpinnings of modern sovereignty. One of the conceptual assumptions of the theory of modern sovereignty, and the idea of law as the command of the sovereign, was its overwhelming emphasis on coercive force as the necessary grounds of legal obligation. However, "just as it is possible to forget the existence of friction in nature and the reality of other motives in society except to get rich, so the pupil of Austin may be tempted to forget that there is more in actual Sovereignty than force, and more in laws which are the commands of sovereigns than can be got out of them by merely considering them as regulated force."[95] For Maine, as even Austin's account of customary law as positive morality implied, there may be a number of different reasons why laws were in fact obeyed. By reducing law to coercive force, Austin not only obscured exactly those sources of obligation dominant in small-scale ancient/primitive societies but also underestimated the influence of other motivating reasons in modern legal systems. The true *history* of sovereignty was constituted by "the whole enormous aggregate of opinions, sentiments, beliefs, superstitions, and prejudices, of ideas of all kinds, hereditary and acquired, some produced by institutions, some by the constitution of human nature" that "perpetually shapes, limits, or forbids the actual direction of the forces of society by its Sovereign."[96] A purely abstract definition of sovereignty could tell us nothing, Maine argued, about how morality determined the way sovereigns "shall exercise or forebear from exercising irresistible force."[97] The link between coercive force and obligation was not a logically necessary one, but rather, again a product of a particular historical and political process, one that self-consciously worked to obscure and replace the motivations and habits of mind that comprised the historical force of custom. It was precisely in the attempt to undermine the tenacity of local usage and custom, through the power of legislation emanating from a centralized authority, that the force of law, as perceived by Hobbes and Austin, became most apparent.[98]

The formation of large, centralized states of the Western kind was historically exceptional. Most ancient empires (with the important exception of Rome) and Eastern empires had been, according to Maine, "taxtaking" empires, in which the "every day religious or civil life of the groups to which their subjects belonged" were left untouched. Traditional empires were perfectly compatible with the flourishing of the "separate local life of the small communities," with only limited intrusion from the distant tax-taking ruler.[99] By contrast, a legislating empire, such as the Roman Empire, increasingly legislated according to its own principles and interests that inevitably hastened the decay of customary rules. In this sense, "legislation, as we conceive it, and the break up of local life appear to have universally gone together,"[100] and it is this model that was becoming universal with the expansion and development of the modern state-system.

State-formation, through the linked processes of centralization and legislation, was the culmination of the "trituration in modern societies of the groups which once lived with an independent life."[101] But whereas Hobbes had hailed this development, comparing privileged corporations and organized local groups to parasites on the body politic, for Maine, "these groups must rather be compared to the primary cells out of which the whole human body has been built up."[102] Here, we glimpse in Maine a stronger, normative commitment to a corporatist critique of sovereignty, one that would become stronger in late conservative writings on popular government. The coming of democracy, argued Maine, tied the project of reforming legislation to the purpose of government, unleashing a new kind of never-ending revolution in customs and manners. This was a more dangerous prospect than the tumult of revolution, for in privileging innovation institutional stability was necessarily undermined and a popular, absolutist state was seen as its inevitable culmination.[103]

Maine's critique of sovereignty linked his work more squarely with the central trajectory of historical jurisprudence, but it was also a commitment that was mitigated by his tempered respect for utilitarian jurisprudence and its spirit of reform. Maine's conservatism was thus a peculiar kind, driven less by a religious, sentimental, or nostalgic appeal to the values of the old regime than by the worry that the expansion of the franchise would threaten the security of property and individual rights, or in other words, the historical achievements of the liberal age. Democracy was an inherently unstable and fragile form of government that naturally tended in its dissolution toward despotism. The machinations of party politics and the manipulation of public opinion by "wire-pullers" were intimations of a despotism in which the naturally irrational and conservative tendencies of the populace would be enervated and unleashed. Maine was never a nostalgic or antiquarian defender of small-scale, self-organizing societies, yet he was concerned about the disappearance of privileged groups—such as aristocracies of knowledge and experience—with the advent of popular government, a development that, for Maine, led to mediocrity in virtue and science, on the one hand, and removed necessary protections against unlimited state power and unmediated sovereignty, on the other. Thus, the conjunction of a fragile, ancient form of government (democracy) with the machinery of the modern centralized state, was "apt to lead to cruel disappointment or serious disaster."[104]

CHAPTER FOUR

THE NINETEENTH-CENTURY DEBATE
ON PROPERTY

> The question is opened whether the older or the later ideas
> are best suited to rule the future; and if the change from the
> one to the other was brought about by circumstances which
> the world has since outgrown—still more if it appears to
> have been in great part the result of usurpation—it may well
> be that the principle, at least, of the older institutions is fitter
> to be chosen than that of the more modern, as the basis of a
> better and more advanced constitution of society.
> —*John Stuart Mill*[1]

IN THE NINETEENTH CENTURY the question of property came to the fore
in a new way. The language of this debate was decidedly historical and
comparative, overturning accepted understandings of the nature and origins of private property rights. Previously dominant philosophical and
juridical accounts of property had sought to establish its theoretical basis
in individual modes of appropriation and occupation. By contrast, Maine
posited an alternative conceptualization and historical sequence in which
property was originally held in common (by a group of families or an
extended household) and gradually over time becoming divided, breaking
apart into forms of individual ownership. The revised evolutionary history of property, with its "discovery" of communal property, challenged
the notion of property rights as necessarily individual and absolute. In
this, Maine's accomplishment was pivotal; Maine's thesis about the communal origins of rights in property (and of modern conceptions of rights
in general) effectively called into question the historical and logical priority of the unitary conception of individual proprietorship, especially as
formulated in Roman law and natural rights theories.

In highlighting the difficult and precarious process by which private
property and individual right came to be established, Maine sought to
justify private property as a progressive historical achievement. No one
was "at liberty to attack several property and to say at the same time that
he values civilization. The history of the two cannot be disentangled."[2]
Yet, Maine's establishment of the historical fact of original communism,

regardless of its supposed place in history of civilization, suggested the relativization of the modern notion of private property and gave alternative communal modes a legitimate historicity. In this way, Maine's evolutionary progressivism, tempered by historicism, engendered skepticism about the legitimacy of modern legal and political institutions, especially the institution of private property rights in land. In doing so, Maine's thesis on communal property became implicated in a variety of normative and historicist arguments that together contested the unmitigated expansion of private property and the free market in land. The former strand, exemplified in socialists and agrarian radicals, straightforwardly proclaimed the independent, normative priority of communal property over individual proprietorship. The latter attempted to correlate forms of property with historical stages and thus construed private property as inappropriate for traditional or premodern societies. In practical terms, Maine's evolutionary historicism made it possible to question the viability and applicability of modern institutions (legal, political, and economic) in societies considered to have not reached the apposite state of social progress.

Maine's thesis on communal property was to have an exceptional salience in British India, as a marked intervention in the vexed debate on Indian land tenure as well as a systematic attempt to privilege the village-community as the characteristic form of traditional society in India. Land revenue was the foundation of imperial rule in India; it was the core of the administrative and financial structure of the Government of India, as well as the most vital instrument through which native social and economic life would be directly affected and transformed. Moreover, in the charged political atmosphere following the 1857 Rebellion, to which agrarian discontent was seen to have lent a critical force, established liberal-utilitarian norms regarding land tenure and economic policy would be subject to renewed debate and revision. In this context, Maine's idea of a village-community founded upon communal modes of land use and appropriation worked in tandem with his methodological strictures against utilitarianism to undermine the applicability of its doctrines to India. But Maine's argument with utilitarianism went further, suggesting that the gravest errors of British rule stemmed from its misapprehension of the customary and communal basis of Indian society.

This chapter explores the origins and implications of Maine's revisionary account of the evolutionary history of property. By, firstly, locating its conceptual roots in the critique of natural law theory (in its Roman and modern incarnations), I reconstruct the theoretical and empirical coordinates of the wider scholarly debate on the historical origins of property. This scholarly debate was both drawn into and stimulated political arguments about land reform and the future of private property on a global scale. Maine's ambitious reconstruction of the origins of private property was premised upon an expansive comparative framework that sought to incorporate an enormous variety of anthropological and historical materials, in which the Indian village-community especially comes to occupy a central theoretical role. Finally, the chapter assesses Maine's influence and involvement in the Indian policy debate, and its culmination in a historicist critique of classical political economy.

Like the domain of law, the question of land tenure—of the rights and customs that organized patterns of land ownership, use, and distribution—was central to debates concerning the essential character of "Indian society." Maine's thesis on communal property was pivotal in cementing a view of native society in which its identity and integrity was closely tied to the shared possession and exploitation of land. While native community and authority in the legal arena was symbolized most evocatively by the concept of native customary law, with land tenure the self-organizing capacity of traditional society would be defined through the customs and practices of the village-community. In Maine's revisionary account of the evolution of property, the structure of the village-community demonstrated the ideological hold of kinship in ancient/primitive society, where kinship in the form of the joint-family, caste, tribe, and/or clan was seen as coextensive with rights in collective property. In addition to being an exemplary instance of the category of traditional society, the village-community *in its dissolution* also provided Maine precise evidence of the transition from status to contract, that is, of the historical processes by which kinship-based communal property breaks apart into modes of private property. The breakdown of the Indian village-community, while in one sense historically inevitable, was also a process that was understood to have been dangerously accelerated with the coming of imperial rule. Maine was anxious that the radical undoing of the customary basis of the village-community under imperial rule augured the ungovernable atomization of Indian society. Maine's warning about the potential trauma that contact with modern society portended for traditional societies led many imperial administrators to seek a solution in an alternative strategy of imperial rule—namely, indirect rule.

COMPARATIVE JURISPRUDENCE AND
THE CRITIQUE OF NATURAL LAW

Alongside the critique of utilitarian jurisprudence, *Ancient Law* contained Maine's insistent antipathy, both political and theoretical, toward "the modern school of natural law" and social contract theory. Maine contended that natural law's doctrine of the fundamental equality of humans was inherently political, and had sustained the most dangerous excesses of the French Revolution (especially through the influence of Rousseau). In *Ancient Law*, a proper understanding of the long history of Roman law was argued to temper and correct these unwarranted abstract claims by demonstrating, from the historical record, the actual nature of primitive or ancient society. Historical and comparative inquiry, according to Maine, would thus shed light on and clarify a stage of society whose study had been overly dominated by philosophical speculations about the so-called state of nature. The irony, for Maine, was that Roman law was itself the historical source for the idea of a law of nature. Thus, in a more direct sense, understanding its modern variants must begin with an assessment of its origins and permutations in the historical development of Roman law.

But the untangling of the intimate connections between ancient and modern theories of natural law ultimately led Maine, paradoxically, to the recognition of the limitations inherent in the historical study of Roman law as a guide to an understanding of primitive law. After *Ancient Law*, the study of Roman legal antiquities never again was as central to Maine's scholarly concerns. In later works, such as *Village-Communities in the East and West*, *The Early History of Institutions*, and *Lectures on Early Law and Custom*, Maine's enterprise was decidedly more comparative in scope, while his substantive concerns moved more directly to the reconstruction of the history of property. In exploring the nature of this shift I suggest that Maine's move to comparative jurisprudence was not only a response to the ever-increasing array of historical and anthropological research in legal antiquities but was also summoned by Maine's awareness of the intrinsic limits of the historical study of Roman law.

Maine's revised account of the early history of Roman law, in *Ancient Law*, aimed to counter rationalist, deductive political theories, which reasoned from an account of "natural" man in an originary "state of nature" (here Maine's chief target was Rousseau). Philosophical speculations about the so-called state of nature tended to project characteristics of the modern individual backward in time:

> these sketches of the plight of human beings in the first ages of the world are effected by first supposing mankind to be divested of a great part of the circumstances by which they are now surrounded, and by then assuming that, in the condition thus imagined, they would preserve the same sentiments and prejudices by which they are now actuated,—although, in fact, these sentiments may have been created and engendered by those very circumstances of which, by the hypothesis, they are to be stripped.[3]

In doing so, these theories became tautological; they took for granted exactly what was in need of explanation, namely the logic and sequence of the historical evolution of ideas, institutions, and practices that led to the very possibility of *individual* contract.

One key strategy for contesting the account of the state of nature in natural law, as we have seen in chapter two, was Maine's delineation of the corporate nature of the ancient patriarchal family, as the fundamental social unit of ancient/primitive society. The evidence from archaic law was proffered to undermine the assumed state of anarchy inherent in primitive society. The Hobbesian idea of a primitive state of war "may be true of the contests of tribe with tribe and of family with family; but it is not true of the relations of individual man with individual man, whom we, on the contrary, first discern living under a regimen . . . of ultra-legality."[4] In Maine's view, this disorder, even it were to have existed, did not function as a motivating factor in the evolution of primitive society. Rather, in the trajectory from ancient to modern society, the despotism of archaic law gradually lost hold over its dependents and family dependency gave way to greater forms of individualism. Roman law of the archaic period, especially as it was expressed in, and developed out of, the Twelve Tables, was the starting point for a more general theoretical reconstruction of the primitive age, augmented importantly by comparative research. Indeed, for Maine, what encouraged unfettered theoretical speculation on primitive society was the relative paucity of knowledge of comparative legal antiquities in the eighteenth century. Lacking a true historical and comparative method, eighteenth-century thought was unhinged from any basis in historical reality. Rather, for its philosophic foundations, eighteenth-century thought turned wholeheartedly to the later Roman jurisprudence of the classical and imperial periods, from which the modern theory of natural law had its conceptual origins.

According to Maine, the conflation of the law of nature, the *ius naturale*, and the law of nations, the *ius gentium*, was the influential achievement of the later and most productive period of Roman jurisprudence— the "golden age" of Stoic jurisprudence under the Antonine Caesars. In the historical development of law, the transformation of the *ius gentium* into the law of nature demonstrated the importance of a crucial form of legal change, equity. Equity was a system of rules or principles that could legitimately supersede the strictures of civil law; its authority, importantly, was based neither on legislative or sovereign authority nor tradition or precedent, but rather referred to the special character of its principles. Well-formed principles of equity are thus the cornerstone of all forms of legal progress; they can function to temper reforming zeal as well as to release the law from an oppressive reliance on ritual and formality.[5] Roman equity in the form of natural law was central to the ability of Roman law to evolve out of the strictures of primitive law and reach the heights of a mature and accomplished jurisprudence.

Ius gentium in early Roman law emerged as a practical response to the question of how to adjudicate disputes between Roman citizens and foreigners, since the latter were excluded from the jurisdiction of the civil law. In this sense, *ius gentium* was initially "a collection of rules and principles, determined by observation to be common to the institutions which prevailed among the various Italian tribes."[6] It was a set of rules appealed to not because they were assumed to be endowed with a higher or inherent authority but as the pragmatic means by which to solve a jurisdictional dilemma. The transformation of *ius gentium* into the more capacious *ius naturale* was in large part actuated, on the one hand, institutionally through the development of the authority of the office of the Praetor bequeathed with the duty of settling jurisdictional disputes and, on the other, philosophically by the importation of the Greek, Stoic idea of nature into Roman law. In the confluence, the Praetor's office and its edicts became the agency in which the law of nature assumed its greatest productivity as a system of equity, as a way of intervening in and overriding the rigid prescriptions of the archaic codes.

The Stoic theory of natural law was the means by which the law of nations was imputed with a new philosophical resonance and a felicitous historical conjuncture that allowed Roman law to liberate itself from the rigidly of primitive law, reaching an excellence unknown in other archaic legal systems.[7] The influence of Stoic philosophy on Roman jurisconsults in its most productive period was also the cornerstone of the success of Roman jurisprudence in the improvement of legal terminology and philosophy. For Maine, the Stoic command "to live according to nature" stimulated juridical reform and the rationalization of the law. Nature's guiding principles—simplicity, symmetry, and harmony—would underpin a jurisprudence that now sought to increasingly systematize and generalize.

In the *modern* history of natural law, however, the admiration of natural law shifted from its beneficial effects in generating principles out of diverse legal sources and axioms to the principles themselves. Generalization and systematization, as well as harmony and simplicity, were valued for their own sake. This unmooring of the law of nature from actual legal practices was the important step in the eventual adoption of natural law as the abstract and undirected norm that could independently generate rational, systematized legal codes.[8] In the philosophical realm, this shift was mirrored, as Maine put it, in the shift in focus from inquiry into the laws of nature to a contemplation of the state of nature itself. And this shift, for Maine, was at the core of natural law theory's many political errors.

The tendency for abstraction in late Roman jurisprudence also had important methodological consequences for Maine's central theoretical project: the reconstruction of ancient or primitive society. For it was precisely in the attempt to generalize and systematize law, indeed to tease out and differentiate legal principles that were truncated and folded in their original form, that later Roman jurisprudence had a tendency to obscure the true face of these primitive forms. This inadequacy was most keenly felt in the law of property. And thus it is in relation to the question of the early history of property that the historical study of Roman law reaches its limit as the primary method for the reconstruction of the earliest forms of ancient society.

For Maine, the origins of property, and specifically the institution of private property, was one of the most difficult and obscure historical questions. In *Ancient Law*, Maine argued that it was also an obscurity that natural law theories had only helped to perpetuate. Indeed, "the popular account of it, that is had its origin in a state of nature, is merely a way of giving expression to our own ignorance."[9] In this case, both Roman and modern natural law accounts suffered from the same drawbacks. In both, the present institutional conditions and conceptual relations in existing property law were read back, as it were, to account for its historical origins. Taking Blackstone's theory of occupancy as a popular natural law argument concerning the origins of property, Maine questioned the adequacy of generalized arguments premised upon individual motivation and actions. For Blackstone, property arose when, out of an original commons, the first user of a thing or of land gained a kind of possession over it, from which it was unjust to remove him by force. Over time this transient and precarious possession was granted a conventional right of appropriation. As we have seen, Maine questioned appeals to individual "instinct" or motive not only because of their reliance on the individual as the unit of analysis (which he viewed as substantively inappropriate for the study of ancient society), but also because of a basic sociological premise, namely that individual action and habitual behavior are forged vis-à-vis institutional change. For Maine, the important question was less why people began to appropriate things individually, but rather why appropriation or occupancy created a sentiment of respect by society. This shifted the question from individual to sociological action, that is, what must have been the institutional conditions by which occupancy came to be seen as a legitimate origin of a right to exclusive property.

Maine unveiled a similar logic at work in relation to the question of property in Roman law, as expressed in Savigny's famous treatise on possession in the civil law.[10] Savigny argued that Roman law protected rights of possession in the form of possessory interdicts that were independent of and prior to property rights. The reason for this unique feature was the general acceptance of the implicit rule that all possession was in the process of developing into property, and the underlying claim that all property began with possession. The thesis on possession was not dissimilar to the idea of occupancy; both rendered the origin of property in the ability of the first possessor to protect his possession. The question remained as to why this possession is recognized and given legal sanction.

In *Ancient Law*, Maine does not provide the answer. Rather, in pointing to the conundrum, Maine exposed what he took to be the central weakness of both theories of property. In his view, both theories reversed the logic of historical development:

> It is only when the rights of property have gained a sanction from long practical inviolability, and when the vast majority of the objects of enjoyment have been subjected to private ownership, that mere possession is allowed to invest the first possessor with dominion over commodities in which no prior proprietorship has been asserted. . . . Its true basis seems to be, not an instinctive bias towards the institution of Property, but a presumption, arising out of the long continuance of that institution, that *everything ought to have an owner.*[11]

In a typical manner, Maine transformed a speculative/logical account of origins into a historical explanation that emphasized slow institutional developments.

In the matter of the historical origins of property, Roman law seemed to shed as little light as modern natural law theories. The significance of Maine's recognition of this limitation was that it made the move to the comparative study of institutions a *methodological* imperative. As Maine notes, the Roman distinction between the law of persons and property was a convenient and important product of later Roman jurisprudence, but it was an artificial one that tended to "divert inquiry on the subject before us from the true direction."[12] Evidence from archaic family law demonstrated the inextricable conflation of the law of persons and property in early law. From this Maine deduced the a priori possibility that the law of property, like that of persons, originally took a communal rather than an individual form. In place of individual proprietorship, Maine argued, one would expect to find forms of communal and joint-ownership in the early history of property. And in demonstrating this fact, "the Roman jurisprudence will not here assist in enlightening us, for it is exactly the Roman jurisprudence which, in the transformed theory of Natural Law, has bequeathed to the moderns the impression that individual ownership is the normal state of proprietary right, and that ownership in common by groups of men is only the exception to the general rule."[13] To authenticate his view of primitive society and law, and the expression of property appropriate to it, Maine immediately moved to an account of the Indian village-community, which seemed to exhibit the exact pattern of ownership proposed:

But though the evidence does not warrant our going so far as this, it renders less presumptuous the conjecture that private property, in the shape in which we know it, was chiefly formed by the gradual disentanglement of the separate rights of individuals from the blended rights of a community. Our studies in the Law of Persons seemed to show us the Family expanding into the Agnatic group of kinsmen, then the Agnatic group dissolving into separate households; lastly, the household supplanted by the individual; and it is now suggested that each step in the change corresponds to an analogous alteration in the nature of Ownership.[14]

In this manner, Maine's account of ancient law generated an important hypothesis about the ways in which private property and individual right historically emerged. Maine's later works, especially *Village-Communities in the East and West* and *Lectures on the Early History of Institutions*, sought to establish in detail the truth of this proposition. Less than fifteen years after *Ancient Law*, Maine announced the clarification of "the beginnings of the great institution of Property in Land"[15] to be the most important achievement of comparative jurisprudence. As the sources of knowledge about primitive societies multiplied, the idea of private property emerging out of initial forms of communal or co-proprietorship had come to be recognized as a universal phenomenon. This historical thesis about the priority of an original or primitive communism in property had a profound effect on the unique ways in which property as a political problem would be debated in the latter half of the nineteenth century.

COMMUNAL PROPERTY AND THE NINETEENTH-CENTURY DEBATE ON PROPERTY

Maine's reconstruction of the history of property, although formulated as a critique of natural law, had surprisingly few direct connections to the substantive arguments about property put forward in the seventeenth- and eighteen-century tradition of natural jurisprudence. What is perhaps most surprising in this is that it was precisely in relation to the question of property that natural lawyers came the closest to formulating evolutionary schemas of legal development.[16] Both Grotius and Pufendorf had postulated something akin to the idea of an original communism with the thesis concerning the priority of a negative community in property in the precivil state. For both, private property was a process of individuation from the commons and developed out of this primitive form through acts of appropriation (via modes of occupation). While Grotius and Pufendorf disagreed on the natural or conventional origin of private property, they both conceived of it as a right that was by definition individual and exclusive. By contrast, the thesis of communal property in the nineteenth century came to dispute this conception of the right to property as an individual, exclusive, and absolute *iure in re*.

Maine's work played a defining role in this challenge, effectively calling into question the logical priority of the unitary conception of individual proprietorship as an *iure in re*, especially as formulated in Roman law. Maine's account not only resulted in a relativization of the modern notion of private property, it also gave alternative communal modes a legitimate historicity. And while Maine's thesis on communal property was put forward mainly in historical terms, and the criticism of Roman law was made primarily in methodological terms, together they were implicated in a set of theoretical and political debates that sought to undermine the normative priority and juridical dominance of property in land as individual, absolute, and exclusive. Thus, the scholarly debate concerning the historical origins of property necessarily intersected concurrent political debates on the nature of land reform and the future of private property.

The debate on property was conducted upon and shaped by the coming together of three different streams of historical and anthropological research: (1) on ancient Rome, (2) on the medieval agricultural community (Germanic), and (3) on contemporary forms of communal landholding (especially in the non-European world and also Russia and Ireland). It was perhaps Maine's singular accomplishment to have incorporated these disparate streams, via a comparative and evolutionary framework, into a more general theory of property.[17] While Maine's work concerned all three formative research domains, it was implicated in each, theoretically and politically, in different ways and around different sets of issues.

Roman law and history was the arena in which the debate on the absolute historical origins of private property was primarily waged. Maine's audacious claim that ancient law knew nothing of individual right implied that it also could not have contained the concept of private property. This claim, especially as it was propagated in the more politically charged work of the Belgian economist Émile de Laveleye was contested most notably (and vehemently) by Fustel de Coulanges.[18] In *The Ancient City*, Fustel had linked the laws of property and inheritance to the primeval cult of ancestors common to the Aryan family. Ancestor worship depended on the protection and delineation of separate lands for the burial of ancestors. These burial grounds were viewed as the first instantiations of bounded territory, the historical kernel of property rights. By contrast, Theodor Mommsen had offered an account of collective landownership by the *gens* in early Rome.[19] Maine relied on Niebuhr's reconstruction of early Roman history to make the case for the imbrication of the law of persons and property in archaic law, and by implication for the original communal proprietorship of the ancient family. Niebuhr's account of the

origins of Roman property law had an independent and more direct impact on property debates, one that was often used as evidence for an
ancient form of communal property linked to state ownership. In this
latter form, Neibuhr's argument was especially central to Marx's account
of communal forms of ownership, thus also confirming the place of ancient Roman history as a particularly important nodal point for the development of nineteenth-century theories of property.

While the debate about the absolute origins of private property, waged
on the terrain of the early history of Roman law, continued throughout
the nineteenth century, it was at times joined to and eclipsed by another
line of inquiry more directly focused on the historical trajectory and future of private property. Here historical research on agricultural village-
communities and their relation to the origins of feudalism was central,
especially the investigations of medieval social and political life around
the German *Markenverfassung*, or village-community. This line of inquiry
had its roots in the work of the Grimm brothers, but it was Konrad von
Maurer's work on the *Mark* that had the widest circulation and impact.
Maurer's work was an enormous fillip to the scholarly study of medieval
antiquities and encouraged the study of remnants of the Germanic agricultural community in other countries (such as in England).[20] Notably, this
form of historical research led one Germanist, August von Haxthausen
to the first scholarly studies of the Slavonic house communities and the
Russian *mir.*

In the debate on medieval village-communities, the historical priority
of communal property was a given; yet the political and normative implications of this fact were manifold and often contradictory. Depending on
one's political program, the village-community in its archaic form exemplified liberal "Teutonic" freedoms and free associationism, libertarian
self-governance, socialist and communist solidarity and cooperation, and/
or hierarchal patriarchy and feudal oppression.[21] For Maine this was the
central social form from which to demonstrate most directly the disentanglement of individual right out of its original communal nexus; understanding its historical development was therefore crucial for understanding the origins of modern property in land. Moreover, this evolutionary
movement from communal to private property was the substantive crux
of the progressive transition from status to contract; the fact of original
communism merely showed how far mankind had advanced on the path
of civilization from its primitive roots. But even as Maine considered the
emergence of private property to be a sign of progress, his historicism
provoked questions about the legitimacy of the central moments in this
process of transformation from the dissolution of communal property
into individuated private tenure. As Mill noted in a review of Maine's
Village-Communities,

the question is opened whether the older or the later ideas are best suited to rule the future; and if the change from the one to the other was brought about by circumstances which the world has since outgrown—still more if it appears to have been in great part the result of usurpation—it may well be that the principle, at least, of the older institutions is fitter to be chosen than that of the more modern, as the basis of a better and more advanced constitution of society.[22]

In raising the specter that the history of private property in land might be construed as a continuing tale of usurpation and oppression, Mill's interest in the question highlights the way in which in the discussion of village-communities the locus of debate shifted from the question of the absolute origins of private property to the legitimacy of these key moments of transition.

Finally, anthropological and ethnological research on extant forms of communal property figured in the debate on property as evidence for the thesis of original communal property, and the locus of a specific imperial debate about the importation of Western theories and institutions of property. The exponential growth of these studies legitimated the use of comparative methodologies to incorporate and subsume these findings into more universal frameworks, and thereby gave sustenance to more daring generalizations and political claims. The increased exposure to anthropological evidence of alternative modes of property bore an important relation to the consolidation of overseas empires and systematization of channels of information (in the form of colonial bureaucrats' reports). The administrative imperatives of expanding empires, in terms of rationalizing modes of rule, confronted alternative economic and landholding systems most dramatically. A similar process took shape in Europe, as various attempts to codify land law brought forth large-scale investigations into the existing systems of land rights. Not only in India and Ireland, but in England and Italy as well, these parliamentary investigations brought to light the immense diversity of legal practices that new standardized property laws were meant to supersede. These latter sources, for example, governmental reports such as the 1844 parliamentary report on enclosures, were especially important as they exposed the practical grounds on which notions of exclusive and individual property competed with and confronted alternative proprietary modes.[23]

The most ambitious political claim made through an expansive use of these kinds of anthropological findings was made in Laveleye's *De la propriété et de ses formes primitives*.[24] Laveleye, an avowed follower of Maine's, attempted to demonstrate the universal existence of communal property by incorporating Mommsen's work on Rome; von Maurer's and Maine's work on Germanic customs; Maine's work on India; as well as a host of other sources on communal landholding in England, Italy, Scandinavia, the Netherlands, Switzerland, Russia, the United States, Algeria, Java, Papua New Guinea, and China. Laveleye, in demonstrating the almost universal existence of communal property across time and space, proved that private appropriation of the bourgeois kind was in fact the true historical aberration. The evidence from past and present primitive societies proved not only the historical priority of communal property but also imputed it with an independent normative significance. However, in imperial political debates, especially around practical questions of land reform and policy, there emerged another distinctive argument about the need to correlate the form of property with the historical stage of the society in question. The integrity and identity of native societies were understood to be especially tied to the collective control of land, such that any interference in this delicate equilibrium would undo native authority and community, leading to social upheaval and anomie. A comparative and evolutionary account of property, like Maine's, could be harnessed to contest the appropriateness of expanding or instituting private property and a free market in land in countries considered to have not reached the appropriate stage of social evolution. This latter argument cut across political lines and was especially prominent in late nineteenth-century debates about land reform in India, Ireland, and Russia. In these debates, the normative argument, rather than eclipsed, would be melded to a deep historicism.

MAINE ON THE ORIGINS OF PRIVATE PROPERTY

In *Village-Communities in the East and West*, Maine began the proof of the hypothesis put forward in *Ancient Law* concerning the development of individual private property out of earlier communal forms. He tied this project to an argument in favor of the comparative method, defining the comparative method for jurisprudence in the following terms:

> We take a number of contemporary facts, ideas, and customs, and we infer the past form of those facts, ideas, and customs not only from historical records of that past form, but from examples of it which have not yet died out of the world, and are still to be found in it.[25]

In this way, "direct observation comes thus to the aid of historical enquiry, and historical enquiry to the help of direct observation."[26]

For comparative jurisprudence, two kinds of knowledge were particularly obligatory: knowledge of India and knowledge of Roman law. The former was essential as "it is the great repository of verifiable phenomena of ancient usage and ancient juridical thought" and the latter "because, viewed in the whole course of its development, it connects these ancient usages and this ancient juridical thought with the legal ideas of our own day."[27] In Maine's work, the ancient laws and usages of India and archaic Rome were rendered nearly identical, specifically as they were seen to have emerged from common roots in the legal form of the patriarchal family. This similarity in archaic form was neither an arbitrary historical fact nor exactly a universal feature of human society. Rather, the institutions of Rome and India could be brought into such an epistemological relation because of a prior ontological fact, namely the unity of the Aryan family of nations, discovered and substantiated in terms of an Indo-European linguistic family. It is important to note that despite this terminology, for Maine, this was not a theory of racial unity. Language and race here, unlike other important accounts of the Indo-European phenomenon, were not equated. Rather the history of language filiation was given an institutional cast.

In terms of a practical agenda, this common institutional genealogy highlighted the centrality of contemporary research in Indian legal forms, for they supplemented, confirmed, and brought to light key elements of early legal history. In *Village-Communities*, Maine pursued this agenda by popularizing historical inquiries into the medieval, Germanic agricultural community (especially the work of von Maurer) and supplementing these findings with extant examples from Indian village-communities (as evinced in Anglo-Indian administrative records). According to Maine, studies of the remnants and traces of the Teutonic village-community in Germany, Scandinavia, and parts of England had demonstrated its influential legacy for understanding aspects of contemporary land law, agricultural customs, and the territorial distribution of landed property. But while the Teutonic agricultural community had a historically direct link with modern law, and had existed in a similar form in many parts of Europe, it was not a living institution. By contrast, in India ancient communal social forms could be directly observed. Moreover, the course of Indian legal development served as an ideal type of the autochthonous, if also arrested, evolution of Aryan ideas and institutions, isolated from outside influence until the coming of British rule.[28] According to Maine,

> two causes have done most to obscure the oldest institutions of the portion of the human race to which we belong: one has been the formation throughout the West of strong centralized governments, concentrating in themselves the public force of the community, and enabled to give to that force upon occasion the special form of legislative power; the other has been the influence, direct and indirect, of the Roman Empire, drawing with an activity of legislation unknown to the parts of the world which were never subjected to it.[29]

While advanced research on the historical German or Teutonic mark-community also uncovered key moments in the legal history of property, it was often inextricably mixed with elements of Roman and feudal law. In reconstructing the features of this European social form with the help of ethnographic accounts from India, one could "correct and amplify the received theories of the origin and significance of English real-property law"[30] and produce a single narrative of the development of distinctively modern proprietary rights. In the "startling coincidence" between Eastern and Western social forms and the joining of the Indian material to those from Europe, "it would seem that light is pouring from many quarters at once on some of the darkest passages in the history of law and society."[31]

The ability of Indian legal practice and custom to augment, correct, and verify the logic of legal development was nowhere more apparent than in the history of property in land. Two Indian institutions in particular demonstrated key historical moments in the establishment of and eventual disintegration of communal property into forms of private ownership, the Hindu joint family and the Indian village-community. Indeed, the transmutation from the one to the other involved that great revolution that Maine named the transition from kinship to locality as the source of social and political obligation. The Hindu undivided or joint family was then the clearest representative of the kinship pattern of social organization.[32] It was an example of the ancient patriarchal family that Maine had established as the original social form out of which ancient law had sprung. Unlike the Roman counterpart, which could only be retrospectively constructed from remnants of archaic Roman law,[33] the joint family was alive and well as a central institution of Hindu law. Like the patriarchal family of Roman law, the Hindu joint family was not a family in the simple sense, but a body of agnatic kinsmen who shared in worship, food, and the collective enjoyment of property. This family had a corporate existence that, in legal terms, perpetuated itself indefinitely. The mode of inheritance involved the appointment of a new head of the household, usually the next in line in terms of agnatic succession. In the strict sense, the head of the modern joint family was not quite the equivalent of the paterfamilias who wields ownership and power over all who are subject to his authority. Rather he was, in practice, the (sometimes elected) manager of the joint estate. Although divisible in principle with each member having a right to a share, in practice, property was always on its way to returning to the communal pot.[34]

While the Hindu joint family may in practice earn its living through cultivation and ownership of land, in Maine, the connection to land was considered to be only accidental and not a necessary relation. As a general pattern of social organization the joint family could also thrive and shape hereditary trades and occupations that had no specific roots in landed property. The real move to landed property began when larger groups of self-styled kinsmen (the tribe or *gens*) settled and worked the land collectively. This was the establishment of the village-community and marked the beginning of the transition from kinship to locality as the source of communal affiliation and obligation. In its original phases, the village-community embodied the pure doubling of kinship and locality; the "Village Community of India is at once an organised patriarchal society and an assemblage of co-proprietors. Personal relationships are confounded with proprietary rights."[35] But over time, "Land begins to be the basis of society . . . at the expense of Kinship, ever more vaguely conceived."[36] And in place of the model of the natural family, communities were held together by mutual rights and obligations in relation to land.

For Maine, the real importance of studying village-communities, in terms of understanding the origins of private property, stemmed less from their initial formation than from their gradual dissolution. In this process lay the first historical differentiation of persons and property and the eventual emergence of individual right and private property in land. In its most basic and generic form, the village-community comprised groups of kinsmen or co-proprietors who exercised common ownership over the village as a whole. They cultivated the lands and shared in its fruits collectively. Eventually, the village land was further divided into village (household), arable, and common or waste lands, over which different forms of use rights and ownership developed. This initial division of arable lands from the common was a crucial moment in the development of separate and private ownership.[37] This was also the order of historical priority by which land rights in these different domains became individuated—first in the separation of village land into individual households, then in the apportionment of individual lots for cultivation in the arable lands, and finally ending in the enclosure of the commons.

In the Teutonic form, "the community inhabited the village, held the common in mixed ownership, and cultivated the arable mark in lots appropriated to the several families."[38] In its more communal forms, for example in the Russian *mir*, this basic division remained intact with the further element that cultivated lands were subject to regular redivision and redistribution. This fact, for Maine, demonstrated that the original division of cultivating lands was based upon a strict egalitarian basis. The current Russian practice of redistribution was a living remnant of this and retained the original sense of an individuation that was always subsumed by communal power. For Maine, "in comparing the two extant types of the Village Community which have been longest examined, the Russian and the Indian, we may be led to think that the traces left on usage and ideas by the ancient collective enjoyment are faint exactly in proportion to the decay of the theory of actual kinship among the co-villagers."[39] In the Indian village-community, there was rarely redivision and redistribution, but the communal element survived in terms of cultivating techniques, inheritance, and alienation, which all were subject to and limited by communal agreement and adjudication. In more advanced forms, the apportionment of the cultivating lands became permanent and was held by families over time and intergenerationally, it came to function more and more like heritable private property. Thus, when this individuation extended not only to arable but also to pasture and waste lands, it represented the final emergence of private property in land.

In this account, Maine stressed the "natural" growth of private property out of collective ownership in the gradual dissolution of ancient cultivating communities. And everywhere village-communities existed as the foundational, ancient social form, such as Western Europe, this process left recognizable marks in current land law and agricultural customs. But for a full account of the specific nature of absolute property in land, exclusive and alienable, two other historical and legal developments had to be understood. In Maine's later works, the original thesis concerning the development of private property out of the dissolution of communal property and communal rights of the family was augmented with an account of the ever-increasing authority of the tribal chief.[40]

> Property in Land, as known to the communities of the Aryan race, has had a twofold origin. It has arisen partly from the disentanglement of the individual rights of the kindred or tribesmen from the collective rights of the Family or Tribe, and partly from the growth and transmutation of the sovereignty of the Tribal Chief.[41]

While the natural process of individuation of collective tenures proceeded along with "the decaying authority of the Tribe over the severalties of the tribesmen," the second form of property emerged from an opposite and independent tendency. The form of property that in its origins can be traced to chiefly power was of a more absolute kind (more akin to, and the source of, the dominant form of landed property in England). As the power of tribal chiefdom grew, through military prowess and/or the absorption of dependent strangers into the community, this power was manifest in the acquisition of material wealth in movables and the encroachment and appropriation of the common waste. Political power was manifested in the exclusive right to land that was once subject to common authority and control.

Most importantly, this account of the tendency for a tribal chiefdom to aggrandize power in the form of land allowed Maine to propose a theory of feudalization as an autochthonous development of the ancient village-community, which Maine demonstrated with evidence from those isolated fringes of the Aryan world, India and Ireland. The growth of tribal chiefdoms exemplified the expansion of forms of hierarchy and inequality unknown in original tribal communities. Inequalities of power were manifested in and through unequal rights and duties to land, which was the hallmark of feudal social organization.[42] Moreover, in the strict imbrication of power and land in the authority of the tribal chief, Maine traced the origins of modern territorial sovereignty.

The second historical and legal transformation that Maine highlighted as contributing to the development of absolute property was tied less to exclusivity than to the alienability of land. In classifications of property in ancient law, property was divided into two distinct categories, one that was subject to great regulation, circumscription, and even outright banning, and another class of things that were more easily transferable. In Roman law this was the important distinction between *res mancipi* and *res nec mancipi*, things that are subject to mancipation (that is, strict legal circumscription and formalities) and things that are not. In the development of ancient law there was a gradual process by which rules governing the lower class of objects come to incorporate and supersede the higher, thus rendering all forms of property more easily alienable. Land was almost always classed within the higher subjects (along with beasts of burden) and was often the last to be incorporated into the law of sales. This process was also closely tied to the historical development of commerce and market society, and reached its fruition in societies dominated by the "law of the market." At this point, people no longer related to one another as members of a community or family but as "strangers," for it was only when kinship bonds had fully receded that modes of exchange are freed from customary limitations and can fully align themselves to the "law of the market."[43]

In short, the main forces at work in the transition from communal to private property can be summarized as follows. Firstly, the dominant process was the "natural," immanent growth of forms of individual proprietary right in the division of communal land and the concomitant dissolution of the village-community. In terms of the motive force that made dissolution a given tendency of village-communities, Maine pointed (somewhat vaguely) to the universal growth in the sense of personal right over property acquired separately. Separate property here refers to the early forms of private accumulation that were allowed as exceptions to the rule of common ownership, for example, the Roman *peculium* (separate property of the son or slave), profits from trade, spoils of war. "The reluctance to surrender individual gains is a sentiment observed in force everywhere," and, Maine contended, "always among the most potent of the influences which began to transform the old world of consanguinity into the new world of economical relation."[44] Energetic and acquisitive members tended to rebel against communal authority, introducing an in-equality that eroded the foundations of natural communism.

Secondly, war and the expansion of commerce were further causes that hastened disintegration by initiating and expanding inequality. Primitive village-communities, while permeated by strict internal order, were never-theless considered to be constantly in a state of conflict with their neigh-bors, whether from the stress of population or fluctuations in economic conditions. Conflict was the circumstance that initiated the ascendancy of the authority of tribal chief, who in his origins was almost always the ablest and most revered military leader. And, as was noted above, it was with the growth and transmutation of the sovereignty of the tribal chief that absolute forms of landed property developed, primarily by claiming exclusive authority over his own lands and the increasing encroachment over the commons.

The theoretical significance of Maine's account of the disentanglement of communal ownership is that despite the variation he imputed to the causes of this gradual development, everywhere it seemingly leads to the same historical endpoint, namely the establishment of absolute private property in land. This transition in the history of property—like that of the general movement from status to contract—was not only unequivo-cally identified with progress but was also conceptualized as entirely uni-directional. The emphasis on the incremental but continuous process of transformation reinforced the idea that the shift from ancient to modern society could, in principle, be internally generated. This aspect was made most conspicuous in Maine's developed position on the process of feudal-ization. Initially thought of as an epochal break (and possibly a regressive one) in the history of legal development, later evidence from the Teutonic *Mark*, Indian village-community, and ancient Irish law revealed how the primitive communal social form of ancient society "had everywhere a tendency, not produced from without, to modify itself in the direction of feudalism."[45] This illustrates how, unlike accounts of modernity (compare with Smith's account of the development of capitalism or Marx's account of primitive accumulation) that stressed the conjunctural nature of the origins of modernity, Maine's construction rendered that movement a product of processes of change that were immanent to the social forma-tion in question.[46] The stress on the ever-present internal inclination of village-communities to dissolve, coupled with a unilinear characterization of the telos of that transition in modern forms of private property, un-derpinned Maine's ideological commitment to the view that the long pro-cess in the evolution of private property was, ultimately, a progressive and legitimate development.

THE INDIAN VILLAGE-COMMUNITY IN DISSOLUTION

The notion of the Indian village-community as a specific socioeconomic formation was the distinct intellectual product of Anglo-Indian administration.[47] Well before Maine's theorization, many of its central features had been delineated and analyzed by a number of key Indian administrators, from the early investigations of Metcalfe and Munro to Elphinstone and Campbell.[48] But it was Maine's work that imputed the Indian village-community a grander theoretical significance, drawing the attention of European scholars to the imperial administrative archive and, most importantly, bringing the Indian and European debate together into a unified field of knowledge. Although Maine's work was substantively indebted to previous Anglo-Indian scholarship, in identifying the communal use and ownership of land as a defining feature of the village-community his revitalized conceptualization would reshape the theoretical debate on Indian land tenure and agrarian social structure. In addition to reconstructing the village-community's essential features as a characteristic form of primitive society, Maine was also keen to understand processes of its dissolution as signs of the transition to modern society. The Indian village-community, therefore, was not only theoretically significant as a "living" remnant of ancient society, but also, with the coming of imperial rule, demonstrated in dramatic fashion its historical undoing.

Indian village-communities, whose observation was crucial for the historical reconstruction of the evolution of property, were everyday disappearing under the impact of imperial rule. Here lay the particular urgency in Maine's plea for comparative jurisprudence, for while British rule in India provided the conditions for sustained observation of these forms of ancient society, it was the very fact of that rule that was also undermining the social basis of these same archaic institutions. India must be studied at once, Maine contended, "for this remarkable society, pregnant with interest at every point, and for the moment easily open to our observations, is undoubtedly passing away. . . . India itself is gradually losing everything which is characteristic of it."[49] While Maine considered it "absurd to deny that the disintegration of Eastern usage and thought is attributable to British dominion," the exact causes of dissolution were complex and multifold. Rarely was it due to "high-handed repression or contemptuous discouragement" at the hands of the ruling power.[50] Rather, the Indian village-community was the fulcrum of debates about Indian land revenue, upon which the entire constitution of British power in India rested. As such, the fate of the village-community was irreparably tied to the political and intellectual controversies that shaped British revenue policy. These controversies, according to Maine, stemmed in part from a fundamental misrecognition of the centrality of the village-community as the original social form of India. But they were also exacerbated by faulty analogizing between English and Indian economic phenomena, especially by administrators working under the sway of doctrines of classical political economy. Misunderstandings about the true nature of native customs in relation to land usage thus led to the application of revenue policies that necessarily altered the basic structure of the village-community, most often in an adverse manner.

Moreover, the very machinery of British revenue and legal administration generated and fixed burgeoning private proprietary rights, hastening the decay of the customary basis of the village-community. In this respect, Maine was articulating a more structural source of conflict between ancient and modern society, in which imperial state formation was seen to necessitate the breakdown of ancient forms of life. Although Maine contended that both ancient and modern "legislating" empires, the most significant classical example of which was the Roman Empire, initiated the destruction of local customs, it was a state form that was particularly ascendant in the modern era. Modern Europe was the pinnacle of the development of "highly centralised, actively legislating, States,"[51] which had in their consolidation evacuated and superseded small-scale, self-regulating societies beneath them. Nowhere was this process more apparent than in the consolidation of the British Empire in India. In relation to Indian village-communities, Maine thus implied that the natural processes of disintegration had been greatly accelerated with the coming of British rule.

The territorial power of the East India Company had begun with the transfer of *diwani*, the right to collect land revenue, from the Mughal emperor. According to Maine, the British, guided in part by the mistaken assumption of the theory of Oriental despotism, believed the Mughal emperor to be owner of all the land, and therefore with the transfer of *diwani*, the British government evolved into the "supreme landowner," which claimed a large share of the produce of the soil. Thus, from its inception, and with the further incorporation of new provinces, the settlement of revenue was the foremost task of imperial governance. The practicalities, however, of designating which person, or class of persons, ought be held responsible for revenue payment required determining "the unit of society for agrarian purposes," and consequently shaped, "the entire political and social constitution of the province."[52] The British resolved to settle with those classes deemed to have the strongest claims to rights of property, and in the settlement process granted full legal recognition of such rights. This recognition in sanctioning some proprietary interests at the expense of others necessarily transformed the relative strength and political future of agrarian classes.

Persistent debates about land tenure and revenue policy divided British administrators into two rival schools: one that sought to invest property rights with the cultivating classes, that is, with the peasantry either as individuals or collectively as village-communities, and another that promoted the claims of landlords or some sort of native aristocracy. These debates developed in two distinct phases. In the early nineteenth century Thomas Munro's *ryotwari* experiment, with the support of utilitarian reformers, successfully challenged Lord Cornwallis and the Permanent Settlement of Bengal (1793), which had conferred property rights on *zamindari* middlemen in order to create large estates and "improving landlords" on a British model. The *ryotwari* model, based on direct settlement with the cultivator, made peasant proprietorship the dominant norm of settlement policy until the Mutiny.[53] It was an egalitarian ideal well suited to the heyday of liberal reform; in promoting the peasantry, reformers sought to simultaneously encourage industry and autonomy through the protection of property and undercut the political power of "parasitical" intermediary classes, from tax gatherers to indigenous aristocrats. The debate reemerged (without any final resolution) after 1857, but in a political and ideological context that was primarily oriented toward the stabilization of the agrarian order. Land tenure and revenue policy would no longer be dominated by controversies about the best models for agrarian "improvement."[54]

As interpreters of true native custom in land usage, Maine argued that both schools of thought were partially right and partially wrong, for when one analyzed Indian land tenure as a whole, "claims to some sort of superior right over land in fact existed which correspond to every single stage through which the conception of proprietorship has passed in the Western world, excepting only the later stages."[55] The real error in English revenue policy was not in the assertion of strong proprietary rights in land but rather in the assumption "of a perfect analogy between rights of property as understood in India and as understood in this country."[56] Thus, while Maine had contended that there were Indian examples of "nascent absolute ownership," none matched exactly the assemblage of powers associated with the English holder of fee-simple. Rather, ownership was communal, and when internally disaggregated, different classes and groups would have differential, shared rights in the soil. Yet, British revenue policy had consistently registered what in fact were layered, communal rights in property as absolute, individual, landownership; a misplaced conferral of rights that entailed serious consequences.

According to Maine, "the Village Community of India is at once an organised patriarchal society and an assemblage of co-proprietors. The personal relations to each other of the men who compose it are indistinguishably confounded with their proprietary rights, and to the attempts of English functionaries to separate the two may be assigned some of the most formidable miscarriages of Anglo-Indian administration."[57] These central controversies continually plagued the Anglo-Indian government, only receiving some clarity, according to Maine, with the settlement of Punjab and the Northwest Provinces (1850s), where the true nature of the village-community was finally discovered and it came to be legally recognized as the propriety unit of agrarian society.

The village-community had been a central motif of British investigations into Indian agrarian society and was given its classic and influential formulation in *The Fifth Report*.[58] This description, the basic features of which were reiterated throughout the nineteenth century (in Maine and Marx most prominently) was based on two overlapping sources, those of Mark Wilks and Thomas Munro.[59] Both Wilks and Munro, however, were defenders and, in the case of Munro, founders of the *ryotwari* settlement based upon individual peasant proprietorship. For both, the village was a *republic* in the sense of an organization of free individuals. While Maine drew upon Munro's and Wilks's evocative portrayal of the independent and self-sustaining village, its communal nature (especially in terms of communal landownership) was derived from the work of George Campbell and Mountstuart Elphinstone.[60] Both Campbell and Elphinstone had intimated the comparison between the Indian and the Tacitean Germanic village-community that would structure Maine's work. The resemblance between Eastern and Western village-communities, however, seems to be have been first noted in 1814 in Francis Ellis's investigation of Mirasi (communal) tenures in the Madras Presidency. But unlike Maine, Ellis as a trained Orientalist relied on textual sources to argue for village settlement in opposition to Munro's plan.[61]

The discovery of the true nature of the village-community was, for Maine, key to settling some of the central quarrels about the nature of ownership in India. Study of village-communities revealed that there was ownership in land but that it was often shared, invested in the community as a whole. Even as village-communities came to be recognized as the true proprietary unit of the country, policymakers still faced difficult questions about how to disentangle the shared rights to property of groups internal to the village-community. This problem was especially acute around the question of *rent*. The settlement process involved not only determining who would be responsible for payment of revenue, but also at what rate land tax or rent would be fixed. For Maine, the original inclination of policymakers to distribute proprietary rights (on an English model of absolute ownership) to classes deemed to have the best claim to superior rights assumed that all other classes were only connected to these "landlords" through payment for use of the land. This view of ownership immediately transformed the status of all other cultivating classes into tenants-at-will. With the recognition of shared rights to property came the acknowledgment of a number of intermediary classes, or "occupancy" tenants, who claimed customary protections against eviction and rack-rent. A proper understanding of the nature of these intermediary, imbricated forms of ownership and rent, Maine argued, was obscured by mistaken analogies to the English system as well as "the phraseology already introduced by the Economists."[62]

For Maine, "all the obscurities of mental apprehension which are implied in the use of Nature as a juridical term cluster in India around the word, Rent."[63] British officers, trained in political economy, had systematically prioritized competitive rents that assumed a free market in land over customary forms of rent (linked to shared rights in property) and thus set the terms for a century of confusions about the nature of economic life in India.[64] Customary rents, which by definition bore no relation to either the productive capacity of the soil or the market value of land, were seen as less "natural" and not true rent in the economic sense. Yet, Maine insisted that customary rents were the norm in India and more ancient than competition rent, which was an economic form only applicable in social systems where the rule of the market has superseded custom as the measure of price.

The idea that human beings are naturally inclined to sell goods and services at the highest possible price was not a given fact of nature but was made possible only in economic systems where the ideology of the market had taken hold. The right to take the highest, competitive rent was, Maine contended, a right derived from the rule of the market (and thus a right of contract). And the rule of the market "only triumphs when the primitive community is in ruins."[65] Maine described the complex patterns of interdependence at the village level to illustrate the web of economic activities that were held together by "nonmarket" principles. In the caste division of labor, or what later anthropologists would term the *jajmani* system, persons were tied to one another through the performance of hereditary services in exchange for fixed appropriations of the common harvest. Even those village members who were not directly tied to the cultivation of land, such as artisans whose livelihood necessarily depended on trade or exchange, produced goods as service to the village as a whole. And when these types of exchange did coincide with payment, prices were fixed by custom rather than a market mechanism. When economic fortunes fluctuated, "the artificer who plies an ancient trade still sells his wares at customary prices, and would always change their quality rather than their price."[66]

Maine was critical of the myriad ways in which the misapplication of Western conceptions of ownership and rent had had a deleterious effect on the traditional Indian village-community, and the communal land customs that had sustained it. He was also adamant that the disintegration itself was part and parcel of the imposition of imperial rule, and thus not easily corrected or forestalled. Settlement processes, even when appropriately attuned to the unique dynamics of Indian economic life, nevertheless instantiated profound transmutations of native institutions, hastening the decay of the village-community.

The settlement of revenue prioritized the task of registering, discovering, and fixing all known rights to land, thus, as we have seen, inaugurating a host of debates about the nature and existence of property rights or concepts of legal ownership in India that were comparable to English real property law. Whatever settlement was reached, the procedure initiated processes of structural change in the arena of legal rights. The initial task of Settlement Officers was to identify classes of persons who would be deemed responsible for the collection and payment of revenue. According to Maine, a critical product of these investigations into the rights in soil that existed on the eve of conquest was the Settlement Report and a detailed registry of these rights known as a Record of Rights. This detailing necessarily produced numerous controversies between different groups and between the state and payer. In attempting to resolve these disputes the duties of the Settlement Officer (and later the Revenue Boards) inevitably took on a quasi-judicial character as they decided upon complaints to this record.[67]

Since the most prevalent modes of settlement conferred property rights on particular individuals (even when deeming certain classes of persons appropriate to this task), settlement introduced alienable property with its related bundle of powers. In Maine's historical scheme, alienable property, private property in its mature sense, was intimately related to individual right and freedom of contract. By contrast, in ancient societies, the law of persons was confounded with the law of property, ownership was always embedded within ties of family and kinship. The introduction of personal right into this form of community, for Maine, necessarily undermined its systematized ties of reciprocal obligation. And even with the legal recognition of the village-community as the true proprietary unit, the attempt to delegate differential, shared rights and obligations in relation to collectively owned property, nevertheless "arrested a process of change which was steadily proceeding" and imposed "a new stiffness to the relations of the various classes."[68]

In other words, Maine argued that the establishment of a revenue administration tied to a legal regime that was meant to recognize and protect property rights in effect created land law for India ex nihilo. And with the creation of a modern land law came the inevitable development of personal, individual rights distinct from those of the community. The growth in the sense of personal right (instantiated and protected by the

English courts) under British rule could be seen in the increase of cases seeking the division and repartition of communal properties and testamentary successions that disinherited the traditional claims of the joint family. With the further encroachment of contract law into personal relations of mutual dependence, the growing sense of personal right in the village-community was "destructive of the authority of its internal rules."[69]

The scientific and historical understanding of the inherited customs of the village-community therefore yielded no simple practical solutions. Because it was the *structural* effect of imperial rule and not only conscious policy choices that exposed ancient society to the forces of its dissolution, practical attempts at protection and reconstitution were limited in effectiveness, even bound to fail.

> If I were to describe the feeling which is now strongest with some of the most energetic Indian administrators, I should be inclined to call it a fancy for reconstructing native Indian society upon a purely native model; a fancy which some would apparently indulge, even to the abnegation of all moral judgement. But the undertaking is not practicable. *It is by its indirect and for the most part unintended influence that the British power metamorphoses and dissolves the ideas and social forms underneath it; nor is there any expedient by which it can escape the duty of rebuilding upon its own principles that which it unwillingly destroys* (emphasis added).[70]

As a policymaker involved in a number of key controversies around land tenure and economic legislation, Maine became increasingly disillusioned with attempts to reconstruct rights in land according to preconquest customs or in respect to so-called original forms. In a number of minutes and speeches related to legal challenges over the distribution of proprietary rights in Bengal, Oudh (Awadh), and Punjab, Maine came to believe that the resort to historical arguments only added confusion to an already controversial and difficult set of questions. Not only was the controversy over land tenure a central battleground for imperial policy since the beginning of Company rule, the problem of agrarian indebtedness and unrest was also considered a key determinant of the Rebellion of 1857. Thus any attempt to radically reform tenure rights had the potential to be politically volatile.

For Maine these two questions were interlinked; in the absence of a general consensus on the original form of proprietary rights in any given province, governmental policy should err in favor of continuity.

> Nobody brought to India a stronger conviction than I did of the policy of abandoning all English or European generalizations in India, and of respecting native usage even though it should be unreasonable. And if there was one

class of usages which I should have supposed more deserving of respect than another, it was the custom which constitutes the tenure of land . . . but I must say that there is now great reason to believe that the doctrines of all schools are founded on partial observation, and that the indistinctness of usage throughout India, taken as a whole, which has tempted and enabled the partisans of each school in turn to attribute to its principles this character of universality. . . . In the existing state of authority and opinion I can see no rule to follow, except to abide by actual arrangements, whether founded or not on an original misconstruction of native usage. I say *let us stand even by our mistakes. It is better than perpetual meddling.*[71]

According to Maine, the search for a universal, scientific basis for tenure rights seemed doomed as references to history or ancient usage proved ultimately to be an unreliable guide to practice. On the one hand, native custom and usages in relation to land had been so severely disrupted by the impact of British rule, by the frequency of revisions to land-revenue policy as well as through the dissolving influence of notions of individual property rights, that reconstituting them in their entirety would prove practically impossible. On the other hand, the dissolution of the village-community signaled the transition, albeit in a telescoped and uncontrolled manner, to modern social and economic institutions, the demands of which could not be met by reviving traditional customs. Furthermore, the practical effects of changing a given revenue settlement (even if those rights were purely the creation of British power) could be as unjust and disruptive. Revolutions even for the sake of restoring ancient rights would lead only to instability and a general sense of insecurity in property rights.[72] In relation to questions of revenue, rent, and land tenure, Maine therefore thought it best "to abandon the historical mode of dealing with a practical question peculiar to the Indian government, to choose the social and economical principles on which it was intended to act, and to adhere to them until their political unsoundness was established."[73]

INDIA, IRELAND, AND THE HISTORICAL TURN IN POLITICAL ECONOMY

Although Maine was equivocal about what the practical implications of the discovery of communal property would be for India, his work enabled attempts to forestall the uncritical imposition of Western property institutions in India. Indeed, Maine's work, in the hands of his many energetic followers in the Indian administration, would instigate a shift in economic policy against the extension of free market in land in favor of protecting the customary practices of the village-community.[74] This shift was enabled by the larger intellectual debate about the historical variety of forms of property, such that modern absolute property rights were seen as unsuitable not just for India, but also for similarly situated traditional societies. The historicist revision would have important implications for imperial policy writ large. While the Indian debate would establish a pattern of economic doctrine and land-tenure policy for later British expansion in Asia and Africa, it was itself shaped by and intersected with a concurrent controversy about British policy in Ireland.

In the latter half of the nineteenth century, there was a heightened sense of the extensive similarity between Indian and Irish society, especially in terms of agrarian social and economic structure. India and Ireland were seen to be primarily peasant economies, in which agricultural village-communities played a key role in coordinating socioeconomic life. For scholars like Maine the analogy was even stronger; India and Ireland were seen as part of the Aryan or Indo-European family of institutions, yet outside the orbit of Rome's imperial presence, and thus prime examples of the autonomous logic of ancient/primitive society. Maine analyzed this connection in detail in his *Lectures on the Early History of Institutions*, in which the recently published Brehon law tracts supplied vital evidence in retracing the institutional history of property.[75] In the nineteenth-century debate on property, Irish evidence was as vital as Indian materials in establishing the thesis of original communism, as the India-Ireland analogy came to play a central role in the comparative project.

Imperial observers (and administrators) had been especially attuned to the potential lessons that Ireland could serve for India (and vice versa) given their common experience of British rule, particularly in the arena again of economic policy.[76] From the 1860s onward, there was a growing sense among imperial policymakers as well as political economists that liberal and utilitarian models had not produced the predicted positive outcomes in either case, that is, neither India nor Ireland looked like they were on the road to becoming "little Englands." Moreover, agrarian strife (such as peasant indebtedness and famine) was seen to have emboldened political upheaval, most dramatically with the Mutiny in India and the Fenian uprisings in Ireland. In this context, there was mounting suspicion of "Anglicization," of policies based on English models and patterns of socioeconomic development. This suspicion, in turn, was enabled by a number of intellectual trends from historicism to the marginalist critique that began to challenge central tenets of classical political economy.[77]

The sense of disillusionment with economic policy had already begun to reshape classical political economy from within. With Ireland in mind, J. S. Mill, in successive editions of *Principles of Political Economy*, had increasingly sought to recognize the force of *custom*, not just as a fetter on productivity and rationality, but also as a legitimate constraint on land legislation.[78] Mill's attempt to modify and rehabilitate classical political economy in this manner, however, also drew attention to its theoretical and practical limitations, and thus emboldened critics to search for alternative methods and principles. The turn to custom would become more radical; anthropological and historical investigations such as Maine's would demonstrate the persistence of customary ideas and practices, themselves taken as signs of the resistance of traditional society to imposed modernization. In India, a growing administrative deference to the imperatives of custom cemented the view that India (and Ireland) could no longer be viewed as a blank slate upon which one could recreate English institutions.

Maine's recognition of the communal customary practices of the Indian and Irish village-community would not only challenge specific policies in favor of individual ownership, freedom of contract, and laissez-faire, but would also culminate in the theoretical undoing of classical political economy. According to Maine, just as the Austinian sovereign was dependent upon the modern principle of territorial sovereignty, the classical economic theory of rent was only applicable in social systems where the rule of the market had superseded custom as the measure of price.[79] And even more than Austin's work, political economy was a deductive philosophy that began by imputing a range of motivations and instincts supposedly grounded in human nature. Evidence from India and Ireland was again particularly useful to raise questions about the philosophical legitimacy of such methodological imperatives as well as the practicality of applying its conclusions universally.

Anglo-Indian functionaries investigating Indian economic facts were "apt to borrow the habit of the English political economists, and to throw aside, under the name of *friction*, all the extraneous influences which clog the action of those wheels of social mechanism to which economical science confines almost wholly its attention." In this process of abstraction, "they greatly underrate the value, power, and interest of that great body of custom and inherited ideas which, they throw aside as friction."[80] For Maine, rather than throw these obstructions aside, one could study them in their own right and reveal the rationale and logic of an older order of ideas, a customary order, which systematically impinged upon market principles.

CHAPTER FIVE

NATIVE SOCIETY IN CRISIS: CONCEPTUAL
FOUNDATIONS OF INDIRECT RULE

There is a double current of influences playing upon this
remarkable dominion. One of these currents has its origin in
this country, beginning in the strong moral and political
conviction of a free people. The other arises in India itself,
engendered among a dense and dark vegetation of primitive
opinion, or prejudice if you please, stubbornly rooted in the
debris of the past. As has been truly enough said, the British
rulers of India are like men bound to make their watches
keep true time in two longitudes at once. Nevertheless the
paradoxical position must be accepted. If they are too
slow, there will be no improvement. If they are too fast,
there will be no security.[1]

It is by its indirect and for the most part unintended influence
that the British power metamorphoses and dissolves the ideas
and social forms underneath it; nor is there any expedient
by which it can escape the duty of rebuilding upon its own
principles that which it unwillingly destroys.[2]
—*Henry Maine*

IN THE CONTEXT OF THE POST-MUTINY IMPERIAL ORDER, one that I have
argued was premised upon the conscious disavowal of many of the key
aspects of the liberal model of empire, Maine's work was to have an exceptional relevance. Maine's account of traditional society, especially his
notion of a native society in dissolution, laid the theoretical foundations
of *indirect rule*, the policy characteristic of late imperial ideology. Maine's
influential portrait of the customary basis of native society, of a society
whose foundations were seen to be diametrically opposed to those of
modern society, called into question the theoretical and practical underpinnings of the liberal agenda. The reformation of native society was seen
as especially ineffective at inculcating loyalty to the empire, as evidenced
most provocatively with the experience of the Mutiny. Maine's notion
that native societies may be necessarily threatened with dissolution by the
structural conditions of modern imperial rule proved crucial in shifting

the grounds of imperial rule. That empire could be simultaneously cause and cure for the crisis of native society provided an alibi for permanent, protective rule; permanent, because the link between empire and the goal of modernizing transformation had been effectively severed with the diminution of the liberal agenda of reform.

Chapter one outlined the nature of this ideological transformation from civilizing justifications to culturalist alibis in terms of shifts in primarily (but not exclusively) metropolitan debates about the nature and purpose of empire. In the late nineteenth century, new imperial alibis redefined the terms of debate about empire; foundational questions about the legitimacy of British rule in India were displaced by a presumption of the necessity of foreign rule given by the "nature" of native societies. On the one hand, as opposed to grand schemes of societal improvement, imperial rule was to accommodate itself to the allegedly unchanging and unchangeable character of native peoples. On the other, impending crises within native society, linked either to endemic forms of internecine conflict (that is, sectarian, tribal, religious conflict) or, more often, to traumatic contact with the West, were put forward as (retroactive) validations for the prolongation of imperial rule. The burden of justification had decidedly shifted from metropole to colony; as Lord Cromer often repeated (paraphrasing Boell), "the real Indian question was not whether the English were justified in staying in the country, but whether they could find any moral justification for withdrawing from it."[3] The ethical dilemma at the heart of late empire was not about what right (and for what ethical purpose) Britain ruled India, but a diminished moral duty to stay, as the lesser evil compared to leaving India to collapse on her own.

This chapter retraces and reexamines this ideological transformation from the vantage point of imperial administrators on the ground, and their articulation of distinct ruling strategies in line with the new alibis of late empire. Building upon the work of Maine, administrators such as Alfred Lyall, Lord Cromer, Arthur Gordon, and Lord Lugard formulated and defended what I will argue can be understood as a distinct theory of indirect rule. They argued broadly for a recognition of, and respect for, the customary basis of native society, which in terms of policy implicated imperial rule in a political logic of protection, preservation, and restoration of traditional society. Significantly, while the discourse of indirect rule presented itself as a kind of defensive realism, as a compromise with and recognition of native agency, it would be the cover for greater expansion and consolidation of direct imperial rule across Africa and Southeast Asia. While the move from direct and indirect rule seemed to imply a pulling back of imperial power, it was, in actuality, an entrenchment of an alternative structure of rule, one that was premised on a repudiation of the assumptions of prior direct/liberal models of empire. Among the architects of late empire, the central assumption of the theory of indirect rule—that the imperial order would be best preserved by the insinuation of imperial power in the customary order of native society rather than through its repudiation and transformation—became the pillar of a political theory of rule, premised on a fundamental critique of modern political models of representation and sovereignty. In its most ambitious articulations, indirect rule as political theory was institutionally grounded in a policy of decentralization and philosophically justified as a form of cosmopolitan pluralism.

One of the central conceptual preconditions for the theory of indirect rule was given in the emergence of the idea of *traditional society*, of native society as an integrated social whole whose basis, while diametrically opposed to modern (Western) societies, was recognized to have a logic and rationale of its own. As I sought to demonstrate in chapter two, it was a reconceptualizion linked to the rise of social theory and, in the work of some of its key proponents, shaped by a self-conscious critique of political models of social cohesion and transformation. Traditional society, as exemplified in Maine's seminal contribution, was characterized as a fundamentally apolitical society, structured by and through kinship ties and customary norms. The practical implication, especially in the context of imperial rule, was that the reformation of native society was, if not impossible, undesirable for a variety of strategic and normative reasons.

This new conceptualization of traditional society was put forward by Maine as a critique of previous understandings of Indian society. In relation to post-Mutiny India, Maine argued that imperial policy had often been misguided in assumptions about the strength and character of native belief and the sources through which correct knowledge of India ought to be sought. In this latter respect, Maine was especially suspicious of Orientalist appeals to textual knowledge as a guide to Indian custom. Rather, Maine had emphasized, as a fundamental epistemological correction, the importance of ethnographic evidence of customs already embodied in the colonial archive, as the repository of actual native practice. In the shift from the historical-textual to the anthropological mode of colonial knowledge formation, the key idea of Maine's Indian anthropology crystallized—the village-community as the central social form of India.

Yet, as we have seen in chapters three and four when Maine approached actual Indian policy situations, armed with the idea of the village-community, he became increasingly concerned that even an epistemological correction that recognized the centrality of custom to the dynamics of Indian social life may not be an effective solution given the pace of destructive change to native society under imperial rule. In the two policy domains of special concern to Maine—the stabilization of law and the debate over land tenure—Maine was increasingly pessimistic about using existing or reconstructed native practices (that is, native law or native property customs) as the basis for imperial policy. Maine's seven-year tenure in the Viceroy's Council, his direct experience of imperial administration, came with a growing recognition that with imperial rule, the structural conditions of native life had dramatically shifted. In this new context, the traditional mechanisms of native society were seen to be thoroughly undermined and/or distorted. Custom, once the elastic glue that allowed for the maintenance and reproduction of native society, if not wholly superseded by legislation, remained only in a degraded, frozen, and stereotyped form without the capacity to meet the new demands of a rapidly modernizing society. Modern imperial rule had forced a direct confrontation between modern and traditional institutions, a confrontation that seemed to necessitate the dissolution of native society.

In Maine's view, the dissolution of native society had been exacerbated by liberal and utilitarian models of progressive imperial reform, and thus, the disavowal of the liberal alternative was both an epistemological and practical necessity. Yet, the impending crisis of native society was also construed by Maine as a *structural*, and thus unintended, consequence of imperial rule. As such, even policies premised on the resurrection or protection of native society, were doomed to failure, precisely because imperial rule had set in motion a process of modernization that overwhelmed the traditional adaptability of native society. Despite Maine's reservations about reconstructing native models as the solution to the crisis, this was one of the central lessons drawn from his work by many of his avowed successors. The fact that Maine had so vividly characterized the extent and dangers posed by the dissolution of native society in India, for many, added to the urgency of the need for protection, especially a kind of preemptive and preventative protection of native institutions in societies seen to have been least touched by Western intrusion.

This notion of a native society in crisis, of the inevitable dissolution of native society under the conditions of modern empire, was Maine's most original innovation and arguably his most important contribution to the theory of indirect rule. While the exact nature of the "crisis" that Maine would identify—the sources, manifestations, and even potential solutions—was subject to various interpretations, imperial administrators of the late nineteenth century were animated by a concern to halt the impending collapse of native societies. The idea that the primary task of empire was containing this crisis presented a wholly new rationale for empire, and implied a new framework for the structure of imperial rule. In other words, for the concept of traditional society to have the impact it was to have, it needed to be tied to a new account of the sources of instability, specifically a theoretical outlook that saw the protection of native society as a prerequisite to imperial order. It was the portrayal of native society as simultaneously *intact* and *vulnerable* that underpinned the paternalistic impulse of indirect rule.

This chapter details how Maine's theoretical portrait of primitive/ ancient society, especially the concept of native society in dissolution, laid the conceptual foundations for the theory and practice of indirect rule. It will examine the specific ways this image of native society was mobilized in the context of late imperial policy, first in post-Mutiny India and later in Southeast Asia and Africa. In India, Maine's influence would trigger what Clive Dewey has termed the "great reversal" in agrarian policy, during which time the Government of India found itself repeatedly legislating against laissez-faire market principles. Maine's legacy was here specifically linked to the criticism of previous utilitarian strategies of agrarian reform and thus signaled the intellectual triumph of historicism over the tenets of classical political economy. For some advocates of these policy reversals, protecting so-called native traditions was a normative priority and, for them, Maine's evocative account of native society, where primitive custom rationally ordered social, political, and economic life, was particularly appealing. Others argued for a policy of protection and/or rehabilitation of the village-community and caste formations on more straightforwardly political grounds, as a safeguard against instability, unrest, and rebellion. The latter line of argument was perhaps even more vehement in its criticism of the destabilizing influence of reform-oriented liberalism for the dependent empire. Alfred Lyall, Maine's closest intellectual successor in India, provided a sophisticated theoretical formulation of this political defense of indirect rule. Lyall proposed a theory of decentralization that marshaled historical and anthropological evidence to argue against the transplantation of modern (Western) representative institutions in India. Lyall, through his influence on Lord Cromer, was one important conduit for the export of the theory of indirect rule beyond India (in this case to Egypt). Finally, the chapter concludes with a closer look at what can be termed the culmination of the theory and practice of indirect rule in colonial Africa in the twentieth century, where Lord Lugard would provide its more influential intellectual articulation and defense. It was in colonial Africa that indirect rule would not only see its more widespread application, it would also receive its most elaborate philosophical justification as a model of a culturally sensitive, cosmopolitan pluralism.

RECONCEPTUALIZING NATIVE SOCIETY, RECONSTITUTING CUSTOM

"The great legacy which Maine left to India," according to Charles Lewis Tupper, "does not consist in positive enactments, but in luminous ideas and comprehensive principles to be gathered less from the statute-book than from his speeches and writings."[4] Tupper, a self-proclaimed follower of Maine's (and key figure in what would become the revisionist lobby in Indian agrarian policy), here expressed the general sense that Maine's influence and legacy was tied less to a specific set of policies, but rather stemmed from an underlying set of principles that enabled a changed perspective. In other words, unlike those of Bentham, Maine's Indian disciples were linked by a common attitude to the way Indian society was to be understood, derived from Maine's ideas, rather by an adherence to specific policy prescriptions or a shared political agenda. Tupper identified two interlinked notions of Maine's as being particularly revolutionary, and the source of Maine's "living and inspiring legacy" in a number of fields of Indian policy and administration: Maine's historical evolutionism and the theory of transition from status to contract. Maine's comparative and evolutionary method, according to Tupper, "had taught us to compare one archaic society with another, and to accept as part of the course of nature some of the differences between tribal and civilised society."[5] These differences could be understood historically as stages in the development of society. Maine's historicism thus served to inculcate a respect for the necessary differences between Indian and English ideas and institutions and, for Tupper, led "directly to the conviction that the institutions of any community should correspond to its existing stage of growth."[6] The implication for ruling was to reject the transplantation of English models in favor of existing custom; "the country must be governed in harmony with the established usages of the people, so far as those usages are not flagrantly opposed to our ideas of right and wrong."[7]

What Tupper was attesting to was Maine's role in what scholars now denote as a fundamental shift in the character of official colonial knowledge—of the kinds of knowledge about native society considered necessary for stabilizing imperial rule (after the 1857 Rebellion).[8] In official quarters the Mutiny was understood to be an epistemic failure, a failure of the state (given its misguided attempts at Anglicization) to comprehend and predict the source and extent of native disaffection. In his own reflections on the causes of the Mutiny, Maine had argued that a general lack of accurate knowledge of native religious beliefs and customs had precipitated revolt. That the Mutiny was instigated by a grievance about the use of rifle cartridges greased with pork and beef fat (thus offending both Hindu and Muslim sentiments) was evidence that "terrified fanaticism" was the true (and not merely incidental) spark of the revolt.[9] It was also the reason that the Mutiny proved to be a shock to the English mind, for the insurrection seemingly sprang from *inscrutable* sentiments. Maine construed the social and religious sentiments that defied British sensibilities as "caste sentiment," grounded in fear of spiritual pollution. This blindness to the strength and persistence of religious sentiments was a sign of a "defect of knowledge or imagination which hides these truths from the English mind."[10] This lacuna in the English mind, however deep, could be overcome through the acquisition of better and more appropriate knowledge of native practices and beliefs. He wrote, "I am not making any confident assertion on a subject so vast and so superficially examined as the character of native Indian religious and social belief. But I insist on the necessity of having some accurate ideas about it, and on the fact that a mistake about it caused the Sepoy Mutiny."[11]

In this manner, fundamental questions about the character and strength of native beliefs were linked to the pragmatic exigencies of imperial governance. In Maine's words, ascertaining the roots of the 1857 Rebellion was not

> a merely historical interest. It is a question of the gravest practical importance for the rulers of India how far the condition of religious and social sentiment revealed by the Mutiny survives in any strength. . . . It is manifest that, if the belief in caste continues unimpaired or but slightly decayed, some paths of legislation and of executive action are seriously unsafe: it may be possible to follow them, but it is imperative to walk warily. The question of the existence or otherwise of this belief has also a direct bearing on the structure of the government which it may be possible to give to the Indian possessions of this country.[12]

The revolt in this sense was read as a specific kind of epistemic failure; as Nicholas Dirks has cogently argued, the rebellion was interpreted "as an anthropological failure rather than as political or economic event."[13] This interpretation, on the one hand, refused to read native disenchantment as a fundamental, and self-consciously political, challenge to the imperial order. On the other hand, it privileged and enabled the expansion of a particular form of knowledge—anthropological and ethnographic—as foundational to the late colonial state.[14]

That India ought to be governed "in conformity with its own notions and customs,"[15] was not, as Maine was quick to concede, entirely novel; a deference to existing custom played a central role in pre-Mutiny policy debates. From Hastings and Burke to the so-called Romantic-paternalist school of Munro, Metcalf, and Malcolm, key policies were advocated and defended in terms of their supposed continuity with custom, history, and tradition.[16] Yet, in his appeal for greater and more accurate knowledge of Indian custom, Maine was critically redefining what in fact Indian custom was and what constituted appropriate knowledge of it. What the Mutiny proved was that past epistemological and methodological assumptions of colonial knowledge were mistaken and/or tangential to the real effective concerns of governance. Maine argued that previous accounts of Indian social, political, and religious customs and practices suffered from a number of drawbacks. According to Maine, what little empirical knowledge eighteenth-century European writers of India had, especially Enlightenment philosophical historians, was limited to India's coastal cultures and trading outposts. Likewise, most colonial officers were based in the Presidency towns along the coasts, which had long histories of contact with the outside world, and thus they mistakenly took the urbanized (and more secularized) natives they encountered as representative of all of India. The "vast interior mass" was where "primitive custom and idea" were particularly well preserved, especially in an intimate relationship with the self-organizing village-community, and thus it was "the real India."[17]

Moreover, early European scholars—Orientalists enraptured by the surprising philological discoveries made through the study of Sanskrit—turned to ancient texts to unlock the secrets of Indian social and religious life. And with their Brahminical native informants, to whose views they easily acquiesced, they falsely assumed that Brahminical norms were representative of existing practices across India. Not only did this give a distorted picture of how key Indian institutions, such as caste, actually functioned, it also hid from view the fact that opposed to a devotion to universal Brahminical ideals, "what the Oriental was really attached to is his local custom."[18] Custom was the true guide to native practices and institutions, the logic of which could not be derived from the study of Sanskrit texts alone. Rather, for Maine, the colonial administrative archive was to be the locus of evidential truth about India's living customs. In this sense, colonial settlement reports, district gazetteers, and annual adjustment reports were by far the most precious sources of colonial knowledge.

Although Maine was what we today may consider to be the archetypical armchair anthropologist, never having directly engaged in fieldwork, in privileging the administrative archive he elevated direct observation as a methodological imperative. Maine's elevation of ethnography, coupled with his evolutionary historicism and the stress on native societies as functional wholes,[19] provided an enormous fillip to anthropological research, especially a genre of official anthropology by civil servants.[20] By the end of the century, as Maine's texts became required reading for the Indian Civil Service, his influence trickled down to all levels of service. By then, Maine's work had already had a determining impact in the intellectual development of many of the leading civil servants of the period, from Sir Denzil Ibbetson, Sir Alfred Lyall, S. S. Thorburn, Sir Lewis Tupper, Sir Raymond West, Sir James Wilson, and W. W. Hunter; all self-styled scholar-administrators who consciously framed their official and public work as learned anthropological treatises. Maine in his own work had made provocative use of colonial administrative records, arguing that they were in effect the great repositories "of verifiable phenomena of ancient usage and ancient juridical thought."[21] As a guide to "fragments of ancient society," this archive was the key to a true picture of the ancient/ primitive world and thus an essential starting point for the development of new sciences such as comparative jurisprudence. In elevating bureaucratic notes to the status of universal significance, Maine had, according to Tupper "prepared the minds of scholars in Europe for the reception of the sort of evidence which Indian revenue officers are able to supply."[22] Officials wholeheartedly embraced the new significance their work was given—as contributing to the advancement of Western science as well as providing the state with the kind knowledge thought necessary for better ruling. This was especially the case in Punjab, whose original settlement Maine had mined for evidence of the village-community and the centrality of customary law. Punjab's civil servants also counted among Maine's most fervent disciples, and many of its landmark Settlement Reports bore the unmistakable marks of his influence.[23]

As anthropology became, in Dirks words, "the principle modality of knowledge and rule,"[24] the making of the *ethnographic state* entailed not only a methodological revolution but also a substantive and normative shift in the characterization of Indian society, of what counted as its essential and animating elements and what the state's position ought to be in relation to them. Maine's methodological innovations provoked an important reconceptualization of native society, one that enabled, if not a wholesale rehabilitation of Indian society, a definite reevaluation of key (often reviled) institutions such as caste and the village-community. The transformation of the normative status of caste in post-Mutiny official discourse was perhaps the most dramatic example of this kind of reevaluation.[25] For the radical reformers of the early nineteenth century (as well as in much missionary discourse), there was no greater sign of India's moral degradation and barbarism than the institution of caste. The strictures of caste—often seen as a well-spun conspiracy meant to preserve the privileges of the priestly class—were reproached for enabling a whole host of societal and psychological ills, from sanctioning inequality and idolatry, stifling autonomy and individuality, to impeding incentives to productive work.[26] In terms of policy, reform was directly associated with and would culminate with the breakdown of the caste order, under pressure from the expansion of Western education, the replacement of customary constraints on caste labor with free contractual relations, and the expansion of a modern legal system based upon individual rights and equality before the law.

By contrast, Maine contended that traditional European understandings of caste, "all too reliant upon Brahminical accounts," had misunderstood this "remarkable institution" and its vital functioning as the bedrock of the social order. Maine argued that the understanding of caste as *varna*, that all social groups could be neatly divided into four universal castes in a theologically fixed hierarchy, was never an empirical reality in India. Rather, caste as a living institution was better understand as

> only the name for a number of practices which are followed by each one of a multitude of groups of men, whether such a group be ancient, natural or modern and artificial. As a rule, every trade, every profession, every guild, every tribe, every clan is also a caste, and the members of a caste not only have their own special objects of worship, selected from the Hindoo pantheon or adopted by it, but they exclusively eat together and exclusively intermarry.[27]

In other words, Maine emphasized caste as *jati*, as the name for an endogamous, horizontal social grouping that was typical of ancient/primitive society in which kinship functioned as the ideological basis of group cohesion. What made caste a "remarkable" and distinctly Indian institution was less its connection to theological doctrine than its ability to preserve this primitive mode of social organization (and the primitive ideas and customs that were integrally tied to its functioning), such that in India all sorts of groups—even modern and artificial groups such as new religious sects—continually dissolve and recombine "on the footing and on the model of the natural family."[28]

Maine's successors furthered this reevaluation of caste and extended the interest to genealogical groups such as the tribe and the clan; together, these corporate groups were seen as representative of the organized patriarchal groups whose historical and sociological importance Maine's work had sought to demonstrate.[29] For example, the scholar-administrators responsible for the Punjab's most famous Settlement Reports were especially keen to document the integral function of caste and these corporate groups in the maintenance and reproduction of social order. They were the cement that gave coherence to rural society, that made sense of and underlaid the economic, political, and social rationale of village customs and institutions. This was a direct application of Maine's stress on viewing native society as a rational, functional whole, where all social spheres exhibit synchronic interdependency. Maine had particularly emphasized the dual nature of the social groups that formed the Indian village-community: a community of self-styled kinsmen *and* co-proprietors. Maine's followers also directed special attention to the ways in which corporate social groups cohered around the exploitation of land, often including minitreatises on the dual evolution of property and kinship patterns in the districts they settled.[30] This emphasis on the interconnectedness between land tenure and group cohesion, implied in policy terms that the misapplication of modern (English) concepts of land tenure in social formations that were proven to be at much earlier evolutionary stages threatened the very fabric of rural society.

The normative rehabilitation of caste was part and parcel of a distinct Mainian methodological investment in social holism and evolutionary historicism. More generally, the anthropological reevaluation of Indian society made possible, perhaps even required as a prior assumption, a kind of cultural relativism or tolerance vis-à-vis the moral valuation and understanding of primitive society. But in Maine's case, it was a relativism of a peculiar sort, enabled by his model of comparison that both bridged and entrenched the divide between the primitive and the modern, India and Britain. While India still remained in a social state that "can only be called Barbarism," he objected strongly to the "unfavorable associations with the word."[31] In this respect, the reevaluation of barbarism was tied to the recognition of the deep divide between primitive and modern society, and thus it was difference that grounded a discourse of cultural toleration. The acceptance of a minimal relativism was a methodological imperative required in the attempt to unveil the unique logic of primitive or ancient societies, whose structuring principles and customs were seen to be radically distant from those of modern society. As Maine wrote in relation to political economy, "the first step towards the discovery of new truth on these subjects (and perhaps the most difficult of all, so obstinate are the prejudices which stand in the way) is to recognize the Indian phenomena of ownership, rent, and price as equally natural, equally respectable, equally interesting, equally worthy of scientific observation, with those of Western Europe."[32] In accepting the radical differences between primitive institutions and their Victorian counterparts, evolutionism could be harnessed to question the propriety of instituting modern institutions in the Indian context. Coupled with a functionalist holism that acknowledged the internal rationality of primitive society, the administrative lesson of evolutionary historicism would be to view caste and the village-community, rather than simply anachronisms, as rational adaptations appropriated to differing historical environments and, thus, worthy objects of imperial patronage and protection.

Yet, Maine and his successors also prided themselves that the new science of comparison contained the potential for encouraging "mutual tolerance" between Indian and Europeans, between subjects and rulers. As such, it was a tolerance that was born of a discourse of resemblance. In this respect, the revaluation of Indian barbarism stemmed from the recognition that it was "a barbarism, which contains a great part of our own civilisation, with its elements as yet inseparate and not yet unfolded."[33] Linguistic and institution filiation, stemming from common membership in the Indo-European or Aryan family, would work to diffuse national prejudices by allowing Europeans to "perceive that India of to-day teems with analogies to the past of Europe."[34] Moreover, recognizing India (and Ireland) as encasing Europe's primitive past would, Maine hoped, temper the arrogance of imperial power, the sense of superiority that had often urged the destruction of native institutions in the name of progress. The popular recognition of the scientific importance of Indian and Irish (living) antiquities could induce a distinct respect for those primitive institutions, and thus lead to better imperial governance.[35]

Maine's reconceptualization of native society could work to underpin the new language of toleration of native custom and tradition, yet its incipient relativism was ultimately constrained by a fixed temporal hierarchy between Eastern and Western institutions. While the deference to native custom in post-Mutiny Indian policy, and Maine's specific influence in this policy shift, is often characterized as a revival of older Oriental and/ or Romantic imperial policy traditions, it would be a mistake to collapse the two.[36] For example, Burke's insistence on a necessary deference to Indian law and custom was tied to rhetorical strategy and worldview that attempted to place India and Western Europe on a proximate civilizational footing. In Burke's discussion of caste, the emphasis on the intricacy of its rules was partly meant to demonstrate the ways in which Indian society, like all civilized societies, was a delicate system of customs and manners, developed through time, and therefore both politically hubristic and normatively iniquitous to overturn.[37] Even in the more orientalizing moments of Burke's discussion of caste, that is, those moments when Burke noted the singularity and uniqueness of caste, he did not conceive of differences between Indian and European institutions in a temporalized manner. Rather than working with a model of reading differences in institutions as differences in stages in a unilinear trajectory, Burke—and many Orientalist scholars as well—was more likely to accept the coexistence of different civilizational trajectories. By contrast, the late nineteenth-century defenders of caste as tradition functioned within a comparative evolutionary framework that assumed the temporal and normative superiority of Western institutions; the endorsement of caste was conditional and paternalistic, deemed valuable and acceptable only for primitive societies.

Maine's revised understanding of custom not only involved a new account of the source of custom, what counted as representative of true customary practices; custom itself was imbued with a structural significance, as the marker of systematicity and another name for the logical order of primitive society. This is another important contrast between eighteenth-century and nineteenth-century views of custom. In his critique of utilitarianism, Maine argued that the abstract theories of political economy (as well as analytic definitions of law and sovereignty) "greatly underrate the value, power, and interest of that great body of custom and inherited ideas which, they throw aside as friction. The best corrective which could be given to this disposition would be a demonstration that this 'friction' is capable of scientific analysis and scientific measurement."[38] Importantly, *custom* here is not understood as way of describing a series of isolated phenomena. Neither is it given a substantive definition, that is, as a name for a particular set of ritual or religious practices. Rather, custom is understood in structural and institutional terms and, in this manner, takes on a more anthropological and sociological resonance. Custom refers then to a customary *order*, with a rationale and systemic logic. Whereas, in the history of legal thought, custom was most often considered to be one among many sources of substantive law, in Maine's work it emerges to signify an entire legal and moral order at odds with a modern contractual and legislative system. The ideological roots of this opposition can be traced to European debates between defenders of the common law/customary law and the advocates of natural law/codified law. But in Maine's more anthropological account the difference between the two systems places less emphasis on a difference in the sources of law than on the interplay and embeddedness of legal norms in the total fabric of political, social, and economic institutions. In this way, the dichotomy of status and contract, in Maine's later works, metamorphoses and structures analogous binary formulations such as custom/market and custom/contract.

NATIVE SOCIETY IN CRISIS:
MAINE'S SOCIOLOGY OF COLONIALISM

Maine's reconceptualization of Indian society underpinned a shift in the normative assessment of native customs and traditions, which sought to repudiate the liberal agenda of reform. In contrast to liberal ruling strategies that could only view traditional social structures as various impediments to civilizing improvement, the anthropological turn reinterpreted them as foundational to the coherence and stability of native society. But what gave the anthropological-historicist argument in favor of protection its practical importance and urgency was its deep affinity with the ideological prioritization of the maintenance of order in the aftermath of the 1857 Rebellion.

In the transition from universalist civilizing justifications to culturalist alibis for the maintenance of empire, social order and stability supplanted agendas of reform as the motivating ground of imperial rule. The anthropological turn in governing knowledge, and within it the Mainian revolution in Indian anthropology, definitively located order with the integrity of "natural" social groups—joint-families, castes, tribes, clans, village-communities—now seen as the elemental units of Indian society. In accepting these traditional groups, and the customs and institutions vital to their functioning, as foundational to political stability, threats to the imperial order would be radically redefined in terms of disruptions to the integrity of native society. If in the early nineteenth century the obstacles to good government in India were found (especially by reformers) in the so-called pathologies of native society, in outmoded and barbarous customs and practices related to caste and religion, post-Mutiny policymakers were animated by a diametrically opposite fear. For them, the great danger lay in the rapid dissolution of the elemental units of native society and the concomitant transformation of India into an inchoate mass of individuals. The need to avert the impending social upheavals occasioned by the disintegration of native society became the sine qua non for the maintenance of imperial rule. Indirect rule therefore did not attain its importance solely on the strength of a normative reassessment of native society, but rather its exigency was premised on an ideological reconstruction of imperial order that made protecting native society an overarching strategic imperative.

For policymakers, Maine's work drew attention to the crisis of native society and provided a theoretical framework through which to understand its origins and consequences. For Tupper, the movement from status to contract that Maine had theorized to be a general law of social evolution was demonstrated to be a *real* movement occurring in India under British rule. Indeed, imperial rule had instigated and dramatically hastened this transition, such that "the movement of centuries of normal growth may be compressed in tens of years."[39] And it was precisely the rapidity of the transformation from an ancient society of corporate groups to a modern society of individuals that had threatened to make India ungovernable. Maine provocatively argued that the dissolution of traditional society, of intermediary associations of caste, tribe, the village, and the joint family and the customary ties that animated them, was a distinct structural consequence of contact with modern institutions under the rubric of imperial rule.

Maine offered a distinctive sociology of colonialism in which the bases of traditional society were seen as increasingly undermined by contact with the modern, where the collapse of traditional society was conceived of in terms of disruptions to a delicate social and cultural equilibrium. Although primitive societies were functional wholes, in Maine's terms, self-acting and self-generating,[40] they were also, paradoxically, under the threat of imminent dissolution. Maine's account of dissolution resembled Durkheim's notion of *anomie* in the sense that it was the necessary counterpart to a holistic view of primitive societies in which the systemic balance among coordinating social spheres could be radically undermined by changes in any one sphere. Maine employed the metaphor of contagion to describe the incremental and indirect ways in which changes in one social sphere, for example, the introduction of contract law in relations between landlord and peasant, would necessarily alter (and in this case, destabilize) the entire structure of customary ties well beyond the economic realm. In this way, British rule in India worked to undercut the social basis of native institutions. The British in India, Maine argued, "do not innovate or destroy in mere ignorance. We rather change because we cannot help it. Whatever be the nature and value of that bundle of influences which we call Progress, nothing can be more certain than that, when a society is once touched by it, it spreads like a contagion."[41] The contagion simile articulated an account of the *structural* impact of colonial rule on native institutions and practices, one in which the disintegration of traditional Indian society was conceived as enacted unwittingly, and thus all the more difficult to reverse.[42] Maine insisted that it was "by its indirect and for the most part unintended influence that the British power metamorphoses and dissolves the ideas and social forms underneath it."[43]

Maine's incipient sociology of colonialism emerged from his critical examination of imperial policy in two key domains: law and land revenue. In the analysis of both, Maine pinpointed two central sources or catalysts responsible for the dissolution of the customary basis of native society. As discussed above, Maine was critical of a number of previous accounts of Indian society—from the Orientalists to the liberal reformers—for fundamentally misunderstanding the nature of native custom and practice. He was especially suspicious of the influence of utilitarianism and the overzealous application of Benthamite legal and economic principles as abetting processes of dissolution. From *Ancient Law* through to his late lectures on *Early Law and Custom*, Maine had consistently criticized utilitarian theories of law and political economy for their inability to capture the corporate and customary logic of primitive society. Benthamism had both a normative and methodological investment in individualism. All individuals were assumed to have a universal psychological structure (the calculus of pains and pleasures) that implied that all peoples could be expected to respond in similar ways to common institutional incentives once they were abstracted and freed from the distorted influence of informal social ties and irrational customs. This implied, in the Indian case, that the state's legal machinery and land-revenue systems could and ought to work to remold, reform, and thus "free" the individual from the fetters of the caste system, the joint family, and the village-community, seen as suspect morally as well as sources of economic stagnation. Maine argued that not only did Benthamism wrongly construe custom as a mere fetter (or "friction"), and thus misjudge the salience of customary beliefs and attachments, but in its aggressive attempts at reform also seemed only to effect a distortion and destabilization of the older customary order (and never producing solid foundations of a new order).

Alongside the specific censure of misguided policies, Maine was especially attuned to the *unintended* consequences of imperial rule, "unintended" here implicating the very structure of imperial rule in the crisis of native society. Maine specifically identified the juridification of social relations—the growth of individual right—to be a necessary, destructive product of the imposition of modern imperial rule. Even when the state recognized custom as a legitimate source of law, the logic of legal sovereignty (and the influence of English rules of precedent) necessarily transformed the nature and function of custom. Once unwritten custom was incorporated into the legal order, it was immediately converted into written law, and its observance was backed by the coercive authority of state. The effect of British power, even when ruling through some deference to native law and custom, necessarily worked to distort and undermine the self-legislative, adjudicative, and sanctioning capacity of customary legal authorities, such as the caste or village *panchayat* or council. Likewise, in the domain of land revenue, revenue settlements (even when settling with corporate groups such as the village-community) necessarily introduced the language and structure of legal right into the domain of customary practices. Controversies about the apportionment of property rights inevitably involved the state in some sort of legal adjudication between rival customary claims. Again, the mere establishment of the legal and administrative machinery of the modern state fundamentally altered the structural context in which native society had functioned.[44]

Most significantly, the combined effect of misguided policies and the structural conditions of imperial rule was to perilously quicken the transition from a customary to a contractual order. The rapid pace of the destruction of the authority of corporate groups such as the village-community led to the unmitigated growth of personal right. The triumph of right without the concomitant emergence of an appropriate, limiting moral framework enabled the equation of right with mere license, egoism, or caprice. The empirical examples of the play of unstructured individual right in India, to which Maine referred, centered on the growing number of claims for the division of joint properties and testamentary successions (the use of wills) that actively encroached on the traditional claims of the joint family. He also pointed to the general rise in litigation, spurred on by agile native lawyers, as enabling a culture of petty competition to take root over customary bonds of reciprocal obligation. Maine concluded, "unfortunately for us, we have created the sense of legal right before we have created a proportionate power of distinguishing good and evil in the law upon which the legal right depends."[45] And it was the "growth on all sides of the sense of individual right" that represented "the greatest change which has come over the people of India and the change which has added most seriously to the difficulty of governing them."[46]

Mainian critics of the Benthamite legal system, who attributed a host of societal and moral ills from its intrusion into native society, sought a remedy in the revival of customary law and courts. More dramatically, in context of land policy, Maine's influence would trigger a wholesale shift in agrarian strategy. Followers of Maine considered the rapid breakdown of the customary order and traditional socioeconomic structures to be specifically responsible for numerous forms of agrarian unrest. For them, the Mutiny's expansion into a general agrarian revolt was enabled by liberal and utilitarian economic policies that sought, on the one hand, to dispossess intermediate quasi-feudal landholders in favor of peasant proprietors, and, on the other, to convert customary tenancy claims into legal rights. Both policy trajectories, driven by arguments from classical political economy for greater efficiency and productivity, instead seemingly spurred mass agrarian discontent and indebtedness. In the context of this debate, Maine's impact—his critique of utilitarianism, his reconceptualization of native society and the warning about the dangers of its dissolution—instigated, according to Dewey, a great reversal in strategies of agrarian reform.[47] Dewey argues that between 1857 and 1906 the Government of India altered its entire agrarian strategy, repeatedly legislating against laissez-faire market relations.[48] This period was marked by an interest in the rehabilitation of native customs and institutions to avert the political and economic instability that supposedly sprang from their erosion; protection of the village-community was thus central to new agrarian strategies. Maine's self-professed disciples, as noted above, rather than disclaim the influence of caste and custom like their utilitarian predecessors, tended to see in traditional institutions such as the village-community forces of social stability. Ibbetson, Tupper, and Wilson would become the central architects of this revisionist strategy. The hallmark achievement of this agrarian strategy was the passage of the Punjab Alienation of Land Act (1900), which prohibited land sales between members of different tribes (thus violating the most basic principle of laissez-faire and confirming caste formations).

In post-Mutiny India, Maine's importance was to undergird a general intellectual shift toward a presumptive suspicion of the practical effects of economic modernization and utilitarian reform. More generally, Maine inaugurated a theoretical framework that predicted social disorder as a necessary by-product of imperial rule. The dissolution of native society under the impact of British imperialism was a vivid example of the ways in which the colonizing process set traditional and modern societies into a dramatic, living, and potentially devastating opposition. In Maine's sociology of colonialism, the encounter between these opposed social forms necessarily led to conflict, a conflict that inevitably hastened the dissolution of older ancient, customary forms of life. Significantly, the conflict was specifically theorized as an apolitical and unintentional one—a structural conflict for which imperial power was never deemed wholly responsible.

This warning about the "dissolution of society" under the imperative of empire served to be the ideological linchpin of the theory and practice of indirect rule. It provided a radically new account of what constituted threats to imperial rule and a new rationale for continued imperial presence. For advocates of native institutions, Maine's cogent account of the disruptive, structural impact of colonial/modern institutions upon native society vividly demonstrated the urgent need for protection. The sympathetic portrayal of native society was coupled with a sociology of colonialism that not only imputed avowed reform and intervention as causes of instability but also implied that everywhere traditional societies were inherently fragile in the context of modernity. In this sense, the new account of threats was intimately tied to a generic characterization of a traditional society in crisis, that is, a society struggling to survive under the traumatic impact of contact with the West.

A. C. LYALL AND THE POLITICAL FOUNDATIONS OF INDIRECT RULE

> The danger of Indian society lies in the prospect of its too
> rapid disintegration, partly under pressure of the restless
> commercial spirit of the West, and partly through the
> hasty exchange, in the sphere of politics and sociology,
> of old lamps for new.[49]

While administrators like Ibbetson and Tupper appropriated Maine's insights to advocate policies reinforcing the socioeconomic functions of caste formations and village-communities, Alfred C. Lyall, Maine's most respected intellectual successor, expanded Maine's warning about the dissolution of native society to the domain of politics and political institutions. In doing so, Lyall developed a sophisticated political theory of indirect rule that worked through the sociology of colonialism to reformulate the appropriate political foundations of British rule in India. If Maine's insights had served to cement a historicist critique of classical political economy and the direct application of Western economic models and concepts to India, Lyall analogously located a growing source of discontent and dislocation in the uncritical transplantation of Western political models, of concepts of representation, self-government, and sovereignty.

Lyall and Maine shared a profound sense of the transformative impact British rule had had upon the character of the people and institutions under its dominion. For Lyall, these processes of change had only increased with the cumulative expansion and consolidation of British rule such that India was now "the scene of the most rapid transitions, morally, materially, and politically, that have ever been recorded in the history of nations."[50] One of Maine's most important accomplishments was to alert administrators to the enormity of the challenge posed by this revolutionary overturning of the old order, and demonstrate the practical means by which to "guide and regulate the process by which the separate groups are very gradually dissolving into a population with some of the rudimentary characteristics of a great territorial nationality, under the pressure of a government that has introduced and enforces certain general principles of modern polity."[51] In this task, Maine carefully mediated between reformers and Indian "officialism," between the innovators "who thought that political institutions could be imported like steam machinery, warranted to stand any climate and to benefit every community" and the conservatives who opposed all change and "gravely distrusted European interference."[52] Maine was especially effective at tempering the "ardour of the ideologist," whom Lyall ridiculed for "avoiding the extremely difficult business of discovering exactly what suited the very special circumstances of modern India" and adopting "the much easier expedient of taking facsimile casts from English models, whereby they saved the trouble of invention and gained credit, as Englishmen, for magnanimity."[53]

But while "Maine's method of finding a *modus vivendi* and a point of conciliation between ancient and modern ideas displayed a political instinct invaluable for legislation for India," for Lyall, "our chief concern should now be . . . to arrest what [Maine] called 'the trituration of societies,' and to retard the dissolution of numerous groups and petty jurisdictions into a vast incoherent multitude under one overburdened foreign government."[54] This process of dissolution and the political instability it produced stemmed in part, for Lyall, from the general political predicament of empires, especially Asiatic empires, and their tendencies toward overcentralization. These tendencies had been perilously exacerbated by the impact of modern principles of education, economy, and politics under British dominion. Together, these processes, in hastening the dissolution of native social forms, unleashed a social and political uniformity and leveling that threatened to undermine the very foundations of British rule.

In contrast to Maine's interest in village-communities as the primary location of dissolution, Lyall focused instead on the fate of Rajput tribal kingdoms to demonstrate the political consequences of this process. These tribal groupings were taken to be an Indian example of the kinds of autonomous, aristocratic orders that were central to the development of Western political institutions. The Rajput states, partly through British protection, had alone resisted the centralizing, destructive power of the Mughal Empire. For Lyall, the fact that Mughal rule had seemingly not penetrated so deeply into Indian society so as to overturn local customs and religious attachments did not mean that it had had no effect on India's political development. The oppressive presence of Mughal rule, coupled with the internal tendency of castes to continuously divide rather than expand beyond the model of a "natural" social group, had obstructed the formation of political institutions in India. In destroying rival intermediary powers, Mughal rule had forced India into an "arrested" state of development; local clans and tribes that ought to have amalgamated into larger, territorial units were stymied.

What made the Rajput states important as models for political development was that not only did "these States contain the only ancient institutions in India which have shown stability," but they were also the only ones "worthy of free men."[55] The recurring contest between chiefs and noblemen that was central to Rajput political history was, albeit in a primitive form, akin to the political antagonisms between the king and his nobles that tempered and checked the growth of sovereign power in the West.[56] In his characterization and assertion of the benefits of the natural equilibrium between rival political orders, Lyall sought to apply Tocqueville's political lessons (especially the Tocqueville of *The Old Regime*) to a set of Indian problems. As Lyall writes, "these Rajput societies, held together by all cumbrous bonds and stays of a primitive organism, present far more promising elements of future development than powerful and well-ordered despotisms of the normal Asiatic type, where a mixed multitude are directly under the sway of one ruler, however able, who degrades or dignifies at his will."[57]

Moreover, like Tocqueville, Lyall saw the most pressing threats to the survival of these societies in the modern presumption toward state centralization. And it was in their desire for order and progress, for a uniform and efficient form of administration, that British officials were in danger of embarking on exactly that kind of program of centralization that destroyed the vitality of mediating political institutions and orders. The natural tendency of the imperial bureaucrat, in the name of peace and standardization, was to strengthen the quasi-sovereign power of the native ruler against these disorderly nobles. But, "if these rough hewn obstructions to helpless equality under the orders of a central government are once smoothed away they will assuredly never be built up again; and as there is nothing that could take their place, the tribal chieftain will have converted himself into a petty autocrat, responsible to his doings only to the paramount power which sustains him."[58] The real danger of this shortsighted policy, besides the potential for consolidating forms of native despotism, was that the destruction of native political forms was undertaken without any idea of "how the void which they will leave can be filled up."[59] Attending to this void was vital, and by ignoring it Britain, Lyall feared, was sowing the seeds of its own destruction. In Lyall's historical schema, empires foundered through a political isolation bred from overcentralization. By leveling out intermediate and local centers of power, empires cut their bonds with subordinate orders, and became "top-heavy towers." And, in times of turbulence, this isolation led to insecurity and instability, leaving no outlets of local support.

Thus, for Lyall, the basic principle of stable government was decentralization of a Tocquevillian kind, based upon, as far as possible, the natural divisions and groupings of the subcontinent. But if these "subdivisions are vanishing," they must be substituted or reconstituted by "other administrative and territorial groupings. . . . Otherwise the English dominion in India may drift towards that condition of over-centralised isolation, with shallow foundations and inadequate support, which renders an empire as top-heavy as an over-built tower, and which is unquestionably an element of political instability."[60] To avoid such a fate, Britain had to embark on a policy of building up native "pillars" to support the British tower, most importantly in alliances with native subpolities like the Rajput states but also through the protection of more informal institutions like caste and religion.[61]

Yet, it was also these same traditional institutions, Lyall here concurring with Maine, that were breaking under the pressure of British rule. Lyall was especially concerned with the cumulative impact of Western education on the transformation of religious belief. The spread of English education seemingly induced a kind of religious malaise and spiritual unrest among the most advanced native populations. With the dissemination of modes of scientific reasoning, English education stimulated religious skepticism and doubt, "the cutting of anchors instead of hauling them up, so that in the next emergency there are none to throw out."[62] Less certain that the destruction of traditional religious belief would lead to a known outcome, namely a secularism of a modern European kind, Lyall argued that without knowing the end point of the current spiritual interregnum, British rule unwittingly advanced the prospects for new and potentially more threatening religious formations. In addition to the introduction of modern education, the other revolutionary impact of British rule lay in modern technological advances, such as the railway, which unleashed unprecedented forms of social contact and coordination. These new social conditions may indeed be allowing for the growth of large-scale (potentially national) religious movements. Religion, which for Lyall had historically been the grounds for endless divisions into and rivalry among castes, sects, and creeds, now could become the greatest unifying force in India, but also one that fundamentally threatened the basis of British rule.

Lyall, like Maine, was not an imperial conservative of the older type. They shared none of the earlier Orientalists' reverence or sympathy with native institutions. While Orientalists often compared Indian and English institutions with a view toward placing both on a proximate civilizational footing, Maine's and Lyall's scholarly studies were premised on the radical distinction between the two. For Maine, village-communities needed to be understood and appreciated precisely in their difference from modern institutions. Lyall, in his study of Rajput society, criticized earlier accounts, such as James Tod's famous *Annals and Antiquities of Rajasthan*,[63] for comparing Rajput institutions to feudal institutions. Rather, for Lyall, these kingdoms were construed as specifically *tribal*, that is, at a stage of clan formation that was far removed from the advanced state of feudal society. Thus Lyall's argument for the necessity of building upon natural divisions and institutions was neither sentimental nor nostalgic; it was premised upon political concerns that their dissolution and leveling would lead to instability. In fact, in many ways, it was much more insidious and circular; Lyall not only premised the justification of British rule on the divisive nature of Indian society that would, without the imperial presence, decay into anarchy and chaos, he also advocated policies to maintain those divisions to underwrite the continuation of British rule.[64]

Lyall (like Maine) recognized as a fundamental fact of modern India that the transition from status to contract, from ancient to modern society, which had been instigated by British rule, could never be fully reversed. What was to be prioritized was the preserving modification of native institutions, and resistance to all attempts at quickening the process:

> All of our European experiments in social science have taught us the unwisdom of demolishing old-world fabrics which no one is yet prepared to replace by anything else. Caste, for instance, looks unnecessary and burdensome, it is wildly abused by Europeans, to whom the Brahmanic rules of behaviour seem unmeaning and unpractical; but these things will tumble quite fast enough without our knocking out their keystones by premature legislation. It is hardly our interest to bring them down with a crash. We have ourselves to overcome the rather superficial contempt which an European naturally conceives for societies and habits of thought different from those within the range of his ordinary experience; and also to avoid instilling too much of the destructive spirit into the mind of young India; remembering that for English and natives the paramount object is now to preserve social continuity.[65]

Lyall, again, targets Western education as an acute and growing concern because contrary to the expectations of "political philosophers like the French economists, and the two Mills in England . . . public instruction, when applied largely and unexpectedly . . . operates as quick solvent of

the old social order."[66] Moreover, in disseminating "ideas of abstract political right, and the germ of representative institutions, among a people
. . . in a country where local liberties and habits of self-government have
been long obliterated or have never existed,"[67] liberal education threatened to breed native "ideologists." Unmoored from traditional religion,
they become instead proselytes of extreme innovation who have "a sort
of metaphysical belief in the absolute efficacy of institutions apart from
the circumstances or character of the people on whom they are to be
conferred."[68] Education was not only contributing to political instability
by undermining the ideational grounds of traditional society, it also generated new forms of discontent and disaffection.

Lyall's trepidation about the effects of Western education in India
serves as a sharp contrast to the crucial place that education had had in
the liberal model of empire, both as the central pivot of its agenda of
social and political reform and as a practical means to inculcate allegiance
to the imperial project. Macaulay had famously argued for the expansion
of English education as the means for the creation of "a class of interpreters between us and the millions whom we govern; a class of persons Indian
in blood and colour, but English in tastes, in opinions, in morals and in
intellect."[69] This westernized native intelligentsia would not just serve as
mediators of imperial dominion but through their active identification
with English civilization could be relied on as natural allies in the imperial
project. Western education sought to instill an investment and attachment
by native subjects to the structures and ideologies of British rule, not only
legitimating empire as a joint project of modernizing reform but also as
the practical grounds of imperial stability.

Advocates of indirect rule, from Lyall to Cromer and Lugard, consistently argued that Western education, and thus the liberal imperial project
as whole, failed in some deep sense, neither producing loyal subjects nor
lending security to the imperial enterprise. For them, the exorbitant enthusiasm for education was part and parcel of a now-discredited faith in the
ability of imperial power to radically reshape native society. It was a prime
example of a kind of naive enthusiasm for policies of assimilation and
anglicization—for the uncritical application of Western models to India—
that had already been proven to foment native disenchantment and unrest. Maine, Lyall, and Cromer were, in different degrees, skeptical of the
ability of education to achieve total assimilation in moral and political
habits. More specifically, Western education seemed unable to convert
assimilation to Western culture into political allegiance and political stability, for it was, of course, these same westernized native classes who
were the most vocal critics of imperial rule and consistent agitators for
greater inclusion in governing structures. Moreover, for Lyall and Cromer,
as well as Lugard, westernized natives had become increasingly alienated

from the average native. They could serve neither as mediators nor inter-preters, and thus were unable to fulfill any true *representative* function.[70] In rejecting assimilation as an achievable or strategic good, the architects of indirect rule sought instead to secure British power through cultivating fidelity from "naturally" conservative classes, in the allegiance of tradi-tional elites and the contentment of the masses.

Apprehension about the dissolution of traditional society under the ru-bric of modern imperial rule, when turned to the political realm, gener-ated a wholesale critique of the importation of Western models of repre-sentation and self-government. The rejection of the liberal project of assimilation, buttressed by an anthropological invocation of the necessary and radical difference between East and West, led to a presumptive dis-avowal of the very possibility of educating subject peoples toward self-government. For Cromer, representative government in the West was founded upon a "complex conception of ordered liberty," which, if it could ever be transplanted to India or Egypt, "will probably be the work, not of generations, but of centuries."[71]

FROM INDIA TO AFRICA: THE CULMINATION OF INDIRECT RULE

By the time of the "scramble for Africa," at the height of Europe's territo-rial expansion into Asia and Africa, liberal endeavors to civilize and mod-ernize native society had been effectively reversed and sidelined by the prioritization of stability and security as the watchwords of late imperial policy. In the wake of 1857, imperial order was thought to be best achieved through a pragmatic policy of least interference in native affairs. By the turn of the century, this incipient principle of noninterference meta-morphosed into a systematic argument for the protection and rehabilita-tion of native institutions. Indirect rule would become the foundational doctrine of late imperial governance, enacting a transcontinental shift in ruling practices in India, Southeast Asia, and Africa. And with its enlarged application, its institutional structure and philosophical justification would receive ever-more-sophisticated elaborations.

In practice, indirect rule would assume a multiplicity of institutional forms, that is, the specific native structures of authority deemed most appropriate for protection would vary from dependency to dependency. Yet, what unified indirect rule was a distinct account of threats to the imperial order—namely, the impending collapse of native societies—and that this disintegration could be remedied by the preservation and incor-poration of native institutions into imperial power structures. And while indirect rule was often, perhaps even primarily, legitimated as a vehicle for stabilizing imperial rule, it would be increasingly defended normatively as a practice of cultural toleration, one that recognized and respected the specificity of native society. Traditional structures of authority were seen to command the natural and spontaneous allegiance of the native and thus thought to provide a more efficient support for imperial authority as well as a better conduit for securing native aspirations. At its limit, with the opposition to the alienating impact of imposing Western institutions, *progress* itself would be redefined as better attained through the gradual modification of the natives' culturally specific traditions and practices.

In British Malaya indirect rule involved the transposition of the Indian residential system, consolidating British power through treaties with native sultans. Sir Frank Swettenham oversaw this transition to formal British control and bluntly defended the maintenance of native rulership as a better alternative to reform-minded policies: "the Malay is a Muhammedan and looks to his Raja as the ruling authority. The ballot box makes no appeal, and self-government has no attractions. If we could order him differently, give him a new idea of life, we should only make him unhappy."[72] As in India, Malaya was to be governed through a plural legal order that demarcated subordinate jurisdictions on the basis of ethnicity and religion. In the same year as Swettenham's treaty that inaugurated the Federated Malay States (1874), Britain formally annexed Fiji. Fiji's first governor, Sir Arthur Gordon, self-consciously sought to implement what he considered to be a new and more principled experiment in native government, anticipating the more expansive normative claims for indirect rule that its twentieth-century defenders would advance.

In the case of Fiji, calls for the protection of native society became the linchpin of a humanitarian argument for direct British rule, and conferral of Crown Colony status. With this in mind, Gordon defended the preservation of native society tout court, not merely as politically expedient—not just in terms of the strategic importance of gaining the support of native chiefs—but also as an endangered, valid form of life in urgent need of imperial protection.[73] Gordon was an enthusiast of historical and comparative methods and a self-styled follower of Maine's who argued for recognition of the integrated character of native society, that native society was a total social system of ideas and practices such that disruptions in one realm (that is, economy or leadership) could undo the coherence of the whole.[74] The disposition to preserve was buoyed by a worldview that, with Maine, warned that contact with the West would inevitably undermine the social basis of native society. In Fiji, this kind of destructive contact with modernity was associated with the influx of European settlers, whose attempt to develop a plantation economy had led to the unregulated appropriation of native lands (and a host of social and political upheavals that underwrote the pleas for accession to direct British rule). Gordon's program of native government began with the reversal of this

trend, reestablishing native authority over land through legislative codification of customary practices that severely restricted the alienation and
sale of communal property.[75] Gordon applied Maine's theories directly in
the construction and codification of chiefly authority and the protection
of communal land linked to the ideal pattern of the village-community.[76]
But rehabilitation was to be the first phase in an alternative schema of
development, for it was "only through the village community system that
Fiji could be civilized." For Gordon, "it was not enough to abstain from
seeking hastily to replace native institutions by unreal imitations of European models, but that it was also of the utmost importance to seize the
spirit in which native institutions had been framed, and develop to the
utmost extent the capacities of the people for the management of their
own affairs, without exciting their suspicion or destroying their self-
respect."[77] Gordon's experiment in Fiji envisaged a model of native government that in rejecting the imposition of Western institutions also
sought to appropriate and append the language of self-determination and
progress to the paternalistic project of cultural protection.

It was in colonial Africa, however, that indirect rule reached its zenith
in terms of the breadth of application, institutional articulation, and theoretical elaboration. The theoretical framework of indirect rule in Africa
was deeply indebted to post-Mutiny debates in India, but with an important difference. As D. A. Low has argued, "in India the actions which
the British took to prevent 'the dissolution of society' were essentially
curative, in Africa preventative."[78] While indirect rule in India was primarily a remedial formula in which attempts to resurrect native institutions were limited in scope, in Africa it took on preemptive, and therefore
more systematic, character.[79] The preventative or preemptive aspect of the
policy attests to how deeply indirect rule was implicated in a transformed
ideological framework that predicted social trauma and upheaval as the
inevitable consequences of modern imperial rule.

Lord Lugard's *The Dual Mandate in British Tropical Africa* (1922) not
only contained the most influential statement of the policy of indirect rule
but also was widely hailed as offering its most cogent moral justification.
Lugard sought to forestall radical and liberal critics of British expansion
in Africa, who had argued that it was exploitative and financially burden-
some.[80] Against these claims, Lugard's *dual mandate* argued for the twofold imperial duty of developing the material resources of Africa "for the
mutual benefit of the people and of mankind in general,"[81] and, at the
same time, shepherding "the native races in their progress to a higher
place."[82] For Lugard, the latter objective was framed not by the principle
of assimilation or the introduction of "progressive self-government on
Western models."[83] Rather than imposing "alien, democratic systems,"
Lugard argued that "liberty and self-development can be best secured to

the native population by leaving them free to manage their own affairs through their own rulers, proportionately to their degree of advancement, under the guidance of the British staff, and subject to the laws and policy of the administration."[84] The "freedom" of self-management was, however, a highly circumscribed affair, where native chiefs were "unfettered in their control over their people" but strictly "subordinate to the control of the protecting Power in certain well-defined directions."[85] The policy of indirect rule elaborated by Lugard was far more complex and systematic than the mere enactment of a principle of noninterference in native affairs. Lugard outlined a specific formula framed by three central elements: a Native Authority or Administration, a Native Court (administering customary law), and a Native Treasury, all coalescing around the power of the tribal chief. The guiding principles of imperial administration were "decentralization" and "continuity" through cooperation with subordinate native authorities at the local level. Lugard's model of indirect rule, as Mahmood Mamdani has argued, embodied a specific state-form, namely, a decentralized despotism in which native authorities were defined by a territorialized form of institutional segregation. The boundaries of local administrative units—the parameters of decentralized rule—were first and foremost *cultural* boundaries, meant to correspond with the authority of the native community (that is, tribal authority).[86] In the implementation of this model of indirect rule, what constituted native community, custom, and tradition were redefined, reified, and territorialized through this mode of institutional segregation.

Trusteeship in Lugard's formulation functioned in tandem with a view of native administration as the most secure method of maintaining law and order. In 1930, Donald Cameron restated the main purposes of native administration as the vehicle that will shape "the political and social future of the natives in a manner which will afford them a permanent share in the administration of the country on lines which they themselves understand and can appreciate, building up at the same time a bulwark against political agitation and averting the social chaos of which signs have already manifested themselves in other countries similarly situated."[87] For Lugard and Cameron, the examples of political agitation and social chaos to be avoided were taken explicitly from what they considered the manifest failures of *direct* rule in British India: the Mutiny of 1857 and the rise of the Indian nationalist movement led by an English-educated elite. While it is certainly true that administrators like Lugard construed the early experiments in indirect rule to be expedient and cost-effective solutions,[88] what was considered practically necessary was itself determined by an underlying worldview that redefined what constituted threats to imperial rule. These perceived threats stemmed, in different ways, from a generic characterization of native society in crisis, that is, a society struggling to survive under the traumatic impact of contact with the West. This transformed view, which saw enforced modernization and transformative reform as potential sources of colonial disorder, was exported from post-Mutiny India to Africa by prominent colonial officers, such as Lord Lugard, Lord Cromer, and Malcolm Hailey.[89]

For Africa, the main source of social dislocation was seen to lay in the decay of tribal authority and tribal institutions with the advent of European intrusion. As opposed to the village-community in India and Fiji, the tribe was taken to be the characteristic unit of African society, and invested with the same generic features of the nineteenth-century model of traditional society. For colonial administrators and social anthropologists alike the tribe appeared as a closed, corporate, and consensual organ whose authority was thought to define the conceptual horizon and identity of the African. The tribal system was marked as simultaneously a cultural unit and a sociopolitical system, founded on kinship and genealogical membership, and institutionalized through common customary law and collective control of land. The break-up of this system was thought to presage nothing short of a social catastrophe; Lugard warned that in the absence of the constraints definitive of the tribal system, all the ruling power would have left to deal with was the "rabble."[90] Like Maine and Lyall, Lugard was concerned that the rapid dissolution of the traditional order would necessitate social atomization and anomie, and "denationalized" and "detribalized" natives would constitute an unstable, undifferentiated mass.[91] Jan Smuts similarly warned that when "freed from all traditional moral and social discipline, the native just emerging from barbarism, may throw all restraints to the winds," native society would be dissolve into "vaste [*sic*] hordes of detribalized natives," "human atoms" unleashing "possibilities of universal Bolshevism and chaos which no friend of the natives, of the orderly civilization of this continent, could contemplate with equanimity."[92]

Lugard identified Western education as not only another contributing cause in the undermining of traditional authority but also one that threatened to be the most politically disruptive. It was argued that nationalist agitation and unrest in India (as well as in Egypt and Ireland) stemmed in part from a wrongheaded, liberal educational policy, which, in emphasizing "a literary education on European lines" had only produced discontent, hostility, and ingratitude.[93] The danger of introducing self-government in India, for Lugard, was that it would be dominated by a minority (or oligarchy) of Europeanized natives who were not only disaffected but also unrepresentative of the mass of native society. This divergence between an educated class and the masses was seen as even more extreme in the case of Africa, such that Lugard liked to claim that the illiterate native was "more ready to give his confidence to a white man than to an educated native."[94] Simultaneously alienated from his traditional life *and* rebuffed from white colonial civil society, the Europeanized native was seen as caught in limbo, psychologically strained and dangerously unsatisfied; the Europeanized natives, in Lugard's vision, were an unstable and untrustworthy class upon whom neither future self-government nor collaborative arrangements could depend. Proper education policy, instead of making natives "unsuited to and ill-contented with their mode of life," should aim to "fit the ordinary individual to fill a useful part of his environment . . . [to] use his abilities for the advancement of the community and not to its detriment" and thus "train a generation able to achieve ideals of their own, without slavish imitation of Europeans."[95]

Proponents of indirect rule in being acutely attuned to the dangers contact with the West posed to the sanctity of native society also, it was argued, recognized the vitality of African society. Marjery Perham defended indirect rule from those critics who wanted to "supersede" rather than conserve native culture by arguing that indirect rule was a more characteristically British political principle,[96] and born of greater knowledge of the true nature of African society:

> we begin to understand how African cultures were integrated and so to recognize the functions of certain customs which seemed to our grandfathers the perverse aberrations of the heathen. We identify in miniature and under primitive disguise the elements common to all human societies, and we begin to question whether those elements, instead of being wholly destroyed, might not be re-expressed in forms more serviceable to the needs of today.[97]

For Perham, the relevant element of African society that could shape its future progress was the tribe that, under the policy of indirect rule, was invested with a new kind of legitimacy and authority. As she writes, "the preservation of native law and custom is . . . a transitional stage by which Africans may in their own right become members of the civilized world, not as individuals, but as communities."[98]

The architects of indirect rule and its most authoritative apologists came to hail the policy as a more progressive alternative to the civilizing mission, now seen as embodying distinctively British principles of moderation and liberal tolerance. In his Rhodes Lectures of 1929, Commonwealth statesman and former Prime Minister of the Union of South Africa Jan Smuts confirmed this revised account: "the British Empire does not stand for assimilation of its peoples into a common type, it does not stand for standardization, but for the fullest freest development of its people along their own specific lines."[99] For Smuts, British policy represented the learned evolution of European thinking about Africa that had previously erred when the "principles of the French Revolution which had emancipated Europe were applied to Africa," and "liberty, equality and fraternity" were thought to be able to "turn bad Africans into good Europeans." But, he argued, "nothing could be worse for Africa than the application of a policy, the object or tendency of which would destroy the basis of this African type, to de-Africanize the African and turn him . . . into a pseudo-European."[100]

> If Africa has to be redeemed, if Africa has to make her own contribution to the world, if Africa is to take her rightful place among the continents, we shall have to proceed on different lines and evolve a policy which will not force her institutions into an alien European mould, but which will preserve her unity with her own past, conserve what is precious in her past, and build her future progress and civilization on specifically African foundations. That should be the new policy, and such a policy would be in line with the traditions of the British Empire.[101]

Indirect rule and its model of native government was heralded as a distinctively British solution to the dilemmas of imperial rule, and proffered as a guiding example for the newly created mandate system of the League of Nations.

NATIVE SOCIETY AS ALIBI

Maine's original account of a native society in crisis was his most innovative and influential contribution to nineteenth-century imperial thought and practice. The provocative notion that modern imperial rule had forced a potentially catastrophic confrontation between traditional and modern societies would undergird a new rationale for the maintenance of empire, one that also implied a new framework for the structure of imperial rule. As the primacy task of empire was redefined as a bulwark against the imminent collapse of native society, imperial rule became implicated in a political strategy of protecting, preserving, and rehabilitating traditional society. Indirect rule was grounded in the conviction that the imperial order would be best sustained by the insinuation of imperial power in the customary order of native society rather than through its repudiation and transformation. That empire could be simultaneously cause and cure for the crisis of native society became an alibi for permanent imperial rule.

Indirect rule functioned to decisively shift the burden of imperial legitimation onto native societies, to constitute native society itself as an alibi of empire. Moreover, with this shift, not only were the moral foundations of empire evacuated and recharacterized as a necessity emergent from the crisis of native society, but also the structure of imperial domination was masked through its insinuation into native structures of authority. As a form of rule, it was often construed as merely an epiphenomenal construct "indirectly" ruling through preexisting native institutions. As castes and tribes became marked as intransigent to modernizing reform and the stabilizing units of social cohesion, they could be incorporated into governing strategies, as a mode through which "to both buttress and displace colonial authority."[102] In its ideological self-understanding, indirect rule would appear as a kind of defensive realism, as a compromise with and recognition of native agency. Even as it enabled the consolidation of direct imperial rule across Africa and Southeast Asia, in its most laudatory representations indirect rule and its deference to the logic of native tradition would be heralded as a practice of cultural tolerance and cosmopolitan pluralism.

——— CODA ———

LIBERALISM AND EMPIRE RECONSIDERED

WITH THE END OF THE COLD WAR and the declining salience of third-worldist defenses of state sovereignty (and the doctrine of sovereign equality), we have witnessed a remarkable resurgence of arguments for empire as a necessary and stabilizing force in global politics. Most strikingly, distinctly liberal arguments seeking to justify imperial projects in normative terms have come to the forefront of political debate with increasing urgency in the aftermath of the events of September 11, 2001 and, most consequentially, in the lead-up to the U.S. invasion of Iraq in 2003. What is particularly conspicuous in the revival of theories of benevolent empire, many of which explicitly draw upon the history of the British Empire for comforting precedents and instructive analogies, is the unabashed moralism and idealism of the defense of the use of force. In the case of Iraq, strategic goals were reconceived as a moral project, namely, the global export of liberal democracy, an ideological reconstitution that was given sustenance by a related set of debates about humanitarian intervention and human rights that likewise sought to inject an ethical framework into foreign policy considerations. Whether we take these discourses to be hopelessly naive or cynical mystifications, I want to suggest that liberal imperialism—as a framework of justification—sets into motion a logic of explanation that inevitably undoes the confidence in and the coherence of liberalism's moral commitments.

The period of aggressive and moralistic rhetoric in favor of military intervention in Iraq, which came to an end as it became clear that the invading army would not be greeted as "liberators," was followed by growing doubts about the "readiness" of Iraqis for the boon of democracy. This was partly expressed as a problem of perception; the good intentions of the so-called liberators were mistakenly viewed as an aggressive demonstration of American power, thus hindering the United States' ability to win the "hearts and minds" of not only Iraqis but also the Arab world more generally. As the conflict escalated and insurgency expanded, this milder hesitation and attempted corrective was eclipsed by elaborate culturalist explanations of the failure of the swift transition to democracy. From ethnographic accounts of the salience of tribal systems of political patronage, histories of entrenched ethnic and sectarian conflicts among Kurds, Sunnis, and Shi'as, to the allegedly deep incompatibility between Islam and secular modernity, these explanations effectively shifted the burden of failure to the cultural capacities (or lack thereof) of Iraqis to reform or accommodate themselves to the norms of liberal democracy. In the most extreme characterizations, resistance was rendered wholly inscrutable or nihilistic, such that political persuasion as a viable strategy had to give way to the language of brute force.

As liberal ambitions for the democratic transformation of Iraqi society came to heel in the face of an emboldened Iraqi resistance, these culturalist explanations also called into question the original moral agenda of the occupation. If the war could not be won in the terms originally set out, that is, once it was admitted that the ambitious criteria of a just intervention could not be met, then the justification of continued U.S. presence had to be recalibrated. No longer framed by a moral imperative to transform Iraq into a "beacon of democracy" in the Middle East, the necessity of continued occupation is understood to be a consequence of the pathologies of Iraqi society, the duty to stay now redefined as a necessary bulwark against impending civil war. The justification of the war has become so dissociated from its initial moral and strategic agenda that the onus of ending the intervention is squarely placed on the shoulders of the Iraqi government and the Iraqi people, increasingly berated for not taking on more of the political and financial responsibility for reconstruction.

This regressive dynamic from high moral ambition, followed by disillusionment, leading finally to disavowal, resonates in revealing ways with the fate of nineteenth-century liberal imperialism analyzed in this book. I want to suggest that the striking similarity between the shifting rhetoric of justification around the Iraq war and the career of nineteenth-century imperial ideology brings to light an important dynamic internal to the political logic of modern empire. It is a logic that is sequentially structured by moral idealism, culturalist explanation, and retroactive alibis for imperial rule. The fragility of norms of universality, equality, and tolerance that is exposed in the practice of liberal imperialism emerges less (or, in any case, not only) from a theoretical inconsistency within but as a contradictory political entailment of liberalism.

One of the central tasks of this book has been to outline the distinctive conceptual foundations of late empire and its most characteristic form of governance, indirect rule. I have sought to demonstrate how indirect rule as an ideological formation emerged as a reaction to, and critique of, liberal models of empire, and thus was strategically, temporally, and logically linked to the collapse of that earlier imperial agenda. In doing so, I want to suggest that understanding the story of late imperial rule as an outcome of a certain kind of liberal predicament yields an alternative stance from which to assess the limits and hazards of liberalism's imperial projects. Focusing on the work of Henry Maine drew attention to how the intellectual coordinates of nineteenth-century liberalism shifted in relation to imperial politics. Not only did Maine play a crucial role in articulating the theoretical agenda of late imperial rule, but his complex relationship to liberalism—as both a defender and prominent critic—also locates him at the center of its discursive reconstitution and political realignment. Throughout his career, Maine would remain committed to the basic components of a recognizably liberal agenda—to free trade, freedom of contract, limited government, that is, to the ideology of laissez-faire individualism. Yet, his defense of liberalism was underscored by theoretical premises, historicist and conservative in nature, that ultimately turned to a frontal assault against notions of equality and the value of democracy. The turn against liberal imperialism was intimately tied to the crisis of Victorian liberalism itself, dramatically revealed in the splitting of the Liberal Party over the issue of Irish Home Rule. Simmering tensions among liberals on questions of empire, evidenced in mounting disillusionment from the Mutiny and the Eyre controversy, to the Ilbert Bill and the Irish Land Acts, culminated in the crisis over Home Rule and the abandonment of the Liberal Party by some of its most prominent intellectuals—most strikingly by intellectuals with deep investments in imperial debates, such as Maine, Stephen, Lyall, and Seeley.

In one sense, the focus on late empire as a distinctively anti- or postliberal formation is offered as a corrective to the overwhelming emphasis, especially among political theorists and intellectual historians, on the liberal imperialism of James and John Stuart Mill as the definitive ideological form of nineteenth-century British empire. This tendency to assume that the liberal civilizing mission was the most important and most potent justification of empire often works to elide from view the variety of forms of imperial legitimation as well as the wider range of imperial political thought (that is, the numerous ways that political thought was shaped by and engaged the question of empire). The issue at stake, however, is not only one of expanding and correcting our historical understanding of the trajectories of nineteenth-century imperial ideology. More importantly, I want to suggest that this privileging of liberal imperialism also invests it as a particular kind of object of criticism. Liberal imperialism comes to be primarily understood as a discrete theoretical formation, with the implication that liberal collusions with empire can be explained and criticized (and perhaps eventually corrected) at the level of theoretical assumptions alone. In this vein, critics have scrutinized the philosophical and anthropological assumptions that made the liberal defense of empire possible, especially emphasizing the ways in which paternalistic, denigrating, or racist attitudes toward native societies functioned as grounds for exclusion from and exceptions to liberal norms. Critics have also shown, in nuanced and persuasive ways, how these attitudes may stem from an underlying set of theoretical commitments (such as, notions of progress, rationalism, universalism) that necessarily call into question the normative status of forms of life construed as nonmodern or nonliberal. In this sense, the critique of liberal imperialism shares a number of concerns about contemporary liberalism and its approach to the problem of cultural difference and diversity that have emerged most tenaciously around the issue of multiculturalism.

These are compelling and important arguments, raising fundamental doubts about the adequacy of liberal approaches to key moral and political dilemmas of living in plural and deeply divided societies. However, I want to point to the possible limits of this strategy of criticism, especially as it relates to the politics of empire. Consider, for example, the important recent studies of empire and political thought by Uday Mehta, Sankar Muthu, and Jennifer Pitts.[1] These studies have been enormously productive for understanding the ways in which major political thinkers have grappled with the question of empire and how modern political theory as an enterprise has been shaped by debates about global political, social, and economic processes concomitant with European expansion. Yet, at the same time, all three elucidate the critical or justificatory stances taken by prominent political thinkers vis-à-vis empire and imperial projects by focusing primarily on theoretical assumptions, especially those that are implicated in the understanding and representation of non-European peoples. This approach, I suggest, engenders a number of explanatory and critical conundrums. At one level, the analysis of philosophical assumptions as the primary grounds for understanding and evaluating a thinker's position on empire can be too abstract to capture important political and historical shifts in imperial ideologies. For example, in Muthu's influential characterization of Enlightenment anti-imperialism, what is taken to enable the skepticism of Kant, Herder, and Diderot toward European expansion was a common philosophical commitment to moral universalism grounded in the recognition of cultural diversity (the recognition of human beings as "fundamentally cultural beings").[2] Yet, Muthu admits that while this philosophical formation was crucial in superseding what he takes to be the more minimal (and more ambiguous and paternalistic) claims to equality contained in eighteenth-century discourses of natural rights or noble savagery, it was not markedly different from nineteenth-century liberal imperialism at the level of philosophical argumentation about human unity and diversity.[3] If the most prominent political theorists of the nineteenth century could reconcile moral universalism, a recognition of cultural diversity, with their defense and support of empire (a point Muthu concedes), then this, I think, casts some doubt on the depth of the anti-imperial valence attributed to Enlightenment philosophy. More importantly, it suggests that understanding and criticizing modes of imperial justification cannot be limited to the level of philosophical assumptions and abstract moral commitments.

Moreover, in attempting to give coherence to a thinker's philosophical vision, and in reconciling views on empire with their more general political theory, scholars have been less attuned to the political entailments of these visions and to how ideas of human unity and diversity emerged out of the practical politics of empire. Pitts is more attentive to the larger historical framework within which imperial positions were articulated and defended. She explicitly rejects the idea that "some set of basic theoretical assumptions in the liberal tradition can possibly explain such flexibility on the question of empire: liberalism does not lead ineluctably either to imperialism or anti-imperialism."[4] Yet, at the same time, while Pitts carefully elaborates the variety of ways that nineteenth-century liberalism accommodated itself to imperialism, these theoretical transformations are understood as *accommodations* to changing historical attitudes and dispositions (especially about the inferiority of non-European peoples). The rise of imperial liberalism is in some important sense understood as an externally induced formation, a development that emerges neither out of the fissures of earlier theoretical formations nor points to any particular crises within liberalism. For example, one of the key changes in historical dispositions that Pitts argues explains in part the liberal turn to empire was the hardening of racial attitudes and the rise of scientific racism.[5] The growing alignment with racialized discourses in the work of Mill, for example, is understood as part of parcel of a general shift in racial attitudes rather than a contribution to that shift or as emergent from the inner tensions of Millian liberalism. While Pitts attends to the "articulation of liberalism as a practice" and the ways in which the consolidation of empire was central to liberal's practical engagement in politics, the question of practice is geared toward giving coherence to each liberal thinker's discrete theoretical commitments, even as liberalism is understood to embody a number of historical variations.

Uday Mehta's *Liberalism and Empire* offers the most sustained interrogation of the philosophical assumptions of nineteenth-century liberalism that underpinned its imperial ambitions. Mehta tracks liberalism's long engagement with empire in India as indicative of liberalism's theoretical response to the problem of unfamiliarity. Mehta is alert to how this liberal formation reaches a kind of limit in the late nineteenth century as the imperial project incorporated more aggressively illiberal positions, for example in Stephen's belligerent critique of Mill and turn to a more authoritarian liberalism.[6] Mehta, however, is less interested in this moment as a reflection of liberalism's exhaustion in imperial practice than as way to mark the outer limits of liberal discourses of empire. My overall contention is that attending to the outer limits of liberalism is as important as understanding its internal coherence to grasp the inner trajectory and political dynamic of liberal empire.

Moreover, an overly strict focus on the theoretical core of liberal imperialism often positions the representations of non-European peoples as the key pivot through which to account for stances for or against empire. This investment in representations and evaluations of difference may prove to be a precarious strategy of criticism. Muthu stresses philosophical arguments about cultural diversity as central to Enlightenment anti-imperialism, specifically whether non-European cultural forms are deemed worthy of a respect that in turn enables a kind of moral commiseration. Likewise, for Pitts, much depends on how notions of progress and nationality are inflected by assumptions about the inferiority of non-European cultures. In Mehta, the question concerning the status of non-European cultures is framed by a deep scrutiny of liberalism's epistemological standpoint with respect to the unfamiliar. Mehta is careful to argue that this question has less to do with the substantive characterization of other societies, but rather is indicative of an a priori stance liberalism takes in its judgment of other cultures, a position taken in advance that seeks to make sense of, and domesticate, difference. For example, Burke's skepticism is seen to make available an anti-imperial stance less because he asserts an alternative, more benevolent portrait of Indian society, but because he assumes a presumptive deference to its integrity.[7] Nevertheless, for all three, there remains a normative investment in notions of pluralism and difference as an important theoretical ground opened up by the exploration of the question of empire.

In this vein, responses to the theoretical problem of liberal empire, implied as much as openly advocated, often gesture toward the revaluing of formally denigrated cultures and, at a more general level, call for a heightened recognition and respect for cultural difference. While there may be a number of reasons to endorse this turn to culture as an antidote to forms of liberal exclusion, I want to point to the limits of invoking culture as a definitively anti-imperial gesture, as indeed the only corrective lesson to be learned from the history of liberalism's vexed relationship to empire. The ways in which the ideological forms of late empire were thoroughly imbricated in, and underpinned by, discourses of cultural difference attests to the uncomfortable fact that there need be nothing contradictory about imperial self-justifications that speak in the name of cultural pluralism and cosmopolitan toleration. The turn to culture in late imperial ideology—the ways in which ideas of cultural difference developed in response to, and out of, a crisis of liberal empire—points to a deep and revealing complicity between liberalism and culturalism. This complicity suggests that the changing moral evaluation and characterization of subject peoples may be as much the consequence and not the originating cause of imperial politics. In other words, the ways societies and peoples are marked as similar or different is subject to oscillations *internal* to the structure of imperial ideology.

To prioritize the representations of others (non-European societies) as the strategic ground of criticism, moreover, too easily allows the justification of empire to turn on (disputed) empirical controversies about the nature of subject societies (such as, their commitments to pluralism, secularism, modernity, and so forth). Similarly, when debates about multiculturalism come to hang on the empirical characterization of those cultures deemed worthy of "accommodation," they effectively elide the more pressing questions of why liberalism engenders culturalist reactions, and of the liberal state's historical role in entrenching and amplifying forms of cultural difference and cultural conflict.[8] Finally, when the nature of subject societies and cultures becomes the terrain on which the necessity of empire is debated and justified—when it becomes the legitimate ground upon which to excavate and evaluate arguments for and against imperial rule—the moral and political consequences of empire are effectively evaded. The turn to culturalism is itself indicative of a distinct imperial pattern whereby a collapsing moralism takes refuge in portraits of subject societies as alibis of empire.

Not only ought the imperial logic of indirect rule caution us against an undue deference to the normative claims of culture, but also the close consideration of the fact and the manner in which liberal models were historically superseded in the consolidation of Victorian empire reveals something fundamental about liberalism and its shifting relationship to empire. The connection I want to highlight between liberalism (universalism) and culturalism, the turn from one to the other, is less a logically necessary one than a relation of political entailment. Given this entailment, a positive investment in culturalism as a compelling alternative to, and adequate critique of, liberal imperialism is not ultimately persuasive. Moreover, I want to insist, a critical understanding of liberal imperialism cannot limit itself to a criticism of the theoretical assumptions of liberalism's norms in abstraction from the ways these ideals play themselves out in the contingent field of political action. To emphasize the political entailments of liberal imperialism is to point less to the way liberal norms are embodied in and make possible (imperial) practices, institutions, and policies than to shift the focus to the field of unintended consequences, to the kinds of reactions, resistances, and failures concomitant with and, in some compelling sense, *intrinsic* to the project of liberal empire.

Historians of the British Empire have been especially attuned to the unintended ideological and political consequences of the decline of early nineteenth-century liberal reformism. In contrast to the focus on the discrete theoretical universe of liberalism, historians of empire have formulated the collapse of liberal reformism as the working out of a series of internal contradictions of liberalism. In relation to empire in India, Thomas Metcalf has offered an influential, overarching formulation of this shift in imperial ideologies (one to which the argument of this book is very much indebted).[9] For Metcalf, liberal ascendance in India, marked by an alliance of free traders, evangelicals, and utilitarians committed to the reform of Indian society, had by midcentury come to encounter "powerful currents of disillusionment."[10] The crisis over the Mutiny served as the death knell to this liberal consensus as a new emphasis on Indian "difference" produced a form of rule based upon a revitalized conservatism, an investment in "traditional" India, and a turn to more authoritarian patterns of governance. For Metcalf, in some important sense, this post-Mutiny turn capitalized upon contradictions internal to the liberal ideal of assimilation.

The radical universalism of liberal idealism, which was premised on a conception of human nature as amenable to education and civilization, entrenched notions of difference in the process of constructing native subjects as objects of reform. As Francis Hutchins cogently argued in an earlier work, liberals like James Mill and evangelicals like Charles Grant built an argument for a "just rule" on a rhetorical strategy that denigrated Indian society in the name of future rejuvenation. For Hutchins, as the ambitious program of reform was abandoned, these harsh portraits retained their hold on the imperial imagination, the long-term effect of which was to embolden the argument for permanent rule.[11] Similarly, for Metcalf, the troubling implication of this kind of liberal idealism was how it required the continuous production of difference to justify its programs of eradication.[12] The notion of a difference produced out of the internal contradictions of the discourse of liberal empire resonates with what Partha Chatterjee has theorized as the contradictory logic of colonial power. For Chatterjee the dynamics of colonial power/knowledge objectified and constituted the "truth of colonial difference" as a limit even to the more universalist projects of transformation. It was a contradiction born out of the imperial project as a whole such that overcoming this difference would supersede the constitutive conditions of colonial rule.[13]

At the same time, while difference underpinned and was incited by the program of liberal reform, it is unclear if these internal contradictions themselves can account for the disillusionment with the project of reform and the forms of culturalism that emerged in the wake of the widespread sense of its practical failure. As I have highlighted in the book, one of the most important and dramatic triggers for this form of liberal disappointment was the experience of political rebellion and resistance.

Imperial historians have marked the importance of the Mutiny and the Morant Bay Rebellion as moments of a deep liberal crisis that initiated more overtly racialized discourse as well as more illiberal and authoritarian models of empire. Perceived failures in a whole set of social and economic experiments, from abolitionism and conversion to models of economic development, induced a similar crisis of expectations. As the work of Thomas Holt and Catherine Hall has so vividly captured, the history of abolitionism offers a particularly resonant example of the arc of disillusionment (in this case, with the results of emancipation).[14] This history also illustrates a similar strategy of explanation in which racial apologia are employed to account for the failure of the Great Experiment in postemancipation Jamaica. The concomitant move from an image of childlike but reformable slaves to depictions of the irredeemable savage nature of ex-slaves, I would argue, is less the coming to light of a preexisting and latent racism in liberal and abolitionist discourse than the articulation of new forms of racialization. Rather than the contradictions inherent in imperial projects of liberal reform, what interests me is how the inconsistencies, failures, and unintended consequences of these projects were ultimately rationalized. For in these rationalizations, a rhetorical apparatus is employed to make sense of resistance or failure as something other than what it is, as stemming from deep anthropological, racial, and cultural imperatives. In other words, the logic of explanation works as a rhetoric of evasion.[15]

Today, we see a resurgence of liberal arguments for empire, from calls for the revival of an imperial mandate system to the institutionalization of humanitarian intervention, that is, a variety of arguments in favor of the use of force for transformative political projects (across borders). While some advocates of empire explicitly evoke British precedents, even without these direct analogies, in an important sense, contemporary imperial forms work in the shadow of the specifically liberal reconstitution of modern empire that took shape in the eighteenth and nineteenth centuries. Like their forbearers, what makes the contemporary argument for empire distinctly liberal is the contrast it draws between its benign agenda of promoting peace and commerce through temporary tutelage from empires of conquest, extraction, and subjugation driven only by a (self-defeating) desire for power and prestige. As critics insistently charge imperial revivalists for ignoring the genocidal and exploitative history of modern empire, the liberal rejoinder has contended that since it has rejected the virulent theories of racial and civilizational hierarchy with which this history is associated, liberal empire can be effectively severed from its recently condemned past. But if violence and racialization are understood as constitutive political entailments of modern empire rather than theoretical assumptions or attitudes that can be corrected, then liberal imperialists cannot so easily rely on the purity of moral intentions or the universalism of liberal ideals as the grounds for judging the legitimacy of empire. If we consider the problem of imperial politics as less a problem of moral intention, idealism, or universalism but more a question of political consequences then the revival of empire cannot be so straightforwardly cleansed of its more troubling associations and responsibility for its calamitous outcomes.

Notes

Introduction: The Ideological Origins of Indirect Rule

1. Henry Sumner Maine, "India," in *The Reign of Queen Victoria: A Survey of Fifty Years of Progress*, vol. 1, ed. Thomas Humphry Ward (London, 1887), 470.

2. For the impact of the rebellion on imperial ideology and policy, see Thomas R. Metcalf, *The Aftermath of Revolt: India, 1857–1870* (Princeton, 1964); Francis Hutchins, *The Illusion of Permanence: British Imperialism in India* (Princeton, 1967); D. A. Low, *Lion Rampant: Essays in the Study of British Imperialism* (London, 1973); Eric Stokes, *The Peasant and the Raj: Studies in Agrarian Society and Peasant Rebellion in Colonial India* (Cambridge, 1978); Thomas R. Metcalf, *Ideologies of the Raj* (Cambridge, 1994); and Nicholas Dirks, *Castes of Mind: Colonialism and the Making of Modern India* (Princeton, 2001). On metropolitan perceptions of, and responses to, the Mutiny, see Gautam Chakravarty, *The Indian Mutiny and the British Imagination* (Cambridge, 2005) and Christopher Herbert, *War of No Pity: The Indian Mutiny and Victorian Trauma* (Princeton, 2008).

3. See Uday Singh Mehta, *Liberalism and Empire: A Study in Nineteenth-Century British Liberal Thought* (Chicago, 1999) and Jennifer Pitts, *A Turn to Empire: The Rise of Imperial Liberalism in Britain and France* (Princeton, 2005). For a critical review of recent literature on liberalism and empire, see also Andrew Sartori, "The British Empire and Its Liberal Mission," *Journal of Modern History* 78 (2006): 623–42.

4. See especially Thomas Holt, *The Problem of Freedom: Race, Labor, and Politics in Jamaica and Britain, 1832–1938* (Baltimore, 1992).

5. Throughout the book I use the terms *late empire* and *late imperial ideology* to refer to the period from 1857 to 1914, extending at times to the interwar years. As such the adjective *late* is used less to denote the *last* historical phase of empire, than as a way to emphasize the temporal nature of the relationship between two distinct imperial formations. Late empire is defined in large part by its self-conscious rejection of earlier forms of (liberal) imperial thought and practice. My use of the term, and its conceptual logic, is indebted to Mahmood Mamdani, *Citizen and Subject: Contemporary Africa and the Legacy of Late Colonialism* (Princeton, 1996).

6. Henry Sumner Maine, *Ancient Law: Its Connection with the Early History of Society, and Its Relation to Modern Ideas* (1861; Tucson, 1986, 166).

7. On Mill's influence on British policy in India consider the classic work by Eric Stokes, *The English Utilitarians and India* (Oxford, 1959).

8. Maine, "India," 474.

9. Ibid., 473.

10. See Herbert's *War of No Pity*.

11. Dalhousie's controversial "doctrine of lapse," renounced after the Mutiny, officially allowed for the annexation of any princely state if no natural heir was available. In privileging "natural" heirs, Maine argued that this policy was based upon a fundamental misrecognition of the importance of adoption to Indian society (and ancient society, more generally).

12. Maine, "India," 476.

13. Ibid.

14. On the transformation in attitudes toward, and depictions of, Jamaica's ex-slave population, see especially Catherine Hall, *Civilising Subjects: Metropole and Colony in the English Imagination, 1830–1867* (Cambridge, 2002). To attest to how widespread this transformed view of native subjects was, consider this contemporary response to the Maori rebellion: "We have dealt with the natives of this country upon a principle radically wrong. We have conceded them rights and privileges which nature has refused to ratify. . . . We have pampered ignorance and misrule, and we now experience their hatred of intelligence and order. The bubble is burst. The Maori is now known to us as what he is, and not as missionaries and philanthropists were willing to believe him. [In reality, the Maori is] a man ignorant and savage, loving darkness and anarchy, hating light and order; a man of fierce, and ungoverned passions, bloodthirsty, cruel, ungrateful, treacherous." Quoted from James Belich, *The Victorian Interpretation of Racial Conflict: The Maori, the British, and the New Zealand Wars* (Montreal, 1989), 328.

15. See Herbert, *War of No Pity*, and Metcalf, *Ideologies of the Raj*. For connections between the Morant Bay/Governor Eyre controversy and the growth of racism, see Bernard Semmel, *Democracy versus Empire: The Jamaica Riots of 1865 and the Governor Eyre Controversy* (New York, 1969); Douglas Lorimer, *Colour, Class, and the Victorians: English Attitudes to the Negro in the Mid-Nineteenth Century* (New York, 1978); and Hall, *Civilising Subjects*.

16. Although with respect to British India, "indirect rule" is more often associated with the residency system of the princely states, it was never used to describe any actual imperial arrangement in India. Indeed, the term *indirect rule* emerged as a name for the specific system of native government inaugurated by Lord Lugard in Northern Nigeria. I use the term more broadly to not only refer to patterns of rule—actual institutional configurations—but more centrally, for my purposes, a distinct philosophy of rule that self-consciously contrasts itself to more direct or interventionist policies. On the origins and uses of the term, see especially the introduction in Michael Fisher, *Indirect Rule in India: Residents and the Residency System, 1764–1858* (Delhi, 1991).

17. For general references to Maine in connection with indirect rule, see Stokes, *The English Utilitarians in India*, 309–10; C. A. Bayly, "Maine and Change in Nineteenth-Century India," in *The Victorian Achievement of Sir Henry Maine: A Centennial Reappraisal*, ed. Alan Diamond (Cambridge, 1995), 391; Mamdani, *Citizen and Subject*, 49.

18. Paul Kennedy, *The Rise and Fall of the Great Powers: Economic Change and Military Conflict from 1500 to 2000* (New York, 1989), 148–49.

19. See Raymond Betts, *Assimilation and Association in French Colonial Theory, 1890–1914* (London, 2004) and Mamdani, *Citizen and Subject*.

20. See Anthony Pagden, *The Fall of Natural Man: The American Indian and the Origins of Comparative Ethnology* (Cambridge, 1982); James Tully, "Rediscovering America: The Two Treatises and Aboriginal Rights," in James Tully, *An Approach to Political Philosophy: Locke in Contexts* (Cambridge, 1993); Barbara Arneil, *John Locke and America: The Defence of English Colonialism* (Oxford, 1996); Richard Tuck, *The Rights of War and Peace: Political Thought and the International Order from Grotius to Kant* (New York, 1999).

21. Bhikhu Parekh, "The Narrowness of Liberalism from Mill to Rawls," *Times Literary Supplement*, February 25, 1994, 11–13; Mehta, *Liberalism and Empire*; Pitts, *A Turn to Empire*; Eileen Sullivan, "Liberalism and Imperialism: J. S. Mill's Defense of the British Empire," *Journal of the History of Ideas* 44, no. 4 (1983); Cheryl Welch, "Colonial Violence and the Rhetoric of Evasion: Tocqueville on Algeria," *Political Theory* 31, no. 2 (2003); Melvin Richter, "Tocqueville on Algeria," *Review of Politics* 25 (1963); George Fredrickson, "Race and Empire in Liberal Thought: The Legacy of Tocqueville," in Fredrickson, *The Comparative Imagination: On the History of Racism, Nationalism, and Social Movements* (Berkeley, 2000).

22. This point is examined further in the coda.

23. Ged Martin's pithy review essay, "Was There a British Empire," *Historical Journal* 15, no. 3 (1972); 562–69, offers a snapshot into this debate. Much of this revisionism, shaped in important ways by the pioneering work of John Gallagher and Ronald Robinson, was directed against Whiggish assumptions of a continuity and unity in imperial purpose and initiated a turn to the the periphery as the key site of imperial dynamism. See R. Robinson, "Non-European Foundations of European Imperialism: Sketch for a Theory of Collaboration," in *Studies in the Theory of Imperialism*, ed. R. Owen and B. Sutcliffe (London, 1972) and R. Robinson and J. Gallagher, with Alice Denny, *Africa and the Victorians: The Official Mind of Colonialism* (London, 1961).

24. On the one hand strategic (political and economic) interest is privileged over ideal or ideological investments and, on the other, however coherent imperial ideologies and policies may seem they are assumed to inevitably fracture, mutate, and/or be undermined in contact with local forces. In Chris Bayly's words, "colonial ideology was broken to fragments on the hard edges of Indian society." Bayly, "Maine and Change in Nineteenth-Century India," 391.

25. See Robinson, "Non-European Foundations of European Imperialism," and the essays in W. R. Louis, ed., *Imperialism: The Robinson and Gallagher Controversy* (New York, 1976).

26. Jacques Derrida, *Without Alibi*, ed. and trans. Peggy Kamuf (Stanford, 2002), xvi.

27. Richard Tuck, "Rights and Pluralism," in *Philosophy in the Age of Pluralism: The Philosophy of Charles Taylor in Question*, ed. James Tully (Cambridge, 1994). See also Tuck, *The Rights of War and Peace*.

28. J. G. A. Pocock, *Barbarism and Religion*, vol. 4, *Barbarians, Savages, Empires* (Cambridge, 2005); Tzvetan Todorov, *On Human Diversity: Nationalism, Racism, and Exoticism in French Thought* (Cambridge, 1993); Sankar Muthu, *Enlightenment against Empire* (Princeton, 2003), Pitts, *A Turn to Empire*; Sunil Agnani, *European Anticolonialism at Its Limit: Denis Diderot and Edmund*

Burke, 1770–1800 (forthcoming); Thomas Macarthy, *Race, Empire, and the Idea of Human Development* (Cambridge, 2009).

29. See Stefan Collini, Donald Winch, and John Burrow, *That Noble Science of Politics: A Study in Nineteenth-Century Intellectual History* (Cambridge, 1983), chap. 7 and Melvin Richter, "The Comparative Study of Regimes and Societies," in *The Cambridge History of Eighteenth-Century Political Thought*, ed. Mark Goldie and Robert Wokler (Cambridge, 2006), 147–71.

30. See John W. Burrow, *Evolution and Society: A Study in Victorian Social Theory* (Cambridge, 1968) and George W. Stocking, *Victorian Anthropology* (New York, 1987).

31. Tönnies names Maine as one of three writers (the others being Gierke and Marx) who had "stimulated, instructed and corroborated" his work. See the preface to Ferdinand de Tönnies, *Community and Civil Society (Gemeinschaft und Gesellschaft)*, trans. Jose Harris and Margaret Hollis (1887; Cambridge, 2001).

32. Émile Durkheim, *The Division of Labor in Society*, trans. W. D. Halls (1893; New York, 1984).

33. George W. Stocking, *Race, Culture, and Evolution: Essays in the History of Anthropology* (Chicago, 1991), chaps. 4 and 9.

34. Margaret Archer, *Culture and Agency: The Place of Culture in Social Theory* (Cambridge, 1996).

35. See Bernard McGrane, *Beyond Anthropology: Society and the Other* (New York, 1989) and David Scott, "Culture in Political Theory," *Political Theory* 13, no. 1 (2003): 92–115.

36. The best scholarly studies of Maine have explored his thought in the context of Victorian intellectual debates, especially in the domains of jurisprudence and social theory. The classic work on Maine's social thought is John W. Burrow's *Evolution and Society: A Study in Victorian Social Theory*. Maine's legal thought is comprehensively examined in Raymond Cocks, *Sir Henry Maine: A Study in Victorian Jurisprudence* (Cambridge, 1988). The collection of essays in Diamond, ed., *The Victorian Achievement of Sir Henry Maine: A Centennial Reappraisal* includes a number of excellent essays on specific aspects of Maine's thought, while George Feaver's essential biography, *From Status to Contract: A Biography of Sir Henry Maine, 1822–1888* (London, 1969), covers the broad range of Maine's political, social, and intellectual connections in Victorian England.

37. Gandhi famously cites Maine (for example in the appendix to *Hind Swaraj*) as an intellectual authority on the democratic pasts of the Indian village-community. See also Minoti Chakravarty-Kaul's innovative use of Maine in *Common Lands and Customary Law: Institutional Change in North India over the Past Two Centuries* (Delhi, 1996).

38. Despite Maine's well-known reputation as a significant Indian policymaker and the recognition of his importance for historians of colonial law as well as Indian anthropology more generally, there are very few expanded studies on Maine's Indian work and legacy. Some key pieces include Ron Inden, *Imagining India* (Oxford, 1990), 136–57, and the essays by Gordon Johnson, Chris Bayly, and Clive Dewey in Diamond, *The Victorian Achievement of Henry Maine*. In terms of Maine's influence in Indian policy, Clive Dewey has provided the most comprehensive assessment in a number of key articles. See especially Dewey,

"The Influence of Sir Henry Maine on Agrarian Policy in India," in Diamond, *The Victorian Achievement of Sir Henry Maine*. Also Alex Kirshner has offered a rare and compelling reading of Maine's Indian thought in terms of his political thought as a whole. See Alexander Kirshner, "Character and the Administration of Empires in the Political Thought of Henry Maine," M.Phil thesis, University of Cambridge, 2002.

Chapter One: The Crisis of Liberal Imperialism

1. T. B. Macaulay provided a classic formulation of British India's "anomalous" status in his 1833 speech on the renewal of charter of the East India Company: "It is true that the power of the Company is an anomaly in politics. . . . But what constitution can we give to our Indian Empire which shall not be strange, which shall not be anomalous? That Empire is itself the strangest of all political anomalies. . . . Reason is confounded. We interrogate the past in vain. General rules are useless where the whole is one vast exception. The Company is an anomaly; but it is part of a system where every thing is anomaly. It is the strangest of all governments; but it is designed for the strangest of all empires." Macaulay, "Government of India," 10 July 1833, in *Macaulay: Prose and Poetry* (Cambridge, 1970), 695–96.

2. Henry Sumner Maine, "The Effect of Observation of India on European Thought," the Rede Lecture of 1875, in *Village-Communities in the East and West* (London, 1876), 233.

3. The precise term *liberal imperialism* emerged in later Victorian political debates, and was especially associated with Lord Roseberry's attempt to carve out a liberal argument in favor of empire and expansionism (in contrast to Gladstone's reticence). See R. Koebner and H. D. Schmidt, *Imperialism: The Story and Significance of a Political Word, 1840–1960* (Cambridge, 1964). I am using the term somewhat anachronistically to denote a particular constellation of liberal thinking on the dependent (nonsettler) empire.

4. The title of this chapter pays homage to and signals my considerable debt to Thomas Metcalf's discussion of "The Crisis of Liberalism" in his wonderfully cogent chapter on "Liberalism and Empire" in *Ideologies of the Raj* (Cambridge, 1995), 28–65.

5. T. B. Macaulay, *Warren Hastings* (London, 1900), 13. Originally published in the *Edinburgh Review*, October 1841.

6. For recent interpretations of Burke's writings and speeches on India, see especially Frederick G. Whelan, *Edmund Burke and India: Political Morality and Empire* (Pittsburgh, 1996); Uday Singh Mehta, *Liberalism and Empire: A Study in Nineteenth-Century British Liberal Thought* (Chicago, 1999); Sunil Agnani, *European Anticolonialism at Its Limit: Denis Diderot and Edmund Burke, 1770–1800* (forthcoming); Jennifer Pitts, *A Turn to Empire: The Rise of Imperial Liberalism in Britain and France* (Princeton, 2005), chap. 3; Richard Bourke, *Empire to Revolution: The Political Life of Edmund Burke* (forthcoming).

7. Revisionary accounts, which attempted to more or less exonerate Hastings, were especially prominent in late Victorian imperial discourse. See Eric Stokes,

"The Administrators and Historical Writing in India," in *Historians of India, Pakistan, and Ceylon*, ed. C. H. Philips (Oxford, 1961), 385–403. Also discussed, on pages 44–48.

8. Edmund Burke, "Speech on Opening of Impeachment," 15 February 1788, in *Writings and Speeches of Edmund Burke, Volume VI, India: The Launching of the Hastings Impeachment*, ed. P. J. Marshall (Oxford, 1991), 271.

9. Edmund Burke, "Speech on Fox's India Bill," 1 December 1873, in *Writings and Speeches of Edmund Burke, Volume V, India: Madras and Bengal, 1774–1785*, ed. P. J. Marshall (Oxford, 1981), 383.

10. Burke, "Speech on Opening of Impeachment," 316–17.

11. Ibid., 285–86. See also Burke, "Speech on Fox's East India Bill," 402.

12. Burke, "Speech on Fox's East India Bill," 385. See also Richard Bourke, "Liberty, Authority, and Trust in Burke's Idea of Empire," *Journal of the History of Ideas* 61, no. 3 (2000): 453–71.

13. Edmund Burke, "Speech on Bengal Judicature Bill," 27 June 1781, in *Writings and Speeches of Edmund Burke, Volume V, India: Madras and Bengal, 1774–1785*, ed. P. J. Marshall (Oxford, 1981), 141.

14. Burke, "Speech on Opening of Impeachment," 302.

15. See Robert Travers, *Ideology and Empire in Eighteen-Century India: The British in Bengal* (Cambridge, 2007).

16. Burke, "Speech on Fox's East India Bill," 390.

17. Mehta emphasizes the potential philosophical resonances of this understanding of sympathy. According to Mehta, it is in Burke's humility and openness to the possible risks of encounter with unfamiliarity that "lies the possibility of *mutual* understanding, *mutual* influence, and *mutual* recognition." Mehta, *Liberalism and Empire*, 23.

18. Burke, "Speech on Opening of Impeachment," 304.

19. Francis G. Hutchins, *The Illusion of Permanence: British Imperialism in India* (Princeton, 1967), chap. 1. In addition to Hutchins, the following discussion of James Mill and Charles Grant relies on the seminal work on this conjuncture of liberal, utilitarian, and evangelical thinking on empire in India by Eric Stokes, *The English Utilitarians and India* (Oxford, 1959) and Raghavan Iyer, "Utilitarianism and All That (the Political Theory of British Imperialism in India)," *St. Anthony's Papers* 8 (1960): 9–71.

20. James Mill, *The History of British India* (1817; New Delhi, 1990). For extended discussions of Mill's *History* and his views on imperial policy, see Stokes, *The English Utilitarians and India*; Javed Majeed, *Ungoverned Imaginings: James Mill's* The History of British India *and Orientalism* (Oxford, 1992); Pitts, *A Turn to Empire*; Duncan Forbes, "James Mill and India," *Cambridge Journal* 5 (1951–52): 19–33.

21. Mill, *The History of British India*, 1:3.

22. Ibid., 1:458.

23. On Mill's relation to the tradition of Scottish conjectural history, see Forbes, "James Mill and India"; Knud Haakonsen, *Natural Law and Moral Philosophy: From Grotius to the Scottish Enlightenment* (Cambridge, 1996), chap. 9; Pitts, *A Turn to Empire*, chap. 5.

24. Mill, *The History of British India*, 1:456.

25. For example, Mill was careful not to construe the "indolent" habits of the natives as products of climate or geography.

26. See especially Majeed, *Ungoverned Imaginings*.

27. Stokes, *The English Utilitarians and India*.

28. Charles Grant, *Observations on the State of Society among the Asiatic Subjects of Great Britain, Particularly with Respect of Morals; and the Means of Improving It, Appendix to Report of the Select Committee of the House of Commons on the Affairs of the East India Company*, 16 August 1832, *Parliamentary Papers* (London, 1832). See also Ainslee T. Embree, *Charles Grant and British Rule in India* (New York, 1962).

29. "In short, a Hindoo, from the hour of his birth, through the different stages of his existence, in infancy, in youth, in manhood, in old age, and in death, in all relations, and in all the casualties of life, is subject to an accumulation of burthemsome rites, with which the preservation of his caste, his credit, and place in society, are strictly connected: nay, for his conduct in former states of being, preceding his birth, these absolute lords of his faith, conscience, and conduct, bring him to account, nor do they resign their dominion over him when he is dead. The return he has for unbounded subjection, is an indulgence in perpetual deviations, even from those few principles of morality which his religion acknowledges. It is thus that abject slavery, and unparalleled depravity, have become the distinguishing characteristics of the Hindoos." Grant, *Observations on the State of Society*, 142–43.

30. Ibid., 149.

31. See Syed Mahmood, *A History of English Education in India, 1781–1893* (Aligarh, 1895) and Gauri Viswanathan, *Masks of Conquest: Literary Study and British Rule in India* (New York, 1998).

32. Grant, *Observations on the State of Society*, 149.

33. Ibid., 218.

34. Ibid.

35. These ideas would be echoed and restated by Macaulay in a number of his speeches and minutes on India. See especially the 1833 speech on charter renewal, "Government of India," 10 July 1833, in Macaulay, *Prose and Poetry* (Cambridge, 1970).

36. Grant, *Observations on the State of Society*, 221.

37. T. B. Macaulay, "Government of India," 717.

38. J. R. Seeley, *The Expansion of England* (London, 1883), 253.

39. This was an important rhetorical strategy among early nineteenth-century British liberals, but it was by no means a logically necessary feature of liberalism. Many liberals from Locke to Mill had justified conquest on liberal grounds. On Locke and the debate on the legitimacy of conquest in the Americas, see especially James Tully, "Rediscovering America: The Two Treatises and Aboriginal Rights," in James Tully, *An Approach to Political Philosophy: Locke in Contexts* (Cambridge, 1993); Barbara Arneil, *Locke and America: The Defense of English Colonialism* (Oxford, 1996); Richard Tuck, *The Rights of War and Peace: Political Thought and the International Order from Grotius to Kant* (New York, 1999); Aziz Rana, *Freedom Without Empire: The Paradox of America's Settler Legacy* (Harvard, forthcoming).

40. See especially volume 3 of Mill, *The History of British India*, or volumes 5 and 6 of the H. H. Wilson edition of 1820.

41. Grant, *Observations on the State of Society*, 15.

42. See also Embree, *Charles Grant and British Rule in India*, chap. 7. The rhetoric of atonement would remain a feature of radical positions of empire, for example in John Bright's views of empire in India and J. S. Mill's late views on Ireland. It was precisely this language of moral responsibility that would be attacked by late Victorian critics of liberal imperialism. See John Bright, *Selected Speeches by Rt. Honble. John Bright, M.P., on Public Questions* (London, 1907); John Stuart Mill, "England and Ireland," in *The Collected Works of John Stuart Mill*, vol. 6, *Essays on England, Ireland, and the Empire*, ed. John M. Robson (Toronto, 1982); and Lynn Zastoupil, "Moral Government: J. S. Mill on Ireland," *Historical Journal* 26, no. 3 (1983): 707–17.

43. As Stokes provocatively argued, "India provided that element of scale and expansiveness to the new middle class-mind, so essential for the deployment of its political and moral ideas." Stokes, *The English Utilitarians and India*, xii.

44. Macaulay, in his speech on the renewal of the charter, articulated this sentiment in the following manner: "The destinies of our Indian empire are covered with thick darkness. It is difficult to form any conjecture as to the fate reserved for a state which resembles no other in history, and which forms in itself a separate class of political phenomenon. . . . It may be that the public mind of India may expand under our system till it has outgrown that system; that by good government we may educate our subjects into a capacity for better government; that, having become instructed in European knowledge, they may, in some future age, demand European institutions. Whether such a day will ever come I know not. But never will I attempt to avert or to retard it. Whenever it comes, it will be the proudest day in English history." Macaulay, "Government of India," 718.

45. John Stuart Mill, *On Liberty*, in *The Collected Works of John Stuart Mill*, vol. 18, *Essays on Politics and Society, Part I*, ed. John M. Robson (Toronto, 1977), 224. (Hereafter *CW*.)

46. John Stuart Mill, *Considerations on Representative Government*, in *The Collected Works of John Stuart Mill*, vol. 19, *Essays on Politics and Society Part II*, ed. John M. Robson (Toronto, 1977), 567–68.

47. A similar trajectory can be seen in Mill's revised understanding of custom in utilitarian political economy. In the long run, the recognition of custom arguably worked to disable rather than rejuvenate the tradition of classical political economy. See the final section of chapter four. On Mill's increasing recognition of custom and history in Mill's approach to India, see especially Lynn Zastoupil, *John Stuart Mill and India* (Stanford, 1994).

48. Mill, *On Liberty*, *CW* 18, 224.

49. Mill, *Considerations*, *CW* 19, chaps. 1–3.

50. John Stuart Mill, "Remarks on Bentham's Philosophy," in *The Collected Works of John Stuart Mill*, vol. 10, *Essays on Ethics, Religion, and Society*, ed. John M. Robson (Toronto, 1985), 10.

51. Mill, "Remarks on Bentham's Philosophy," *CW* 10, 10.

52. Ibid.

53. Mill, *Considerations*, *CW* 19, 393–94.

54. Mill, *On Liberty*, CW 18, 224.

55. See Haakonsen, *Natural Law and Moral Philosophy*, chap. 8, and Pitts, *A Turn to Empire*, chap. 5.

56. John Stuart Mill, "Civilization," in *The Collected Works of John Stuart Mill*, vol. 18, *Essays on Politics and Society Part I*, ed. John M. Robson (Toronto, 1977), 120.

57. Ibid., 122.

58. John Stuart Mill, "A Few Words on Non-Intervention," in *The Collected Works of John Stuart Mill*, vol. 21, *Essays on Equality, Law and Education*, ed. John M. Robson (Toronto, 1984), 119.

59. Mill, *Considerations*, CW 19, 394, 567.

60. Mill, *On Liberty*, CW 18, 272; *Considerations*, CW 19, 567.

61. Mill, *Considerations*, CW 19, 567.

62. Mill, *On Liberty*, CW 18, 224.

63. Mill, *Considerations*, CW 19, 395.

64. Ibid., 568.

65. Ibid. Mill never specified in great detail what kinds of policies would educate a subject population toward greater individuality. Even in his defense of the East India Company and the superiority of rule through an apolitical and expert bureaucracy, Mill offered a predominately institutionalist account of the appropriate mechanisms of imperial governance. See ibid., 568–77.

66. Mill, *On Liberty*, CW 18, 224.

67. Mehta, *Liberalism and Empire*, 46–77.

68. Ibid., 49.

69. John Stuart Mill, *A System of Logic Ratiocinative and Inductive*, in *The Collected Works of John Stuart Mill*, vol. 8, *A System of Logic; Ratiocinative and Inductive*, ed. John M. Robson (Toronto, 1974), 860–74.

70. John Stuart Mill, "The Negro Question," in *The Collected Works of John Stuart Mill*, vol. 21, *Essays on Equality, Law, and Education*, ed. John M. Robson (Toronto, 1984), 93. See Iva Jones, "Trollope, Carlyle, and Mill on the Negro: An Episode in the History of Ideas," *Journal of Negro History* 52 (1967): 185–99; David Theo Goldberg, "Liberalism's Limits: Carlyle and Mill on 'the Negro Question,'" *Nineteenth Century Contexts* 22 (2000); and Georgios Varouxakis, "Empire, Race, Euro-Centrism: John Stuart Mill and his Critics," in *Utilitarianism and Empire*, ed. Bart Schultz and Georgios Varouxakis (Lanham, 2005).

71. On the shifting nature of the categories of race, culture, and nation in Victorian discussions, see Peter Mandler, "'Race' and 'Nation' in Mid-Victorian Thought," in *History, Religion, and Culture: British Intellectual History, 1750–1950*, ed. S. Collini, R. Whatmore, and B. Young (Cambridge, 2000), and Douglas A. Lorimer, *Colour, Class, and the Victorians: English Attitudes to the Negro in the Mid-Nineteenth Century* (Leicester, 1978).

72. Mill, "A Few Words on Non-Intervention," CW 21, 119.

73. For general accounts of the Morant Bay Rebellion, the debates about the ensuing controversy, and Mill's role in the Jamaica committee, see Gad J. Heuman, *"The Killing Time": The Morant Bay Rebellion in Jamaica* (Knoxville, 1994); Bernard Semmel, *Democracy versus Empire: The Jamaica Riots of 1865 and the Governor Eyre Controversy* (New York, 1969); Catherine Hall, *Civilizing*

Subjects: Metropole and Colony in the English Imagination, 1830–1867 (Cambridge, 2002); Thomas Holt, *The Problem of Freedom: Race, Labor, and Politics in Jamaica and Britain, 1832–1938* (Baltimore, 1992); Geoffrey Dutton, *Edward John Eyre: The Hero as Murderer* (New York, 1977); Lorimer, *Colour, Class, and the Victorians*, chap. 5; Arvel B. Erickson, "Empire or Anarchy: The Jamaica Rebellion of 1865," *Journal of Negro History* 44, no. 2 (1959): 99–122.

74. Gordon, having played no immediate role in the riots, had been forcibly removed from Kingston to Morant Bay (where martial law was in effect) and hastily convicted of treason under the law of court-martial.

75. John Stuart Mill, "The Disturbances in Jamaica [2] 31 July, 1866," *The Collected Works of John Stuart Mill*, vol. 28, *Public and Parliamentary Speeches Part I*, ed. John M. Robson (Toronto, 1988), chap. 33.

76. According to Collini, "this was one of those great moral earthquakes of Victorian public life whose fault lines are so revealing of the subterranean affinities and antipathies of the educated classes." Stefan Collini, Introduction to John Stuart Mill, *The Collected Works of John Stuart Mill*, vol. 21, *Essays on Equality, Law, and Education*, ed. John M. Robson (Toronto, 1984), xxvi.

77. See especially Semmel, *Democracy versus Empire*, 134–48. Also Catherine Hall, "The Nation Within and Without," in *Defining the Victorian Nation: Class, Race, and Gender and the British Reform Act of 1867*, ed. Catherine Hall, Keith McClelland, and Jane Rendall (Cambridge, 2000).

78. On the emergence of the distinction between *old* and *new* liberals see the seminal work of John Roach, "Liberalism and the Victorian Intelligentsia," *Cambridge Historical Journal* 13, no. 1 (1957): 58–81.

79. See especially Metcalf, *Ideologies of the Raj*, 52–59.

80. See Hall, *Civilizing Subjects*, Lorimer, *Colour, Class, and the Victorians*, and Semmel, *Democracy versus Empire*.

81. See Edwin Hirschmann, *"White Mutiny": The Ilbert Bill Crisis and the Genesis of the Indian National Congress* (New Delhi, 1980); Mrinalini Sinha, *Colonial Masculinity: The "Manly" Englishman and the "Effeminate" Bengali* (New York, 1995); Uma Dasgupta, "The Ilbert Bill Agitation, 1883," in *We Fought Together for Freedom: Chapters from the Indian Nationalist Movement*, ed. Ravi Dayal (New Delhi, 1995); Christine Dobbin, "The Ilbert Bill: A Study in Anglo-Indian Opinion in India, 1883," *Historical Studies* 12, no. 45 (1965): 87–104.

82. Maine had famously tried to warn Lord Ripon (through the Secretary of State, Lord Hartington) about the potential crisis the proposed act would instigate. George Feaver, *From Status to Contract: A Biography of Sir Henry Maine, 1822–1888* (London, 1969), 205.

83. A similar controversy emerged in response to Macaulay's so-called Black Act (1836), which likewise sought to institutionalize legal equality in civil jurisdictions outside Presidency towns (like Calcutta). English residents had long fought this equalization, arguing that in making them Indian subjects (equally subject to the Empire's despotic power) it would in effect deprive them of a host of political liberties associated with the inherited rights of Englishmen (such as the right to trial by jury, and the separation of executive and legislative power). This argument

was especially prominent in the debate on the Ilbert Bill, even as the idea of a privileged set of rights for *Englishmen* took on a more racial character.

84. The 1884 Bill allowed European settlers in the rural districts to appeal for jury trials (comprised of Europeans) to compensate for their acceptance of the jurisdiction of native judges.

85. Ripon was appointed Viceroy during Gladstone's second ministry. His tenure bore the signs of Gladstone's distrust of militaristic expansion as well as a brief revival of the liberal agenda in post-Mutiny India.

86. Branson was one of most vocal opponents of the bill. His inflammatory speeches against the bill did much not only to fan the flames of settler rebellion, but in polarizing the debate along racial lines his speeches also instigated and emboldened a coordinated native opposition (one that eventually led to the creation of the Indian National Congress). See Hirschmann, "*White Mutiny.*"

87. Lord Ripon, Letter to Forster, 6 March 1883. Citation from Hirschmann, "*White Mutiny,*" 70.

88. J. F. Stephen, *The Times*, 1 March 1883, 8. This extract is also reprinted in J. F. Stephen, "Foundations of the Government of India," *Nineteenth Century* 80 (October 1883): 541–68.

89. Stephen, "Foundations of the Government of India," 551.

90. Ibid., 558.

91. Ibid., 561.

92. See the preface to James Fitzjames Stephen, *Liberty, Equality, Fraternity, and Three Brief Essays* (1874; Chicago, 1991).

93. Stephen, *Liberty, Equality, Fraternity*, 68–69.

94. Ibid., 69.

95. See Jeanne Morefield's excellent discussion of this point in relation to the international thought of interwar British liberalism in *Covenants without Swords: Idealist Liberalism and the Spirit of Empire* (Princeton, 2006). Morefield is especially convincing in demonstrating how attempts to integrate fuller notions of community within liberalism have often entailed pulling back from ideals of equality, expressed most dramatically in the realm of international and imperial affairs.

96. This is again to emphasize the temporal underpinnings of this ideological shift, one that Stephen's increasingly conservative views epitomize. Indeed, one can see the arc of disillusionment in the generational history of the Stephen family's long and intimate connection to the liberal project of empire. Stephen's grandfather, James Stephen, was a prominent abolitionist and the chief draughtsman of the 1807 Act abolishing the slave trade. Stephen himself was the chief legal counsel for the Jamaica committee in their attempted prosecution of Eyre. See K. J. M. Smith, *James Fitzjames Stephen: Portrait of a Victorian Rationalist* (Cambridge, 2002), chap. 6, and Roach, "Liberalism and the Victorian Intelligentsia."

97. See especially Roach, "Liberalism and the Victorian Intelligentsia," and Stokes, *The English Utilitarians and India*. In addition to Stephen and Maine, intellectuals with deep connections to India, such A. C. Lyall, Lord Curzon, and John Strachey, were at the forefront of the political realignment sparked by the debate over Irish Home Rule.

98. For Stokes, Stephen best illustrated "how the authoritarian element in utilitarianism, which had found in India so much more congenial a field for its development and which was given a working expression in the machine of the Indian bureaucracy, was carried back into English thought and helped produce the crisis within English liberalism which occurred in 1886. . . . Stephen contributed to the outcome of this intellectual crisis of liberalism by coming forward with a political philosophy which generalized and rendered articulate the British middle-class experience of efficient and progressive autocracy in India" (288). Stokes, *English Utilitarians and India*.

99. Evelyn Baring, Earl of Cromer, "Some Indian Problems," *Political and Literary Essays, 1908–1913* (London, 1913), 418. Cromer here is paraphrasing a passage from Paul Boell that in the original reads as follows: "La question qui se pose n'est pas de savoir si l'Angleterre a le droit de conserver l'Inde, mais bien plutôt *si elle a le droit de la quitter*." Paul Victor Boell, *L'Inde et le question indien* (Paris, 1901), 289.

100. James Fitzjames Stephen, *The Story of Nuncomar and the Impeachment of Sir Elijah Impey* (London, 1885).

101. Other notable attempts to challenge the Burke-Mill-Macaulay consensus were John Strachey, *Hastings and the Rohilla War* (Oxford, 1892) and A. C. Lyall, *Warren Hastings* (London, 1889).

102. Impey was a close associate of Hastings and the controversial first Chief Justice of the Supreme Court in Calcutta who presided over the trial and execution of Maharaja Nandakumar. Hastings and Impey were accused of colluding in the "judicial murder" of Nandakumar and brought up on charges related to the case in their respective impeachment proceedings.

103. *The Expansion of England* was an extraordinarily popular and influential work, enabling a popular imperial consciousness and, in the long run, shaping a distinct tradition of imperial historiography. See Duncan Bell, *The Idea of Greater Britain: Empire and the Future of World Order* (Princeton, 2007) and Koebner and Schmidt, *Imperialism*, chap. 7.

104. Seeley, *The Expansion of England*, 193.

105. Ibid., 202.

106. Ibid., 208.

107. Ibid., 205.

108. Mill, "A Few Words on Non-Intervention," *CW* 21, 119.

109. See John Strachey, *India: Its Administration and Progress* (London, 1888); A. C. Lyall, "Government of the Indian Empire," *Edinburgh Review*, January 1884, 1–40; J. F. Stephen, "Foundations of the Government in India"; W. W. Hunter, *A History of British India* (London, 1899).

110. Seeley, *The Expansion of England*, 222. Maine also claims India to be a mere "geographical expression," having no real political unity or identity larger than the caste, tribe, clan, or sect. See Henry Sumner Maine, "Indian Government," *Saturday Review* 4 (3 October 1857), 295.

111. Ibid., 234.

112. Maine, "The Effects of Observation of India on Modern European Thought," in *Village-Communities*, 206.

113. See especially Lyall, "Government of the Indian Empire," and Cromer, "The Government of the Subject Races," in *Political and Literary Essays*.

114. The transfer of India from Company to Crown authority took place on 2 August 1858. The Queen's Proclamation was delivered on 1 November 1858. Excerpts of the speech are taken from C. H. Philips, H. L. Singh, and B. N. Pandey, eds., *The Evolution of India and Pakistan, 1858 to 1947: Select Documents* (London, 1962), 11.

115. Ibid.

116. Some of the other most prominent contemporary explanations focused on Dalhousie's aggressive policy of annexation of princely states (e.g., Awadh in 1856), expansion and government sanction of missionary activities, and agrarian unrest and indebtedness.

117. Henry Sumner Maine, "India," in *The Reign of Queen Victoria: A Survey of Fifty Years of Progress*, ed. Humphry Ward (London, 1887), 460–528.

118. See also Henry Sumner Maine, "Indian Statesmen and English Scribblers," *Saturday Review* 4 (24 October 1857): 361.

119. Maine, "India," 474. Nicholas Dirks has characterized reactions to the Mutiny similarly as an "anthropological failure." This argument will be explored more fully in chapter five. Nicholas B. Dirks, *Castes of Mind: Colonialism and the Making of Modern India* (Princeton, 2001), 148.

120. Maine, "India," 478.

121. Henry Sumner Maine, *Village-Communities in the East and West* (London, 1876), Lecture One.

122. Maine, "The Effects of Observations of India on Modern European Thought," 215.

123. Maine, *Village-Communities*, 22.

124. David Cannadine, in his controversial book *Ornamentalism: How the British Saw Their Empire*, criticizes the notion that the British primarily viewed native subjects through a racialized lens and/or as irretrievably other, a view he sees as having become the dominant view in imperial studies since Said's *Orientalism*. Thus, in direct contrast to Metcalf, Cannadine argues that the late nineteenth-century turn toward the preservation of Indian society as "traditional and organic" was premised upon a nostalgic identification with the (lost) past of Europe, and thus was primarily a discourse of similarity. As a projection onto the empire of an aristocratic ideal of a hierarchal, ordered society, Cannadine sees this ideal as more sympathetic than earlier liberal models to the workings of traditional society, and moreover, that as an ideology it was more thoroughly imbued by a strategy of (upper) class identification rather than racial difference. I follow Metcalf, Hutchins, and Stokes, and their emphasis on the ways in which this ideal was in fact founded in a more fundamental account of difference. David Cannadine, *Ornamentalism: How the British Saw Their Empire* (Oxford, 2001); Metcalf, *Ideologies of the Raj*, 66–112; Hutchins, *The Illusion of Permanence*, chap. 10; Eric Stokes, "The Administrators and Historical Writing on India," in *Historians of India, Pakistan, and Ceylon*, ed. C. H. Philips (London, 1961), 392–94.

125. See Clive Dewey, "The Influence of Sir Henry Maine on Agrarian Policy in India," in *The Victorian Achievement of Sir Henry Maine: A Centennial Reappraisal*, ed. Alan Diamond (Cambridge, 1995), 353–75. See especially Lyall's and

Hunter's works on caste and clan formation: A. C. Lyall, *Asiatic Studies: Religious and Social* (1882; London, 1899) and W. W. Hunter, *The Annals of Rural Bengal* (London, 1868). See also chapter five for a more detailed analysis of Maine's impact on imperial policy.

126. Maine, "India," 476.

127. Maine's most detailed account of the structural impact on British rule on native institutions appears in *Village-Communities in the East and West*, and will be further explored in chapters three, four, and five.

128. Metcalf, *Ideologies of the Raj*, and Thomas R. Metcalf, *The Aftermath of Revolt, India 1857–1870* (Princeton, 1964).

129. Dewey, "The Influence of Sir Henry Maine on Agrarian Policy in India."

130. Seeley, *The Expansion of England*, 190–91.

131. Ibid., 12–13.

132. Ibid., 176.

133. Ibid., 190.

134. D. A. Low, *Lion Rampant: Essays in the Study of British Imperialism* (London, 1973), 39–82.

Chapter Two: Inventing Traditional Society

1. Henry Sumner Maine, *Village-Communities in the East and West* (1871; London, 1876), 6–7.

2. Raymond Schwab, *The Oriental Renaissance: Europe's Rediscovery of India and the East, 1680–1880*, trans. Gene Patterson-Black and Victor Reinking (New York, 1984), 16.

3. See John W. Burrow, *Evolution and Society: A Study in Victorian Social Theory* (Cambridge, 1968); Kenneth E. Bock, "The Comparative Method of Anthropology," *Comparative Studies in Society and History* 8 (1966): 269–80; George W. Stocking, *Victorian Anthropology* (New York, 1987).

4. See especially Burrow, *Evolution and Society*; Edward Shils, "Henry Maine in the Tradition of the Analysis of Society," in *The Victorian Achievement of Sire Henry Maine*, ed. Alan Diamond (Cambridge, 1991); Kenneth E. Bock, "Comparison of Histories: The Contribution of Henry Maine," *Comparative Studies of Society and History* 16 (1974): 232–62.

5. Henry Sumner Maine, *Ancient Law: Its Connection with the Early History of Society, and Its Relation to Modern Ideas* (1861; Tucson, 1986); Ferdinand de Tönnies, *Community and Society (Gemeinschaft und Gesellschaft)* (1887; Cambridge, 2001); Émile Durkheim, *The Division of Labor in Society* (1893; New York, 1984), Herbert Spencer, *Principles of Sociology* (New York, 1897); Otto Friedrich von Gierke, *Natural Law and the Theory of Society, 1500–1800* (Cambridge, 1950).

6. As Anthony Pagden has argued, the sixteenth- and seventeenth-century Spanish scholastic debates over the status of the Amerindian initiated a fundamental shift away from the standard Aristotelian dichotomy of civilization and barbarism as the theoretical framework by which differences in human behavior and practice were to be understood. This shift resulted in the abandonment of the

Aristotelian conception of natural slavery, and its static, binary classificatory conception of human natures upon which it was based, toward a more dynamic theory of habituation in which human diversity would be explained in terms of social conditioning. The new "comparative ethnologies" of Las Casas and José Acosta, in this sense, undid the static contrast between civilization and barbarism by diversifying the definition of the barbarian. Establishing new hierarchies required a theory of cultural evolution, an explanation of how some peoples had in fact advanced toward civilization. Divergence in customs and human diversity, now seen as cultural diversity, were conceptualized temporally as differences in time. This framework for comparison not only introduced an anthropological time frame for relating peoples but also inaugurated a new historical account of the origins and development of human societies as a series of successive stages from barbarism to civilization. Anthony Pagden, *The Fall of Natural Man: The American Indian and the Origins of Comparative Ethnology* (Cambridge, 1982). See also Ronald L. Meek, *Social Science and the Ignoble Savage* (Cambridge, 1976).

7. Meek, *Social Science and the Ignoble Savage,* J. G. A. Pocock, *Barbarism and Religion*, vol. 4, *Barbarians, Savages, Empires* (Cambridge, 2005); Istvan Hont, "The Language of Sociability and Commerce: Samuel Pufendorf and the Theoretical Foundation of the 'Four-Stages Theory,'" in *Jealousy of Trade: International Competition and the Nation-State in Historical Perspective* (Cambridge, 2005); Hont, "Adam Smith's History of Law and Government as Political Theory," in *Political Judgement: Essays in Honour of John Dunn*, ed. Raymond Geuss and Richard Bourke (Cambridge, 2009); Christopher Berry, *The Social Theory of the Scottish Enlightenment* (Edinburgh, 1997); Jennifer Pitts, *A Turn to Empire: The Rise of Imperial Liberalism in Britain and France* (Princeton, 2005), chap. 1; Sankar Muthu, *Enlightenment against Empire* (Princeton, 2004).

8. Commentators such as Robert Nisbet have noted the link between the rise of social theory and postrevolutionary debates about politics and society, noting the conservative origins of organic conceptions of society in the antirevolutionary thought of Burke, de Maistre, and Bonald, on the one hand, and the romantic rediscovery of the medieval concept of the corporate group as a bulwark against atomized individualism and the growth of state power, on the other. But while these analyses rightly highlight concepts that would become central to social theory—such as the prioritization of the concept of social order, the critique of the ideal of individualism, as well as an emphasis on pre- or nonrational belief as the foundation of authority—they do not account for the characteristic, dichotomous form that modern social theory would come to take. In this respect, what seems of crucial importance are a related but distinct set of postrevolutionary debates that likewise were framed by a rejection of Enlightenment perfectionism and the ideals of the French Revolution, but conducted in terms of a political, historical, and sociological reevaluation of ancient society. See Robert A. Nisbet, "The French Revolution and the Rise of Sociology in France," *American Journal of Sociology* 49, no. 2 (1943): 156–64; Nisbet, "Conservatism and Sociology," *American Journal of Sociology*, 58, no. 2 (1952): 167–75; Leon Bramson, *The Political Context of Sociology* (Princeton, 1961).

9. Benjamin Constant, "The Liberty of Ancients Compared with That of the Moderns," speech given at the Athénée Royal in 1819, in Benjamin Constant, *Political Writings* (Cambridge, 1988), 309–28.

10. Constant, "The Liberty of the Ancients," 311.

11. Ibid., 312. Constant himself cites Condorcet as the originator of this claim.

12. Ibid., 311.

13. Ibid., 317.

14. Ibid., 318.

15. Ibid., 317–20.

16. For an examination of the impact of the Terror in constructing an unbridgeable gap between ancient and modern liberty, see Martin Thom, *Republics, Nations, Tribes* (London, 1995), 13–30, 87–150.

17. Constant, "The Liberty of the Ancients," 312.

18. Barthold Georg Niebuhr, *The History of Rome*, trans. Julius Charles Hare and Connop Thirlwall (Philadelphia, 1835). Originally published as *Römische Geschichte* between 1811 and 1832.

19. A. D. Momigliano, "New Paths of Classicism in the Nineteenth-Century," in *A. D. Momigliano: Studies on Modern Scholarship* (Berkeley, 1994), 230.

20. This interpretation of the agrarian law as the basis for the equal distribution of property was a central theme of republican discourses from Machiavelli and Harrington to Rousseau. The crucial misconception, for Niebuhr, stemmed from the fact that republican proponents of the agrarian law had generalized the idea of limiting property from what was a specific rule relating only to the precarious tenures in the *ager publicus*, or public lands. Over time possession in the *ager publicus* became inheritable and exclusive and thus for practical purposes was treated like true proprietary right. Initially this right to possession in the *ager publicus* was limited to original Roman citizens (patricians), but with the growth of plebeian incorporation and power, the call for a more equitable distribution of public lands was increasingly heard. For Niebuhr, the agrarian law in its formulation from the Servian and Licinian laws to the reforms of the Gracchi, rather than attempts to undermine property were promulgated for the purpose of allowing more citizens a share in lands that had been usurped by a few. The true purpose of the agrarian law was thus to raise the status of this possession to real property, especially in relation to plebian tenures. Niebuhr claimed his insight into the nature of the *ager publicus* in ancient Rome came to light through his comparative study of leasehold property among different countries, most notably the study of feudalism in the East Indies. Niebuhr's friend James Grant, a tax official and major figure in the debate on the permanent settlement of Bengal, in *An Inquiry into the Nature of Zemindary Tenures in the Landed Property of Bengal* (London, 1791), had argued that the *zamindars* (who were given property rights under Cornwallis's scheme) were not true owners but appeared as such because they had over time usurped public lands to which they were meant to act as tax-collecting agents of the sovereign. It was this debate on permanent settlement and the characterization of the *zamindar* in Indian land tenure that clarified Niebuhr's understanding of the kind of hereditary occupation linked to the *ager publicus*. For Niebuhr, like Eastern sovereigns (according to accepted theory of Oriental despotism) who were the real owner of all the lands, the ancient polis was also

the absolute owner in a similar way. See B. G. Niebuhr, *Lectures on the History of Rome*, trans. Leonhard Schmitz [based on lectures given in 1823–29] (London, 1873), chap. 30, and Niebuhr, *The History of Rome*, 2:97–130. See especially Momigliano, "New Paths of Classicism in the Nineteenth Century," 232–36.

21. Niebuhr, *The History of Rome*, 1:xx.

22. Ibid., 1:xiii.

23. Niebuhr, *Lectures on the History of Rome*, 80.

24. Ibid.

25. Ibid., 103.

26. Ibid., 101.

27. Ibid.

28. Ibid., 104–8. Morgan had argued that the plebs had no *gentes*, but likewise construed the conflict of the orders as pertaining to gaining access to the gentile order and thus the state. See Lewis Henry Morgan, *Ancient Society; or, Researches in the Lines of Human Progress from Savagery through Barbarism to Civilization* (1877; Tucson, 1985).

29. Niebuhr, *Lectures on the History of Rome*, 100.

30. Niebuhr, *The History of Rome*, 1:297–330, and Niebuhr, *Lectures on the History of Rome*, 82–112.

31. Niebuhr, *Lectures on the History of Rome*, 101–3.

32. Niebuhr's account also influenced Marx's analysis of ancient forms of collective property. See especially Norman Levine, "The German Historical School of Law and the Origins of Historical Materialism," *Journal of the History of Ideas* 48, no. 3 (1987): 431–51.

33. See Thomas R. Trautmann, *Lewis Henry Morgan and the Invention of Kinship* (Berkeley, 1987); Adam Kuper, *The Invention of Primitive Society: Transformations of an Illusion* (London, 1988); Stocking, *Victorian Anthropology*. Maine's connection to Niebuhr was forged through his close association with Thirwall and Hare (Niebuhr's English translators) at Cambridge. See Nick O'Brien, "'Something Older than Law Itself': Sir Henry Maine, Niebuhr, and 'the Path Not Chosen,'" *Journal of Legal History* 26, no. 3 (2005): 229–51.

34. Numa Denis Fustel de Coulanges, *The Ancient City* (New York, 1873). Originally published as *La cité antique* (Paris, 1864). Fustel had no knowledge of Maine's work when this work was published. The two thinkers later dissented most importantly on the question of whether or not archaic Roman law had a conception of private property (Fustel thought it did, while Maine thought ownership if it existed was communal). Nevertheless, Fustel was an admirer of Maine's and, indeed, delivered Maine's eulogy upon his death in France in 1888.

35. Fustel de Coulanges, *The Ancient City*, 11.

36. Ibid., 12.

37. After 1870 and the experience of the Paris Commune, Fustel directed his attention to a more pointed defense of private property (from ancient and medieval examples), and was less preoccupied with the religious aspects of ancient society. Durkheim, a student of Fustel's, would strikingly take up Fustel's structural analysis of religion and kinship in *The Elementary Forms of Religious Life* (1912; New York, 1995).

38. Fustel de Coulanges, *The Ancient City*, 220.

39. Ibid., 219.
40. Maine, *Ancient Law*, 250.
41. Ibid., 121.
42. Ibid.; Fustel de Coulanges, *The Ancient City*; Morgan, *Ancient Society*; and Durkheim, *The Elementary Forms of Religious Life*.
43. Wolin formulates the development of modern social theory as a tradition of thinking that worked toward "the erosion of the distinctively political." For Wolin, this is not simply a methodological claim that delineates and divides the domains appropriate for political philosophy, on the one hand, and modern social science, on the other. Rather, it is a not-so-innocent substantive claim about the status of the political itself. In privileging the role of sociological, economic, and cultural factors in the explanation of modern society, social theory views politics as "a derivative form of activity, one that is to be understood in terms of more 'fundamental' factors." Whether these fundamental factors are construed as primarily economic, cultural, or even psychological in character, the implication is that political phenomena (ideas, institutions, and practices) have no unique identity or purpose that is not ultimately dependent upon an underlying set of social processes and imperatives. See Sheldon S. Wolin, *Politics and Vision: Continuity and Innovation in Western Political Thought* (Princeton, 2004), chap. 9.
44. Arendt's understanding of the rise of the "social" and the threat it poses to political freedom was specified in quite different (almost opposite) terms. The social question in a strict sense was "what we may better and more simply call the existence of poverty"(60) and its effect on politics was not to restrict but dangerously expand the domain of politics. Thus, Arendt's warning concerned the proper *limitations of politics*, for "every attempt to solve the social question with political means leads into terror" (112). See especially Hannah Arendt, *On Revolution* (New York, 1963), 59–114.
45. For Montesquieu, republican government required strict limitations of contract for the purpose of maintaining and promoting equality and frugality. In land law this meant that the initial equal division of land could not be altered or divided easily. Even upon succession, inheritance was regulated in such a way as to disallow free testamentary succession and thus preclude disruptions to the fundamental laws of republics. In Montesquieu, *patria potestas*—a principle of power seemingly at odds with republican equality—is rendered an "auxiliary" power, necessary to supplement the lack of repressive power in republics. Also, the domestic sphere, as the prime location for the reproduction of republican mores, is understood as justifiably constrained by patriarchal power. Thus the tutelage of women, the institutional view of women as under a perpetual guardianship of father, husband, or kinsmen, is construed as the appropriate counterpart to republican equality in the public sphere. See Montesquieu, *The Spirit of the Laws* (Cambridge, 1989), 44–46, 50–51, 107.
46. Émile Durkheim, *Montesquieu and Rousseau: Forerunners of Sociology* (Ann Arbor, 1965), 4–5. On Montesquieu's comparative method, see Melvin Richter, "The Comparative Study of Regimes and Societies," in *The Cambridge History of Eighteenth-Century Political Thought*, ed. Mark Goldie and Robert Wokler (Cambridge, 2006), 147–71.
47. Durkheim, *Montesquieu and Rousseau*, 3–4.

48. Ibid., 24–35.
49. Ibid., 13. In the Latin original, the term is *political science*. See Émile Durkheim, *Montesquieu: Quid Secundatus Politicae Scientae Instituendae Contulerit/ Montesquieu's Contribution to the Establishment of Political Science* (Oxford, 1997), 20–20e.
50. Durkheim, *Montesquieu and Rousseau*, 18.
51. Maine, *Ancient Law*, 110–13.
52. John Stuart Mill, "Remarks on Bentham's Philosophy," in *The Collected Works of John Stuart Mill*, vol. 10, *Essays on Ethics, Religion, and Society*, ed. John M. Robson (Toronto, 1985), 10.
53. Durkheim, *Montesquieu and Rousseau*, 17.
54. Maine, *Ancient Law*, 85.
55. Ibid., 22–23.
56. Durkheim, *Montesquieu and Rousseau*, 3–4.
57. The key figure in intimating the connection between these ancient languages was William Jones in his 1786 presidential address to the Asiatic Society in Calcutta. Thomas R. Trautmann, *Aryans and British India* (Berkeley, 1997). See also Schwab, *The Oriental Renaissance*; Thomas R. Trautmann, *Languages and Nations: The Dravidian Proof in Colonial Madras* (Berkeley, 2006); Maurice Olender, *The Languages of Paradise: Race, Religion, and Philology in the Nineteenth Century*, trans. Arthur Goldhammer (Cambridge, 1992). The discovery of the Indo-European language family was also crucial in displacing eighteenth-century comparative models based upon forms of government and property with ones that sought affinities and contrasts in terms of genealogical connections among languages, races, and nations. On how theses linguistic models and the Indo-European idea worked to displace earlier schemas of comparison, see especially Thom, *Republics, Nations, and Tribes*.
58. Maine, *Village-Communities*, 6. Also Maine, *Ancient Law*, 118.
59. Henry Sumner Maine, "The Effects of Observation of India on Modern European Thought," the Rede Lecture of 1875, reprinted in *Village-Communities*, 209.
60. Maine, *Village-Communities*, 22.
61. Maine, *Ancient Law*, 3.
62. Ibid., 116.
63. Maine, "The Effects of Observation of India," in *Village-Communities*, 215.
64. Johannes Fabian, *Time and the Other: How Anthropology Makes Its Object* (New York, 1983). Fabian's work explores the ethical implications of this kind of temporal distancing.
65. Maine, *Village-Communities*, 6–7.
66. See Trautmann, *Aryans and British India*. Most tellingly, in all his works, Maine never once treats Aryan societies as essentially different from or in opposition to non-Aryan histories or institutions.
67. Maine, *Village-Communities*, 8.
68. Henry Sumner Maine, *Lectures on the Early History of Institutions* (London, 1875), 11.
69. Maine, *Village-Communities*, 9.

70. Maine, "The Effects of Observation of India," in *Village-Communities*, 211.

71. Maine, *Ancient Law*, 165–66.

72. Ibid., 119.

73. "The group consists of animate and inanimate property, of wife, children, slaves, land, and goods, all held together by subjection to the despotic authority of the eldest male of the eldest ascending line, the father, grandfather, or even more remote ancestor. The force which binds the group together is Power." Maine, *Early History of Institutions*, 310.

74. Maine, *Ancient Law*, 119.

75. Ibid., 165–67.

76. This was a point also emphasized by Constant.

77. Maine, *Ancient Law*, 140–45.

78. Robert Filmer, the seventeenth-century defender of absolute monarchy, is most famously remembered as the central antagonist of Locke's *First Treatise*. For Filmer, sovereign power was in essence a fatherly authority that, as in the case of the first patriarch Adam, was drawn, not from the consent of his subjects/descendants, but from God. See R. Filmer, *Patriarcha and Other Writings*, ed. Johann P. Sommerville (Cambridge, 1991).

79. Trautmann, *Lewis Henry Morgan and the Invention of Kinship*, 136.

80. Maine, *Village-Communities*, 15.

81. In Maine's words, there was "nothing in the superficial passions, habits, or tendencies of human nature which at all sufficiently accounts for it." Maine, *Village-Communities*, 15.

82. Maine explicitly criticized Morgan and McLennan for assuming the absence of power in the early history of society. See Henry Sumner Maine, *Dissertations on Early Law and Custom* (1883; New York, 1886), chap. 7.

83. Maine, *Early History of Institutions*, 247.

84. Maine, *Ancient Law*, 124.

85. Ibid., 127.

86. Ibid., 124.

87. Ibid., 103–4. Or in an alternative formulation: "England was once the country which Englishmen inhabited. Englishmen are now the people who inhabit England." Maine, *Early History of Institutions*, 73–74.

88. Henry Sumner Maine, *International Law: The Whewell Lectures* (London, 1888).

89. Maine, *Early History of Institutions*, 72.

90. Maine, *Ancient Law*, 261.

91. Ibid.

92. Ibid., 252.

93. Bernard McGrane, *Beyond Anthropology: Society and the Other* (New York, 1989), chap. 3.

94. Burrow sees Maine as oscillating between being an evolutionist and a dichotomist. But in relation to Maine's dichotomism, Burrow focuses less on the status/contract binary than on Maine's claims about the difference between stationary and progressive societies, a distinction that Maine indeed does waver on quite significantly. See Burrow, *Evolution and Society*, chap. 5.

95. As I will argue in chapter five, it is this spatial vision that underpins the theory and practice of indirect rule.

96. Fortes saw Morgan as another fruitful source for the structural analysis of kinship (once shorn of his heavy investment in evolutionism). See Meyer Fortes, *Kinship and the Social Order: The Legacy of Lewis Henry Morgan* (London, 1970).

97. Maine, *Village-Communities*, 175.

98. See A. L. Kroeber, *The Nature of Culture* (Chicago, 1952), A. L. Kroeber and C. Kluckhohn, "Culture: A Critical Review of Concepts and Definitions," *Papers of the Peabody Museum of American Archaeology and Ethnology* 47 (1952), and George W. Stocking, *Race, Culture, and Evolution: Essays in the History of Anthropology* (Chicago, 1968).

99. See Stocking, *Race, Culture, and Evolution*, chap. 9.

100. Ibid.

101. See Franz Boas, *Race, Language, and Culture* (New York, 1940); Boas, *The Mind of Primitive Man* (New York, 1913); and Boas, *Anthropology and Modern Life* (Westport, 1962).

102. They also contested the view that the shift from kinship to locality as ordering principles of society was a universal development.

103. See especially A. R. Radcliffe-Brown, *Structure and Function in Primitive Society: Essays and Addresses* (New York, 1965).

104. I have been emphasizing an equivalence between the *social* and the *cultural* as quasi-autonomous spheres, and indeed often use the terms interchangeably. Given the important differences between social and cultural anthropology, where the tradition of British social anthropology with which Maine was most strongly associated was especially critical of the use of culture (and its emphasis on meaning), my usage can be misleading. My main concern has been to point to some of the ways that the social and the cultural function in similar ways as modes of explanation, a similarity that has been reinforced in contemporary invocations of the *culture*, especially in political theory and political science.

105. Maine, *Ancient Law*, 22–24. See also chapter three for a detailed analysis of Maine's view of legal change.

106. Maine, *Early History of Institutions*, 228.

107. Maine's insistence on this point became ever more politically charged, culminating in his critique of democracy in *Popular Government*.

108. Margaret Archer, *Culture and Agency: The Place of Culture in Social Theory* (Cambridge, 1996).

109. Stocking, *Victorian Anthropology*, 236–37. Also see Dirks for an account of the impact of anthropological methods on colonial governance: Nicholas Dirks, *Castes of Mind: Colonialism and the Making of Modern India* (Princeton, 2001).

110. Stocking, *Victorian Anthropology*, 236.

111. See Max Gluckman, *The Ideas in Barotse Jurisprudence* (New Haven, 1965) and Meyer Fortes and E. E. Evans-Pritchard, *African Political Systems* (London, 1940).

112. Talal Asad, "Two European Images of Non-European Rule," in *Anthropology and the Colonial Encounter*, ed. Asad (New York, 1973).

Chapter Three: Codification in the East and West

1. See Bernard Cohn, *Colonialism and Its Forms of Knowledge* (Princeton, 1998); Radhika Singha, *A Despotism of Law: Crime and Justice in Early Colonial India* (Delhi, 1998); Jon E. Wilson, *The Domination of Strangers: Modern Governance in Colonial India, c. 1780–1835* (London, 2008).

2. The position of Law Member was established by the Charter Act of 1833, first as consultant to the Governor-General's Council and then, after 1861, as a full member of the Viceroy's Legislative Council.

3. J. F. Stephen, "Legislation under Lord Mayo," in *The Life of the Earl of Mayo, Fourth Viceroy of India, Volume II*, ed. W. W. Hunter (London, 1876), 168–69.

4. See Michael Lobban, *The Common Law and English Jurisprudence, 1760–1850* (Oxford, 1991) and Lobban, "How Benthamic Was the Criminal Law Commission?" *Law and History Review* 18, no. 2 (2000): 427–32.

5. See M. E. Lang, *Codification in the British Empire and America* (Amsterdam, 1924).

6. Lindsay Farmer, "Reconstructing the English Codification Debate: The Criminal Law Commission," *Law and History Review* 18, no. 2 (2000): 397–425.

7. This assessment, of course, depends on whether one views the French and German codes (or for that matter the Indian Penal Code) as attaining their self-professed goals as models of enlightened codification. For skepticism of this achievement, see Lang on the French and German codes, and Skuy on the Indian Penal Code. Lang, *Codification in the British Empire and America*, and David Skuy, "Macaulay and the Indian Penal Code of 1862: The Myth of the Inherent Superiority and Modernity of the English Legal System Compared to India's Legal System in the Nineteenth Century," *Modern Asian Studies* 32, no. 3 (1998): 513–57.

8. Whitley Stokes, ed., *The Anglo-Indian Codes* (London, 1891).

9. J. F. Stephen, "Codification in India and England," *Fortnightly Review* 12 (1872): 650.

10. Frederic Harrison, "The English School of Jurisprudence," *Fortnightly Review* 25 (1879): 130.

11. Ibid., 118–19.

12. T. B. Macaulay, "Government of India," 10 July 1833, in *Macaulay: Prose and Poetry* (Cambridge, 1970), 675.

13. Ibid., 679.

14. Ibid.

15. Ibid.

16. See Eric Stokes, *The English Utilitarians and India* (Oxford, 1959), 184–218.

17. Letter to Lord Auckland, Governor-General of India in Council, from Indian Law Commissioners (T. B. Macaulay, J. M. Macleod, G. W. Anderson, F. Millet), dated 2 May 1837. Reprinted in C. D. Dharkar, ed., *Lord Macaulay's Legislative Minutes* (London, 1946), 259–71. This quote is from page 260.

18. Letter to Lord Auckland [Dharkar, *Lord Macaulay's Legislative Minutes*, 263]. See also Skuy on how despite Macaulay's claim to originality, the Penal Code bore the mark of drafts of the envisioned English criminal code. Skuy, "Macaulay and the Indian Penal Code of 1862."

19. See Stokes for a full discussion of Macaulay's connections to Bentham in this regard. Stokes, *The English Utilitarians and India*, 219–20.

20. Letter to Lord Auckland [Dharkar, *Lord Macaulay's Legislative Minutes*, 263]. There were traces of this idea in Bentham's "Specimen for a Penal Code" and in Austin's proposed code for Malta, but Macaulay's was arguably the first use of "illustrations" in enacted legislation. See W. Stokes's Introduction, in *The Anglo-Indian Codes* (Oxford, 1891).

21. See Lobban, *The Common Law and English Jurisprudence*, chap. 7.

22. See Elizabeth Kolsky, "Codification and the Rule of Colonial Difference: Criminal Procedure in British India," *Law and History Review* 23, no. 3 (2005): 631–83.

23. T. B. Macaulay, Minute of 3 March 1836, No. 5. Reprinted in Dharkar, ed., *Lord Macaulay's Legislative Minutes*, 190.

24. Macaulay, "Government of India."

25. Gordon Johnson, "India and Henry Maine," in *The Victorian Achievement of Sir Henry Maine: A Centennial Reappraisal*, ed. Alan Diamond (Cambridge, 1991). See also Sandra den Otter, "'A Legislating Empire': Victorian Political Theorists, Codes of Law, and Empire," in *Victorian Visions of Global Order: Empire and International Relations in Nineteenth-Century Political Thought*, ed. Duncan Bell (Cambridge, 2007).

26. Friedrich Karl von Savigny, "Vom Beruf unserer Zeit für Gesetzgebung und Rechtswissenschaft," in *Thibaut und Savigny*, ed. Jacques Stern (Munich, 1973). References are to the English translation by Abraham Hayward of Savigny, *Of the Vocation of Our Age for Legislation and Jurisprudence* (London, 1831).

27. Savigny, *Of the Vocation of Our Age*, 20.

28. Ibid., 21.

29. Ibid., 58–60.

30. Henry Sumner Maine, "Roman Law and Legal Education," in *Village-Communities in the East and West* (London, 1876), 365. Originally published in *Cambridge Essays* in 1856.

31. This 1856 essay, like his more famous Rede lecture of 1875, was partly pedagogic in nature in arguing for the necessity of a historical knowledge of Roman law for the practical training of English lawyers. At the time Maine was involved in a larger debate about the need for fundamental reform in legal education, which reached a consensus of sorts with the 1846 Report of the Select Committee on Legal Education. The findings emphasized the need for more formal training in the history of both English and Roman law. The academic training for lawyers at the time was negligible, with the one exception being University College London, where Austin had given his lectures on jurisprudence. On recommendation from the Report, the Council of Legal Education attempted to formally integrate training in jurisprudence at the Inns of Court in London, the central institution for gaining professional accreditation to practice law. Five readerships were established at the Inns, one of which on Jurisprudence and Civil Law was offered

and accepted by Maine. Maine's lectures at Middle Temple between the years 1853 and 1860 formed the basis of *Ancient Law*. See R. C. J. Cocks, *Sir Henry Maine: A Study in Victorian Jurisprudence* (Cambridge, 1988), 39–51.

32. Maine, "Roman Law and Legal Education," 333.

33. Ibid., 332.

34. See David Lieberman, *The Province of Legislation Determined: Legal Theory in Eighteenth-Century Britain* (Cambridge, 1989), chaps. 2 and 3; Michael Lobban, "Blackstone and the Science of Law," *Historical Journal* 30 (1987): 311–35.

35. John Austin, *Province of Jurisprudence Determined*, ed. Wilfrid E. Rumble (1832; Cambridge, 1995), 161. Austin was no stranger to the study of Roman law, having studied in Göttingen under Thibaut (Savigny's main antagonist in the German codification debate).

36. Savigny, *Of the Vocation of Our Age*, 29.

37. Ibid., 24–27.

38. Henry Sumner Maine, *Lectures on the Early History of Institutions* (London, 1875), 44–50. See also Henry Sumner Maine, *Ancient Law: Its Connection with the Early History of Society and Its Relation to Modern Ideas* (1861; Tucson, 1986), chaps. 1–3.

39. Maine, "Roman Law and Legal Education," 340.

40. Savigny, *Of the Vocation of Our Age*, 50–51.

41. Maine, "Roman Law and Legal Education," 365.

42. Maine, *Ancient Law*, 1.

43. Maine arguably invented the term *analytical jurisprudence* to describe the work of Austin and Bentham (whose fundamental views of law Maine often took as interchangeable). See especially W. E. Rumble, "John Austin and His Nineteenth-Century Critics: The Case of Sir Henry Maine," *Northern Ireland Legal Quarterly* 39, no. 2 (1988): 119–49. Also W. E. Rumble, *The Thought of John Austin: Jurisprudence, Colonial Reform, and the British Constitution* (London, 1985) and Philip Schofield, "Jeremy Bentham and Nineteenth-Century English Jurisprudence," *Journal of Legal History* 12, no. 1 (1991): 58–88.

44. Austin, *Province of Jurisprudence Determined*, Lecture One.

45. Maine, *Early History of Institutions*, 369.

46. Maine, *Ancient Law*, 7.

47. Ibid., 15.

48. Ibid., 21–24.

49. Ibid., 18–19.

50. Ibid., 17.

51. Ibid., 19.

52. Ibid., 72.

53. Although Maine thought that "few national societies have had their jurisprudence menaced by this peculiar danger of precocious maturity and untimely disintegration," he saw something akin to that instability with rise of popular government (which Maine saw as a revival of ancient democracy and all its defects). Maine, *Ancient Law*, 78. See also Henry Sumner Maine, *Popular Government* (1885; Indianapolis, 1976).

54. Maine, *Ancient Law*, 20–24.

55. Ibid., 23.

56. Ibid., 25 and chap. 2.

57. Ibid., chap. 3.

58. Ibid., 76.

59. Ibid., 82.

60. Ibid., 28.

61. See especially Cocks for an erudite account of the Maine's jurisprudence as a whole. Cocks, *Sir Henry Maine.*

62. Maine, *Village-Communities,* 75.

63. Hastings, the first Governor-General, had introduced a bifurcated legal system, one system for Presidency towns involving English litigants with the Supreme Court at its apex and generally administering English law and another set of Company courts (known as the *Sadr Diwani Adalat*), which eventually were established in every administrative district, administering native law, Mughal criminal law, and Muslim and Hindu personal law. These two sets of courts would eventually be fused in 1861, after the transfer of rule to the Crown.

64. The most well known include William Jones, noted originator of the idea of an Indo-European linguistic family; Nathaniel Halhed, whose 1776 publication of *A Code of Gentoo Laws; or, Ordinations of the Pundits* served to shape the field; H. T. Colebrooke who completed the translation upon Jones's death of *The Digest of Hindu Law on Contracts and Successions.* See B. S. Cohn, "Law and the Colonial State in India," in his *Colonialism and Its Forms of Knowledge* and J. D. M. Derrett, *Religion, Law, and the State in India* (London, 1968).

65. Maine, *Village-Communities,* 31–62.

66. Ibid., 45.

67. See Cohn, "Law and the Colonial State in India"; Derrett, *Religion, Law, and the State in India*; Marc Galanter, *Law and Society in Modern India* (Delhi, 1989).

68. Maine, *Ancient Law,* 33–39; Maine, *Village-Communities,* 41.

69. Maine, *Village-Communities,* 45.

70. Ibid., 75.

71. Ibid., 53.

72. Ibid., 71–72.

73. Ibid., 75.

74. Ibid., 76; Henry Sumner Maine, "Memorandum on Codification in India," *Papers of Sir Henry Maine,* India Office Collections, Mss.Eur.C.179. Reprinted as "Indian Codification," in *Minutes by Sir H. S. Maine, 1862–69: With a Note on Indian Codification, Dated 17th July, 1879* (Calcutta, 1892), 231–39.

75. Maine, *Village-Communities,* 59.

76. Reenacted in 1954 as the Special Marriage Act.

77. Letter to Grant Duff, 22 December 1868, reprinted in George Feaver, *From Status to Contract: A Biography of Sir Henry Maine, 1822–1888* (London, 1969), 102–3.

78. See especially Maine's minutes of 28 January 1864, 11 September 1866, 22 September 1868, 6 October 1868, in *Minutes by Sir H. S. Maine, 1862–69,* 25, 93–94, 204–10, 219.

79. Maine, "Indian Codification," in *Minutes by Sir H. S. Maine, 1862–69*, 232.

80. Ibid.

81. Henry Sumner Maine, "Note on Revival of the Indian Law Commission," Proceedings of the Council of India, India Office Collections, C/138/136–37.

82. Henry Sumner Maine, "Memo on Proposed Appellate Courts in Bengal," 2 May 1879, Proceedings of the Council of India, India Office Collections, C/142/414–15.

83. Maine, "Indian Codification," in *Minutes by Sir H. S. Maine, 1862–69*, 232.

84. Henry Sumner Maine, "Legal Education of Civil Servants," 2 December 1863, in *Minutes by Sir H. S. Maine, 1862–69*, 20.

85. In his most theoretical writing on law and sovereignty, Maine began to call for a "new philosophy of law." See Maine, *Early History of Institutions*, Lecture Twelve.

86. Ibid., Lecture Thirteen.

87. Ibid., 392.

88. Maine, *Village-Communities*, 67–69.

89. Maine, *Early History of Institutions*, Lecture Thirteen.

90. Austin, *Province of Jurisprudence Determined*, 34–36, 141.

91. Ibid., 35.

92. See Rumble, "John Austin and His Nineteenth Century Critics."

93. Maine, *Early History of Institutions*, 364.

94. Ibid., 390.

95. Ibid., 361.

96. Ibid., 359–60.

97. Ibid., 360.

98. Ibid., Lectures Eleven and Twelve.

99. Ibid., 384.

100. Ibid., 389.

101. Ibid., 387.

102. Ibid., 396.

103. Maine, *Popular Government*, Essay Three.

104. Maine, *Popular Government*, 25.

Chapter Four: The Nineteenth-Century Debate on Property

1. J. S. Mill, "Mr. Maine on Village-Communities," *Fortnightly Review* 9 (May 1871): 544.

2. Henry Sumner Maine, "The Effects of Observation of India on Modern European Thought," the Rede Lecture of 1875, in *Village-Communities in the East and West* (London, 1876), 230.

3. Henry Sumner Maine, *Ancient Law: Its Connection with the Early History of Society and Its Relation to Modern Ideas* (1861; Tucson, 1986), 247.

4. Henry Sumner Maine, *Lectures on the Early History of Institutions* (London, 1875), 357.

5. Maine, *Ancient Law*, chap. 3.

6. Ibid., 48.

7. See the discussion in chapter three.

8. Maine also referred to legal development in early modern France as an example of natural law functioning as an arbitrating principle over bifurcated systems of Roman law and customary law. See *Ancient Law*, chap. 4.

9. Ibid., 247.

10. Friedrich Karl von Savigny, *Das Recht des Besitzes* (1803; Vienna, 1865). References are to the English version titled *Von Savigny's Treatise on Possession*, trans. Erskine Perry (London, 1848). For Maine's discussion of Savigny on property, see *Ancient Law*, chap. 8.

11. Maine, *Ancient Law*, 249. (Emphasis in original.)

12. Ibid., 251.

13. Ibid., 252. Marx similarly noted the conflict between the "hybrid, indeterminate forms of property" in customary understandings and the unitary view of property in civil law derived from Roman property law. See Karl Marx, "Debates on the Law of Thefts of Wood," *Collected Works*, vol. 1 (London, 1976), 233.

14. Maine, *Ancient Law*, 252.

15. Maine, *Early History of Institutions*, 1.

16. See Peter Stein, *Legal Evolution: The Story of an Idea* (Cambridge, 1980) and Istvan Hont, "The Language of Sociability and Commerce: Samuel Pufendorf and the Theoretical Foundations of the 'Four-Stages Theory,'" in *Jealousy of Trade: International Competition and the Nation-State in Historical Perspective* (Cambridge, 2005).

17. The other key scholars who combined the literature on "Eastern" and "Western" village-communities were M. M. Kovalevsky and Marx. Kovalevsky was deeply influenced by Maine's work and was an acquaintance of Marx's. It was Kovalevsky who brought Marx a copy of Morgan's *Ancient Society* back from a visit to America. See M. M. Kovalevsky, *Communal Landholding: Causes, Courses, and Consequences of Its Disintegration* (London, 1879).

18. Fustel de Coulanges did not confront Niebuhr directly, but rather focused on the refutation of Mommsen, and, in later works, Fustel turned to a more universal defense of private property. As a classicist and historian, Fustel attacked the major interpretations of the primary sources that undergirded Laveleye's synthesis, most importantly von Maurer's and Maine's reading of *Tacitus* and Mommsen's use of Cicero and Plutarch. But as the thesis on the historical priority of communal property came to be almost universally accepted in the late nineteenth century, Fustel's insistence on an original private property was a lone, but determined, dissenting voice. Numa Denis Fustel de Coulanges, *The Origin of Property in Land* (London, 1891). Originally published in *Revue des Questions Historiques* (April 1889).

19. Numa Denis Fustel de Coulanges, *The Ancient City* (New York, 1874) (originally published as *La cité antique* [Paris, 1864]), and Theodor Mommsen, *A History of Rome*, trans. William Purdie Dickson (London, 1894) (originally published as *Römische Geschichte* [1854]). See also A. D. Momigliano, "New Paths of Classicism in the Nineteenth Century," in *A. D. Momigliano: Studies on Modern Scholarship* (Berkeley, 1994).

20. The theory of the mark-community, in the English context, was first taken up by Kemble in *The Saxons in England* (1849). Later constitutional historians (Stubbs, Freeman, Green) in treating the mark as the basis of medieval politics and the direct ancestor of parliamentary democracy and Westminster-style government, construed their political conclusions through notions of historical right and/or continuity. See John W. Burrow, "'The Village Community' and the Uses of History in Late Nineteenth-Century England," in *Historical Perspectives: Studies in English Thought and Society in Honour of J. H. Plumb*, ed. Neil McKendrick (London, 1974), 255–85.

21. See Burrow, "'The Village Community and the Uses of History," and Clive Dewey, "Images of the Village Community: A Study of Anglo-Indian Ideology," *Modern Asian Studies* 6, no. 3 (1972): 291–328.

22. Mill, "Mr. Maine on Village-Communities," 544.

23. See especially Paolo Grossi, *An Alternative to Private Property: Collective Ownership in the Juridical Consciousness of the Nineteenth Century* (Chicago, 1981). Grossi traces the fascinating story of how Maine's and Fustel's works came to be evoked in parliamentary debates about agrarian land reform in post-Unification Italy.

24. Émile de Laveleye, *De la propriété et de ses formes primitives* (1874; Paris, 1901).

25. Maine, *Village-Communities*, 6–7.

26. Ibid.

27. Ibid., 22.

28. Ibid., Lecture One.

29. Maine, *Early History of Institutions*, 11. "The great difference between the Roman Empire and all other sovereignties of the ancient world lay in the activity of its legislation, through the Edicts of the Praetor and the Constitutions of the Emperors. For many races, it actually repealed their customs and replaced them by new ones. For others, the results of its legislation mixed themselves indistinguishably with their law. With others, it introduced or immensely stimulated the habit of legislation; and this is one of the ways in which it has influenced the stubborn body of Germanic custom prevailing in Great Britain." Ibid., 20–21.

30. Maine, *Village-Communities*, 10.

31. Ibid., 61.

32. The other main example of this form of social organization was the East European House Community. See Henry Sumner Maine, *Dissertations on Early Law and Custom* (1883; New York, 1886), chap. 8, and *Early History of Institutions*, Lecture Three.

33. Most importantly from Niebuhr's discovery of Gaius's Institutes in 1814.

34. Maine, *Early History of Institutions*, 107–18.

35. Maine, *Ancient Law*, 252.

36. Maine, *Early History of Institutions*, 72–73.

37. Maine, *Village-Communities*, 79.

38. Ibid., 78.

39. Maine, *Early History of Institutions*, 81.

40. Ibid., Lectures Four and Five.

41. Ibid., 120.

42. Maine, *Ancient Law*, 102.

43. Ibid., chap. 8.

44. Maine, *Early Law and Custom*, 253.

45. Maine, *Village-Communities*, 21. Also Maine, *Early History of Institutions*.

46. Marx specifically criticized Maine's "twofold" account of the origins of private property that Maine construed as arising from the natural disentanglement of the rights of individual members from the collective whole and the growth of the proprietary and political authority of the tribal chief. For Marx, these were not separate developments, but rather two sides of a single process. Marx emphasized the latter, that is, the history of expropriation, as the dominant and formative cause of the dissolution of communal tenures. For Marx, private property did not emerge naturally from, and thus could not be simply derived from, the process of dissolution of communal forms. Rather the historical rise of private property signifies the replacement tout court of one institutional form of property with another. This stress on the fundamental discontinuity between ancient and modern forms was also echoed in Marx's critique of Maine's account of the rise of the nuclear family and his intimation of the origins of territorial sovereignty in tribal sovereignty. See Marx's excerpts and notes on Maine in *The Ethnological Notebooks of Karl Marx*, ed. Lawrence Krader (The Netherlands, 1972).

47. See Dewey, "Images of the Village Community: A Study of Anglo-Indian Ideology."

48. See Louis Dumont, "The 'Village-Community' from Munro to Maine," *Contributions to Indian Sociology* 9 (1966): 67–89.

49. Maine, *Village-Communities*, 24.

50. Ibid., 26–27.

51. Maine, *Early History of Institutions*, 390.

52. Maine, *Village-Communities*, 149.

53. For more general accounts of these debates on land tenure and rival revenue systems see Ranajit Guha, *A Rule of Property for Bengal: An Essay on the Idea of Permanent Settlement* (Paris, 1963); Eric Stokes, *The English Utilitarians and India* (Oxford, 1959); Burton Stein, ed., *The Making of Agrarian Policy in British India, 1770–1900* (Delhi, 1992); Stein, *Thomas Munro: The Origins of the Colonial State and His Vision of Empire* (Delhi, 1989).

54. Thomas R. Metcalf, "The Struggle over Land Tenure in India, 1860–1868," *Journal of Asian Studies* 21, no. 3 (1962): 295–307; Metcalf, *The Aftermath of Revolt: India, 1857–1870* (Princeton, 1964); Peter Robb, *Ancient Rights and Future Comfort: Bihar, the Bengal Tenancy Act of 1885, and British Rule in India* (London, 1997); Eric Stokes, *The Peasant and the Raj: Studies in Agrarian Society and Peasant Rebellion in Colonial India* (Cambridge, 1978).

55. Maine, *Village-Communities*, 157.

56. Ibid., 158.

57. Maine, *Ancient Law*, 252.

58. "A village, geographically considered, is a tract of country comprising some hundreds or thousands of acres of arable and waste land. Politically viewed, it resembles a corporation or township. Its proper establishment of officers and servants consists of the following descriptions. The *Potail*, or head inhabitant,

who has the general superintendence of the affairs of the village, settles the disputes of the inhabitants, attends to the police, and performs the duty of collecting the revenue within the village;—the *Curnum*, who keeps the accounts of cultivation, and registers everything connected with it;—the *Tallier* and *Totie*—the duty of the former appearing to consist in a wider and more enlarged sphere of action, in gaining information of crimes and offences, and in escorting and protecting persons travelling from one village to another; the province of the latter appearing to be more immediately confined to the village—consisting, among other duties, in guarding the crops and assisting in measuring them; the *Boundaryman* who preserves the limits of the village, and gives evidence respecting them in cases of dispute;—the *Superintendent of Tanks* and *Water-Courses*, who distributes the water for purposes of agriculture;—the *Bramin*, who performs the village worship;—the *Schoolmaster*, who is seen teaching the children in the villages to read and write in the sand;—the *Calendar Bramin*, or astrologer, who proclaims the lucky or unpropitious periods for sowing and threshing;—the *Smith* and *Carpenter*, who manufacture the implements of agriculture, and build the houses of the ryots;—the *Potman*, or Potter; the *Washerman*; the *Barber*; the *Cowkeeper*; who looks after the cattle; the *Doctor*; the *Dancing-Girl*, who attends at rejoicings; the *Musician*; and the *Poet*. . . . Under this simple form of municipal government, the inhabitants of the country have lived, from time immemorial. The boundaries of the village have been but seldom altered; and though the villages themselves, have been sometimes injured, and even desolated, by war, famine, and disease; the same name, the same limits, the same interests, and even the same families, have continued for ages. The inhabitants give themselves no trouble about the breaking-up and division of kingdoms; while the village remains entire, they care not to what power it is transferred, or to what sovereign it devolves; its internal economy remains unchanged; the Potail is still the head inhabitant, and still acts as the petty judge and magistrate, and collector or renter of the village." W. K. Firminger, ed., *The Fifth Report from the Select Committee of the House of Commons on the Affairs of the East India Company Dated 28th July, 1812* (Calcutta, 1917), 157–58. See also Dumont, "The 'Village Community' from Munro to Maine."

59. Wilks claims to have taken his description from Munro's settlement "Report on Anantapur" of 1806. See Mark Wilks, *Historical Sketches of the South of India in an Attempt to Trace the History of Mysoor from the Origins of the Hindoo Government of That State to the Extinction of the Mohammedan Dynasty in 1799*, vol. 1 (1810; Mysore, 1930), 139.

60. George Campbell, *Modern India: A Sketch of the System of Civil Government with Some Accounts of the Natives and Native Institutions* (London, 1852) and Mountstuart Elphinstone, *History of India* (London, 1839).

61. See C. P. Brown, ed., *Three Treatises on Mirasi Right: By Francis W. Ellis, Lieutenant Colonel Blackburne, Sir Thomas Munro, with Remarks by the Court of Directors, 1822 and 1824* (Madras, 1852).

62. Maine, *Village-Communities*, 182.

63. Ibid., 183.

64. Henry Sumner Maine, "Talookdaree Bill, Waste Lands, and Redemption of Land Revenue in Oudh," 10 July 1864, *Papers of Sir Henry Maine*, India Office Collections, Mss.Eur.C.179; and Maine, *Village-Communities*, chap. 6.

65. Maine, *Village-Communities*, 197.

66. Ibid., 191.

67. Ibid., 33.

68. Ibid., 151.

69. Ibid., 112–13.

70. Ibid., 26–28.

71. Henry Sumner Maine, "Prinsep's Punjab Theories," in *Minutes By Sir H. S. Maine* (Calcutta, 1892), 105–6.

72. Henry Sumner Maine, "Tenant Right in Punjab," 5 April 1867, *Papers of Sir Henry Maine*, India Office Collections, Mss.Eur.C.179.

73. Maine, *Village-Communities*, 181.

74. Clive Dewey, "The Influence of Sir Henry Maine on Agrarian Policy in India," in *The Victorian Achievement of Sir Henry Maine: A Centennial Reappraisal*, ed. Alan Diamond (Cambridge, 1995), 353–75. This will also be discussed in chapter five.

75. Maine's formulations about chiefly property and tribal sovereignty were primarily drawn from Irish sources. See Maine, *Early History of Institutions*.

76. See especially S. B. Cook, *Imperial Affinities: Nineteenth-Century Analogies and Exchanges between India and Ireland* (New Delhi, 1993).

77. Cook, *Imperial Affinities*; A. W. Coats, "The Historist Reaction in English Political Economy, 1870–90," *Economica* 21 (May 1954): 143–53.

78. E. D. Steele, "J. S. Mill and the Irish Question: The Principles of Political Economy, 1848–65," *Historical Journal* 13, no. 2 (1970); E. D. Steele, "J. S. Mill and the Irish Question: Reform and the Integrity of Empire, 1865–70," *Historical Journal* 13, no. 3 (1970); R. D. Collison Black, *Economic Thought and the Irish Question* (Cambridge, 1960); Bruce Kinzer, *England's Disgrace? J.S. Mill and the Irish Question* (Toronto, 2001).

79. John W. Burrow, *Evolution and Society: A Study in Victorian Social Theory* (Cambridge, 1968).

80. Maine, "The Effects of Observation of India," 233.

Chapter Five: Native Society in Crisis

1. Henry Sumner Maine, "The Effects of Observation of India upon European Thought," the Rede Lecture of 1875, *Village-Communities in the East and West* (London, 1876), 236–37.

2. Maine, *Village-Communities*, 22–23.

3. Evelyn Baring, Earl of Cromer, "Some Indian Problems," in *Political and Literary Essays, 1908–1913* (London, 1913), 418. Cromer here is paraphrasing a passage from Paul Boell that in the original reads as follows: "La question qui se pose n'est pas de savoir si l'Angleterre a le droit de conserver l'Inde, mais bien plutôt *si elle a le droit de la quitter.*" Paul Victor Boell, *L'Inde et le question indien* (Paris, 1901), 289.

4. Sir Charles Lewis Tupper, "India and Sir Henry Maine," *Journal of the Society of Arts* 46 (1898): 391.

5. Ibid., 396.

6. Ibid., 399.

7. Ibid., 395.

8. See especially Nicholas B. Dirks, *Castes of Mind: Colonialism and the Making of Modern India* (Princeton, 2001) and Thomas R. Metcalf, *Ideologies of the Raj* (Cambridge, 1994).

9. Henry Sumner Maine, "India," in *The Reign of Queen Victoria: A Survey of Fifty Years of Progress*, ed. Thomas Humphrey Ward (London, 1887), 474. See also Henry Sumner Maine, "Indian Statesmen and English Scribblers," *Saturday Review* 4 (24 October 1857): 361.

10. Ibid., 474.

11. Ibid., 478.

12. Ibid., 476.

13. Dirks, *Castes of Mind*, 148.

14. As Dirks has argued, "there was an explosion of ethnographic research, collection, and writing in the last decades of the nineteenth century, as the state sought to accumulate the knowledge necessary both to explain the occurrence of the rebellion and to assure that it would never happen again. Victoria's proclamation of noninterference further necessitated a detailed catalogue of what had to be preserved and protected, even as various agencies of the colonial state—from the magistracy and the courts to the police and the army—came to assume the foundational character of ethnographic knowledge." Dirks, *Castes of Mind*, 148. More generally see Part Three on "The Ethnographic State," 125–228.

15. Queen's Proclamation of 1 November 1858. Excerpts of the speech are taken from C. H. Philips, H. L. Singh, and B. N. Pandey, eds., *The Evolution of India and Pakistan, 1858 to 1947: Select Documents* (London, 1962), 11.

16. Although Maine is often associated with this earlier school, I think such a close identification is mistaken. This is partly based on a mischaracterization of the so-called Romantic school (see note 36 below). Unlike the Burkean, Scottish, and Romantic schools, Maine had a distinct ethnographic understanding of tradition. This view also shaped his sharper (civilizational) distinction between ancient and modern societies.

17. Maine, "The Effects of Observation of India," 214–16.

18. Maine, *Village-Communities*, 39.

19. See chapter two for an extended duscussion of this point.

20. For this argument, I rely heavily on Clive Dewey's detailed and striking analysis of Maine's impact in Indian administrative circles. See especially Clive Dewey, "The Influence of Sir Henry Maine on Agrarian Policy in India," in *The Victorian Achievement of Sir Henry Maine: A Centennial Reappraisal*, ed. Alan Diamond (Cambridge, 1995) and Clive Dewey, "A Brief Introduction to the Settlement Literature," in *The Settlement Literature of the Greater Punjab: A Handbook* (Delhi, 1991).

21. Maine, *Village-Communities*, 22.

22. Tupper, "India and Sir Henry Maine," 396.

23. Such as E. G. Wace, *Report of the Land Revenue Settlement of the Hazara District of the Punjab* (Oxford, 1876); S. S. Thorburn, *Report of the First Regular Land Revenue Settlement of the Bannu District in the Derajat Division of the Punjab* (Oxford, 1879); D. C. Ibbetson, *Report on the Revision of Settlement of the Panipat Tahsil & Karnal Parganah of the Karnal District, 1872–1880* (Ann

Arbor, 1883); James Wilson, *Final Report on the Revision of Settlement of the Sirsá District in the Punjáb* (London, 1884); Ibbetson, *Census Report for the Punjab* (1883). See Dewey, "A Brief Introduction to the Settlement Literature."

24. Dirks, *Castes of Mind*, 43.

25. Ibid., chaps. 7, 8, and 9.

26. See the discussion of James Mill and Charles Grant in chapter one.

27. Maine, "The Effects of Observation of India," 219.

28. Ibid., 220.

29. See especially Lyall's and Hunter's works on caste and clan formation: A. C. Lyall, *Asiatic Studies: Religious and Social* (1882; London, 1899), and W. W. Hunter, *The Annals of Rural Bengal* (London, 1868).

30. Dewey, "A Brief Introduction to the Settlement Literature," 27.

31. Maine, "The Effects of Observation of India," 215.

32. Ibid., 224.

33. Ibid., 215.

34. Tupper, "India and Sir Henry Maine," 399.

35. Maine thought this could be the case for both for India and Ireland. See *Early History of Institutions*, 18–19.

36. For the view of Maine as a reviver of older Indian administrative traditions, see C. Bayly, "Maine and Change in Nineteenth-Century India," in *The Victorian Achievement of Sir Henry Maine*, ed. Diamond, and Eric Stokes, *The English Utilitarians and India* (Oxford, 1959). I think this is a misperception of Maine and stems in part from a mischaracterization of this earlier school of paternalism. This earlier school—especially Munro, Malcolm, and Elphinstone—was less formed by a conservative romanticism than an enlightened liberalism of a Scottish kind. See Martha McLaren, *British India and British Scotland, 1780–1830: Career Building, Empire Building, and a Scottish School of Thought on Indian Governance* (Akron, 2001).

37. See especially Edmund Burke, "Speech on Opening of Impeachment," 15 February 1788, in *Writings and Speeches of Edmund Burke*, vol. 6, *India: The Launching of the Hastings Impeachment*, ed. P. J. Marshall (Oxford, 1991), 303–5.

38. Maine, "The Effects of Observation of India," 233.

39. Tupper, "India and Sir Henry Maine," 391.

40. Maine, *Village-Communities*, 101.

41. Maine, "The Effects of Observation of India,' 237–38.

42. Maine detailed this process in reference to two key institutions: the Indian village-community and customary law, both accounts can be found in *Village-Communities*. See chapters three and four.

43. Maine, *Village-Communities*, 22–23.

44. Again the details of Maine's account in these arenas are given in chapters three and four, respectively.

45. Maine, *Village-Communities*, 73.

46. Ibid., 74.

47. Dewey, "The Influence of Sir Henry Maine on Agrarian Policy in India," 353–75.

48. Some of the key acts that were founded upon violations of basic market principles include: The Deccan Agriculturists' Relief Act (1879), Bengal Tenancy Act (1885), Punjab Alienation of Land Act (1900), Bengal Settled Estates Act (1904), Indian Cooperative Societies Act (1904), and Punjab Panchayats Act (1912). See Dewey, "The Influence of Sir Henry Maine on Agrarian Policy in India," 368–70.

49. A. C. Lyall, "Life and Speeches of Sir Henry Maine," *Quarterly Review* 176 (April 1893): 316.

50. Ibid., 288.

51. A. C. Lyall, "Sir Henry Maine," *Law Quarterly Review* 14 (April 1888): 132.

52. Lyall, "Life and Speeches of Sir Henry Maine," 290.

53. Ibid.

54. Ibid., 316.

55. Lyall, *Asiatic Studies*, 223.

56. Ibid., 225.

57. Ibid., 224. For Lyall's interpretation and use of Tocqueville, see also A. C. Lyall, "Government of the Indian Empire," *Edinburgh Review* 325 (January 1884): 1–41.

58. Lyall, *Asiatic Studies*, 225.

59. Ibid., 225.

60. Lyall, "Government of the Indian Empire," 37.

61. See Roger Owen, "Anthropology and Imperial Administration: Sir Alfred Lyall and the Official Use of Theories of Social Change Developed in India after 1857," in *Anthropology and the Colonial Encounter*, ed. Talal Asad (London, 1975), and Eric Stokes, "The Administrators and Historical Writing on India," in *Historians of India, Pakistan, and Ceylon*, ed. C. H. Philips (London, 1961).

62. Lyall, *Asiatic Studies*, 302.

63. James Tod, *The Annals and Antiquities of Rajasthan or the Central and Western Rajpoot States on India* (1829–32; London, 1972).

64. See Owen on Lyall's influence on Cromer's policies in Egypt, specifically the idea of strengthening British power by stressing internal divisions, accommodating and incorporating traditional classes, and abstaining from interference in native customs. Roger Owen, "Anthropology and Imperial Administration," and Roger Owen, "The Influence of Lord Cromer's Indian Experience on British Policy in Egypt, 1883–1907," *St. Antony's Papers* 17 (1965).

65. Lyall, *Asiatic Studies*, 302–3.

66. Lyall, "Government of the Indian Empire," 16.

67. Ibid., 15.

68. Lyall, "Life and Speeches of Sir Henry Maine," 290.

69. Thomas B. Macaulay, "Minute on Indian Education," 2 February 1835, in *Macaulay: Prose and Poetry* (Cambridge, 1970), 729.

70. See Cromer, "The Government of the Subject Races," "Sir Alfred Lyall," "The French in Algeria," "Rome and Municipal Government," and "Some Indian Problems," in Evelyn Baring, Earl of Cromer, *Political and Literary Essays, 1908–1913* (London, 1913); Evelyn Baring, Earl of Cromer, *Ancient and Modern Impe-*

rialism (New York, 1910); F. D. Lugard, *The Dual Mandate in British Tropical Africa* (London, 1922).

71. Cromer, "The Government of the Subject Races," 26. Cromer went on to argue, "it may be said that it will probably never be possible to make a Western silk purse of out of an Eastern sow's ear; at all events, if the impossibility of the task be called into question, it should be recognised that the process of manufacture will be extremely lengthy and tedious" (25).

72. Frank Swettenham, *British Malaya: An Account of the Origin and Progress of British Influence in Malaya* (1906; London, 1948), xii.

73. Legge makes a strong case for viewing Gordon as an early innovator of indirect rule. See J. D. Legge, *Britain in Fiji: 1858–1880* (London, 1958).

74. His other main source of inspiration was J. W. B. Money's *Java: Or How to Manage a Colony; Showing a Practical Solution of the Questions Now Affecting British India* (London, 1861). Money examined the Dutch system in Java to recommend indirect rule for British India, especially as a solution to the crisis following the Mutiny. On Gordon's interest in Maine (and Money) see J. K. Chapman, *The Career of Arthur Hamilton Gordon, First Lord Stanmore, 1829–1912* (Toronto, 1964) and Legge, *Britain in Fiji*.

75. Legge, *Britian in Fiji*, chap. 8.

76. Gordon also followed the work of Lorimer Fison on tribal land tenure in Fiji. Fison is perhaps better known for his later work (with Alfred Howitt) on Australian aboriginal kinship and clan formation, which greatly influenced the theoretical study of kinship (and especially totemism) from Morgan and Durkheim to Frazer and Freud.

77. Quoted from Legge, *Britian in Fiji*, 198.

78. D. A. Low, *Lion Rampant: Essays in the Study of British Imperialism* (London, 1973), 68.

79. See especially Mahmood Mamdani's influential elaboration of this argument in *Citizen and Subject: Contemporary Africa and the Legacy of Late Colonialism* (Princeton, 1996).

80. *The Dual Mandate* was conceived in part as a response to Leonard Woolf's *Empire and Commerce in Africa* (London, 1920).

81. Lugard, *The Dual Mandate in British Tropical Africa*, 58.

82. Ibid., 617.

83. Ibid., 46.

84. Ibid., 94.

85. Ibid., 197.

86. Mamdani, *Citizen and Subject*, chap. 2.

87. Donald Cameron, *Principles of Native Administration and Their Application* (Tanganyika, 1930).

88. See Mamdani for a critical view of the argument that indirect rule was "just a commonsense, pragmatic, and cost-efficient administrative strategy." Mamdani emphasizes that even the primary condition that recommended some form of decentralization—the scarcity of (European) personnel—was artificially created, itself a product of a "decisive shift in the policy orientation of European powers on the continent at the turn of the century, as they dropped the alliance with literate

Africans and began a search for culturally more legitimate allies." Mamdani, *Citizen and Subject*, 74.

89. Many of these officials who would become the chief architects of policies of indirect rule in Britain's "Third Empire," significantly, spent time in Northwest India during the period of the policy reversals discussed above. Lugard was born in post-Mutiny Punjab and started his career as an army officer there. Lord Cromer, the future British Resident in Egypt, had a long career in India, which reached its zenith as Finance Member under Ripon. Cromer was an admirer of Maine's and a friend and close associate of Lyall's, whose work was a major influence. And later, Hailey who was initially mentored by S. S. Thorburn had spent almost thirty years in the Indian Civil Service (as Governor of Punjab and Governor of the United Provinces) before directing the *African Survey*.

90. Lugard, *The Dual Mandate in British Tropical Africa*, 214–29.

91. Ibid., 229.

92. J. C. Smuts, *Africa and Some World Problems, Including the Rhodes Memorial Lectures Delivered in Michaelmas Term, 1929* (Oxford, 1930), 88.

93. Lugard, *The Dual Mandate in British Tropical Africa*, 426–28.

94. Ibid., 88.

95. Ibid., 425–26.

96. "Indirect rule is the characteristically British reaction to the political problem of Africa. It derives partly from our conservatism, with its sense of historical continuity and its aristocratic tradition. Our experience has not taught us to believe in fresh constitutional starts, or in the existence of political principles of universal applicability. . . . But indirect rule derives equally from liberalism with its respect for the freedom of others and its conscious reaction from the old selfish type of imperialism." Marjery Perham, "A Re-Statement of Indirect Rule," *Africa* 7 (1934).

97. Ibid.

98. Marjery Perham, *Colonial Sequence, 1930–1949* (London, 1967).

99. Smuts, *Africa and Some World Problems*, 78. Hailey wrote of the shift in terms of a distinction between the doctrines of *identity* and *differentiation*; the former was motivated by the desire to replant European institutions in Africa, while the latter sought the evolution of separate institutions appropriate for Africa. See Malcolm Hailey, *An African Survey* (London, 1956).

100. Smuts, *Africa and Some World Problems*, 78.

101. Ibid., 78.

102. Dirks, *Castes of Mind*, 15.

Coda: Liberalism and Empire Reconsidered

1. Uday Singh Mehta, *Liberalism and Empire: A Study in Nineteenth-Century British Liberal Thought* (Chicago, 1999); Sankar Muthu, *Enlightenment against Empire* (Princeton, 2003); and Jennifer Pitts, *A Turn to Empire: The Rise of Imperial Liberalism in Britain and France* (Princeton, 2005).

2. Muthu, *Enlightenment against Empire*, 268.

3. Ibid., 280.

4. Pitts, *A Turn to Empire*, 4.

5. Ibid., introduction.

6. Mehta, *Liberalism and Empire*, chap. 6.

7. Ibid., chaps. 5 and 6.

8. See Courtney Jung, *The Moral Force of Indigenous Politics: Critical Liberalism and the Zapatistas* (Cambridge, 2008), and Jung, "The Burden of Culture and the Limits of Liberal Responsibility," *Constellations* 8, no. 2 (2001): 219–35.

9. Thomas R. Metcalf, *Ideologies of the Raj* (Cambridge, 1994).

10. Ibid., 43.

11. Francis Hutchins, *The Illusion of Permanence: British Imperialism in India* (Princeton, 1967), chaps. 1–2, 10.

12. Metcalf, *Ideologies of Raj*, chap. 2.

13. Partha Chatterjee, *The Nation and Its Fragments: Colonial and Postcolonial Histories* (Delhi, 1994), chap. 2.

14. Thomas Holt, *The Problem of Freedom: Race, Labor, and Politics in Jamaica and Britain, 1832–1938* (Baltimore, 1992), and Catherine Hall, *Civilising Subjects: Metropole and Colony in the English Imagination, 1830–1867* (Cambridge, 2002).

15. This evocative phrase is taken from Cheryl Welch, "Colonial Violence and the Rhetoric of Evasion: Tocqueville on Algeria," *Political Theory* 31, no. 2 (2003).

Bibliography

Manuscript Collections

Maine Collection, British Library of Economic and Political Science, London School of Economics.

Maine, Sir Henry, Papers. European Manuscripts: MSS.Eur.C.179. India Office Collections, the British Library.

Published Sources

Aarsleff, Hans. 1983. *The Study of Language in England, 1780–1860*. Minneapolis: University of Minnesota Press.

Adams, William Yewdale. 1998. *Philosophical Roots of Anthropology*. Stanford, CA: CSLI Publications.

Agnani, Sunil. 2007. "*Doux Commerce, Douce Colonisation:* Diderot and the Two Indies of the French Enlightenment." In *The Anthropology of the Enlightenment*, edited by Larry Wolff and Marco Cipolloni. Stanford, CA: Stanford University Press.

———. forthcoming. *European Anticolonialism at Its Limit: Denis Diderot and Edmund Burke, 1770–1800*.

Alter, Stephen G. 1999. *Darwinism and the Linguistic Image: Language, Race, and Natural Theology in the Nineteenth Century*. Baltimore: Johns Hopkins University Press.

Ambirajan, S. 1978. *Classical Political Economy and British Policy in India*. Cambridge: Cambridge University Press.

Anghie, Antony. 2005. *Imperialism, Sovereignty, and the Making of International Law*. Cambridge: Cambridge University Press.

Antoni, Carlo. 1959. *From History to Sociology: The Transition in German Historical Thinking*. Detroit: Wayne State University Press.

Archer, Margaret. 1996. *Culture and Agency: The Place of Culture in Social Theory*. Cambridge: Cambridge University Press.

Arendt, Hannah. 1963. *On Revolution*. New York: Penguin Press.

———. 1976. *The Origins of Totalitarianism*. New York: Harcourt Brace.

Armitage, David. 2000. *The Ideological Origins of the British Empire*. Cambridge: Cambridge University Press.

Arneil, Barbara. 1996. *John Locke and America: The Defence of English Colonialism*. Oxford: Clarendon Press.

Asad, Talal. 1970. *The Kababish Arabs: Power, Authority, and Consent in a Nomadic Tribe*. New York: Praeger.

———. 1975. "Two European Images of Non-European Rule." In *Anthropology and the Colonial Encounter*, edited by Talal Asad. London: Ithaca Press.

———. 1993. *Genealogies of Religion: Discipline and Power in Christianity and Islam*. Baltimore: Johns Hopkins University Press.

Asad, Talal, ed. 1973. *Anthropology and the Colonial Encounter.* New York: Humanities Press.

Augé, Marc. 1979. *The Anthropological Circle: Symbol, Function, History.* Cambridge: Cambridge University Press.

Austin, John. 1995. *The Province of Jurisprudence Determined.* Cambridge: Cambridge University Press.

Bachofen, Johann Jakob. 1967. *Myth, Religion, and Mother Right: Selected Writings of J. J. Bachofen.* Princeton, NJ: Princeton University Press.

Baden-Powell, B. H. 1892. *The Land Systems of British India.* Oxford: Clarendon Press.

———. 1896. *The Indian Village Community.* London: Longman.

———. 1899. *The Origin and Growth of Village Communities in India.* London: Swan Sonnenschein.

Bailey, Anne M., and Josep R. Llobera, eds. 1981. *The Asiatic Mode of Production: Science and Politics.* London: Routledge and Kegan Paul.

Ballantyne, Tony. 2002. *Orientalism and Race: Aryanism in the British Empire.* New York: Palgrave Macmillan.

Baring, Evelyn, Earl of Cromer. 1910. *Ancient and Modern Imperialism.* New York: Longmans, Green.

———. 1913. *Political and Literary Essays, 1908–1913.* London: Macmillan.

Barker, Ernest. 1951. *The Ideas and Ideals of the British Empire.* Cambridge: Cambridge University Press.

———. 1963. *Political Thought in England, 1848–1914.* London: Oxford University Press.

Barringer, T. J. 2005. *Art and Labor in Victorian Britain.* New Haven, CT: Yale University Press.

Bayly, C. A. 1991. "Maine and Change in Nineteenth-Century India." In *The Victorian Achievement of Sir Henry Maine: A Centennial Reappraisal,* edited by Alan Diamond. Cambridge: Cambridge University Press.

———. 1996. *Empire and Information: Intelligence Gathering and Social Communication, 1780–1870.* Cambridge: Cambridge University Press.

Bearce, George D. 1961. *British Attitudes towards India, 1784–1858.* London: Oxford University Press.

Beer, George Louis. 1915. "Lord Milner and British Imperialism." *Political Science Quarterly* 30: 301–8.

Belich, James. 1989. *The Victorian Interpretation of Racial Conflict: The Maori, the British, and the New Zealand Wars.* Montreal: McGill-Queen's University Press.

Bell, Duncan. 2007. *The Idea of Greater Britain: Empire and the Future of World Order.* Princeton, NJ: Princeton University Press.

Bell, Duncan, ed. 2007. *Victorian Visions of Global Order: Empire and International Relations in Nineteenth-Century Political Thought.* Cambridge: Cambridge University Press.

Bellamy, Richard, ed. 1990. *Victorian Liberalism: Nineteenth-Century Political Thought and Practice.* London: Routledge.

Benhabib, Seyla. 2002. *The Claims of Culture: Equality and Diversity in the Global Era.* Princeton NJ: Princeton University Press.

Bentham, Jeremy. 1982. *An Introduction to the Principles of Morals and Legislation*. London: Methuen.

———. 1988. *A Fragment on Government*. Cambridge: Cambridge University Press.

Benton, Lauren. 1999. "Colonial Law and Cultural Difference: Jurisdictional Politics and the Formation of the Colonial State." *Comparative Study of Society and History* 41: 563–88.

———. 2002. *Law and Colonial Cultures: Legal Regimes in World History, 1400–1900*. Cambridge: Cambridge University Press.

Berkowitz, Roger. 2005. *The Gift of Science: Leibniz and the Modern Legal Tradition*. Cambridge, MA: Harvard University Press.

Bernal, Martin. 1987. *Black Athena: The Afroasiatic Roots of Classical Civilization*, vol. 1, *The Fabrication of Ancient Greece, 1785–1985*. London: Vintage.

———. 2001. "The British Utilitarians, Imperialism, and the Fall of the Ancient Model." In *Black Athena Writes Back*, edited by David Chioni Moore. Durham, NC: Duke University Press.

Bernasconi, Robert, and Tommy L. Lott, eds. 2000. *The Idea of Race*. Indianapolis: Hackett.

Berry, Christopher J. 1997. *Social Theory of the Scottish Enlightenment*. Edinburgh: Edinburgh University Press.

Berry, Sara. 1993. *No Condition Is Permanent: The Social Dynamics of Agrarian Change in Sub-Saharan Africa*. Madison: University of Wisconsin Press.

Betts, Raymond F. 1971. "The Allusion to Rome in British Imperialist Thought of the Late Nineteenth and Early Twentieth Centuries." *Victorian Studies* 15: 149–59.

———. 2004. *Assimilation and Association in French Colonial Theory, 1890–1914*. Lincoln: University of Nebraska Press.

Bhabha, Homi K. 1994. *The Location of Culture*. London: Routledge.

Black, R. D. Collison. 1960. *Economic Thought and the Irish Question, 1817–1870*. Cambridge: Cambridge University Press.

———. 1968. "Economic Policy in Ireland and India in the Time of J. S. Mill." *Economic History Review* 21: 321–36.

Boas, Franz. 1913. *The Mind of Primitive Man*. New York: Macmillan.

———. 1940. *Race, Language, and Culture*. New York: Macmillan.

———. 1962. *Anthropology and Modern Life*. Westport, CT: Greenwood Press.

Bock, Kenneth E. 1956. *The Acceptance of Histories: Towards a Perspective for Social Science*. Berkeley: University of California Press.

———. 1966. "The Comparative Method of Anthropology." *Comparative Studies in Society and History* 8: 269–80.

———. 1974. "Comparison of Histories: The Contribution of Henry Maine." *Comparative Studies in Society and History* 16: 232–62.

Bodelson, C. A. 1960. *Studies in Mid-Victorian Imperialism*. London: Heinemann.

Boell, Paul Victor. 1901. *L'Inde et le probleme indien*. Paris: Fontemoing.

Bourke, Richard. 2000. "Liberty, Authority, and Trust in Burke's Idea of Empire." *Journal of the History of Ideas* 61: 453–71.

Bourke, Richard. 2000. "Edmund Burke and Enlightenment Sociability: Justice, Honour, and the Principles of Government." *History of Political Thought* 21: 632–56.

———. 2007. "Edmund Burke and the Politics of Conquest." *Modern Intellectual History* 4: 403–32.

———. forthcoming. *From Empire to Revolution: The Political Life of Edmund Burke*. Princeton, NJ: Princeton University Press.

Bramson, Leon. 1961. *The Political Context of Sociology*. Princeton, NJ: Princeton University Press.

Breckenridge, Carol A., and Peter van der Veer, eds. 1993. *Orientalism and the Postcolonial Predicament: Perspectives on South Asia*. Philadelphia: University of Pennsylvania Press.

Bright, John. 1907. *Selected Speeches by Rt. Honble. John Bright, M.P., On Public Questions*. London: J. M. Dent.

Bromwich, David. 2009. "Moral Imagination." *Raritan* 27: 4–35.

Brown, Charles Philip, ed. 1852. *Three Treatises on Mirasi Right: By Francis W. Ellis, Lieutenant Colonel Blackburne, Sir Thomas Munro, with Remarks by the Court of Directors, 1822 and 1824*. Madras: D. P. L. C. Connor.

Brown, Wendy. 2006. *Regulating Aversion: Tolerance in the Age of Identity and Empire*. Princeton, NJ: Princeton University Press.

Bryce, James. 1901. *Studies in the History and Jurisprudence*. London: Oxford University Press.

Buckler, F. W. 1922. "The Political Theory of the Indian Mutiny." *Transactions of the Royal Historical Society*: 71–100.

Burke, Edmund. 1981. *The Writings and Speeches of Edmund Burke*, vol. 5, *India: Madras and Bengal, 1774–1785*. Oxford: Clarendon Press.

———. 1987. *Reflections on the Revolution in France*. Indianapolis: Hackett.

———. 1991. *The Writing and Speeches of Edmund Burke*, vol. 6, *India: The Launching of the Hastings Impeachment, 1786–1788*. Oxford: Clarendon Press.

———. 2000. *The Writings and Speeches of Edmund Burke*, vol. 7, *India: The Hastings Trial, 1789–1794*. Oxford: Clarendon Press.

Burrow, John W. 1967. "The Uses of Philology in Victorian England." In *Ideas and Institutions of Victorian Britain: Essays in Honour of George Kitson Clarke*, edited by Robert Robson. London: Bell.

———. 1968. *Evolution and Society: A Study in Victorian Social Theory*. Cambridge: Cambridge University Press.

———. 1974. "'The Village Community' and the Uses of History in Late Nineteenth-Century England." In *Historical Perspectives: Studies in English Thought and Society in Honour of J. H. Plumb*, edited by Neil McKendrick, 255–85. London: Europa Publications.

———. 2000. *The Crisis of Reason: European Thought, 1848–1914*. New Haven, CT: Yale University Press.

Bury, J. B. 1932. *The Idea of Progress: An Inquiry into Its Origins and Growth*. New York: Dover.

Cain, P. J., and A. G. Hopkins. 2001. *British Imperialism, 1688–2000*. London: Longman.

Cameron, Donald. 1930. *Principles of Native Administration and Their Application.* Tanganyika.

Campbell, George. 1853. *India as It May Be: An Outline of a Proposed Government and Policy.* London: John Murray.

———. 1853. *Modern India: A Sketch of the System of Civil Government with Some Accounts of the Natives and Native Institutions.* London: John Murray.

———. 1869. *The Irish Land.* London: Trubner.

———. 1881. "The Tenure of Land in India." In *Systems of Land Tenure in Various Countries. A Series of Essays Published under the Sanction of the Cobden Club,* edited by J. W. Probyn. London: Cassell et al.

———. 1893. *Memoirs of My Indian Career.* London: Macmillan.

Cannadine, David. 2001. *Ornamentalism: How the British Saw Their Empire.* Oxford: Oxford University Press.

Cannon, Garland Hampton. 1990. *The Life and Mind of Oriental Jones: Sir William Jones, the Father of Modern Linguistics.* Cambridge: Cambridge University Press.

Cell, John W. 1992. *Hailey: A Study in British Imperialism, 1872–1969.* Cambridge: Cambridge University Press.

Chakrabarty, Dipesh. 2000. *Provincializing Europe: Postcolonial Thought and Historical Difference.* Princeton, NJ: Princeton University Press.

———. 2002. *Habitations of Modernity: Essays in the Wake of Subaltern Studies.* Chicago: University of Chicago Press.

Chakravarty, Gautam. 2005. *The Indian Mutiny and the British Imagination.* Cambridge: Cambridge University Press.

Chakravarty-Kaul, Minoti. 1996. *Common Lands and Customary Law: Institutional Change in North India over the Past Two Centuries.* Delhi: Oxford University Press.

Chanock, Martin. 1982. "Making Customary Law: Men, Women, and Courts in Colonial Northern Rhodesia." In *African Women and the Law: Historical Perspectives,* edited by Margaret Hay and Marcia Wight. Boston: Boston University Press.

———. 1985. *Law, Custom, and Social Order: The Colonial Experience in Malawi and Zambia.* New York: Cambridge University Press.

Chapman, J. K. 1964. *The Career of Arthur Hamilton Gordon, First Lord Stanmore, 1829–1912.* Toronto: University of Toronto Press.

Chatterjee, Partha. 1994. *The Nation and Its Fragments: Colonial and Postcolonial Histories.* Delhi: Oxford University Press.

Chauduri, Sashi Bhusan. 1979. *English Historical Writings on the Indian Mutiny, 1857–1859.* Calcutta: World Press.

Chew, Ernest. 1968. "Sir Frank Swettenham and the Federation of the Malay States." *Modern Asian Studies* 2: 51–69.

Clammer, John. 1975. "Colonialism and the Perception of Tradition in Fiji." In *Anthropology and the Colonial Encounter,* edited by Talal Asad. London: Ithaca Press.

Clifford, James. 1988. *The Predicament of Culture: Twentieth-Century Ethnography, Literature, and Art.* Cambridge, MA: Harvard University Press.

Coats, A. W. 1954. "The Historist Reaction in English Political Economy, 1870–90." *Economica* 21: 143–53.

Cobden, Richard. 1853. *How Wars Are Got Up in India: The Origin of the Burmese War.* London: Cash.

Cocks, R. C. J. 1988. *Sir Henry Maine: A Study in Victorian Jurisprudence.* Cambridge: Cambridge University Press.

Cohn, Bernard. 1961. "From Indian Status to British Contract." *Journal of Economic History* 21: 613–28.

———. 1987. *An Anthropologist among the Historians and Other Essays.* Delhi: Oxford University Press.

———. 1998. *Colonialism and Its Forms of Knowledge.* Princeton, NJ: Princeton University Press.

Colaiaco, James A. 1983. *James Fitzjames Stephen and the Crisis of Victorian Thought.* New York: St. Martin's Press.

Collini, Stefan. 1979. *Liberalism and Sociology: L. T. Hobhouse and Political Argument in England, 1880–1914.* Cambridge: Cambridge University Press.

———. 1980. "Political Theory and the 'Science of Society' in Victorian Britain." *Historical Journal* 23: 203–31.

———. 1984. "Introduction." In *Essays on Equality, Law, and Education: Collected Works XXI,* edited by Stefan Collini. Toronto: University of Toronto Press.

———. 1991. *Public Moralists: Political Thought and Intellectual Life in Britain, 1850–1930.* Oxford: Clarendon Press.

Collini, Stefan, Donald Winch, and John Burrow. 1983. *That Noble Science of Politics: A Study in Nineteenth-Century Intellectual History.* Cambridge: Cambridge University Press.

Collins, Robert O., James MacDonald Burns, and Erik Kristopher Ching, eds. 1996. *Historical Problems on Imperial Africa.* Princeton, NJ: Markus Wiener.

Condorcet, Jean-Antoine-Nicolas de Caritat, Marquis de. 1979. *Sketch for a Historical Picture of the Progress of the Human Mind.* Westport, CT: Hyperion Press.

Conklin, Alice L. 1997. *A Mission to Civilize.* Stanford, CA: Stanford University Press.

Constant, Benjamin. 1988. *Political Writings.* Cambridge: Cambridge University Press.

Cook, S. B. 1993. *Imperial Affinities: Nineteenth Century Analogies and Exchanges between India and Ireland.* New Dehli: Sage.

Cooper, Frederick, and Ann Laura Stoler, eds. 1997. *Tensions of Empire: Colonial Cultures in a Bourgeois World.* Berkeley: University of California Press.

Darwin, Charles. 1859. *On the Origin of Species.* London: John Murray.

Darwin, John. 1997. "Imperialism and the Victorians: The Dynamics of Territorial Expansion." *Economic History Review* 112: 614–42.

Dasgupta, Uma. 1995. "The Ilbert Bill Agitation, 1883." In *We Fought Together for Freedom: Chapters from the Indian Nationalist Movement,* edited by Ravi Dayal. New Delhi: Oxford University Press.

Derrett, J. D. M. 1959. "Sir Henry Maine and Law in India." *Juridical Review* 4: 4–55.

————. 1968. *Religion, Law, and the State in India*. London: Faber and Faber.

Derrida, Jacques. 2002. *Without Alibi*. Stanford, CA: Stanford University Press.

Deschamps, H. 1963. "Et Maintentant, Lord Lugard." *Africa* 33.

Dewey, Clive. 1972. "Images of the Village Community: A Study in Anglo-Indian Ideology." *Modern Asian Studies* 6: 291–328.

————. 1973. "The Education of a Ruling Caste: The Indian Civil Service in the Era of Competitive Examination." *English Historical Review* 88: 262–85.

————. 1974. "Celtic Agrarian Legislation and the Celtic Revival: Historicist Implications of Gladstone's Irish and Scottish Land Acts, 1870–1886." *Past and Present* 64: 30–70.

————. 1974. "The Rehabilitation of the Peasant Proprietor in Nineteenth-Century Economic Thought." *History of Political Economy* 6: 17–47.

————. 1991. "A Brief Introduction to the Settlement Literature." In *The Settlement Literature of the Greater Punjab: A Handbook*, edited by Clive Dewey. Delhi: Manohar.

————. 1991. "The Influence of Sir Henry Maine on Agrarian Policy in India." In *The Victorian Achievement of Sir Henry Maine: A Centennial Reappraisal*, edited by Alan Diamond. Cambridge: Cambridge University Press.

Dharkar, C. D., ed. 1946. *Lord Macaulay's Legislative Minutes*. Oxford: Oxford University Press.

Diamond, Alan, ed. 1991. *The Victorian Achievement of Sir Henry Maine: A Centennial Reappraisal*. Cambridge: Cambridge University Press.

Dirks, Nicholas B., ed. 1992. *Colonialism and Culture*. Ann Arbor: University of Michigan Press.

————. 1993. *The Hollow Crown: Ethnohistory of an Indian Kingdom*. Ann Arbor: University of Michigan Press.

————. 2001. *Castes of Mind: Colonialism and the Making of Modern India*. Princeton, NJ: Princeton University Press.

Dobbin, Christine. 1965. "The Ilbert Bill: A Study in Anglo-Indian Opinion in India, 1883." *Historical Studies* 12: 87–104.

Dumont, Louis. 1966. "The 'Village-Community' from Munro to Maine." *Contributions to Indian Sociology* 9: 67–89.

————. 1986. *Essays on Individualism: Modern Ideology in Anthropological Perspective*. Chicago: University of Chicago Press.

————. 1998. *Homo Hierarchicus: The Caste System and Its Implications*. Delhi: Oxford University Press.

Dungen, P. H. M. van den. 1972. *The Punjab Tradition: Influence and Authority in Nineteenth-Century India*. London: George Allen and Unwin.

Durkheim, Émile. 1951. *Suicide: A Study in Sociology*. New York: Free Press.

————. 1965. *Montesquieu and Rousseau: Forerunners of Sociology*. Ann Arbor: University of Michigan Press.

————. 1984. *The Division of Labor in Society*. New York: Free Press.

————. 1995. *The Elementary Forms of Religious Life*. New York: Free Press.

————. 1997. *Montesquieu: Quid Secundatus Politicae Scientae Instituendae Contulerit/Montesquieu's Contribution to the Establishment of Political Science*. Oxford: Durkheim Press.

Dutton, Geoffrey. 1977. *Edward John Eyre: The Hero as Murderer*. New York: Penguin Books.

Elias, Norbert. 1978. *The Civilizing Process: The History of Manners*. New York: Urizen Books.

Elphinstone, Mountstuart. 1839. *History of India*. London: John Murray.

Embree, Ainslee T. 1962. *Charles Grant and British Rule in India*. New York: Columbia University Press.

Emerson, Rupert. 1937. *Malaysia: A Study in Direct and Indirect Rule*. New York: Macmillan.

Engels, Friedrich. 1972. *The Origin of the Family, Private Property, and the State*. London: Lawrence and Wishart.

Erickson, Arvel B. 1959. "Empire or Anarchy: The Jamaica Rebellion of 1865." *Journal of Negro History* 44: 99–122.

Evans, Morgan O. 1896. *Theories and Criticisms of Sir Henry Maine*. London: Steven and Haynes.

Evans-Pritchard, E. E. 1981. *A History of Anthropological Thought*. London: Faber and Faber.

Fabian, Johannes. 1983. *Time and the Other: How Anthropology Makes Its Object*. New York: Columbia University Press.

Farmer, Lindsay. 2000. "Reconstructing the English Codification Debate: The Criminal Law Commissioners, 1833–45." *Law and History Review* 18: 397–425.

Farrell, H. P. 1917. *An Introduction to Political Philosophy*. London: Longmans, Green.

Feaver, George. 1965. "The Political Attitudes of Sir Henry Maine: Conscience of a 19th Century Conservative." *Journal of Politics*: 290–317.

———. 1969. *From Status to Contract: A Biography of Sir Henry Maine, 1822–1888*. London and Harlow: Longmans, Green.

———. 1991. "The Victorian Values of Sir Henry Maine." in *The Victorian Achievement of Sir Henry Maine: A centennial reappraisal*, edited by Alan Diamond. Cambridge: Cambridge University Press.

Filmer, Robert. 1991. *Patriarcha and Other Writings*. Cambridge: Cambridge University Press.

Finley, M. I. 1976. "Colonies: An Attempt at a Typology." *Transactions of the Royal Historical Society* 26: 167–88.

———. 1977. "The Ancient City: From Fustel de Coulanges to Max Weber and Beyond." *Comparative Studies in Society and History* 19: 305–27.

Firminger, W. K., ed. 1917. *The Fifth Report from the Select Committee of the House of Commons on the Affairs of the East India Company Dated 28th July, 1812*. Calcutta: R. Cambray.

Fisher, Michael. 1991. *Indirect Rule in India: Residents and the Residency System, 1764–1858*. Delhi: Oxford University Press.

Forbes, Duncan. 1951–52. "James Mill and India." *Cambridge Journal* 5: 19–33.

Fortes, Meyer. 1970. *Kinship and the Social Order: The Legacy of Lewis Henry Morgan*. London: Routledge and Kegan Paul.

Fortes, Meyer, and E. E. Evans-Pritchard, eds. 1940. *African Political Systems*. London: Oxford University Press.

Foucault, Michel. 1972. *The Archaeology of Knowledge*. New York: Barnes and Noble.

———. 1977. *Discipline and Punish: The Birth of the Prison*. London: Penguin Books.

———. 1978. *The History of Sexuality: An Introduction*. New York: Vintage.

———. 1991. "Faire vivre et laisser mourir: La naissance du racisme." *Les Temps Modernes* 46.

———. 1991. "Governmentality." In *The Foucault Effect: Studies in Governmentality*, edited by Graham Burchell, Colin Gordon, and Peter Miller. London: Harvester Wheatsheaf.

———. 1994. *The Order of Things: An Archaeology of the Human Sciences*. New York: Vintage.

Francis, Mark. 1980. "The Nineteenth-Century Theory of Sovereignty and Thomas Hobbes." *History of Political Thought* 1: 517–40.

Fredrickson, George. 2000. *The Comparative Imagination: On the History of Racism, Nationalism, and Social Movements*. Berkeley: University of California Press.

Fuller, C. J. 1989. "Misconceiving the Grain Heap: A Critique of the Concept of the Indian Jajmani System." In *Money and the Morality of Exchange*, edited by Jonathan P. Parry and Maurice Bloch. Cambridge: Cambridge University Press.

Furnivall, J. S. 1948. *Colonial Policy and Practice: A Comparative Study of Burma, Netherlands, India*. Cambridge: Cambridge University Press.

Fustel de Coulanges, Numa Denis. 1874. *The Ancient City: A Study on the Religion, Laws, and Institutions of Greece and Rome*. New York: Doubleday Anchor.

———. 1890. *The Origin of Property in Land*. London: George Allen and Unwin.

Galanter, Marc. 1989. *Law and Society in Modern India*. Delhi: Oxford University Press.

Gallagher, John. 1982. *The Decline, Revival, and Fall of the British Empire*. Cambridge: Cambridge University Press.

Gandhi, M. K. 1958. *The Collected Works of Mahatma Gandhi*. Delhi: Government of India.

———. 1997. *Hind Swaraj and Other Writings*. Cambridge: Cambridge University Press.

Geertz, Clifford. 1993. *The Interpretation of Cultures: Selected Essays*. London: Fontana.

Gierke, Otto Friedrich von. 1950. *Natural Law and the Theory of Society, 1500–1800*. Cambridge: Cambridge University Press.

Gilmour, David. 2005. *The Ruling Caste: Imperial Lives in the Victorian Raj*. New York: Farrar, Straus and Giroux.

Gluckman, Max. 1965. *The Ideas in Barotse Jurisprudence*. New Haven, CT: Yale University Press.

Goldberg, David Theo. 2005. "Liberalism's Limits: Carlyle and Mill on 'the Negro Question.'" In *Utilitarianism and Empire*, edited by Bart Schultz and Georgios Varouxakis. Lanham, MD: Lexington Books.

Gopal, S. 1965. *British Policy in India, 1858–1905*. Cambridge: Cambridge University Press.

Gordon, Arthur. 1883. "Native Councils in Fiji, 1875–80." *Contemporary Review* 43.

Gossman, Lionel. 1983. *Orpheus Philologus: Bachofen versus Mommsen on the Study of Antiquity*. Philadelphia: American Philosophical Society.

Grant, Charles. 1832. "Observations of the State of Society among the Asiatic Subjects of Great Britain, Particularly with Respect to Morals; and on the Means of Improving It, Appendix to Report of the Select Committee of the House of Commons on the Affairs of the East India Company." *Parliamentary Papers*.

Grant Duff, Sir Monstuart Elphinstone. 1892. *Sir Henry Maine: A Brief Memoir of His Life . . . With Some of His Indian Speeches and Minutes*. London: Murray.

Grant, James. 1791. *An Inquiry into the Nature of Zemindary Tenures in Landed Property in Bengal*. London: J. Debbit.

Grossi, Paolo. 1981. *An Alternative to Private Property: Collective Property in the Juridical Consciousness of the Nineteenth Century*. Chicago: University of Chicago Press.

Guha, Ranajit. 1963. *A Rule of Property for Bengal: An Essay on the Idea of Permanent Settlement*. Paris: Mouton.

Haakonsen, Knud. 1996. *Natural Law and Moral Philosophy: From Grotius to the Scottish Enlightenment*. Cambridge: Cambridge University Press.

Habibi, Don. 1999. "The Moral Dimensions of J. S. Mill's Colonialism." *Journal of Social Philosophy* 30: 125–46.

Hailey, Malcolm. 1943. *Great Britain, India, and the Colonial Dependencies in the Post-War World*. Toronto: University of Toronto Press.

———. 1943. *The Future of Colonial Peoples*. London: Oxford University Press.

———. 1956. *An African Survey: A Study of Problems Arising in Africa South of the Sahara*. London: Oxford University Press.

Halévy, Elie. 1966. *The Growth of Philosophic Radicalism*. Boston: Beacon Press.

Hall, Catherine. 2002. *Civilising Subjects: Metropole and Colony in the English Imagination, 1830–1867*. Cambridge: Polity Press.

Hall, Catherine, Keith McClelland, and Jane Rendall, eds. 2000. *Defining the Victorian Nation: Race, Class, Gender, and the British Reform Act of 1867*. Cambridge: Cambridge University Press.

Hamburger, Joseph. 1962. "James Mill on Universal Suffrage and the Middle Class." *Journal of Politics* 24: 167–90.

Harrison, Frederic. 1879. "The English School of Jurisprudence." *Fortnightly Review* 25: 114–30.

Hawthorn, Geoffrey. 1976. *Enlightenment and Despair: A History of Sociology*. Cambridge: Cambridge University Press.

Hay, Margaret, and Marcia Wright, eds. 1982. *African Women and the Law*. Boston: Boston University Press.

Herbert, Christopher. 1991. *Culture and Anomie: Ethnographic Imagination in the Nineteenth Century*. Chicago: University of Chicago Press.

———. 2008. *War of No Pity*. Princeton, NJ: Princeton University Press.

Heuman, Gad J. 1994. *"The Killing Time": The Morant Bay Rebellion in Jamaica*. London: Macmillan.

Hirschman, Albert. 1977. *The Passions and the Interests: Political Arguments for Capitalism before Its Triumph*. Princeton, NJ: Princeton University Press.

———. 1991. *The Rhetoric of Reaction: Perversity, Futility, Jeopardy*. Cambridge, MA: Belknap Press.

Hirschmann, Edwin. 1980. *"White Mutiny": The Ilbert Bill Crisis in India and the Genesis of the Indian National Congress*. New Delhi: Heritage Publishers.

Hobbes, Thomas. 1994. *Leviathan*. Cambridge: Cambridge University Press.

Hobsbawm, Eric, and Terence Ranger, eds. 1983. *The Invention of Tradition*. Cambridge: Cambridge University Press.

Hodgen, Margaret T. 1964. *Early Anthropology in the Sixteenth and Seventeenth Centuries*. Philadelphia: University of Pennsylvania Press.

Holdsworth, William. 1982. *A History of English Law*. London: Methuen.

Holt, Thomas. 1992. *The Problem of Freedom: Race, Labor, and Politics in Jamaica and Britain, 1832–1938*. Baltimore: Johns Hopkins University Press.

Hont, Istvan. 2005. *Jealousy of Trade: International Competition and the Nation-State in Historical Perspective*. Cambridge, MA: Belknap Press of Harvard University Press.

———. 2009. "Adam Smith's History of Law and Government as Political Theory." In *Political Judgement: Essays in Honour of John Dunn*, edited by Richard Bourke and Raymond Geuss. Cambridge: Cambridge University Press.

Horrut, Claude. 1982. *Frédéric Lugard et la pensée coloniale britannique de son temps*. Bordeaux: Institute d'études politiques de Bordeaux.

Hostettler, John. 1995. *Politics and Law in the Life of Sir James Stephen*. Chichester: Barry Rose Law Publishers.

Hunter, W. W. 1868. *The Annals of Rural Bengal*. London: Smith, Elder.

———. 1899. *A History of British India*. London: Longmans, Green.

Hunter, W. W., ed. 1876. *A Life of the Earl of Mayo, Fourth Viceroy of India*. London: Smith, Elder.

Hussain, Nasser. 2003. *The Jurisprudence of Emergency: Colonialism and the Rule of Law*. Ann Arbor: University of Michigan Press.

Hutchins, Francis G. 1967. *The Illusion of Permanence: British Imperialism in India*. Princeton, NJ: Princeton University Press.

Ibbetson, Denzil. 1974. *Punjab Castes*. Lahore: Mubarak Ali.

Inden, Ronald. 1990. *Imagining India*. Oxford: Oxford University Press.

Iyer, Raghavan. 1960. "Utilitarianism and All That (the Political Theory of British Imperialism in India)." *St. Antony's Papers* 8: 9–71.

Jhering, Rudolf von. 1880. "The Value of the Roman Law to the Modern World." *Virginia Law Journal* 4: 453–63.

Johnson, Douglas H. 1982. "Evans-Pritchard, the Nuer, and the Sudan Political Service." *African Affairs* 81: 231–46.

Johnson, Gordon. 1991. "India and Henry Maine." In *The Victorian Achievement of Sir Henry Maine: A Centennial Reappraisal*, edited by Alan Diamond. Cambridge: Cambridge University Press.

Johnson, Gordon. 1993. "India and Henry Maine." In *India's Colonial Encounter: Essays in Memory of Eric Stokes*, edited by Mushirul Hasan and Nrayani Gupta. Delhi: Manohar.

Jones, Gareth Stedman. 2002. "Introduction." In *The Communist Manifesto*, edited by Gareth Stedman Jones, 3–187. London: Penguin Classics.

Jones, Iva G. 1967. "Trollope, Carlyle, and Mill on the Negro: An Episode in the History of Ideas." *Journal of Negro History* 52: 185–99.

Jung, Courtney. 2001. "The Burden of Culture and the Limits of Liberal Responsibility." *Constellations* 8: 219–35.

———. 2008. *The Moral Force of Indigenous Politics: Critical Liberalism and the Zapatistas*. Cambridge: Cambridge University Press.

Kantorowicz, H. U. 1937. "Savigny and the Historical School of Law." *Law Quarterly Review* 53.

Kaviraj, Sudipta. 1991. "On State, Society, and Discourse in India." In *Rethinking Third World Politics*, edited by James Manor. London: Longman.

———. 1992. "Marxism and the Darkness of History." *Development and Change* 23: 79–102.

———. 2005. "Outline of a Revisionist Theory of Modernity." *European Journal of Sociology* 46: 497–526.

Kaviraj, Sudipta, and Sunil Khilnani, eds. 2001. *Civil Society: History and Possibilities*. Cambridge: Cambridge University Press.

Kelley, Donald R. 1978. "The Metaphysics of Law: An Essay on the Very Young Marx." *American Historical Review* 83: 350–67.

———. 1984. "The Science of Anthropology: An Essay on the Very Old Marx." *Journal of the History of Ideas* 45: 245–62.

———. 1990. *The Human Measure: Social Thought in the Western Legal Tradition*. Cambridge, MA: Harvard University Press.

Kelley, Donald R., and Bonnie G. Smith. 1984. "What Is Property? Legal Dimensions of the Social Question in France (1789–1848)." *Proceedings of the American Philosophical Society* 128: 200–230.

Kemble, John. 1849. *The Saxons in England: A History of the English Commonwealth till the Period of the Norman Conquest*. London: Green and Longmans.

Kennedy, Duncan. 2003. "Two Globalizations of Law and Legal Thought: 1850–1968." *Suffolk University Law Review* 36: 631–79.

Kennedy, Paul. 1989. *The Rise and Fall of the Great Powers: Economic Change and Military Conflict from 1500 to 2000*. New York: Vintage.

Kinzer, Bruce L. 2001. *England's Disgrace? J. S. Mill and the Irish Question*. Toronto: University of Toronto Press.

Kirk, Russell. 1953. "The Thought of Sir Henry Maine." *Review of Politics* 15: 86–96.

Kirk-Greene, A. H. M., ed. 1965. *The Principles of Native Administration in Nigeria: Selected Documents, 1900–1947*. London: Oxford University Press.

Kirshner, Alexander. 2002. "Character and the Administration of Empires in the Political Thought of Henry Maine." M.Phil thesis. University of Cambridge.

Koebner, Richard. 1961. *Empire*. Cambridge: Cambridge University Press.

Koebner, Richard, and Helmut Dan Schmidt. 1964. *Imperialism: The Story and Significance of a Political Word, 1840–1960*. London: Cambridge University Press.

Kolsky, Elizabeth. 2005. "Codification and the Rule of Colonial Difference: Criminal Procedure in British India." *Law and History Review* 23: 631–83.

Koskenniemi, Martti. 2002. *The Gentle Civilizer of Nations: The Rise and Fall of International Law, 1870–1960*. Cambridge: Cambridge University Press.

Kovalevsky, M. M. 1879. *Communal Landholding: Causes, Courses, and Consequences of Its Disintegration*. London: N.p.

Krader, Lawrence. 1975. *The Asiatic Mode of Production: Sources, Development and Critique in the Writings of Karl Marx*. Assen: Van Gorcum.

Krader, Lawrence, ed. 1972. *The Ethnological Notebooks of Karl Marx (Studies of Morgan, Phear, Maine, Lubbock)*. Assen: Van Gorcum.

Kroeber, A. L. 1952. *The Nature of Culture*. Chicago: University of Chicago Press.

Kroeber, A. L., and Clyde Kluckhohn. 1952. "Culture: A Critical Review of Concepts and Definitions." *Papers of the Peabody Museum of Archaeology and Ethnology* 47, Harvard University.

Kuklick, Henrika. 1991. *The Savage Within: The Social History of British Anthropology, 1885–1945*. Cambridge: Cambridge University Press.

Kuper, Adam. 1988. *The Invention of Primitive Society: Transformations of an Illusion*. London and New York: Routledge.

———. 1999. *Culture: The Anthropologist's Account*. Cambridge, MA: Harvard University Press.

Kuttner, Stephan. 1991. "The Revival of Jurisprudence." In *Renaissance and Revival in the Twelfth Century*, edited by Robert L. Benson, Giles Constable, and Carol D. Lanham. Toronto: University of Toronto Press.

Kymlicka, Will. 1995. *Multicultural Citizenship: A Liberal Theory of Minority Rights*. Oxford: Oxford University Press.

Lackner, Helen. 1973. "Social Anthropology and Indirect Rule. The Colonial Administration and Anthropology in Eastern Nigeria: 1920–1940." In *Anthropology and the Colonial Encounter*, edited by Talal Asad. New York: Humanities Press.

Laitin, David. 1986. *Hegemony and Culture: Politics and Religious Change among the Yoruba*. Chicago: University of Chicago Press.

Landauer, Carl. 2002. "From Status to Treaty: Henry Sumner Maine's *International Law*." *Canadian Journal of Law and Jurisprudence* 15: 219–54.

Lang, Maurice Eugen. 1924. *Codification in the British Empire and America*. Amsterdam: H. J. Paris.

Laveleye, Émile de. 1901. *De la propriété et de ses formes primitives*. Paris: F. Alcan.

Legge, J. D. 1958. *Britain in Fiji: 1858–1880*. London: Macmillan.

Leopold, Joan. 1974. "British Applications of the Aryan Theory of Race to India, 1850–1870." *English Historical Review* 276: 578–603.

Leslie, T. E. C. 1875. "Maine's *Early History of Institutions*." *Fortnightly Review* 17: 303–20.

Letourneau, Charles. 1892. *Property: Its Origins and Development*. London: W. Scott.

Lévi-Strauss, Claude. 1962. *The Savage Mind*. London: Weidenfeld and Nicolson.

Levine, Norman. 1987. "The German Historical School of Law and the Origins of Historical Materialism." *Journal of the History of Ideas* 48: 431–51.

Levitt, Cyril. 1975. "Anthropology and Historical Jurisprudence: An Examination of the Major Issues Raised in Marx's Excerpts from Henry Sumner Maine's 'Lectures on the Early History of Institutions.'" In *Philosophischen Fakultät*. Berlin: Freien Universität Berlin.

Lewis, Andrew, and Michael Lobban, eds. 2004. *Law and History: Current Legal Issues 2003, Volume 6*. Oxford: Oxford University Press.

Lewis, George Cornewall. 1841. *An Essay on the Government of Dependencies*. Oxford: Clarendon.

Lichtheim, George. 1963. "Marx and the 'Asiatic Mode of Production.'" *St. Antony's Papers* 14.

Lieberman, David. 1989. *The Province of Legislation Determined: Legal Theory in Eighteenth-Century Britain*. Cambridge: Cambridge University Press.

———. 2005. "Legislation in a Common Law Context." *Zeitschrift für Neuere Rechtsgeschichte* 27, nos. 1–2: 107–23.

Lingat, Robert. 1998. *The Classical Law of India*. Delhi: Oxford University Press.

Lippincott, Benjamin Evans. 1964. *Victorian Critics of Democracy: Carlyle, Ruskin, Arnold, Stephen, Maine, Lecky*. New York: Octagon Books.

Lobban, Michael. 1987. "Blackstone and the Science of Law." *Historical Journal* 30, no. 3: 11–35.

———. 1991. *The Common Law and English Jurisprudence, 1760–1850*. Oxford: Oxford University Press.

———. 2000. "How Benthamic Was the Criminal Law Commission?" *Law and History Review* 18: 427–32.

Locke, John. 1988. *Two Treatises of Government*. Cambridge: Cambridge University Press.

Lorimer, Douglas A. 1978. *Colour, Class, and the Victorians: English Attitudes to the Negro in the Mid-Nineteenth Century*. Leicester: Leicester University Press.

Louis, William Roger, ed. 1976. *Imperialism: The Robinson and Gallagher Controversy*. New York: New Viewpoints.

Low, D. A. 1973. *Lion Rampant: Essays in the Study of British Imperialism*. London: Frank Cass.

Lowith, Karl. 1949. *Meaning in History*. Chicago: University of Chicago Press.

Lubbock, John. 1978. *The Origin of Civilisation and the Primitive Condition of Man*. Chicago: University of Chicago Press.

Ludden, David. 1993. "Orientalist Empiricism: Transformation of Colonial Knowledge." In *Orientalism and the Postcolonial Predicament: Perspectives on South Asia*, edited by Carol A. Breckenridge and Peter van der Veer. Philadelphia: University of Pennsylvania Press.

Lugard, Lord. 1965. *The Dual Mandate in British Tropical Africa*. London: Frank Cass.

Lukes, Steven. 1973. *Émile Durkheim: His Life and Work*. London: Allen Lane.

Lyall, Alfred C. 1882. *Asiatic Studies: Religious and Social*. London: John Murray.

———. 1884. "Government of the Indian Empire." *Edinburgh Review* 325: 1–41.

———. 1888. "Sir Henry Maine." *Law Quarterly Review* 4: 129–38.

———. 1889. *Warren Hastings.* London: Macmillan.

———. 1893. "Life and Speeches of Sir Henry Maine." *Quarterly Review* 176: 287–316.

———. 1894. *The Rise and Expansion of the British Dominion in India.* London: John Murray.

Macarthy, Tom. 2009. *Race, Empire, and the Idea of Development.* Cambridge: Cambridge University Press.

Macaulay, T. B. 1970. *Macaulay: Prose and Poetry.* Cambridge, MA: Harvard University Press.

Macfarlane, Alan D. J. 1991. "Some Contributions of Maine to History and Anthropology." In *The Victorian Achievement of Sir Henry Maine: A Centennial Reappraisal,* edited by Alan Diamond. Cambridge: Cambridge University Press.

Macpherson, C. B. ed. 1978. *Property: Mainstream and Critical Positions.* Oxford: Basil Blackwell.

Mahmood, Syed. 1895. *A History of English Education in India, 1781–1893.* Aligarh: The Muhammadan Anglo-Oriental College.

Maine, Henry Sumner. 1855. "The Conception of Sovereignty and Its Importance in International Law." *Papers of the Juridical Society*: 26–45.

———. 1857. "Indian Government." *Saturday Review* 4 (3 October): 295.

———. 1857. "Indian Statesmen and English Scribblers." *Saturday Review* (24 October): 361.

———. 1857. "Mr. Disraeli on India." *Saturday Review* 4 (1 August): 97.

———. 1858. "The Middle Classes and the Abolition of the East India Company." *Saturday Review* 5 (9 January): 31.

———. 1858. "The Petition of the East India Company." *Saturday Review* 5 (23 January): 899.

———. 1875. *Lectures on the Early History of Institutions.* London: John Murray.

———. 1876. *Village-Communities in the East and West: Six Lectures Delivered at Oxford.* London: John Murray.

———. 1880. "Imaginary Indian Grievances." *St. James Gazette* 1 (27 July): 796.

———. 1886. *Dissertations on Early Law and Custom.* New York: Holt.

———. 1886. "Mr. Godkin on Popular Government." *Nineteenth Century*: 266–79.

———. 1886. "The Patriarchal Theory." *Quarterly Review* 162: 181–209.

———. 1887. "India." In *The Reign of Queen Victoria: A Survey of Fifty Years of Progress,* edited by Thomas Humphry Ward, 460–528. London: Smith, Elder.

———. 1888. *International Law: The Whewell Lectures.* London: John Murray.

———. 1892. *Minutes by Sir Henry Maine, 1862–69: With a Note on Indian Codification, Dated 17th July, 1879.* Calcutta: Government of India, Legislative Department.

———. 1976. *Popular Government.* Indianapolis: Liberty Classics.

———. 1986. *Ancient Law: Its Connection with the Early History of Society, and Its Relation to Modern Ideas.* Tucson: University of Arizona Press.

Majeed, Javed. 1992. *Ungoverned Imaginings: James Mill's* The History of British India *and Orientalism.* Oxford: Clarendon Press.

Majeed, Javed. 1999. "Comparativism and References to Rome in British Imperial Attitudes to India." In *Roman Presences: Receptions of Rome in European Culture, 1789–1945*, edited by Catherine Edwards, 88–109. Cambridge: Cambridge University Press.

Mamdani, Mahmood. 1996. *Citizen and Subject: Contemporary Africa and the Legacy of Late Colonialism*. Princeton, NJ: Princeton University Press.

Mamdani, Mahmood, ed. 2000. *Beyond Rights Talk and Culture Talk*. New York: St. Martin's Press.

Mandelbaum, Maurice. 1971. *History, Man, and Reason: A Study in Nineteenth-Century Thought*. Baltimore: Johns Hopkins University Press.

Mandler, Peter. 2000. "'Race' and 'Nation' in Mid-Victorian Thought." In *History, Religion, and Culture: British Intellectual History, 1750–1950*, edited by Stefan Collini, Richard Whatmore, and Brian Young. Cambridge: Cambridge University Press.

Mantena, Karuna. 2004. "Law and 'Tradition': Henry Maine and the Theoretical Origins of Indirect Rule." In *Law and History*, edited by Andrew Lewis and Michael Lobban. Oxford: Oxford University Press.

———. 2006. "Fragile Universals and the Politics of Empire." *Polity* 38.

———. 2007. "Mill and the Imperial Predicament." In *J. S. Mill's Political Thought: A Bicentennial Reassessment*, edited by Nadia Urbinati and Alex Zakaras. Cambridge: Cambridge University Press.

Manuel, Frank E. 1962. *The Prophets of Paris*. Cambridge, MA: Harvard University Press.

———. 1965. *Shapes of Philosophical History*. Stanford, CA: Stanford University Press.

Marcuse, Herbert. 1954. *Reason and Revolution: Hegel and the Rise of Social Theory*. New York: Humanities Press.

Marriott, McKim, ed. 1955. *Village India: Studies in the Little Community*. Chicago: University of Chicago Press.

Marshall, P. J. 1964. "The First and Second British Empires: A Question of Demarcation." *History* 49: 13–23.

———. 1965. *The Impeachment of Warren Hastings*. Oxford: Oxford University Press.

———. 1987. "Empire and Authority in the Later Eighteenth Century." *Journal of Imperial and Commonwealth History* 15.

———. 2005. *The Making and Unmaking of Empires: Britain, India, and America, c. 1750–1783*. Oxford: Oxford University Press.

Martin, David E. 1981. *John Stuart Mill and the Land Question*. Hull: University of Hull Publications.

Marx, Karl. 1964. *Pre-Capitalist Economic Formations*. London: Lawrence and Wishart.

———. 1968. *Karl Marx on Colonialism and Modernization*. New York: Doubleday.

———. 1971. *Marx's Grundrisse*. New York: Macmillan.

———. 1977. *Capital: A Critique of Political Economy*. New York: Vintage.

Marx, Karl, and Friedrich Engels. 1876. *Collected Works*. London.

———. 1960. *The First Indian War of Independence, 1857–1859*. Moscow: Foreign Languages Publishing House.

Matson, J. N. 1993. "The Common Law Abroad: English and Indigenous Laws in the British Commonwealth." *International and Comparative Law Quarterly* 42: 753–79.

Maurer, G. L. von. 1854. *Einleitung zur Geschichte der Mark-, Hof-, Dorf-, und Stadtverfassung und der offentlichen Gewalt*. Munich: Kaiser.

———. 1856. *Geschichte der Markenverfassung in Deutschland*. Erlangen: F. Enke.

Mauss, Marcel. 1990. *The Gift: The Form and Reason for Exchange in Archaic Societies*. New York: W. W. Norton.

Mazlish, Bruce. 1988. *James and John Stuart Mill: Father and Son in the Nineteenth Century*. New Brunswick, NJ: Transaction Books.

McGrane, Bernard. 1989. *Beyond Anthropology: Society and the Other*. New York City: Columbia University Press.

McLaren, Martha. 2001. *British India and British Scotland, 1780–1830: Career Building, Empire Building, and a Scottish School of Thought on Indian Governance*. Akron, OH: University of Akron Press.

McLennan, John. 1865. *Primitive Marriage: An Inquiry into the Origin of the Form of Capture in Marriage Ceremonies*. Edinburgh: A. & C. Black.

———. 1885. *The Patriarchal Theory*. London: Macmillan.

Meek, C. K. 1949. *Land Law and Custom in the Colonies*. London: Oxford University Press.

Meek, Ronald L. 1976. *Social Science and the Ignoble Savage*. Cambridge: Cambridge University Press.

Mehta, Pratap Bhanu. 1996. "Liberalism, Nation, and Empire: The Case of J. S. Mill." Unpublished paper presented at the Annual Meeting of the American Political Science Association. San Francisco.

———. 2000. "Cosmopolitanism and the Circle of Reason." *Political Theory* 28: 619–39.

———. 2003. *The Burden of Democracy*. New Delhi: Penguin.

Mehta, Uday Singh. 1992. *The Anxiety of Freedom: Imagination and Individuality in Locke's Political Thought*. Ithaca, NY: Cornell University Press.

———. 1999. *Liberalism and Empire: A Study in Nineteenth-Century British Liberal Thought*. Chicago: University of Chicago Press.

Menski, Werner F. 2003. *Hindu Law: Beyond Tradition and Modernity*. Delhi: Oxford University Press.

Metcalf, Thomas R. 1962. "The Struggle Over Land Tenure in India, 1860–1868." *Journal of Asian Studies* 21: 295–307.

———. 1964. *The Aftermath of Revolt: India, 1857–1870*. Princeton, NJ: Princeton University Press.

———. 1994. *Ideologies of the Raj*. Cambridge: Cambridge University Press.

———. 2007. *Imperial Connections: India in the Indian Ocean Arena, 1860–1920*. Berkeley: University of California Press.

Mill, James. 1990. *The History of British India*. New Delhi: Atlantic Publisher and Distributors.

Mill, James. 1992. *The Collected Works of James Mill: Essays from the Supplement to the Encyclopedia Britannica*. London: Routledge/Thoemmes Press.

———. 1992. *Political Writings*. Cambridge: Cambridge University Press.

Mill, John Stuart. 1859. *Dissertations and Discussions: Political, Philosophical, and Historical*. London: John W. Parker and Son.

———. 1871. "Mr. Maine on Village-Communities." *Fortnightly Review* 9: 543–56.

———. 1963–. *The Collected Works of John Stuart Mill*. Toronto: University of Toronto Press.

———. 1972. *Utilitarianism, On Liberty, Considerations on Representative Government*. London: Everyman.

———. 1973. *A System of Logic, Racionative and Inductive: Being a Connected View of the Principles of Evidence and the Methods of Scientific Investigation*. Toronto: University of Toronto Press.

———. 1982. *Essays on England, Ireland, and the Empire*. Toronto: University of Toronto Press.

———. 1984. *Essays on Equality, Law, and Education*. Toronto: University of Toronto Press.

———. 1990. *Writings on India*. Toronto: University of Toronto Press.

———. 1994. *Principles of Political Economy*. London: Oxford Classics.

Millar, John. 1986. *The Origin of the Distinction of Ranks: An Inquiry into the Circumstances Which Give Rise to the Influence and Authority in Different Members of Society*. Aalen: Scientia Verlag.

Miller, W. Watts. 1993. "Durkheim's Monstesquieu." *British Journal of Sociology* 44: 693–712.

Moir, Martin I., Douglas M. Peers, and Lynn Zastoupil, eds. 1999. *J. S. Mill's Encounter with India*. Toronto: University of Toronto Press.

Momigliano, Arnaldo. 1977. "The Ancient City of Fustel de Coulanges." In *Essays in Ancient and Modern Historiography*, 325–44. Middleton, CT: Wesleyan University Press.

———. 1994. *A. D. Momigliano: Studies on Modern Scholarship*. Berkeley: University of California Press.

Mommsen, Theodor. 1894. *A History of Rome*. London: R. Bently.

Mommsen, W. J., and J. A. de Moor, eds. 1992. *European Expansion and Law: The Encounter of European and Indigenous Law in 19th- and 20th-Century Africa and Asia*. Oxford: Berg.

Money, J. W. B. 1861. *Java: Or How to Manage a Colony; Showing a Practical Solution of the Questions Now Affecting British India*. London: Hurst and Blackett.

Montesquieu, Charles de Secondat, Baron de. 1989. *The Spirit of the Laws*. Cambridge: Cambridge University Press.

———. 1999. *Considerations on the Causes of the Greatness of the Romans and Their Decline*. Indianapolis: Hackett.

Moore, Sally Falk. 1986. *Social Facts and Fabrications: "Customary" Law on Kilimanjaro, 1880–1980*. Cambridge: Cambridge University Press.

Morefield, Jeanne. 2006. *Covenants without Swords: Idealist Liberalism and the Spirit of Empire*. Princeton, NJ: Princeton University Press.

———. 2008. "Empire, Tragedy, and the Liberal State in the Writings of Niall Ferguson and Michael Ignatieff. *Theory and Event* 11, no. 3.

Morgan, Lewis Henry. 1985. *Ancient Society.* Tucson: University of Arizona Press.

———. 1997. *Systems of Consanguinity and Affinity of the Human Family.* Lincoln: University of Nebraska Press.

Morley, John. 1884. "The Expansion of England." *Macmillan's Magazine* 49: 241–58.

———. 1886. "Sir H. Maine on Popular Government." *Fortnightly Review* 39: 152–73.

Morris, H. F., and James S. Read. 1972. *Indirect Rule and the Search for Justice: Essays in East African Legal History.* Oxford: Clarendon Press.

Mukerjee, Radhakamal. 1923. *Democracies of the East: A Study in Comparative Politics.* London: P. S. King and Son.

Mukherjee, Rudrangshu. 2001. *Awadh in Revolt, 1857–1858: A Study in Popular Resistance.* Delhi: Permanent Black.

Müller, F. Max. 1864. *Lectures on the Science of Language.* London: Longman.

———. 2002. *India: What Can It Teach Us?* Delhi: Rupa Publishers.

Murray, Robert H. 1929. *Studies in the English Social and Political Thinkers of the Nineteenth Century.* Cambridge: W. Heffer and Sons.

Muthu, Sankar. 2003. *Enlightenment against Empire.* Princeton, NJ: Princeton University Press.

Nasse, Erwin. 1872. *On the Agricultural Community of the Middle Ages: And Inclosures of the Sixteenth Century in England.* London: Williams and Norgate.

Niebuhr, Barthold Georg. 1835. *The History of Rome.* Philadelphia: Thomas Warble.

———. 1873. *Lectures on the History of Rome.* London: Lockwood.

Nielsen, Donald A. 1972. "The Sociological Theories of Sir Henry Maine: Societal Transformation, Cultural Modernization, and Civilization in Sociocultural Perspective." Ph.D. Thesis. New School for Social Research.

Nisbet, Robert A. 1943. "The French Revolution and the Rise of Sociology in France." *American Journal of Sociology* 49: 156–64.

———. 1952. "Conservatism and Sociology." *American Journal of Sociology* 58: 167–75.

———. 1966. *The Sociological Tradition.* New York: Basic Books.

O'Brien, Karen. 1997. *Narratives of Enlightenment: Cosmopolitan History from Voltaire to Gibbon.* Cambridge: Cambridge University Press.

O'Brien, Nick. 2005. "'Something Older than Law Itself': Sir Henry Maine, Niebuhr, and 'The Path Not Chosen.'" *Journal of Legal History* 26: 229–51.

O'Leary, Brendan. 1989. *The Asiatic Mode of Production: Oriental Despotism, Historical Materialism, and Indian History.* Oxford: Basil Blackwell.

Olender, Maurice. 1992. *The Languages of Paradise: Race, Religion, and Philology in the Nineteenth Century.* Cambridge, MA: Harvard University Press.

Otter, Sandra den. 2001. "Rewriting the Utilitarian Market: Colonial Law and Custom in mid-Nineteenth-Century British India." *European Legacy* 6: 177–88.

Otter, Sandra den. 2007. "'A Legislating Empire': Victorian Political Theorists, Codes of Law, and Empire." In *Victorian Visions of Global Order: Empire and International Relations in Nineteenth-Century Political Thought*, edited by Duncan Bell. Cambridge: Cambridge University Press.

Owen, Roger. 1965. "The Influence of Lord Cromer's Indian Experience on British Policy in Egypt, 1883–1907." *St. Antony's Papers* 17.

———. 1973. "Imperial Policy and Theories of Social Change: Sir Alfred Lyall in India." In *Anthropology and the Colonial Encounter*, edited by Talal Asad. Atlantic Highlands, NJ: Humanities Press.

———. 2004. *Lord Cromer: Victorian Imperialist, Edwardian Proconsul.* Oxford: Oxford University Press.

Owen, Roger, and Bob Sutcliffe, eds. 1972. *Studies in the Theory of Imperialism.* London: Longman.

Padmore, George. 1936. *How Britain Rules Africa.* London: Wishart Books.

Pagden, Anthony. 1982. *The Fall of Natural Man: The American Indian and the Origins of Comparative Ethnology.* Cambridge: Cambridge University Press.

———. 1995. *Lords of All the World: Ideologies of Empire in Spain, Britain, and France c. 1500–c. 1800.* New Haven, CT: Yale University Press.

Panikkar, K. M. 1969. *Asia and Western Dominance.* New York: Collier Books.

Parekh, Bhikhu. 1994. "The Narrowness of Liberalism from Mill to Rawls." *Times Literary Supplement*, 11–13.

Parel, Anthony, and Thomas Flanagan, eds. 1979. *Theories of Property: Aristotle to the Present.* Waterloo: Wilfrid Laurier University Press.

Pels, Peter, and Lorraine Nencel, eds. 1991. *Constructing Knowledge: Authority and Critique in Social Science.* London: Sage.

Pels, Peter, and Oscar Salemink, eds. 1999. *Colonial Subjects: Essays in the Practical History of Anthropology.* London: Sage.

Perham, Marjery. 1934. "A Re-Statement of Indirect Rule." *Africa* 7.

———. 1967. *Colonial Sequence, 1930–1949.* London: Methuen, 1967.

Perreau-Saussine, Amanda, and James Bernard Murphy, eds. 2007. *The Nature of Customary Law: Legal, Historical, and Philosophical Perspectives.* Cambridge: Cambridge University Press.

Phear, John B. 1880. *The Aryan Village in India and Ceylon.* London: Macmillan.

Philips, C. H., H. L. Singh, and B. N. Pandey, eds. 1962. *The Evolution of India and Pakistan, 1858–1947: Select Documents.* London: Oxford University Press.

Pilling, N. 1970. "The Conservatism of Sir Henry Maine." *Political Studies* 18: 107–20.

Pitts, Jennifer. 2005. *A Turn to Empire: The Rise of Imperial Liberalism in Britain and France.* Princeton, NJ: Princeton University Press.

Pocock, J. G. A. 1957. *The Ancient Constitution and the Feudal Law: A Study of English Historical Thought in the Seventeenth Century.* Cambridge: Cambridge University Press.

———. 1999. *Barbarism and Religion: The Enlightenments of Edward Gibbon, 1737–1764.* Cambridge: Cambridge University Press.

———. 1999. *Barbarism and Religion: Narratives of Civil Government.* Cambridge: Cambridge University Press.

———. 2003. *Barbarism and Religion: The First Decline and Fall.* Cambridge: Cambridge University Press.

———. 2005. *Barbarism and Religion: Barbarians, Savages, Empires.* Cambridge: Cambridge University Press.

Pollock, F. 1893. "Sir Henry Maine as a Jurist." *Edinburgh Review* 178: 100–121.

Porter, Andrew, ed. 1999. *The Oxford History of the British Empire: The Nineteenth Century.* Oxford: Oxford University Press.

Prakash, Gyan, ed. 1995. *After Colonialism: Imperial Histories and Postcolonial Displacements.* Princeton, NJ: Princeton University Press.

Probyn, J. W., ed. 1881. *Systems of Land Tenure in Various Countries: A Series of Essays Published under the Sanction of the Cobden Club.* London: Cassell.

Proudhon, Pierre-Joseph. 1994. *What Is Property?* Cambridge: Cambridge University Press.

Pufendorf, Samuel. 1991. *On the Duty of Man and Citizen According to Natural Law.* Cambridge: Cambridge University Press.

Radcliffe-Brown, A. R. 1965. *Structure and Function in Primitive Society: Essays and Addresses.* New York: Free Press.

Rai, Mridu. 2004. *Hindu Rulers, Muslim Subjects: Islam, Regional Identity and the Making of Kashmir.* Princeton, NJ: Princeton University Press.

Rana, Aziz. forthcoming. *Freedom Without Empire: The Paradox of America's Settler Legacy.* Cambridge, MA: Harvard University Press.

Ranger, Terence. 1983. "The Invention of Tradition in Colonial Africa." In *The Invention of Tradition*, edited by Eric Hobsbaum and Terence Ranger. Cambridge: Cambridge University Press.

Redfield, R. 1950. "Maine's *Ancient Law* in Light of Primitive Societies." *Western Political Quarterly* 3: 574–89.

Rich, Paul B. 1986. *Race and Empire in British Politics.* Cambridge: Cambridge University Press.

Richter, Melvin. 1963. "Tocqueville on Algeria." *Review of Politics* 25.

———. 2006. "The Comparative Study of Regimes and Societies." In *The Cambridge History of Eighteenth-Century Political Thought*, edited by Mark Goldie and Robert Wokler. Cambridge: Cambridge University Press.

Roach, John. 1957. "Liberalism and the Victorian Intelligentsia." *Cambridge Historical Journal* 13: 58–81.

Robb, Peter. 1997. *Ancient Rights and Future Comfort: Bihar, the Bengal Tenancy Act of 1885, and British Rule in India.* London: Curzon.

Robb, Peter, ed. 1995. *The Concept of Race in South Asia.* Delhi: Oxford University Press.

Roberts, Richard, and Kristin Mann, eds. 1991. *Law in Colonial Africa.* Portsmouth, NH: Heinemann Educational Books.

Robertson, William. 1822. *An Historical Disquisition concerning the Knowledge Which the Ancients Had of India, and the Progress of Trade with Country Prior to the Discovery of the Passage to It by the Cape of Good Hope.* Albany: E. & E. Hosford.

Robinson, Ronald. 1950. "Why 'Indirect Rule' Has Been Replaced by 'Local Government' in the Nomenclature of British Native Administration." *Journal of African Administration* 2.

———. 1972. "Non-European Foundations of European Imperialism: Sketch for a Theory of Collaboration." In *Studies in the Theory of Imperialism*, edited by Roger Owen and Bob Sutcliffe. London: Longman.

Robinson, Ronald, and John Gallagher, with Alice Denny. 1961. *Africa and the Victorians: The Official Mind of Imperialism*. London: Macmillan.

Rose, Gillian. 1981. *Hegel Contra Sociology*. London: Atholone.

Roth, G. K. 1951. *Native Administration in Fiji during the Past 75 Years*. London: The Royal Anthropological Institute of Great Britain and Ireland.

Rousseau, Jean-Jacques. 1997. *The Discourses and Other Early Political Writings*. Cambridge: Cambridge University Press.

———. 1997. *The Social Contract and Other Later Political Writings*. Cambridge: Cambridge University Press.

Rumble, Wilfrid E. 1985. *The Thought of John Austin: Jurisprudence, Colonial Reform, and the British Constitution*. London: Athlone Press.

———. 1988. "John Austin and His Nineteenth-Century Critics: The Case of Sir Henry Sumner Maine." *Northern Ireland Legal Quarterly* 39: 119–49.

Runciman, Walter G. 1963. *Social Science and Political Theory*. Cambridge: Cambridge University Press.

Ryan, Alan. 1984. *Property and Political Theory*. Oxford: Basil Blackwell.

———. 1987. *The Philosophy of John Stuart Mill*. London: Macmillan.

Ryan, Alan, ed. 1979. *The Idea of Freedom: Essays in Honour of Isaiah Berlin*. Oxford: Oxford University Press.

Said, Edward. 1979. *Orientalism*. New York: Vintage Books.

———. 1994. *Culture and Imperialism*. New York: Knopf.

Sangari, Kumkum, and Sudesh Vaid, eds. 1989. *Recasting Women: Essays in Colonial History*. New Delhi: Kali for Women.

Sartori, Andrew. 2006. "The British Empire and Its Liberal Mission." *Journal of Modern History* 78: 623–42.

Sarvadhikari, Rajkumar. 1985. *The Taluqdari Settlement in Oudh*. New Delhi: Usha.

Savigny, Friedrich Karl von. 1831. *Of the Vocation of Our Age for Legislation and Jurisprudence*. London: Littlewood.

———. 1848. *Von Savigny's Treatise on Possession; Or, the Jus Possessionis of the Civil Law*. Westport, CT: Hyperion Press.

———. 1979. *The History of the Roman Law during the Middle Ages*. Westport, CT: Hyperion Press.

———. 1979. *System of the Modern Roman Law*. Westport, CT: Hyperion Press.

Sawer, Marian. 1977. *Marxism and the Question of the Asiatic Mode of Production*. The Hague: Martinus Nijhoff.

Schofield, Philip. 1991. "Jeremy Bentham and Nineteenth-Century Jurisprudence." *Journal of Legal History* 12: 58–88.

Schwab, Raymond. 1984. *The Oriental Renaissance: Europe's Rediscovery of India and the East, 1680–1880*. New York: Columbia University Press.

Scott, David. 1995. "Colonial Governmentality." *Social Text* 43: 191–220.

———. 1999. *Refashioning Futures: Criticism after Postcoloniality.* Princeton, NJ: Princeton University Press.

———. 2003. "Culture in Political Theory." *Political Theory* 13: 92–115.

———. 2004. *Conscripts of Modernity: The Tragedy of Colonial Enlightenment.* Durham, NC: Duke University Press.

Schultz, Bart, and Georgios Varouxakis, eds. 2005. *Utilitarianism and Empire.* Lanham, MD: Lexington Books.

Seeley, J. R. 1883. *The Expansion of England.* London: Macmillan.

Seidman, Steven. 1983. *Liberalism and the Origins of European Social Theory.* Berkeley: University of California Press.

Semmel, Bernard. 1969. *Democracy versus Empire: The Jamaica Riots of 1865 and the Governor Eyre Controversy.* New York: Anchor.

———. 1993. *The Liberal Ideal and the Demons of Empire: Theories of Imperialism from Adam Smith to Lenin.* Baltimore: Johns Hopkins University Press.

Sen, Sudipta. 2002. *Distant Sovereignty: National Imperialism and the Origins of British India.* New York: Routledge.

Shanin, Teodor, ed. 1983. *Late Marx and the Russian Road: Marx and the "Peripheries of Capitalism."* New York: Monthly Review Press.

Shils, Edward. 1991. "Henry Sumner Maine in the Tradition of the Analysis of Society." In *The Victorian Achievement of Sir Henry Maine: A Centennial Reappraisal*, edited by Alan Diamond. Cambridge: Cambridge University Press.

Singha, Radhika. 1998. *A Despotism of Law: Crime and Justice in Early Colonial India.* Delhi: Oxford University Press.

Sinha, Mrinalini. 1995. *Colonial Masculinity: The "Manly Englishman" and the "Effeminate Bengali."* New York: Manchester University Press.

Skorupski, John, ed. 1998. *The Cambridge Companion to Mill.* Cambridge: Cambridge University Press.

Skuy, David. 1998. "Macaulay and the Indian Penal Code of 1862: The Myth of the Inherent Superiority and Modernity of the English Legal System Compared to India's Legal System in the Nineteenth Century." *Modern Asian Studies* 32: 513–57.

Smith, Adam. 1978. *Lectures on Jurisprudence.* Indianapolis: Liberty Fund.

———. 1981. *An Inquiry into the Nature and Causes of the Wealth of Nations.* Indianapolis: Liberty Fund.

Smith, K. J. K. 1988. *James Fitzjames Stephen: Portrait of a Victorian Rationalist.* Cambridge: Cambridge University Press.

Smuts, J. C. 1930. *Africa and Some World Problems, Including the Rhodes Memorial Lectures Delivered in Michaelmas Term, 1929.* Oxford: Clarendon Press.

Spencer, Herbert. 1897. *The Principles of Sociology.* New York: Appleton.

———. 1981. *The Man versus the State: With Six Essays on Government, Society, and Freedom.* Indianapolis: Liberty Classics.

Spivak, Gayatri Chakravorty. 1999. *A Critique of Postcolonial Reason: Toward a History of the Vanishing Present.* Cambridge, MA: Harvard University Press.

Srinivas, M. N. 1975. "The Indian Village: Myth and Reality." In *Studies in Social Anthropology*, edited by J. Beattie and R. Lienhardt. Oxford: Clarendon Press.

Steele, E. D. 1968. "Ireland and the Empire in the 1860s: Imperial Precedents for Gladstone's First Irish Land Act." *Historical Journal* 11: 64–83.

———. 1970. "J. S. Mill and the Irish Question: The Principles of Political Economy, 1848–1865." *Historical Journal* 13: 216–36.

———. 1970. "J. S. Mill and the Irish Question: Reform, and the Integrity of the Empire, 1865–1870." *Historical Journal* 13: 419–50.

Stein, Burton. 1989. *Thomas Munro: The Origins of the Colonial State and His Vision of Empire*. Delhi: Oxford University Press.

———. 1992. *The Making of Agrarian Policy in British India, 1770–1900*. Delhi: Oxford University Press.

Stein, Peter. 1980. *Legal Evolution: The Story of an Idea*. Cambridge: Cambridge University Press.

Stepan, Nancy. 1982. *The Idea of Race in Science: Great Britain, 1800–1860*. London: Macmillan.

Stephen, James Fitzjames. 1861. "English Jurisprudence." *Edinburgh Review* 114: 456–86.

———. 1872. "Codification in India and England." *Fortnightly Review* 12: 644–72.

———. 1876. "Legislation under Lord Mayo." In *The Life of the Earl of Mayo, Fourth Viceroy of India*, edited by W. W. Hunter. London: Smith, Elder.

———. 1883. "Foundations of the Government of India." *Nineteenth Century* 80: 541–68.

———. 1885. *The Story of Nuncomar and the Impeachment of Sir Elijah Impey*. London: Macmillan.

———. 1991. *Liberty, Equality, Fraternity, and Three Brief Essays*. Chicago: University of Chicago Press.

Stephen, Leslie. 1900. *The English Utilitarians*. London: Duckworth.

Stern, Jacques, ed. 1973. *Thibaut und Savigny*. Munich: Vahlen.

Stocking, George W., Jr. 1982. *Race, Culture, and Evolution: Essays in the History of Anthropology*. Chicago: University of Chicago Press.

———. 1987. *Victorian Anthropology*. New York: Free Press.

Stocking, George W., ed. 1991. *Colonial Situations: Essays on the Contextualization of Ethnographic Knowledge*. Madison: University of Wisconsin Press.

———. 1996. *Volksgeist as Method and Ethic: Essays on Boasian Ethnography and the German Anthropological Tradition*. Madison: University of Wisconsin Press.

Stokes, Eric. 1959. *The English Utilitarians and India*. Oxford: Oxford University Press.

———. 1960. *The Political Ideas of English Imperialism: An Inaugural Lecture Given in the University College of Rhodesia and Nyasaland*. London: Oxford University Press.

———. 1961. "The Administrators and Historical Writing on India." In *Historians of India, Pakistan and Ceylon*, edited by C. H. Philips, 385–403. London: Oxford University Press.

———. 1978. *The Peasant and the Raj: Studies in Agrarian Society and Peasant Rebellion in Colonial India*. Cambridge: Cambridge University Press.

Stokes, Whitley. 1891. *The Anglo-Indian Codes*. Oxford: Clarendon.

Stoler, Ann Laura. 1995. *Race and the Education of Desire: Foucault's History of Sexuality and the Colonial Order of Things.* Durham, NC: Duke University Press.

Strachey, John. 1892. *Hastings and the Rohilla War.* Oxford: Clarendon Press.

———. 1903. *India: Its Administration and Progress.* London: Macmillan.

Sullivan, Eileen P. 1983. "Liberalism and Imperialism: J. S. Mill's Defense of the British Empire." *Journal of the History of Ideas* 44: 599–617.

Swettenham, Frank. 1948. *British Malaya: An Account of the Origin and Progress of British Influence in Malaya.* London: George Allen and Unwin.

Tacitus. 1999. *Germania.* Oxford: Clarendon.

Tambiah, Stanley. 2002. *Edmund Leach: An Anthropological Life.* Cambridge: Cambridge University Press.

Taylor, Charles. 1994. "The Politics of Recognition." In *Multiculturalism: Examining the Politics of Recognition,* edited by Amy Gutmann. Princeton, NJ: Princeton University Press.

Taylor, Miles. 1991. "Imperium et Libertas? Rethinking the Radical Critique of Imperialism during the Nineteenth Century." *Journal of Imperial and Commonwealth History* 19: 1–23.

Thom, Martin. 1995. *Republics, Nations, and Tribes.* London: Verso.

Thorner, Daniel. 1966. "Marx on India and the Asiatic Mode of Production." *Contributions to Indian Sociology* 9: 33–66.

Thornton, A. P. 1985. *The Imperial Idea and Its Enemies: A Study in British Power.* London: Macmillan.

Tigor, Robert L. 1963. "The 'Indianization' of the Egyptian Administration under British Rule." *American Historical Review* 68: 636–61.

Tocqueville, Alexis de. 1955. *The Old Regime and the French Revolution.* New York: Doubleday.

———. 2000. *Democracy in America.* New York: Perennial Classics.

———. 2001. *Writings on Empire and Slavery.* Baltimore: Johns Hopkins University Press.

Tod, James. 1972. *The Annals and Antiquities of Rajasthan or the Central and Western Rajpoot States of India.* London: Routledge and Kegan Paul.

Todorov, Tzvetan. 1993. *On Human Diversity: Nationalism, Racism, and Exoticism in French Thought.* Cambridge, MA: Harvard University Press.

———. 1999. *The Conquest of America: The Question of the Other.* Norman: University of Oklahoma Press.

Tönnies, Ferdinand. 2001. *Community and Civil Society (Gemeinschaft und Gesellschaft).* Cambridge: Cambridge University Press.

Trautmann, Thomas R. 1987. *Lewis Henry Morgan and the Invention of Kinship.* Berkeley: University of California Press.

———. 1997. *Aryans and British India.* Berkeley: University of California Press.

———. 2006. *Languages and Nations: The Dravidian Proof in Colonial Madras.* Berkeley: University of California Press.

Travers, Robert. 2007. *Ideology and Empire in Eighteenth-Century India: The British in Bengal.* Cambridge: Cambridge University Press.

Tuck, Richard. 1979. *Natural Rights Theories: Their Origin and Development.* Cambridge: Cambridge University Press.

Tuck, Richard. 1994. "Rights and Pluralism." In *Philosophy in the Age of Pluralism: The Philosophy of Charles Taylor in Question*, edited by James Tully. Cambridge: Cambridge University Press.

———. 1997. "The Dangers of Natural Rights." *Harvard Journal of Law* 20: 683–93.

———. 1999. *The Rights of War and Peace: Political Thought and the International Order from Grotius to Kant*. New York: Oxford University Press.

Tully, James. 1980. *A Discourse on Property: John Locke and His Adversaries*. Cambridge: Cambridge University Press.

———. 1993. *An Approach to Political Philosophy: Locke in Contexts*. Cambridge: Cambridge University Press.

———. 1995. *Strange Multiplicity: Constitutionalism in an Age of Diversity*. Cambridge: Cambridge University Press.

Tupper, Charles Lewis. 1898. "India and Sir Henry Maine." *Journal of the Society of Arts* 46: 390–405.

Tylor, E. B. 1871. "Maine's *Village-Communities*." *Quarterly Review* 131: 176–89.

———. 1877. *Primitive Culture: Researches into the Development of Mythology, Philosophy, Religion, Language, Art, and Custom*. New York: Henry Holt.

Unger, Roberto Mangabeira. 1976. *Law in Modern Society: Towards a Criticism of Social Theory*. New York: Free Press.

———. 1987. *Social Theory: Its Situation and Its Task*. Cambridge: Cambridge University Press.

Urbinati, Nadia, and Alex Zakaras, eds. 2007. *J. S. Mill's Political Thought: A Bicentennial Reassessment*. Cambridge: Cambridge University Press.

Varouxakis, Georgios. 2005. "Empire, Race, Euro-Centrism: John Stuart Mill and His Critics." In *Utilitarianism and Empire*, edited by Bart Schultz and Georgios Varouxakis. Lanham, MD: Lexington Books.

Vinogradoff, Paul. 1904. "The Teaching of Sir Henry Maine." *Law Quarterly Review* 20.

Viswanathan, Gauri. 1998. *Outside the Fold: Conversion, Modernity, and Belief*. Delhi: Oxford University Press.

———. 1998. *Masks of Conquest: Literary Study and British Rule in India*. New York: Columbia University Press.

Ward, Thomas Humphry, ed. 1887. *The Reign of Queen Victoria: A Survey of Fifty Years of Progress*. London: Smith, Elder.

Washbrook, David A. 1981. "Law, State, and Agrarian Society in Colonial India." *Modern Asian Studies* 15: 649–721.

———. 1999. "India, 1818–1860: The Two Faces of Colonialism." In *The Oxford History of the British Empire*, vol. 3, *The Nineteenth Century*, edited by Andrew Porter. Oxford: Oxford University Press.

Weber, Max. 1946. *From Max Weber: Essays in Sociology*. New York: Oxford University Press.

———. 1978. *Economy and Society: An Outline of Interpretive Sociology*. Berkeley: University of California Press.

Welch, Cheryl. 2003. "Colonial Violence and the Rhetoric of Evasion: Tocqueville on Algeria." *Political Theory* 31.

Whelan, Frederick G. 1996. *Edmund Burke and India: Political Morality and Empire*. Pittsburgh: University of Pittsburgh Press.

Whitman, James Q. 1990. *The Legacy of Roman Law in the German Romantic Era: Historical Vision and Legal Change*. Princeton, NJ: Princeton University Press.

Wilks, Mark. 1930. *Historical Sketches of the South of India in an Attempt to Trace the History of Mysoor from the Origins of the Hindoo Government of That State to the Extinction of the Mohammedan Dynasty in 1799*. Mysore: Government Press.

Williams, Raymond. 1958. *Culture and Society, 1780–1950*. New York: Columbia University Press.

Wilson, Jon E. 2008. *The Domination of Strangers: Modern Governance in Colonial India, c. 1780–1835*. London: Palgrave.

Wilson, Woodrow. 1898. "A Lawyer with a Style." *Atlantic Monthly* 82: 363–74.

Wolff, Hans Julius. 1951. *Roman Law: An Historical Introduction*. Norman: University of Oklahoma Press.

Wolff, Larry, and Marco Cipolloni, eds. 2007. *The Anthropology of the Enlightenment*. Stanford, CA: Stanford University Press.

Wolin, Sheldon S. 1960. *Politics and Vision: Continuity and Innovation in Western Political Thought*. Boston: Little, Brown.

Woolf, Leonard. 1920. *Empire and Commerce in Africa: A Study in Economic Imperialism*. London: Labour Research Department.

Yack, Bernard. 1997. *The Fetishism of Modernities: Epochal Self-Consciousness in Contemporary Social and Political Thought*. Notre Dame, IN: University of Notre Dame Press.

Yavetz, Zvi. 1976. "Why Rome? Zeitgeist and Ancient Historians in Early 19th Century Germany." *American Journal of Philology* 97: 276–96.

Young, Crawford. 1994. *The African Colonial State in Comparative Perspective*. New Haven, CT: Yale University Press.

Zammito, John H. 2002. *Kant, Herder, and the Birth of Anthropology*. Chicago: University of Chicago Press.

Zastoupil, Lynn. 1983. "Moral Government: J. S. Mill on Ireland." *Historical Journal* 26: 707–17.

———. 1994. *John Stuart Mill and India*. Stanford, CA: Stanford University Press.

Index

abolition of slavery, 2, 38, 187

adoption, 78, 105, 190n11

Africa, 7, 152, 171, 173–76

agency, 86, 87

ager publicus (public lands), 204n20

agrarian reform, 164; *See also* land revenue and land tenure issues

alibis of empire: allowing deferral and disavowal of responsibility, 12; crisis containment as primary task, 151; ethical dilemma in diminished moral duty, 149; housed in language of expediency, 55; for insinuation of imperial power into native society, 177; native societies as, 12, 177–78, 185; necessitated by "nature" of native society, 56; as pretext and solution, 11; as protection and reinvigoration of native societies, 11, 177; as rationale for permanent imperial rule—staying as lesser evil, 149, 177; social, cultural, and racial theories supporting, 9, 17; transformation from moral justifications to retroactive alibis, 55, 56, 180; from universalist justifications to culturalist alibis, 9, 160; *See also* civilizing mission; imperial ideology; indirect rule

alienability of land and "law of the market," 136, 142, 147

analytical jurisprudence, 212n43; *See also* utilitarianism/utilitarian jurisprudence/analytical jurisprudence

anthropology and evolutionary anthropology: as ambitious comparative endeavor, 13, 57, 73, 83, 121; and colonialism, 87–88; conceptualizing culture as humanistic cultivation, 84; cultural versus social, 209n104; expanding scope of colonial knowledge, 12–14; exponential growth of, 130, 154; focus on origins of civilization, 87; and imperial rule in India, 88, 154, 155, 156–57; justifying imperial ideology, 87; Maine's efforts spurring development of, 50–52, 155–56; origins and authors of, 64; as principle modality of knowledge and rule,

156; retaining hierarchical savagery-barbarism-civilization triad, 82; varying conceptualizations of culture, 84–85

Archer, Margaret, 86–87

Arendt, Hannah, 68

Arnold, Matthew, 38

Aryan peoples: branches as India, Ireland, Rome and Germany, 81; in evolutionary history of development, 74; having Indo-European language family in common, 73, 74, 132, 207n57; idea of unity spurring research, 65; importance of India and Ireland, 135, 146; as incorporative framework for global comparison, 73, 207n57; primeval cult of ancestors common to, 66, 128; recognition of common Indo-European heritage diffusing national prejudice, 158; study of Indian society and institutions casting light upon, 51, 75, 132; substantiated through Indo-European linguistic family, 132

assimilation, 10, 17–18, 28, 170–71, 176

Austin, John, 90, 100, 115

Bachofen, Johann Jakob, 64

barbarism: caste system as evidence of, 156; civilization/barbarism duality, 6, 202–3n6; despotism as legitimate mode of dealing with, 30, 47; England's civilizing duty to erase, 41; Maine's reevaluation of, 74, 158; Mill's analyses as sociopsychological or culturally oriented, 32–36; as pre-agricultural, pastoral and shepherding stage, 26, 59; as product of political despotism and religious tyranny, 27; reevaluation of, 158; Smuts's fear of "hordes of detribalized natives," 175; Stephen's argument for vigorous authoritarianism, 41, 42–43; as superstition and moral degradation, 28

Bayly, Chris, 191n24

Belich, James, 190n14

Bentham, Jeremy and Benthamism, 31, 94, 95, 100, 105, 112, 162

Bentinck, Lord William (William Henry Cavendish), 29

Black Act (1836), 95–96, 198n83
Blackstone, Sir William, 100, 125
Boas, Franz, 84, 85
Boell, Paul, 149, 200n99, 219n3
Brahminical norms and texts, 108, 113, 155
burial grounds, 128
Burke, Edmund, 22–25, 159, 194n17
Burrow, John W., 208n94

Cameron, Donald, 174
Campbell, George, 141
Cannadine, David, 201n124
Carlyle, Thomas, 36, 38
case law, 105
caste system: as acceptable for primitive societies, 159; buttressing colonial authority, 168, 169, 178; as cause of host of societal ills, 156; confirmed in Punjab Land Alienation Act, 164; endorsed by Brahmin view, 104, 155, 156; as evidence of premodern corruption and degradation, 10; fears of pollution from beef/pork fat on rifle cartridges, 4; as force for social stability, 164, 169; as hereditary division of labor, 142; as kinship and natural social group, 121, 160; liberal desires to reform and overcome, 156; need to reconcile policy to, 5, 52, 154, 156–57, 161; as part of customary village legal authorities, 163; as rational adaptations to historical environments, 158; rehabilitation as safeguard against unrest atomization, 154; significance and persistence eluding British policymakers, 50, 153–54; tendency to divide internally, 167
character, 35–36
Charter Act (1833), 94, 95
Chatterjee, Partha, 186
civilization: and barbarism duality, 6, 202–3n6; as humanistic cultivation, 84; India's as morally degraded, 25–29; Mill's characterization of stages of, 32–33; Mill's contrast with barbarism, 32–34, 42–43; as precarious and collective, 36; scale of assessment and stages of progress, 26
civilizing mission: ambitions curtailed and assumptions repudiated, 2, 5; as central to liberal imperialism, 17; expressing England's virtue, honor, and superiority,

41; improvement.progress dependent on natives' readiness for, 31–36; as misguided and leading to instability, 48–53; as moral justification of empire, 11; obstacles and failures ascribed to cultural impediments, 36–37; as reparation for crimes of conquest, 29, 41, 195n39, 196n42; *See also* liberal imperialism
clans, 157; *See also* kinship
Code Napoléon (French Civil Code) (1804), 91, 98
codification of laws: *See* legal reform of Indian law under British rule; legal reform — background, concepts, and debates
Colebrooke, H. T., 213n63
Collini, Stefan, 198n76
colonialism, 87–88, 160–65; *See also* empire
common law, 97, 99, 100
communal property, 127–31; *See also* land revenue and land tenure issues; legal evolution from status to contract; village-communities
communism, 119–20, 127, 129, 137, 146
comparative jurisprudence, 74, 75, 121–27, 131–32, 138
comparative method: comments on Montesquieu's use of, 70; critique of, 85; as methodological revolution, 126; as model in social theory, 57; revealing differences between tribal and civilized society, 153; spurred by anthropology and ethnology, 130; for study of antiquity, 65; temporal horizon accentuating contrasts, 82; use by Niebuhr, 62, 204n20
conquest: atonement and reparation for, 29, 196n42; attempts to cleanse empire of unsavory associations with, 46; followed by reconstitution of kinship associations, 79; justifications and critiques of, 29, 195n39; as misleading and misnomer, 47; as political affront only upon recognizable community or nationality, 47; as proof of inherent right to rule, 45–47
consent of governed, 24–25
Constant, Benjamin, 60–61
contract: *See* legal evolution from status to contract
Contract Act (passage stalled), 110–11

Cromer Lord (Evelyn Baring), 7, 20, 44, 149, 152, 170, 171, 175, 223n71, 224n89
cultural relativism, 85, 157, 159
culture: complicity between liberalism and culturalism, 8–9, 184–85; conceptualization, relationship with politics, and dynamics of imperial rule, 2–3, 15–16, 87–88, 176, 184, 185; culturalism as inadequate critique of liberal imperialism, 185; culturalism indicative of collapsing moralism, 185; as determinative of behavior and institutions, 15, 85; East and West differing only in degree, 86; evolution and comparative method, 203n6; as historical, plural, integrative, and relative, 85; as holistic, 2, 14, 57, 60, 82–87; as humanistic cultivation, 84; Iraqi, as source of failure of transition to democracy, 179–80; as mode of differentiation, 36; natives' intransigence to universal norms of civilization due to, 9; as perfectionist and progressive, 85; premised on theses of traditional society, 86; redefinitions superseding universalist stance, 2; "social" and "culture" as interchangeable terms, 209n104; as social learning, institutional conditioning, and custom, 86–87; as systemic social whole, 84
curiae (in early Roman society), 63–64
custom: binding traditional societies, 3, 14–15, 56, 57–58; as culture, 86–87; as "despotism" emasculating individuality, 33; eroding in rapidly modernizing society, 151; expanding from ancient law, 103; as fetters or "friction," 147, 159, 162; importance of caste system, 156–57; as legal and moral order at odds with modern systems, 160; as logical order of primitive society, 159; Maine's redefinition/reconstitution of, 7, 50, 51, 81, 152–60; persistence in resistance to modernization, 147; with rationale and systemic logic, 160; reconstituting in native societies, 152–60; as true guide to native practices, 155; in utilitarian political economy, 196n47; well preserved in village-communities, 155
customary law: of India, 107–10, 163; inherent flexibility accounting for longevity, 109; as legal order contrasted to modern, 114, 115, 116, 117; as "positive

morality" in Austin's view, 115; as ritualistic, unwritten, aristocratic monopolization of rules, 103; as scanty yet overly detailed, 110; as stage of law's evolution, 19, 90

Dalhousie, Lord (James Andrew Broun-Ramsay, 1st Marquess of), 4, 29, 201n116
democracy: fears of, 38, 42, 43–44; leading to mediocrity in virtue and science, 118; Maine's fears of, 51, 106, 117, 118, 212n53; removing protections against unmediated sovereignty, 118; representative and constitutional in age of commerce, 60; rift between proponents and critics of, 38; as unstable, fragile, and tending toward despotism, 51, 117; US hopes of global export of, 179
despotism: barbarism as product of, 27; benevolent, as legitimate form of government, 30, 42; decentralized form in tribal Africa, 174; democracies tending toward, 51, 117; French Revolution succumbing to notion of ancient liberties, 60–61; as legitimate mode of dealing with barbarism, 30, 47; Oriental, 25, 27, 28; ruling elites preferring, 97; teaching obedience, discipline, and bringing improvement, 33–35
Dewey, Clive, 152, 164, 220n20
Dirks, Nicholas, 154, 201n119
diversity of human life, 12–13, 57, 71, 203n6; *See also* culture; human nature
"doctrine of lapse," 4, 190n11
Durkheim, Émile, 14, 69, 70, 72, 78–79, 205n37

East India Bill (1783), 24
East India Company, 3, 22–25, 139, 193n1, 201n114
economic policies: challenges to classical tenets, 146–47; development of natural resources, 173; differences as rational adaptations, 158; disillusionment with, 146; laissez-faire, 30, 52, 152, 164, 222n48; Maines' criticisms of classical political economy, 51, 103, 113, 139, 142, 145–47, 152, 158, 162, 164, 171; *See also* land revenue and land tenure issues

education, Western-style: breeding native "ideologists," discontent, hostility, and ingratitude, 170, 175; breeding religious malaise and spiritual unrest, 168; contributing to undermining of traditional authority, 175; in English language, use of reason and argument, 28; hope of creating native allies and mediators of imperial dominion, 170; in jurisprudence for England's lawyers, 211n31; missionaries taking lead in, 30; as naive enthusiasm for assimilation and anglicization, 170–71; nationalist movement led by English-educated elite, 174; as quick solvent of old social order, 169–70; in Roman law for England's lawyers, 99–100, 211n31; westernized natives alienated from average natives, 170–71
egalitarianism, 71
Egypt, 7, 152
Ellis, Francis, 141
Elphinstone, Mountstuart, 141, 221n36
empire: as bulwark against collapse of native society, 177; conflicting aims of improvements and security, 148; disorder, conflict, and dissolution as inevitable by-product of, 19–20, 148, 164–65; expansion and consolidation under alibi of indirect rule, 149; Indian, as anomalous, 53–55, 193n1; intellectual history of, and relationship to modern political theory, 7–8; land revenue as ideological and practical basis of, 89, 120; "late" defined, 189n5; in paradoxical relationship with liberalism, 8; as simultaneously cause and cure of crises, 149, 177; "tax-taking" versus legislating, 116–17, 139, 216n29; tendency toward overcentralization, 166, 168; See also alibis of empire; imperial ideology; indirect rule; land revenue and land tenure issues; liberal imperialism; rebellions and crises of the British Empire
English language instruction, 28
Enlightenment, 13, 28, 70, 73, 155, 182
equity, 123
equity jurisprudence, 106
ethnographic state, 156
ethnography, 14, 57, 130, 154, 155, 220n14; See also anthropology and evolutionary anthropology
Eyre, Edward John, 37–39

family, 77, 83, 123; See also kinship
Federated Malay States (1874), 172
Fenian Rising (Ireland), 1, 146
feudalism, 80, 135–36, 137
fictions, role of, in legal change, 105
Fiji, 172–73
Filmer, Robert, 77, 208n78
Fison, Lorimer, 223n76
Fortes, 87
French Civil Code (Code Napoléon) (1804), 91, 98
French Revolution: erroneous notions of ancient liberties, human perfectibility, natural law, and equality, 60–61, 65, 68, 122; fervor for land redistribution, 62; inaugurating ancient/modern binary and re-evaluation, 59–60, 203n8; principles applied to Africa, 176–77
Fustel de Coulanges, Numa Denis, 61, 64, 65–66, 69, 78, 128, 205n34, 215n18

Gallagher, John, 10, 191n23
Gandhi, 192n37
gens (patrilineal family), 63–64, 79, 134
gentile society (early Roman), 62, 63
German Markenverfassung, 129
Gluckman, 87
Gordon, George William, 37, 198n74
Gordon, Sir Arthur, 20, 149, 172–73
government: benevolent despotism as legitimate, 30; British model for "settlement colonies," 54; British rule in India taking on unique and experimental character, 54; Burke on institutional checks, 23–24; Burke on unlawful beginnings, 23; coercion necessary for law and order, 41; consent of governed, 24–25; corresponding to society's stage of growth, 153; essence of government in trust, 24–25; ethnographic state, 156; government working toward improvement of subject race, 29; Hobbes's theory of modern state formation, 115–16, 117; as principle of progressive improvement, 31; rejecting transplantation of English models, 153; state of society or civilization, 32; Stephen's preference for benevolent imperial despotism and coercion, 42, 43; varying definitions of "good" government, 23; See also imperial ideology; indirect rule; self-government

Grant, Charles, 25, 27–28, 29, 186, 195n29
Grant, James, 204n20
Greek society, 61, 62–64, 65–66
Greek/Stoic theory of natural law, 124
Grossi, Paolo, 216n23
Grotius, Hugo, 127

Hailey, Malcolm, 175, 224n89 & 99
Halhed, Nathaniel, 213n63
Hall, Catherine, 187
Harrison, Frederic, 92–93
Hastings, Warren, 22–25, 45, 213n63
Haxthausen, August von, 129
Hindu law: Brahminical texts erroneously assumed to represent native custom, 108, 155; commentaries as vital instruments, 108; as distorted, outmoded, and based on Brahmin monopoly, 113; religious and scriptural character of, 108; as rigidified or displaced by common law, 107–9
historical jurisprudence, 18, 90, 98–107, 117
historicism: of legal evolution, progress, and codification, 102–7; Maine emphasizing slow institutional developments, 126; in Maine's anthropological timescale, 74; of Maine's investigations of law and property, 89, 90; of Maine's mining of law's transformative epochs, 19; of Maine's thesis on property, 128–30; in relativity of modern legal and political forms and private property, 19; respecting differences in ideas and institutions, 153; of transition from status to contract, 75–76; triumph of, over classical political economy, 152; See also legal evolution from status to contract; property, history of
Hobbes, Thomas, 115–16, 117, 123
Holt, Thomas, 187
human nature: bound by ritualized communal obligation, 78; bound by social learning, institutional conditioning, and custom, 58, 72, 86; critique of transformability, 68–69; as inhibited in field of politics, 73; man as malleable and perfectible, 27, 30, 37, 69, 70; man as pure ego motivated by uncontainable desire, 78; man as selfish and unruly, 42; man as stable, immobile, and resistant to

change, 51, 71, 86; theory of habituation, 203n6; See also culture; universalism
Hunter, W. W., 155
Hutchins, Francis, 25, 186

Ibbetson, Denzil, 155, 164
Ilbert, Courtney, 39
Ilbert Bill crisis (1883), 39–44, 199n84, 199n86
imperial ideology: conundrums and new studies in political theory of, 182–83; dual mandate of developing natural resources and helping natives progress, 173–74; fundamental rethinking of, 1–5, 160–61; historiographic trends, 10; "late" defined, 189n5; Maine's role in shaping, 5, 6, 7, 31, 48–53, 89, 148–65; moral constraints explored in Hastings' trial, 22–25; prioritizing protection, preservation, maintenance of stability, and collaboration, 48, 58, 160–61; requiring invention of view of native society, 10; waning of ethical justifications in, 17, 22, 44, 46, 56; See also alibis of empire; civilizing mission; indirect rule; legitimacy; liberal imperialism
Impey, Sir Elijah, 45, 200n102
improvement or "progress," 31
incommensurability, 14
India: as anomalous within the British Empire, 53–55, 193n1; belief in tendency to devolve into communal divisions, 48; British rule taking on unique and experimental character, 54; direct observation of ancient communal social forms, 132–34; lacking political unity or identity, 200n110; lacking sense of community necessary for nationality, 47–48; as morally degraded, corrupt, corrupting, and barbaric, 25, 27; Mughal Empire, 167; nationalist movement, 174; from noninterference to rehabilitation of native institutions, 6–7; Permanent Settlement of Bengal (1793), 141; as point of entry for discussion of primitive law and society, 75; Punjab, 156, 157; Rajput tribal kingdoms, 166–67; rapid settlement of Europeans in interiors, 95; transfer from East India Company to Crown Colony, 201n114; See also legal reform of Indian law under British rule; Mutiny (1857);

India (*cont'd*)
native societies; traditional society; village-communities
Indian Penal Code (1861), 91–92, 94–95, 210n7
indirect rule: in Africa, 173–76; articulation by imperial administrators, Maine's adherents, 149, 224n89; building up native "pillars" to support British tower, 168; burden of legitimation shifted onto native societies, 53, 55, 177; as characteristic of late imperial ideology, 7, 9, 55, 148, 180; as characteristically British political principle, 176; claims of self-determination and progress along with paternalistic protections, 173; as cosmopolitan pluralism, cultural tolerance, and decentralization, 6, 20, 150, 152, 172, 178, 184; as cover for expansion and consolidation of empire, 149; as critique of representation and sovereignty, 150; as decentralized despotism, 174; as defensive realism, 178; disclaiming ideologies, moral agendas, liberal models, or interventionism, 2, 55, 149, 165, 171, 190n16; dual mandate of developing natural resources and helping natives progress, 173; as efficient, nonintrusive rule through native institutions, 6, 171; emphasis on stability and order rather than ethics, 11, 152, 171, 173; emulation by other colonial powers, 7; in Fiji, 172–73; goal of eventual self-government forgotten, 11, 171; Maine's contribution in theoretical foundations of, 3, 6, 7, 19, 49–53, 83, 89, 148–65; maintaining divisive aspects for continuation of British rule, 169; multiplicity of institutional forms in, 171–77; as paternalistic protection of native societies, 2, 6, 10–11, 55, 151, 161, 165; political foundations of, 165–71; as pragmatic, nonideological response to conceptualization of traditional/native society, 9–10, 17, 22, 89, 150; as progressive, evolved, moderate, respectful, and tolerant, 149, 176–77; race defining sectors of nonrepresentative government, 6; as reaction to liberal predicament, 180; seeking fidelity from "naturally" conservative classes and elites, 171; as transcontinental shift in ruling practices with profound impact on indigenous societies, 7, 171

individualism: corporate groups as bulwark against, 203n8; emasculated in despotism of custom, 33; growth of, in village-communities, 80; modern social order of free agreement between, 77–82; *See also* legal evolution from status to contract

Indo-European language family, 73, 74, 132, 207n57; *See also* Aryan peoples

interventionism/noninterventionism, 30, 49, 52

Iraq, 179–80

Ireland, 1, 146, 158, 159

Irish Home Rule, 181

ius gentium, 123, 124

ius naturale, 123, 124

Jamaica, 1, 5–6, 37–39, 54, 187

Jones, William, 25, 207n57, 213n63

judicial legislation ("judge-made law"), 93, 95, 99, 111–12

kinship: as aggregation of families, not of individuals, 77; bound with hierarchy/power, property rights, and religion, 65; as caste, forming basis of group cohesion, 157; as central to primitive political theory, 79; as constitutive of social order, 83; containing artificial, fictive relationships bound by structures of power, 78, 79; as cornerstone of society, 14, 57, 76; corporate character of family in early jurisprudence, 77; displacement by locality, territoriality, or local contiguity, 79–80; in early Roman society, 63–64; households as kingdoms/sovereignties in miniature, 77; as key structural and comparative concept, 67; leading to rights of property and contract, 67, 121; making political communities possible, 79; marking community of worship, 66; patriarchal power slowly losing hold over dependents, 77–78; patriarchy as nearly universal, 76; as political institution marking subjection to common authority, 78; power as formative cause of sociability, 79; providing basis to concept of "social," 69; as reciprocal rights and duties, 14; rights and duties conferred upon families, not individuals,

66–67; sociopolitical groupings based on common lineage, 64; structural-functionalism reinforcing synchronic coherence, 85; transition to locality as basis for political obligation, 133–34

Kovalevsky, M. M., 215n17

laissez-faire, 30, 52, 152, 164, 222n48
land revenue and land tenure issues: administration generating private proprietary rights, 139–40; administrators misunderstanding native land customs, 139, 140–43; agrarian law and land reform, 62; attempts at protection and reconstitution bound to fail, 144; British rule creating land law ex nihilo, 143–44; doubling of sovereignty and dominion, 80; at ideological and practical basis of the British Empire, 89; Maine's recommendation to stand by mistakes, cease meddling in, 144–45; private property, primogeniture, *patria potestas*, 66, 69, 76, 206n45, 208n73; proprietary interests of peasantry/communities versus landlords/aristocracy, 139–44; Punjab Alienation of Land Act (1900), 164; rent as foundation of imperial rule in India, 120; rent question as acute problem, 141–43; revenue, land and tax policy, 27; reversal in strategies of agrarian reform, 164; rights of collection transferred to East India Company, 139; Roman law's tenets of proprietorship, 80; *ryotwari* experiment as egalitarian ideal of liberal imperialism, 140, 141; settlement causing structural changes in legal rights, 143–44; shift to protection of village-communities, 145–46; unintended consequences of "writing" unwritten custom into law, 163; village-communities at fulcrum of debates on, 138; *See also* property, history of; village-communities
languages: English, 28; Indo-European, 73, 74, 132, 207n57
"late" defined, 189n5
Laveleye, Émile de, 128, 130–31
League of Nations, 177
legal evolution from status to contract: analogizing custom/market and custom/contract, 160; circumscribed by diversity of historical sources, 81; codification's centrality to evolution of law, 102–4; cul-

minating in undoing of classical political economy, 147; culminating in undoing to classical political economy, 147; as development of private property, freedom of contract, and individual right, 76, 81, 126, 129; evidence supplied by village-communities in dissolution, 121; evolution of law, 3, 105, 114; freedom of contract, societal establishment of, 51; as irreversible but slowable, 169; leading to unmitigated growth of personal right, 163; legal evolution connected to political transformations, 104, 113; Maine remembered for, 3, 75–76; as metaframe for Maine's investigations, 82–83; "mixed" cases seen as traces, or survivals, or transitional, 81–82; as precarious accomplishment of progressive societies, 72; revealing differences between tribal and civilized society, 153; rise in claims on testamentary successions, litigiousness, and petty competition, 163; societies as spatial frontier in different temporalities, 83, 209n95; transformation threatening to make India ungovernable, 161; transition as parallel for kinship, communal property, and rights, 67; as typical dualistic construction of modern social theory, 14
legal reform — background, concepts, and debates: codes as modes for institutional development, 104–5; codification, resistance to, 91; codification movement's failure in England, 91, 93; criticized as pretense toward perfectibility through codification, 98; criticized as threat to local authorities, 98; danger of judicial legislation ("judge-made law"), 93, 95, 99, 111–12; dangers of rigidity and loss of formality, 105; debates on common law of India and England, 91; dispute over ultimate source of legal authority and obligation, 115; early Roman law, 62, 204–5n20; equity as cornerstone of legal progress, 123–24; family as starting point of law, 78; government through consent, grounded in "empire of opinion," 24–25; hopes for scientific jurisprudence, 91; at ideological and practical basis of the British Empire, 89, 90–91; importance of primitive legal ideas, 75; law as "command of the sovereign,"

legal reform (*cont'd*)
18–19, 90; law as first necessity of human society, 37; law as mechanism for transformation of conduct, 27; law linked to life of a nation, 100–101; law undermined by absolute commitment to liberty, 42; legislation, not courts/judges, as sole instrument of law making, 94–95; legislation and break-up of local life, 116–17; Maine's contribution, 99–107; natural law criticized, 121–27; need for rational, generalizable legal principles, 101; need for technical expertise to correct imprecision, 101; recommendation for lawyers' study of Roman law, 99–100; requiring humility in face of history, 102; role of equity jurisprudence in legal change, 106; role of fictions in legal change, 105; role of legislation in legal change, 106–7; Roman patriarchal family with legal identity, 77; society "in advance of " law, 86; transition from family to individual obligation, 77–82; unease at state of common law in England, 91; *See also* customary law; historical jurisprudence; legal evolution from status to contract; utilitarianism/utilitarian jurisprudence/analytical jurisprudence

legal reform of Indian law under British rule: absolute government suited to, 93; Black Act (1836), 95–96, 198n83; cascade of legal interventions by colonial system, 109; challenges of "judge-made law," 93, 95; Charter Act (1833), 94, 95; codification from Macaulay to Maine, 90–97; colonial court system intruding at village level, 109; Contract Act (passage stalled), 110 11; conundrums in success of codification, 92; critics seeking widened sphere of executive authority and patriarchal despotism, 111; danger of judicial legislation ("judge-made law"), 111–12; Ilbert Bill crisis (1883), 39–44, 199n84, 199n86; "illustrations" by Macaulay, 95; India as testing ground for institutional reforms, 95–97; Indian Penal Code (1861), 91–92, 94–95, 210n7; law regrounded upon command, sovereignty, sanction, and right, 109; Macaulay's contributions, 93–96; Maine's contributions, 97, 110–13; as motley, distorted amalgam of custom and English law, 109–10; Native Marriages Act (1872), 110; prospect of harmonizing law with modernization, 97; question of equality between Britons and Indians, 39–44; resisted by ruling elites preferring paternal despotism, 97; Stephen's contributions, 110; transformation of law and custom, 107–13; transition from custom into written law, 109–10, 163; *See also* Hindu law

Legge, J. D., 223n73

legislative jurisprudence, 94–95, 106–7

legitimacy of empire: concern for, as misplaced and dangerous to stability, 49; concerns displaced by protective, restorative role, 19–20, 149; in ethical character and elevated ideals of imperial regime, 12, 21; subject societies as displaced site of, 53, 55, 177; through conquest as proof of inherent right to rule, 45–47; through consent of governed, 24–25

liberal imperialism—promise of: advantages of anglicization, 196n44; appeal of social experiment to middle class mind, 196n43; belief in temporary, benevolent nature of British rule, 48; civilizing mission as reparation for crimes of conquest, 29, 41, 195n39, 196n42; civilizing mission, moral and material progress as justifications, 1–2, 9, 11, 22–31, 40, 44–48; derivation of term, 193n3; disavowal of conquest and force, 29, 45; education to create native allies and mediators of imperial dominion, 170; as interventionist, 30; legal codification and land reform as elemental to, 89; legal reform bringing uniformity, certainty, and equality, 95–97; Mill's contribution to, 35; pressure on caste system, 156, 160–61; racialized discourses contributing to, 183; tensions and contradictions in, 11, 34, 35, 36–37, 43; *See also* legal reform — background, concepts, and debates

liberal imperialism—rejection of: complicity between liberalism and culturalism, 184–85; contradictions of power, 186; criticisms reflecting general crisis of liberalism, 38, 152; discredited by rebellions and imperial scandals, 1, 4, 17, 21–22, 37–43, 54, 186–87; disruptive impact of promoting representation and self-government, 165–66; giving way to authoritarian prioritization of security and order, 41–43, 54–55; giving way to disillusionment and disavowal, 9, 186–87, 199n96; giving way to protection and conservation of native society, 54–55; giving way to racial and cultural premises, 8–9, 44; incorrectly understood as discrete theory, 181; logic of explanation as rhetoric of evasion, 187; moral vision criticized as sentimental and anarchic, 38, 44–48, 196n42; natives' impediments to progress as permanent, 35, 160, 161; normative investment in pluralism, 184, 185; precarious focus on representations of non-European peoples, 184–85; reconstitution into guise of development in 20th century, 29; unintended consequences intrinsic to, 185–86; *See also* indirect rule; land revenue and land tenure issues; legal reform of Indian law under British rule

liberal imperialism—resurgence in 21st century: in arguments for use of force for transformative political projects, 187; in calls for institutionalization of humanitarian intervention, 187; example in US-led invasion of Iraq (2003), 179; as explanation, undoing confidence and coherence, 179; moralism and idealism in defense of use of force, 179; as question of political consequences, troubling associations, and calamitous outcomes, 188; regression from moral ambition to disillusionment to disavowal, 180; relationship between benign agenda and concomitant violence and racialization, 187–88; responsibility for failure shifted to Iraqi cultural capacities, 179–80; strategy of persuasion giving way to use of force, 180

Liberal Party split (1886), 38, 43–44, 181

liberalism: accommodating to hardening of racial attitudes and scientific racism, 183; as coeval with theories of empire, 8; in crisis, 38, 43–4, 152, 184–85, 187, 200n98; dilemmas of living in plural, deeply divided societies, 182; importance of attending to outer limits of, 183–84; tenets of equality, democracy, and laissez-faire individualism, 181; viewed as sentimental and anarchic, 38, 42

liberty: ancient versus modern, 60; applicability only to mature individuals and societies, 34; communal versus individual, 66; French Revolution's erroneous notions of, 60–61, 65, 68, 122

Low, A. D., 54, 173

Lugard, Lord (Frederick Lugard), 7, 20, 149, 152, 173–75, 190n16, 224n89

Lyall, Alfred, 20, 149, 152, 155, 165–71, 181

Macaulay, Thomas Babington, 22, 28, 90, 93–96, 170, 193n1, 196n44

Maine, Henry Sumner: abandoning Liberal Party, 181; background and achievements, 3, 14, 16; criticized as well for inaction as for "overlegislation," 96–97, 111; as dichotomist, 83, 208n94; disciples as influential, 20, 153, 155, 156, 164, 165–66, 172; disillusionment with land rights situation, 144–45; few studies on Indian work and legacy of, 192–93n38; importance as Law Member of Viceroy's Council, 19, 90, 96; on India lacking political unity or identity, 200n110; interpretive paradox of oeuvre, 16–17; on Mutiny's causes, 4–5, 49–50, 153–55; pessimism about assimilative purposes of education, 170; pessimism about democracy, 51, 106, 117, 118, 212n53; pessimism about reconstructing native practices, 150–51; as pivotal figure, 7, 18, 50–52, 57, 83, 87, 119, 148, 151, 153; praise of Montesquieu, 70; privileging administrative archives, 155–56; reshaping debate on land tenure, 19, 138; reversing civilizing mission, 48–52; on tradition, modernity, and comparative imagination, 73–82

Maine, Henry Sumner—themes: codification of English law, 113; codification of Indian law, 19, 90, 113; connection between good laws and social practices, 107, 113; criticism of classical political economy, 51, 103, 113, 139, 142, 145–47, 152, 158, 162, 164, 171; criticism of common law, 97; criticism of democracy, 117–18; criticism of impracticability of codification of English common law, 99; criticism of natural law, 121–27; criticism of social contract theory and utilitarianism, 68; criticism of "speculative"

Maine, Henry Sumner (*cont'd*)
jurisprudence, 92; criticism of utopianism of political philosophy, 68; denial of existence of ideal political types, 72; evolutionary history of law and property, 16–17, 18, 19, 114, 128, 131–37, 138; historical jurisprudence, 18, 92; sociology of colonialism, 6, 18, 84, 90, 160–65; study of Roman law in Victorian legal education, 99–100; *See also* legal evolution from status to contract
Malaya, 7, 172
Malcolm, John, 154, 221n36
Mamdani, Mahmood, 174, 189n5, 223n88
Maori Wars, 1, 190n14
mark-communities, 216n20
market, law of, 136, 142, 147
marriage, 78, 85, 110
Marx, Karl, 129, 205n32, 217n46
McLennan, John, 64, 78, 208n82
Mehta, Uday Singh, 34, 182, 183, 184, 194n17, 224n1
Metcalf, Thomas, 186, 193n4, 225n9
methodological revolution of Maine, 155; *See also* comparative method
Mill, James, 25–27, 29, 94, 186
Mill, John Stuart, 8, 30–37, 71–72, 119, 129–30, 146–47
missionary activity, 4, 27–28
modernization: as aspect of universalist theory, 17–18; impact on custom, 147, 151, 160; Maine on tradition, modernity, and comparative imagination, 73–82; native societies endangered by, 19, 52, 90, 148, 151, 160–65; as socially disruptive and politically unwieldy, 10; traditional society undermined by, 2, 15, 57, 65–66, 72, 73, 82, 84, 86, 147, 161–62; village-communities undermined by, 52
Momigliano, Arnaldo, 62
Mommsen, Theodor, 128
Money, J. W. B., 223n74
Montesquieu, 69, 70, 71, 206n45
Morant Bay Rebellion, Jamaica (1865), 1, 37–39, 54
Morefield, Jeanne, 199n95
Morgan, Lewis Henry, 59, 64, 67, 78, 82, 205n28, 208n82, 209n96
Mughal Empire, 167
multiculturalism, 182, 185
Munro, Thomas, 140, 141, 154, 221n36

Muthu, Sankar, 182
Mutiny (1857): agrarian discontent causing, and land tenure reforms following, 120, 144, 146, 164; dampening ambition for legislative reform, 96; as definitive turning point, 1; as "greatest fact in all Anglo-Indian history," 1; hardening racial attitudes towards non-European peoples, 5, 6; leading to practice of "indirect rule," 6, 174; privileging anthropological knowledge in policy development, 154–55, 156; proving native reformation's failure to instill loyalty to empire, 148; representative government disavowed for nonwhite populations, 6; as sign of failure of liberal, utilitarian, and evangelical reforms, 4–5, 181, 186; as symptom of fundamental "defect of knowledge," 50, 153–54; as "terrified fanaticism," perverse, irrational, ungrateful, and inscrutable, 4, 5, 49–50; as widespread, disillusioning, and brutally suppressed, 1

Nandakumar, Maharaja, 200n102
Napoleonic Code (1804), 91, 98
nationality: dismissed as lacking in India, 43; as equivalency for self-government, 47–48; as form of cultural achievement equivalent to civilization, 36; India lacking sense of community necessary for, 47–48; presuming exclusive ownership of land, 80; in slow shift from kinship to locality, 80; as united community of race or religion, 48
Native Marriages Act (1872), 110
native societies: as corrupt, corrupting, and barbaric, 27, 28, 195n29; customs and traditions as rigid, 56; in dissolution under conditions of modern empire, 19, 90, 148, 151, 160–65; exhibiting synchronic interdependency, 157; as functional wholes, ordered by primitive custom, 51, 157, 201n124; as intact but vulnerable, 6, 151; Maine's plea for more knowledge, 50–52; as pretext, solution, and alibi for empire, 11, 52, 149, 172; protection of, as safeguard against instability, 52, 149; protection of, in Crown Colony status, 172; reconceptualizing, 50, 150, 152–60, 164; reformation as ineffective in inculcating loyalty to em-

pire, 148; shift of responsibility for imperial project to, 12, 35, 52, 55; as subject of ethnographic and sociological investigations, 5, 53; as sympathetic, aristocratic ideal of hierarchical and ordered, 201n124; transition from status to contract, from ancient to modern, 52; *See also* India; kinship; traditional society; village-communities

natural law, 106, 121–27

Niebuhr, Barthold Georg, 62–65, 128–29, 204n20

Nisbet, Robert, 203n8

obedience, 33

Oriental despotism, 25, 27, 28

Orientalism, 26, 27, 28, 29, 150, 169

Pagden, Anthony, 202n6

patria potestas (power of father), 66, 69, 76, 206n45, 208n73

patriarchy: family as corporate group, 76; guardianship of women in, 206n45; as nearly universal, 76; *patria potestas* (power of father), 66, 69, 76, 206n45, 208n73; slowly losing hold over dependents, 77–78

patricians and plebeians, 63

peculium (separate property), 136–37

Perham, Marjery, 176

Permanent Settlement of Bengal (1793), 141

philology, 74

Pitts, Jennifer, 182, 183, 184

plebeians and patricians, 63

political economy: classical, 139, 142, 144–47, 152, 158–60, 164; Maine's criticisms of, 51, 145–47, 158–60, 162; *See also* utilitarianism

political theory or political philosophy: British, 21, 44; conundrums and new studies of, 7–8, 12–13, 181–83; criticism of idealism and utopianism of, 67–68, 72–73; deductive, 122; Enlightenment, 18th century, 13, 31, 68, 169, 182; feudalism, 80, 135–36, 137; history of, 7–8, 12–13, 79; imperial, 11, 181; indirect rule as, 20, 150, 165, 171, 174, 176; Maine's, 3, 17; natural law, 106, 121–27; 19th century, 8, 13, 32, 71, 169, 181, 183; primitive, 78–79; relationship of, to intellectual history of empire, 7–8;

republican, 62; shaped by experience of human diversity, 12–13; social theory, contrast with, 15, 67–68, 206n43; *See also* alibis of empire; democracy; despotism; government; human nature; imperial ideology; indirect rule; liberal imperialism; liberalism; self-government; universalism; utilitarianism

politics or political practice: accepting possibility of rational, willed transformation of society, 68–69; criticism of tight-knit systematicity of the social, 72; derivative of the social, 69; emphasizing limits of political thought and action, 58; Enlightenment, 18th century view of, 68, 70, 73, 182; institutions expressing underlying social relations, 68; kinship as central to, 67, 78, 79; kinship leading to rights of property and contract, 67; limits of political thought and action, 58; Niebuhr's desire to stem revolutionary ideas of, 62; power as patriarchal in Rome, 66; reframed in relationship to society's imperatives, 15; rights and duties conferred upon families, not individuals, 66; "social" as threat to "political," 68, 70, 72, 73; "social" as threat to political freedom, 206n44; transition from kinship to locality as basis for political obligation, 64, 80, 133; *See also* indirect rule; liberal imperialism

primogeniture, 66

private property: *See* property, history of

Proclamation, Queen's (1858), 49, 201n114, 220n14&15

progress, 31, 137, 162, 172

property, history of: agrarian discontent as partial cause of 1857 Mutiny, 120, 144, 164; alienability of land and "law of the market," 136, 142, 147; challenging future of private property on global scale, 120–21; challenging liberal-utilitarian norms, 120; communal property and 19th century debate, 127–31; from communal to individual private property, 19, 119, 131–37; communality eroded by separate property (Roman *peculium*), 136–37; communality eroded by war and expansion of commerce, 137; as continuing tale of usurpation and oppression, 130; controversy about policy in Ireland, 146; debates by socialists and

property, history of (*cont'd*)
agrarian radicals, 120; debates contesting private property and free market in land, 120, 142, 147; debates leading to modern theories of sovereignty and property, 7–8; debates overturning understanding of appropriation and occupation, 119; dispossession of quasi-feudal landholders in favor of peasant proprietors, 164; diversity of practices revealed by anthropology and ethnology, 130; diversity of practices revealed in colonial bureaucrats' reports, 130; evolution of private property as progressive and legitimate, 137; Indian village-communities in dissolution, 138–45; interconnectedness between land tenure and group cohesion, 157; Maine as pivotal figure in property debates, 119; Marx's account of private property, 217n46; misapprehension of communalism as grave error of British rule, 120; modern rights as unsuitable for traditional societies, 146; natural law theory obscuring, 19, 121–27; private property as separation of individual rights from those of community, 80; private property's origins in ancestor worship, 66; question of viability of modern institutions in premodern societies, 19, 120; relativity of modern legal and political forms and private property, 19, 120, 128; role of village-communities, 121; shift away from private property rights back to "traditional," 52; suspicion of "Anglicization" of policies, 146; tribal chiefdoms aggrandizing power in form of land, 135–36, 137; *See also* land revenue and land tenure issues; legal evolution from status to contract
public lands: *See* land revenue and land tenure issues; legal evolution from status to contract; property, history of
Pufendorf, Samuel von, 127
Punjab, 156, 157
Punjab Alienation of Land Act (1900), 164

Queen's Proclamation (1858), 49, 201n114, 220n14&15

racism: accommodated in Millian liberalism, 183; challenges to explanatory value of race, 85; in condemnation of Hindu society and culture, 195n29; deepening sense of cultural difference between rulers and ruled, 39; in depictions of savage nature of ex-slaves, 187; in idea of privileged set of rights for Englishmen, 198n83; instigating coordinated native opposition, 199n86; in justifications for imperialism, 8; in opposition to Ilbert Bill and legal equality of Europeans and natives, 199n86; rebellions fostering, 5–6; in theory of traditional society, 2; in transformed, postrebellion view of native subjects, 190n14
Radcliffe-Brown, 87
railway, 168
Rajput tribal kingdoms, 166–67
rebellions and crises of the British Empire: Fenian Rising, 1, 146; Ilbert Bill crisis (1883), 39–44; Maori Wars, 1; Morant Bay, Jamaica (1865), 37–39; perceptions by British public, 4, 5, 38, 148, 153–54; as sign of failure of liberal, utilitarian, and evangelical reforms, 4–5, 181, 186; *See also* Mutiny (1857)
relativism, cultural, 85, 157, 159
religion: ancestor worship, 128; as basis for patriarchal family, 78; as foundational set of beliefs for ancients, 66; Grant's condemnation of Hinduism, 28; Indian Mutiny's cause in "terrified fanaticism," 4, 49, 153; missionary activity, 4, 27–28; post-Mutiny noninterference policy, 4; as potential unifier also threatening British rule, 168; Western education inducing malaise and spiritual unrest, 168
rent, 141–43; *See also* land revenue and land tenure issues
revolutions, 23
Ripon, Lord (George Frederick Robinson), 39–40, 199n85
Robertson, William, 25
Robinson, Ronald, 10, 191n23
Roman Empire, 116–17
Roman law: *ager publicus* (public lands), 204n20; connecting ancient with modern, 131–32; *gens* (patrilineal family), 63–64, 79, 134; historical origins of private property, 128; influence on local custom and habit of legislation, 216n29; influences of, 132–33; lessons of, 98–107; Maine's analyses of natural law and pri-

vate property in, 121–27; *patria potestas* (power of father), 66, 69, 76, 206n45, 208n73; *peculium* (separate property), 136–37; recommendation for training in, for English lawyers, 99–100, 211n31
Roman societies, 61, 62–64, 65–66, 69, 72, 75
Romantic-paternalism, 154, 159, 220n16, 221n36
Rousseau, Jean-Jacques, 66
Russian village-communities, 134
ryotwari experiment, 140, 141

Savigny, Karl Friedrich von, 98, 101, 125
scientific jurisprudence/scientific codification, 91, 92–93, 94, 102, 106
Seeley, J. R., 46–48, 181, 195n39
self-government: as cause of disruptions, 165; danger of oligarchies of unrepresentative Europeanized natives, 175; as forgotten goal of liberal imperialism, 11, 48–49, 171; hingeing upon question of nationality, 48; from self-governing to Crown colony, 54; Stephen's disapproval of, 41–42; viewed as possible after "education" of natives, 30, 196n44; white settler colonies on path toward, 54; *See also* democracy
separate property (Roman *peculium*), 136–37
Sepoy Mutiny (1857): *See* Mutiny (1857)
September 11, 2001, 179
Servius Tullius, 64
"settled view" as authoritarian consensus, 54–55
"settlement colonies," 54
Smuts, Jan, 175
social anthropology, 84
social theory, origins (19th century): analytic uses of, 59; ancient/modern dichotomy as radical and fundamental, 58–67, 69; as critique of political philosophy, 67–68; four-stage or stadial model of progress, 59; French Revolution inaugurating ancient/modern binary and reevaluation, 59–60, 203n8; Fustel as central figure, 67; Fustel de Coulanges, 61, 64, 65–66; Greco-Roman societies as foreign, primitive, and inimitable, 61–64; imperial context of, 15; Maine as central figure, 66, 67, 83; Maine's theories of colonialism, 160–65; as methodological

revolution, 67, 69–70, 126; as narrative of transition from historical forms of society, 58–59; Niebuhr, 62–65; "social" and "culture" as interchangeable terms, 209n104; social phenomena as "natural" and independent of human will, 73; structure of contrast and comparative imagination, 73–82; toward holistic models of culture and society, 82–85; *See also* comparative method; kinship; traditional society
social theory/sociology/social science: concept of traditional society as central innovation of, 56; as critique of political, 58; emphasizing nonrational bases of sociability, 15; expanding scope of colonial knowledge, 12–14; Maine as central figure, 57; reciprocal relationship with empire, 57; rethinking "the primitive," 57; sociological privileged over political, 206n43; structural-functionalism, 84–85; structure/agency problem as mirror of culture/agency problem, 87; *See also* comparative method; kinship
society, 2, 15; *See also* culture
sovereignty, 7, 8, 165, 179
"speculative" jurisprudence, 92, 96
stadial model of human progress, 59
status: *See* legal evolution from status to contract
Stephen, James, 199n96
Stephen, James Fitzjames, 40–44, 90, 92, 181, 199n96
Stoic theory of natural law, 124
Stokes, Eric, 27, 44, 194n19, 196n43, 200n98
Strauss, Leo, 68
structural-functionalism, 84–85, 86, 87, 88
Swettenham, Sir Frank, 7, 172

"tax-taking" versus legislating empires, 116–17
technological advances, 168
temporality: accentuating contrasts in comparisons, 82; challenges to assessments of "early" or "primitive" versus "advanced" or "developed," 85; challenges to claims of sequential stages of social progress, 85–86; in Maine's anthropological timescale, 74; producing equivalence between medieval West and contemporary East, 82; *See also* historicism

Teutonic village-communities, 129, 132
The Fifth Report, 141, 217–18n58
Thorburn, S. S., 155
time: *See* historicism; temporality
Tocqueville, Alexis de, 8, 167
Tod, James, 169
Tönnies, Ferdinand, 14
traditional society: African tribal structures as, 175; ancient/modern dichotomy, 65–66; as apolitical, integrated whole, bounded by custom and kinship, 3, 14–15, 57–58, 150; as cohesive, communal culture resisting modernity, 2, 15, 57, 72, 86, 147; concept anticipating models of culture and society, 2, 58, 83, 87; concept of "traditional" as premodern, 82; dangers of despotism in administrative centralization, 167–68; defined through opposition to industrialization/modernization, 73; disintegration under modern impacts as contagion, 162; Maine as model's articulator, 3; as precondition of indirect rule, 89, 150; Rajput tribal states having promising equilibrium, 166–67; as simultaneously intact and vulnerable, 6, 151; undermined with contact with modern, 84, 161–62; Western education inducing religious malaise and spiritual unrest, 168; *See also* native societies; village-communities
tribes, 79, 134, 157, 169, 175, 176; *See also* kinship
trusteeship, 9, 11, 24–25
Tuck, Richard, 13
Tupper, Charles Lewis, 152–53, 155, 156, 161, 164
Tylor, E. B., 84

universalism: as assimilating and modernizing native peoples, 17–18; believing in malleability and perfectibility of human nature, 27, 30, 37; denigrating Indian society in name of future rejuvenation, 186; errors and contradictions in, 11, 31–32, 42–43; exclusion of politically immature, 34–35; giving way in face of natives' intransigence and rebellions, 9, 39; in Maine's views of codification, 97; Mill's skepticism of egalitarianism, 71; as natural freedom, moral equality, and reason, 34; requiring "difference" to justify eradication, 186; superseded by culturalist stance, 2

utilitarianism/utilitarian jurisprudence/analytical jurisprudence: Austin as leading figure of, 18, 90; authoritarianism and crisis within English liberalism, 200n98; belief in sovereign/command, coercion, and force of law, 41, 113–17; holding mistaken views of Indian society, 50; legitimating modern sovereignty, 116; Maine's tempered respect for, 117, 159–60; providing scientific systematization and consistent terminology, 103; skepticism and criticisms of, disillusionment with, 44, 51, 92, 102–3, 113; supposed universality obscuring variations in basic principles, 103

village-communities: at center of debates over property rights, 121; as central social form in India, 150; classic description in *The Fifth Report*, 141, 217–18n58; defined by corporate or communal character, 83; development of varieties of rights and ownership, 134; disappearing under impact of imperial rule, 138–39, 142–43; in dissolution, 138–45; dissolution of family dependency, growth of individual rights and private property, 80, 134; division of labor by nonmarket principles and caste system, 142; duties as those of kinship legitimated by patriarchy, 114; at fulcrum of debates about land revenue, 138; German, 129, 132; as independent, self-acting, self-organized social groups, 114; as kinsmen and co-proprietors, 157; as land-based groups in transition to modern societies, 80; mark-community, 216n20; medieval, as libertarian, socialist/communist cooperatives, 129; medieval, as oppressive feudal patriarchies, 129; as midway point between kinship and locality, 81, 133–34; originating with tribal groups settling upon land, 80; policy shift to protection of customary practices of, 145–46, 164; premised on, and reinforcing, temporal and spatial contrast, 82; Russian, 134; as self-sustaining, functional wholes with communal purpose, 84; stages of land domain differentiation, 134–35; threatened by in-

terference in collective control of land, 131; village elders as quasi-judicial and -legislative, 114; *See also* native societies; traditional society
von Maurer, Konrad, 129, 215n18

Welch, Cheryl, 225n15
West, Raymond, 155
Wilks, Mark, 141
Wilson, James, 155, 164
women, 206n45